W9-ADH-245

Universities and Global
Diversity

Routledge Research in Education

Universities and Global Diversity
Preparing Educators for Tomorrow

Edited by Beverly Lindsay and Wanda J. Blanchett

Routledge
Taylor & Francis Group

NEW YORK AND LONDON

First published 2011
by Routledge
270 Madison Avenue, New York, NY 10016

Simultaneously published in the UK
by Routledge
2 Park Square, Milton Park, Abingdon, Oxon OX14 4RN

Routledge is an imprint of the Taylor & Francis Group, an informa business

© 2011 Taylor & Francis

Typeset in Sabon by Swales & Willis Ltd, Exeter, Devon
Printed and bound in the United States of America on
acid-free paper by IBT Global

Library of Congress Cataloging in Publication Data
A catalog record has been requested for this book

ISBN13: 978–0–415–88287–3 (hbk)
ISBN13: 978–0–203–83969–0 (ebk)

Contents

Tables

Foreword

Preparing educators for tomorrow may seem like an audacious undertaking for a book on global diversity, but the editors and scholars who contribute to this work rise to the challenge. The book demonstrates from the first chapter to the last that diversity need not divide, that pluralism rightly understood and rightly practiced is a benefit and not a burden, that the fear of difference is a fear of the future. The studies and cases of this book provide an essential understanding regarding the fundamental social, geopolitical, and economic dynamics pertaining to education as a local, national, and international enterprise. The inclusion of studies from a wide range of countries, and a variety of institution-types, provides the bases for the first basic lesson from this volume: As yet, globalization has not resulted in comprehensive education programs and policies that embrace and address diversity as an imperative of practice.

The urgent message of this book is very clear. Despite the many attacks on diversity and globalization, those engaged in education can no longer ignore the multiple legitimate ways of knowing, doing, and being. Many leaders in higher education now acknowledge that diversity is an important component of the education and research mission of their institutions. They are the ones who suggest, with validation from objective research, that a diverse faculty produces a wider range of questions in research, a broader range of topics, and bring more to bear on pre-existing topics from different perspectives. The same is now known about the value of a diverse student body. Excellence requires a search for talent from all places on the globe, but it is not enough to simply bring students of different cultures, communities, and color together. Education is best served when these students intersect and interact.

That interaction, however, cannot be coerced. It must be cultivated. Educators, of all disciplines, who work in organizations of learning from preschool to postgraduate, must know how to practice in a manner that exemplifies this pedagogical principle. It was just a few years ago that many scholars and people of goodwill were concerned that the more interdependent our world was becoming, the more people were turning inward to smaller communities of meaning and memory. While some saw this as reason for despair, it now appears that the emphasis on remembering and even the practice on our campuses of regrouping may be a necessary stage of the search for common ground. As we travel around the world, we can still hear people saying that until there is respect for their primary community of identity they will find it difficult to embrace the larger community in which they function. They will, thus, find it difficult to form a more perfect world community as long as the focus of some on the well-being of their primary group is called remembering their roots and honoring their heritage, while for others it is called identity politics.

At the time of writing this, telecommunication technology is forcing worldwide reflection on global interdependence and diversity. On January 12, 2010, we learned that a massive 7.0 force earthquake had hit the small, poverty-stricken island nation of Haiti. Almost real-time accounts of the quake's destruction and the horror of the inevitable aftershocks makes these events a part of life for the entire world. In the few days since the quake hit, an impressive international relief effort has been initiated. The Internet and cell phones are being used to support fund-raising. While logistical challenges make delivery of relief very difficult, the outpouring of compassion is an important indicator that the global village cares—at least in the immediate term. Looking a bit closer, however, the issue of diversity within the Haitian population raises additional perplexing problems. While the entire world has been mobilized to help with recovery and healing, economic differences among the Haitian population define what is needed most. Those who live in the capital city of Port-au-Prince are largely poor, and now destitute. They want the world to send medical care, food, and water. Given the inevitable looting that follows such disasters, they also need security. These requirements are in stark contrast with the priorities expressed by those who live in the nearby suburb of Petionville. This is where the well-connected, middle-class, and wealthy have homes that are luxurious and largely undamaged by the quake. They are better educated, own businesses, and they have generators. Their priority is security.

The rebuilding of Haiti will present the issue of education, and teacher education and higher education will be strategic components of any plan for long-term recovery. More specifically, the physical and economic redevelopment of the country will require more individuals who are better educated and prepared for citizenship and new employment opportunities. Can a country long accustomed to the harsh divide between the haves and the have-nots unite to create a community and economy that supports all? This question challenges the most advanced economies of the world, including, and especially, the United States of America.

Becoming an educator in our global village requires a genuine respect for the power of difference. Jonathon Sacks, the British Rabbi who wrote the book, *The Home We Build Together*, could have been speaking to our universities when he argued that if we were all the same we would have nothing unique to contribute, nor anything to learn from each other. Yet, if we were completely different, we could not communicate, and if we were exactly alike, we would have nothing to say. So the Rabbi concludes that we need to see our differences as gifts to the common good; for without a compelling sense of the common good, difference spells discord and creates, not music, but noise.

Globalization is in many ways the twin, but not always the same as diversity. It brings not just different people to the table, but different ideas and insights as well. Many in South Africa, for example, have been seeking to build a new society based on a traditional concept of community called Ubuntu that is now presented in some American business and education professional development seminars (Nelson & Lundin, 2010). It is best expressed by the Xhosa proverb "People are people through other people."It is this powerful sense of shared interdependence that spawned the spirit of forgiveness and reconciliation that literally stunned the world. It was the ability of people like Nelson Mandela and Desmond Tutu to say that your pain is my pain that allowed them to say that if your humanity is assaulted, my humanity is assaulted; if your dignity is denied, my dignity is denied. It was not "I think, therefore, I am." It was "I am human because I belong." "I participate; I share because I am made for community." It was this commitment to Ubuntu among early Southern African tribes that led them to appoint war-healers to restore respect for the humanity of the combatants after the conflict was over. It was often said that the members of the tribe were brought up to have a short memory of hate. Nelson Mandela carries that tradition forward by reminding us that unless we solve the problems of the world with our brains, we will ultimately solve them with our blood.

Traditions like Ubuntu must be on the radar screen of those who develop curriculum for educators; because these insights are as significant and as critical to the future as any from the Western literature and learning we celebrate as "the" great books. In the years ahead, educators will need to develop increased respect for the many traditions and cultures now shaping a new academic ethos, an approach to education that seeks to put knowledge at the service of society and society at the service of knowledge. We can only hope that the contributors to this book will spark intellectual curiosity and a public dialogue that will result in additional research and writing about educators and global diversity.

Ambassador James A. Joseph
Professor and Director
United States – Southern Africa Center for Leadership and
Public Values, Duke University
Sharon Porter Robinson, Ed.D.
President and Chief Executive Officer
American Association of Colleges for Teacher Education

References

Sacks, Jonathon. (2007). *The Home We Build Together*. United Kingdom, Continuum International Publishing Group Ltd.

Nelson, Bob and Lundin, Stephen (2010). *Ubuntu: An inspiring story about an African tradition of teamwork and collaboration*. New York: Random House/ Crown Business.

Preface to the New Decade

As we begin the second decade of the 21st Century, portraits of globalization abound from the instant communication via Facebook and Twitter among people throughout the world to artistic performances that are viral within minutes such as the incredibly melodic voice of a former obscure singer from "Britain's Got Talent" (television broadcast) to sights of Indian University students in Australia struggling to grapple with racism in what some view as one of the world's most progressive countries. Further, we observe massive migrations as diverse populaces move around the world seeking new family and personal economic opportunities. Howling winds blowing from the West Coast of Africa and the Cape Verde Islands spawned hurricanes that extended throughout the Gulf Coast of the United States causing the worst natural disaster in modern history in the New Orleans metropolitan area. About 300,000 involuntary migrants moved due to devastating effects of hurricanes. The tsunamis in Indonesia and other parts of Asia caused countless migrants and about 300,000 deaths. Global climate conditions hurled forces far beyond original political boundaries.

Saving lives via global connections occurs as illustrated by an anecdote shared by a young physician in an initial hospital assignment after completing medical training. A patient was rushed to a hospital emergency room with life-threatening conditions when no experienced senior physicians were available or on call. "What should I do to save the patient's life?" the young physician queried himself. His dilemma was abated by YouTube where he quickly located an illustrated medical procedure that he then utilized to save the patient.

Simultaneously, while such portraits of globalization are present, the formation and strengthening of regional economic blocs, some that began at the close of the 20th Century, now begin to appear as commonplace in geopolitical regions in Asia, Africa, the Caribbean, Europe, North America, and South America. What is apparent is that individual national and jurisdictional boundaries are not the sole features that determine what had previously been direct international relations between specific nations. Instead, global matters that are not limited to one nation, or even region, become the salient variables.

How do we view such aforementioned illustrative phenomena, especially in relation to the roles of universities? Should we begin to link closely the macro-level geopolitical realities to universities and move beyond academic institutional concerns? Which macro-level conditions should the academy analyze as we observe the vast demographic diversities that exist within and among nations? The question of how to capture useful distinct frameworks of disciplinary scholarship faces us as we ponder our preliminary questions in light of an overarching mission of universities—preparing current and future generations of professional educators.

As the American Association of Colleges of Teacher Education (AACTE) Global Diversity Committee, of which we are both members, struggled with such topics, we began to ponder how we and others, as scholars and university administrators, could contribute to an analysis and understanding of external global forces affecting universities. How can universities also affect globalization and diversity? What challenges do universities face as they attempt to affect globalization and diversity? How might we then pose solutions? Meanwhile, both of us are active scholars and hold leadership roles in national and international professional organizations, like Chair, International Relations Council of the American Educational Research Association (AERA); former president, Comparative and International Education Society (CIES), and presenting scholarly papers at major international scholarship forums (for example, the World Council of Comparative Education and International Association of Special Education).

Our collective formal and informal communications with colleagues in these bodies and our communications with domestic and international colleagues led us to develop a comprehensive project involving global colleagues. The AACTE Global Diversity Committee and the President and Chief Executive Officer of AACTE enthusiastically supported the plan with a funded AACTE project. As our project crystallized, we contacted university colleagues and policymakers throughout the world in order to represent global perspectives—at least from representative geopolitical arenas in the G-8, the G-20, and emerging regions. Thus, we were able to tap into new and ongoing programs and projects in Asia, Africa, Australia, the Caribbean, Europe, New Zealand, North America, and South America.

Conversations then ensued at an annual AERA Conference in New York with Routledge editors. Receptiveness was expressed. Our book proposal was then developed to portray how universities can and should continue and/or begin to initiate and interact with global phenomena in relation to myriad types of diversity. In short, we sought to explore, in a novel manner, how universities can begin and continue to prepare educators for the ensuing decades where globalization and diversity will become increasingly intertwined. Thus, the development and positive uses of YouTube and other, as yet unknown, instructional devices by professionals would be widespread among various global groups.

We express special appreciation to the contributors of our volume who provide explications from interdisciplinary conceptual frameworks from the social sciences, education, and technological fields. They lent their expertise and devoted significant time to writing chapters. We are quite appreciative of Duke University Professor and Ambassador James Joseph (former United States Ambassador to South Africa during the era when that nation struggled through the early decade of independence when diversity was a paramount issue) who exemplifies diplomatic and scholarly expertise. Similarly, we are grateful to AACTE President and CEO Sharon Porter Robinson for endorsing the project. Their co-authored foreword lends an imprimatur to our volume.

In addition to contributing authors, a variety of people contributed behind the scenes including reviewers, doctoral and research assistants, support staff and the like. Hence we would like to acknowledge: David Conner; Beverly Cross; J. Martin Giesen; Suzanne Hickey; Frederick Hickling; Zellyne Jennings-Craig; Sally Kelley; Elias Mpofu; Ronyelle Bertrand Ricard; Arlindo Sitoe; Nathan Sorber; Ann Sanders; Gordon Shirley; Mwalimu Shujaa; Mark Warner; and Shelly Zion. We would also like to thank Max Novick and other Routledge editors and staff who helped bring our volume to fruition.

Overall, we envision and hope that our work will enhance positive solutions and present innovative paradigms regarding the continuing and new challenges for the second and future decades of the 21st Century— via university and public policies and programs to prepare educators for a globally diverse world. Global diversity encompasses national capacity building and development among various ethnic populaces, skills for new professions far beyond the educational milieus, university engagement with diverse domestic and international populations seeking to enhance learning, and balanced re-alignments of geopolitical arenas in order to ensure equity and justice that are evident in porous global borders.

Beverly Lindsay
Visiting Professor – Institute of Education
University of London
Inaugural University Fellow and Professor – Dillard University
and
Wanda J. Blanchett
Dean, Professor and Ewing Marion Kauffman/
Missouri – Endowed Chair in Teacher Education
University of Missouri, Kansas City

Abbreviations

ABET	Accreditation Board for Engineering and Technology
ADPP	Ajuda de Desenvolvimento Povo para Povo (*People to People Development)*
ATN	Australian Technology Network
CARICOM	Caribbean Community
CFL	Centro de Formação Local (Local Training Centre)
CFPP	Centro de Formação de Professores Primários (Primary Teacher Training Centers)
CPD	Continuing Professional Development
CPS	Centro Provincial de Superação *(*Provincial Upgrading Centers*)*
CSME	Caribbean Single Market and Economy
CUPU	Commuter Urban Public Universities
DPE	Direcção Provincial de Educação (Provincial Directorate of Education)
EMP	Escola do Magistério Primário (Teacher Training Shool)
EPF	Escola de Professores do Futuro (Teacher Training College for the Future)
EP1	Ensino Primário do 1 Grau–1ª–5ª Classe (1st Level of Primary Education–Grades 1–5)
EP2	Ensino Primário do 2 Grau—6ª–7ª Classe (2nd Level of Primary Education—Grades 6–7)
EU	European Union
FOE	Faculty of Education
G-8	Group of Eight (Industrialized Nations)
G-20	Group of Twenty (Industrialized National with notable portions of world's GDP)
GER	Gross Enrollment Rate
GPS	Global Positioning System
HBCUs	Historically Black Colleges and Universities
HEIs	Higher Educational Institutes
HSRC	Human Sciences Research Council

IAP	Instituto de Aperfeiçoamento de Professores (Institute for Teacher Upgrading)
IEDA	Instituto de Educação à Distância e Aberta (Institute for Open and Distance Education)
IFP	Institutos de Formação de Professores (Teacher Training Institutes)
IIE	Institute of International Education
INDE	Instituto Nacional de Desenvolvimento da Educação (National Institute for Education Development)
INE	Instituto Nacional de Estatística
INSET	In-service Teacher Training
ISCED	Instituto Superior de Ciências da Educação (Higher Educational Science Institute)
MEC	Ministério da Educação e Cultura (Ministry of Education and Culture)
MED	Ministério da Educação (Ministry of Education)
OSC	Omani Studies Center
PWI	Predominately White Institution
SADC	Southern African Development Community
SARUA	Southern African Regional Universities Association
UAE	United Arab Emirates
UAN	Universidade Agostinho Neto
UEM	Universidade Eduardo Mondlane (Eduardo Mondlane University)
UNESCO	United Nations Educational, Scientific and Cultural Organization
UNICEF	United Nations Children's Fund
UP	Universidade Pedagógica (Pedagogical University)
ZIP	Zona de Influência Pedagógica (Zone of Pedagogical Influence)

1 Universities and Global Diversity: Preparing Educators for Tomorrow

Beverly Lindsay and Wanda J. Blanchett

In February 2009, the then Governor of New York addressed the Council on Foreign Relations (one of the world's preeminent international policy and think tanks) regarding the effects of the contemporary economic crisis on a range of socioeconomic and cultural institutions. Soft laughter bubbled throughout the auditorium and from the electronic audience after he paraphrased the statement that, along with New York, "It's Shanghai, Dubai, Mumbai, or goodbye" (Paterson, 2009). What appears to be an overwhelming financial crisis for the United States cannot be separated from other current and emerging world economic epicenters.

As we composed this volume, two thoughts dominated that further illustrate Paterson's quote. Both might seem, on the surface, to have little relationship to postsecondary education. First, the terrorist attacks in Mumbai dominated the news in late fall 2008 (Bookman, 2008; Lakshmi, 2008). According to initial sources, the attacks appeared to have been undertaken by young men—the age of some seemed to be that of many university students or relatively recent graduates. Second, various recent works analyze the roles of postsecondary education vis-à-vis social challenges. The volume, *Ralph Johnson Bunche: Public Intellectual and Nobel Peace Laureate* (Lindsay, 2008a), explicates essential roles of universities in relation to social problems and analyzes the functions that universities may undertake, or at least consider, in preventing young people from engaging in violent activities. Similarly, Watson (2007) articulates civic engagement roles for universities within the local and global milieu, including gleaning international lessons from universities on several continents.

The aforementioned illustrations are precipitated by the changing phenomena of globalization, especially the economic aspects. Extensive literature exists regarding positive effects of globalization such as the ability to communicate instantly via the Internet and share scholarship (Bhagwati, 2005; Nye, 2005; NASULGC, 2004; Wilson, 2003). Face-to-face personal meetings can be convened anywhere in the world usually within 24 hours given air travel. Only seconds delay visual communication via new video technologies utilizing office or home computer connections to the Internet with an inexpensive camera or even a personal cell phone. Other works explicate the negative effects of globalization, like the widening income discrepancies between developed and developing nations (Henry, 2008; Ball, 2006; Rizvi, 2004; Stromquist, 2002). Or the same technologies that permit instantaneous communications quickly portray vast differentials in educational and career or professional attainment among diverse sectors within the same country such as India or across the border in Pakistan. Still additional publications discuss positive and negative aspects of globalization as multidimensional realities and that the central matters for educational institutions are how to prepare students and faculty to function effectively in domestic and international environments (Dodds, 2008; Friedman, 2007, 2000; Lindsay, 2004). *An alternative mode is to analyze global interconnectivity and responsibility of universities, particularly administrators, and faculty, by taking into account the changing dynamics of globalization and the relationship to diverse demographic groups and regions.*

The attacks in Mumbai further appear to demonstrate a profound discomfort with diversity and globalization at the most fundamental levels. Mumbai may have represented to the young men who attacked the city the combination of diversity and globalization, and thus a direct affront to tradition. A modern city that attracted tourists from around the world and housed the major production houses of India's world-renowned film industry, Bollywood, Mumbai was chosen rather than another city in India. Several sites in the city were attacked. The Taj Mahal and the Oberoi-Trident hotels are located in the heart of Mumbai's financial district in which the city's and the world's business elite often gather to engage in business transactions (BBC News, 2008a). The Leopold Cafe is a major tourist attraction in the city of Mumbai, while the Nariman House houses a Jewish center of worship that attracts Jews from around the world to engage in spiritual worship and growth (BBC News, 2008b). Combined, these four sites represent a clear attack on diversity and globalization. In short, such illustrative sites were attacked where Americans and Westerners resided and/or their cultural and economic influences were readily apparent. Bollywood, which is sometimes called the "Hollywood" of India that captured world attention via the 2009 continental award winning movie, *Slumdog Millionaire*, and the financial centers were under siege. Somewhat unbelievable violence was directed toward a hospital where the wounded might be readily treated (CNN. com/Asia, 2008; BBC News, 2008c). Yet it is a facility where women and children from particular ethnic groups or socioeconomic classes are patients.

Multiple factors are at play raising basic issues about globalization, diversity, and which people and institutions are affected. How are they affected immediately and likely to be affected in the intermediate and distant future? How might universities examine such phenomena? Simultaneously, universities are concerned with their *raisons d'être*—teaching, scholarship/research, and public engagement/service. Moreover, these reasons encompass preparing professionals in a range of fields as academic, civic, corporate, and political leaders who attempt to address current and future challenges, as declared in the newly named Association of Public and Land-Grant Colleges and Universities (formerly the National Association of State Universities and Land-Grant Colleges) publications, *A National Action Agenda for Internationalizing Higher Education* (2007) and *Expanding the International Scope of Universities: A Strategic Vision Statement for Learning, Scholarship, and Engagement in the New Century* (2000). The Longview Foundation report, *Teacher Preparation for the Global Age: The Imperative for Change* (2008), explicated endeavors for colleges and universities in preparing professional educators and teachers. Similarly, Knight in his volume, *Higher education in turmoil* (2008) and Lindsay (2010) expound how universities' missions encompass current analysis and future projections in order to prepare professionals for an array of educational milieus. Within the American environment, Smith (2009) presents imperatives for incorporating diversity in domestic higher education as she moves beyond the previous rationales of the value-added aspects for the inclusion of various demographic groups and multiple frameworks into domestic postsecondary institutions.

If we couple the aforementioned factors with the critical emergence of economic blocs and regions, the re-alignment of nation-states, and altered postsecondary educational structures and objectives, we may observe that various types of universities have diverse foci as they seek to fulfill their basic functions—foremost among them is the preparation of educators—and presenting models for moving forward. *Our volume seeks to articulate and analyze universities' roles in preparing professional educators for changing global diversity via explications of current trends in select geographical regions and nations and positing paradigms to ameliorate global challenges.* Hence, we identified different types of universities in the United States and select nations or geopolitical environments throughout the world and how these sites are addressing mega trends that move beyond international relations between specific nations.

Regarding new and emerging economic powers, the G-8 nations, consisting of eight of the world's highly industrialized nations—Canada, France, Germany, Italy, Japan, Russia, the United Kingdom, and the United States of America—still exert tremendous clout. Nevertheless, the roles of the G-20 nations—consisting of the G-8 nations plus Argentina, Australia, Brazil, China, India, Indonesia, Mexico, Saudi Arabia, South Africa, South Korea, Turkey, and the European Union (EU) —are paramount in affecting salient components of globalization. The G-20 nations account for approximately 90% of the world's gross national product (GNP), 80% of world trade, and two-thirds of the world's population (Brown, 2008; United Kingdom 2009, 2009). Hence our volume examines postsecondary education in a number of G-20 nations and regions, rather than limiting it to G-8 and/or Western modes of education. Moreover, we examine the preparation of professional educators in light of new and emerging blocs in the European Union and the Southern African Development Community (SADC) with select illustrations from South Africa, the dominant nation in SADC. This nation, along with other Southern African ones, is thrust into the throes of postmodern globalization. Only in 1993 was a new constitution promulgated. Other SADC nations such as Mozambique threw off the formal yoke of colonialism in 1975 followed by a protracted Civil War ending in 1992. Thus, postsecondary institutions in SADC face globalization, capacity building, and new economic realities as they attend to traditional and emerging roles for universities with diverse demographic profiles.

Simultaneously historical university roles need to be continued and further enhanced as global emigration and immigration occur among SADC nations, the Caribbean Community (CARICOM), consisting of 15 nations and focusing on economic, cultural, and political issues of the West Indies, the East Asia Summit (consisting of 16 Asian and Pacific nations) that concentrate on economic, energy, security, and other geopolitical issues, and the European Union (South African Development Community, 2009; CARICOM Secretariat, 2009; Europa, 2009). While such regional entities encourage immigration to bolster regional economic independence and security, the new immigrants face cultural challenges as indigenous populations see positive and negative aspects of new arrivals. Yet the emigrant nation may, indeed, be losing part of its skilled populace and thus not observing immediate benefits of the new economic community. In essence, universities enroll endogamous and exogamous students who need preparation for current and emerging features of globalization.

Principles and Organization of the Volume

While macro level global matters are overarching, universities are faced with translating such phenomena into viable policies, programs, and practices at their respective sites. How universities accomplish the translation in view of globalization and diversity is a focus of this volume. Our volume builds upon the works on globalization such as Stromquist (2007) regarding the roles and preparation of faculty, Altbach (2004), and Neave (2000) concerning universities' responsibilities for the local and international environments. We further take into account the works on multi-cultural education such as Banks (2007) on diversity and citizenship in global settings, Banks & Banks (2006) on various cultures and diversity, and Hahn (2005) on diversity in England and the United States. Salient sociological literature involving international aspects of race, culture, and ethnicity in diverse areas include historical works by Bobo & Fox (2003), Van den Berghe (1967), Wilson (1978), and Etzioni (2004).

A seminal essay written by Dodds (2008) elucidates a range of conceptual perspectives on globalization; yet she quotes Amin (1997) that "the more we read about globalization from the mounting literature on the topic, the less clear we seem to be about what it means what it implies" (p. 23). Globalization concepts appear to center around 1) global flows and/or pressures (whether of people, information, or culture); 2) policy trends often associated with markets and capital as exemplified with the G-20; and 3) ideologies often associated with political and/or geopolitical structural arrangements. Indeed, the introduction to this chapter and the 'Issues and Questions' section elucidates material that can be categorized into the three main areas identified by Dodds. Further the concepts may be manifested in generic and unique ways in diverse higher education sites and are noted in the following chapters. In short, the definitions and conceptual perspectives of globalization and diversity delineate characteristics and how such parameters may be analyzed.

Dodds (2008) maintains, in one sense, that relatively few publications examined by her discuss how higher education influences globalization. However, a myriad of publications encompassing Rizvi (2004, 2008) and Rhoads, Saenz, & Carducci (2005) place higher education within the context of dominant Western globalization trends and furthermore buttress, foster, and innovate new or altered ideologies. Our volume seeks to move beyond such publications by utilizing a multi-disciplinary approach drawing upon anthropology, international relations, sociology, political science, psychology, and education as we present combined motifs of how globalization and diversity become global diversity—or sometimes absence thereof—at the institutional level in the preparation of professional educators. *This volume posits interactive effects, that is, how universities respond (to) and initiate globalization and diversity resulting in global diversity.*

This chapter further articulates contemporary global matters and outlines central questions and issues that are explored in three thematic sections in the book: 1) "Geopolitical and Regional Matters in Higher Education;" 2) "Unique Colleges and Universities and Global Influences;" and 3) "University Students and Colleges and Schools of Education." A fourth section, "Global Environments and Diversity," consists of the final chapter, wherein we synthesize tenets gleaned from the various chapters and elucidate aspects of globalization and diversity with the aim of highlighting "best practices and modes" that may enhance country-specific and/or cross-national lessons and paradigms.

Within the various sections, the illustrative issues and questions featured in the chapters are as follows.

Issues and Questions

The chapters seek to articulate and respond to an array of issues *inter alia*:

1) Because a myriad of perspectives exist concerning globalization and diversity, authors will pose the question: How is globalization articulated and/or defined in various types of universities, nation-states, and geopolitical regions? How is diversity articulated and/or defined in these same entities?

2) Even more basic, are globalization and diversity prominent concerns or foci in the universities and postsecondary sites that we examine? If not, why not since manifestations of globalization are ever present?

3) Have the objectives and tenets of major foundations like Carnegie and Ford affected higher education within the two superpowers of the United States and Russia since the shifting World Order of the 1990s? To what extent have such Foundation Reports and those of national Ministries of Education/Higher Education been internalized in universities as professional educators are prepared? Chapters by Nelly Stromquist and Anna Smolentseva and Mouzinho Mario and Beverly Lindsay tackle such illustrative questions.

4) How will universities within the largest populated nations seek to respond to diverse domestic populations while simultaneously enrolling students from various Asian and Pacific nations? How will university academic programs be fostered while offshore university programs are being established as those in select Asian nations such as China and South Korea? Kiwan Sung's chapter explores such questions.

5) How are aspects of globalization and diversity manifested in the university milieu(s), via academic and strategic plans and the curriculum of universities in the Middle East and Australia that advanced, on the surface, technologically during the advent of the current era of globalization? How has the establishment of comprehensive American university branch campuses co-existed with domestic Middle Eastern Universities where indigenous and foreign cultures and curriculum inter-mix, while more Asian and Middle Eastern students are studying in Australian universities. Such matters are presented in chapters by Issam Khoury and Beverly Lindsay and Anne Hickling-Hudson and Ravinder Sidhu.

6) Might foci, which do not appear to concentrate on globalization and/ or diversity, be unrecognized aspects of globalization and diversity? For example, in the senior author's recent field research in Jamaican postsecondary institutions, several faculty stated that globalization and diversity were not real concerns. Nevertheless, they explained how they were preparing graduates to work in the United States and Canada as counselors, nurse educators, and teachers. Or they shared the likely impact of CARICOM (a regional Caribbean Economic Community) that attempts to address economic and political realities. These are features of globalization and diversity that are examined in Beverly Lindsay's chapter.

7) Will original roles of particular types of universities such as Historically Black Colleges and Universities (HBCUs) be altered via globalization? HBCUs have, since their inception, been open to diverse demographic groups, though originally designed to provide postsecondary opportunities for African Americans who were denied entrance to Predominately White Institutions (PWIs). For instance, when Hurricane Katrina devastated New Orleans many immigrant workers, who helped rebuild the city, hailed from Spanish-speaking countries and regions of the United States. Such workers and their families stayed on and entered postsecondary institutions. In their chapter, Beverly Lindsay and Tara Scales Williams present how HBCUs might respond in light of new global demographics caused by massive migration and new demands on urban universities?

8) First or Native Americans were essentially eliminated. Less than 1% still exist; yet for these there should be colleges? Are there parallel components across vastly diffuse geographical arenas that prepare students for global diversity? John W. Tippeconnic, III and Susan C. Faircloth's, Anne Hickling-Hudson and Ravinder Sidhu's, and Joyce King and her co-authors' chapters explore responses.

9) How will unique types of traditional and evolving colleges and universities address globalization and diversity? For example, comprehensive American urban universities essentially evolved since the 1960s coinciding with waves of diverse immigrants (often caused by deteriorating work conditions in their home country and recent formal country independence, facets of globalization). Urban universities which prepare those often nontraditional, first-generation, and commuter students for careers—nurses, social workers, and teachers—that support their immediate communities, ——struggle with the tensions between serving the community and a rapidly globalized world. The chapter by Jorgelina Abbate-Vaughn and Donna DeGennaro provides illustrations.

10) How do the global themes of harmonization and integration of diverse student bodies present new or different options for the postsecondary sites? What kind of amalgamations, mergers, and consortia are emerging? How have students' attitudes in a range of disciplines been affected in various nations? Responses to such queries are observed in chapters by Lani Florian and by Luanna H. Meyer and her co-authors.

11) Why are particular sociocultural and geopolitical features of globalization and diversity examined and not others? For example, in the senior author's Distinguished Fulbright Fellowships to Mozambique and Zimbabwe, she observed considerable discussion regarding Southern African Development Community (SADC) and the call for postsecondary institutions to prepare professionals for the SADC community. This is a geopolitical phenomenon. Yet within

the respective region, the sociopolitical and educational needs of the Portuguese-speaking nations of Mozambique and Angola are often absent in the analyses and discussions. Simultaneously, within SADC, there are to be porous borders that may or may not promote regional economic growth, but increase demographic tensions, particularly among various linguistic groups. Mouzinho Mario and Beverly Lindsay discuss such matters in their chapter.

13) What models and/or paradigms may need to be altered? Are realistic and innovative roles considered and developed and then implemented in light of continuing global changes for the particular region where the universities are situated? The majority of the chapters expand such questions and provide illustrations via analytical summaries and synthesis.

Geopolitical and Regional Matters in Higher Education

In Chapter 2, "The University in Turbulent Times: A Comparative Study of the United States and Russia," Nelly P. Stromquist and Anna Smolentseva contend that the influence of globalization on universities has been primarily through its economic and technological forces, the first opening the university to the market, and the second making it possible for knowledge to cross space inexpensively and with great speed. This chapter compares Russia and the United States. Although the two countries are at very different points in their insertion into the capitalist economy and have traversed contrasting historical trajectories. Their study shows that many contemporary changes are moving their universities into significant convergence, despite some elements that still reflect individual contexts. Common trends include the following. One, the search for excellence or the aspiration to become research universities. Two, the search for efficiency, translated into such measures as mergers of departments and institutions—actions that aim at reducing administrative expenditures, but often end up eliminating important fields of study that by nature are not income-generating, and a shift away from tenure track positions and toward more part-time employment for faculty members. In Russia, most faculties are hired full-time, but many are forced to take on additional part-time jobs to supplement their regular salaries, resulting in higher teaching loads. Three, the competition for student markets, which is leading to internationalization strategies, is often defined as increasing the number of international students who are able to pay full tuition and fees. Four, the competition for research funds, which, on the one hand, promotes attention to social and economic problems, but on the other, focuses on a narrow set of these problems and frames their solutions primarily to address practical needs that have tangible markets and buyers.

The comparative study by Stromquist and Smolentseva seeks to prepare faculty to face shifting realities. In the current state of affairs, the challenges for the professoriate are considerable. Within U.S. universities, the dominance of strategic plans has *de facto* constrained traditional academic governance as institutions are steered by decisions made by central administrators. Within Russian universities, administrative plans at all levels have been traditionally essential, and academic governance has had an insignificant role. It might seem, thus, that governance is moving toward convergence between the two countries. Given these developments in universities, how can faculty respond to changing situations? What venues and strategies are possible for their engagement in the ongoing transformation of the university?

In Chapter 3, "Beyond Globalization: Possibilities and Challenges in Korea and China," Kiwan Sung elucidates significant changes in Higher Educational Institutes (HEIs) in Asia, especially, those being made by the Republic of Korea and the People's Republic of China in order for HEIs to meet the new world order of globalization and internationalization (Altbach & Peterson, 1999). More specifically, he expounds how Western countries such as the United States (Altbach, 2001; Kim, 2004), the International Monetary Fund (IMF) crisis in the 1990s, and recent economic downturns have influenced Korean and Chinese HEIs. In both countries, merging their administrative offices and budgetary efficiency are evinced to help ensure more rigorous accountability in administrative, academic, and research performances in hopes of producing better educators and professionals in various disciplines.

This chapter also considers and identifies key changes on both national and institutional levels in Korea and China in view of various political, sociocultural, and economical factors, which are shaping current efforts to restructure and revitalize HEIs. For example, revitalization in both countries is manifested in curricular revisions to serve students from other countries, mandatory offerings of English courses, and funding for young scholars and recent graduates. Such domestic changes are appearing in light of the influx of professional programs offered by foreign universities and the necessity of sending domestic students overseas for both academic and cultural experiences to enhance their international competitiveness (Ihm, 2006; Kim, 2004).

In this chapter, existing literature studies and documents related to university educational policies and changes are utilized, along with a comparative approach that highlights some characteristics of changes and key challenges occurring in Korea and China. Furthermore, a case study method (Stake, 2005) was employed to examine one of the top-10 Korean universities and a Chinese university's ongoing engagements and efforts in globalizing their campuses and programs, and also to highlight how these universities cope with new challenges and what opportunities they have in process for their academic and administrative restructuring. It is found that, although the two countries have been restructuring their educational systems for better academic and research performances through both centralizing and decentralizing their universities' governances, they continue to face difficulties in meeting students' needs and enhancing their global competitiveness. The difficulties are due, in part, to a rapid increase in domestic student enrollment in China and the lack of systemic efforts to improve HEI's administrative and educational performance and effectiveness in Korea.

For Chapter 4, "Globalization and Higher Education in the Middle East," Issam Khoury and Beverly Lindsay point out that internationalizing campuses to promote global diversity and interconnectedness remained on the agendas of national organizations such as the American Council of Education (2009), the Association of Public and Land-Grant Universities (2009), and the National Association for Equal Opportunity in Higher Education (NAFEO) (2007). Simultaneously, globalization forces, declining economic resources in home countries, and expanding student age populations in other nations, led to a number of Western universities establishing programs or campuses in other nations, including those in the Middle East. Such establishments should be viewed with various concepts of globalization such as those by Dodds (2008) and Rizvi (2008).

It is within this environment that an initial focus of this chapter emerges, that is, higher education was globalized in the Arabian (Persian) Gulf by Western nations. Education City was established in Qatar in 1995 as the cornerstone of the Qatar Foundation's (2009) project to transform mineral wealth into human capital. The City brings together the branch campuses of six American institutions: Texas A&M, Georgetown, Carnegie Mellon, Virginia Commonwealth, Cornell, and Northwestern Universities. Each campus specializes in only one or two majors, with a liberal arts education undergirding each of those programs. Examining Education City as one block, they seek to ascertain how students and nationals in the region have received American-style education.

The second focus of this chapter is on how globalization has, in turn, affected the curricula of Arab universities in the region. The curricular content and programmatic initiatives of major universities in the Arabian Gulf, namely Qatar University, Zayed University (United Arab Emirates [UAE]), and Sultan Qaboos University (Oman) are analyzed in an effort to ascertain the effect of globalization on shaping future generations. To accomplish these tasks, content and web analyses of various university websites and news sources were employed, along with participant observation by the first author and a range of communications with associates in Qatar by both authors. The authors maintain that what appears to be a symbiotic higher education relationship between the West and Gulf States seems to be emerging.

Within Chapter 5, "Shifting Tides in Jamaican Higher Education," Beverly Lindsay discusses how during the past decades, monumental economic and sociocultural changes occurred in Jamaica that have tremendously impacted colleges and universities (Lindsay, 2008b). Foremost among these are the contemporary regional and global economic crises such that in the 1980s about six Jamaican dollars were equivalent to one American dollar. By fall 2008, it was about 76 Jamaican dollars to 1 American dollar. In the 1990s and 2000s, Jamaica and other Caribbean countries faced the growing HIV/AIDS crisis thus curtailing the activities of university individuals and professionals primarily in the 16 to 45 year age cohorts thus affecting socioeconomic development (USAID, 2008).

Against this backdrop of challenges, a central issue emerges concerning how university and college programs and polices prepare Jamaican and Caribbean professionals who will engage in educational enterprises. While local and/or national domestic concerns are paramount and must be addressed for the preparation of educators, what simultaneous measures exist or should be created to ensure that global parameters are part of comprehensive educational equations, since many Jamaicans assume careers in diverse Commonwealth countries and the United States? (U.S. Census Bureau, 2006; Department of Homeland Security, 2007).

How are globalization and diversity explicated, implemented, and/or evaluated in postsecondary educational sites by those integrally involved in tertiary education? In response to this key query, central purposes of this chapter are to: 1) explicate conceptual and programmatic features of globalization and diversity; 2) ascertain and define principles undergirding the aforementioned in Jamaican higher education; and 3) posit motifs which may best facilitate globalization and diversity in a transnational era so cross-national university lessons may be developed. To accomplish the three aims, participant observations at four colleges and universities—especially during fall 2008 and summer 2009—and interviews of administrators, faculty, counselors, and students along with examinations of primary and secondary university and Ministry of Education data sources were undertaken. The observations and interviews sought to answer questions *inter alia:* 1) What is the overall stated mission or purpose of the University or College? 2) Are faculty aware of this mission? Is it implemented? 3) How do particular colleges and universities prepare students and current educators for roles that encompass diversity and globalization? (Arnot & Dillabough, 2000; Cowen, 2000; The University of the West Indies at Mona, 2007a; The University of the West Indies at Mona, 2007b).

Unique Colleges and Universities and Global Influences

Chapter 6, penned by Beverly Lindsay and Tara Scales Williams, is titled, "Historically Black Colleges and Universities in New Orleans: Domestic and Global Engagement in the Post-Katrina Era." In this chapter, the authors review the impact of globalism on HBCUs generally, how HBCUs are addressing global challenges, particularly as it relates to preparing professional educators, and recommend future directions for HBCUs in a globalized world. Particular illustrations are presented for the New Orleans metropolitan area HBCUs that are undergoing rapid changes in the aftermath of Hurricane Katrina where the economic and demographic bases evidenced profound changes. Initiatives for and responses to the effects of Hurricane Katrina, migration, globalism, and diversity, are analyzed at Dillard University, Southern University of New Orleans, and Xavier University based upon participant observations and interviews.

The authors posit several ongoing and possible future strategic plans and directions that the HBCUs may undertake. These include *inter alia*: Curricular and structural changes within the academy, cooperative endeavors within civic and political leaders within the metropolitan and state arenas; innovative public engagement roles with new demographic groups while fostering continued relations with African Americans, and active interactions with national professional organizations and policy organizations that engage in university global programs among various nations.

In Chapter 7, "Native American Tribal Colleges and Universities: Utilizing Indigenous Knowledges and Ways of Knowing to Prepare Native Peoples to Meet the Demands of an Increasingly Globalized Community," John Tippeconnic, III and Susan Faircloth discuss how globalization poses a number of challenges and opportunities for Indigenous communities around the world. Indigenous controlled colleges, first established in the United States in the 1960s, provide a unique mechanism through which Native peoples are able to build their economic and educational capital, thereby increasing their chances for sustainability in an increasingly globalized world. Indigenous knowledges and ways of knowing inform the work of these colleges in ways that are unique to their individual tribes and communities. These colleges provide an opportunity for Native peoples to obtain higher education without losing sight of who they are as a people or being forced to leave their local communities. Founded on principles of sovereignty and self-determination, Indigenous controlled colleges and universities provide an opportunity for students to obtain higher education while maintaining physical and ideological connections to the places from which they come. The opportunity to maintain such connections to place is something rarely available to individuals seeking higher education in mainstream colleges and universities.

Although this chapter focuses primarily upon the ways in which Indigenous knowledges and ways of knowing are utilized by Indigenous controlled colleges and universities in the United States, examples of the ways in which this movement is impacting Indigenous education across the globe, are provided. Implications for policy, practice, and future research are also discussed.

In Chapter 8, "Urban Support Networks: Commuter Urban Public Universities in Global Times," Jorgelina Abbate-Vaughn and Donna DeGennaro, concentrate on commuter urban public universities (CUPU) as one type of university that meets the educational needs of commuter students—those who live with their parents, in rental housing, or are older students with jobs and/or children. They can be located in small urban enclaves or in large urban conglomerates. Nationwide, there are hundreds of colleges and universities that serve large percentages of, or solely, commuters. CUPUs serve significant percentages of economically diverse and older students, and students from cultural, ethnic, and linguistically diverse backgrounds, as their local constituencies primarily draw from the cities in which they are nested.

Many CUPUs rank high in enrollments of low-income students. Other CUPUs main feature is the large population of undergraduates aged 25 or above. As with other urban public universities, CUPUs provide a reliable pipeline for local high school completers and community college transfers. In general, they pioneer community engagement efforts as well as health disparity research and health-promoting partnerships. Emphasis on service to one's local community is similarly evident in the mission that CUPUs such as City University of New York, University of the District of Columbia, Florida International University, and the University of Massachusetts Boston have recently exhibited very publicly on their web pages.

Such institutions are typically committed to researching and offering potential solutions for the complexities of urban sustainability, in ever-growing diverse communities. As with most urban public universities, CUPUs have begun to increasingly engage in the process of thinking globally, but primarily acting locally. The commendable local goals and global engagement, however, might not be enough for CUPUs to respond successfully to 21st-century challenges. All college graduates, some contend, must be able to navigate the increasingly global economies and job markets. Pioneering new programs are appealing because they can potentially attract national and international investments that widen the urban nesting area's job markets. Yet, growth may come at the expense of traditional careers that together form an irreplaceable urban support network; balancing local and global enterprises is necessary.

In Chapter 9, "Australian Universities and the Challenges of Internationalization," Anne Hickling-Hudson and Ravinder Sidhu examine the challenges for Australia's universities as they build an international profile and, strive to produce graduates with global competencies. Embedded within their examination is the phenomena of large numbers of students from India, in particular, and other Asian and Middle Eastern nations who experience notable tensions within Australian higher education. Contextualizing their discussion with an overview of the rise of the education export industry, they analyze the internationalization of university missions and academic practices in two case-study universities within the Australian Technology Network (ATN) where they engaged in participant observations and interviews.

Hickling-Hudson and Sidhu identify the strengths and limitations of existing approaches to internationalization in Australian universities, against a continuum ranging from "symbolic" to "transformative" expressions of internationalization. This allows them to consider the postcolonial query of how far contemporary university education, substantially shaped by its role as a carrier of imperial ideas and introduced to many countries through European colonialism, is likely to carry out its globalizing vision. They conclude by proposing a series of changes that would enable a new model for the international university, one which would play a bigger part in addressing global inequalities and in doing so contribute to a more ethical globalization for the 21st century.

University Students and Colleges and Schools of Education

Regarding Chapter 10, "An International Survey of Higher Education Students' Perceptions of World-Mindedness and Global Citizenship," Luanna H. Meyer, Christine E. Sleeter, Kenneth Zeichner, Hyun-Sook Park, Garry Hoban, and Peter Sorensen raise a fundamental matter, the global awareness of students. In citing Mansilla and Gardner (2007), the co-authors argue that educators should cultivate global consciousness among students, which they define as "The capacity and the inclination to place our self and the people, objects, and situations with which we come into contact within the broader matrix of our contemporary world" (p. 58). However, not only is there no consensus about what globalization means (Dodds, 2008); we also do not have a clear idea about how college students understand globalization, multiculturalism, and their role as citizens. If higher education seeks to prepare educators for tomorrow, we need an understanding of our current students' global consciousness, as mediated by factors such as students' national contexts and disciplinary majors.

Their chapter reports a study undertaken by a team of researchers from a dozen major universities in four countries (the United States, the United Kingdom, Australia, and New Zealand), who have collaboratively undertaken a multi-year, multi-method, and multi-national research project to inform evidence-based practice towards nurturing global consciousness in higher education. Via an overview of the project and selected data from the first stage of the research, this chapter compares the perspectives of undergraduate students in various disciplines: humanities, business, law, social sciences, and education, and compares perspectives across national contexts. Preliminary results are based on more than 1,000 surveys. Factor analysis of responses to the project's *Citizenship & World-Mindedness Survey* reveals five overarching dimensions: 1) Social Responsibility; 2) Skilled Dispositions and Open-Mindedness; 3) Ethnocentrism and Nationalism; 4) Personal Efficacy; and 5) Global Kinship. Business students were least likely to believe that personal actions can make a difference; business and law students were more negative than education and humanities students on ethnocentrism and nationalism; and all student groups tended to agree with the social responsibility and skill-disposition dimensions. On global kinship, all groups scored just under "agreement." The authors discuss the implications of their findings about the attitudes and experiences of young adults for higher education curricula directed toward preparing future citizens in a diverse, multicultural, and inequitable world.

Within Chapter 11, "European Union Universities and Teacher Preparation," Lani Florian discusses how the increasing mobility and migration of people across the 27 member countries of the European Union raise particular issues for global diversity. For example, the increasing mobility and migration of people raise particular issues for global diversity. Declining populations in some parts of Europe mean that immigrant citizens of Member States travel between countries to work and study in other Member States. Such migrants are needed to fill essential jobs. Consequently, issues of global diversity are reflected in an increasing multicultural and multilingual student population in both urban and non-urban schools.

Florian considers how EU reforms have promoted globalization, both *in* and *of* education through initiatives that are aimed at increasing cohesion within Europe via multi-national projects and exchanges aimed at improving understanding and tolerance of differences, on the one hand; and the alignment of national systems of education for the purposes of comparability, collaboration and exchange on the other. The chapter will provide examples of EU education initiatives that support teachers in responding to diversity issues within schools and classroom, as well as initiatives that encourage teacher mobility.

In Chapter 12, "Engaged Research/ers, Transformative Curriculum and Diversity Policy for Teacher Education in the Americas: the United States, Brazil, and Belize," Joyce King, Melissa Speight Vaughn, Petronilha Beatriz Gonçalves e Silva, Regina Conceição, Tatiane Cosentino Rodrigues, and Evaldo Ribeiro Oliveira collaborated on various education and action-research activities in their respective universities and communities in the United States, Belize, and Brazil. Writing among senior faulty and their doctoral students who are also educators, the chapter describes and compares engaged research, curriculum change strategies, diversity policies, and teacher education reforms that address the identity and consciousness of people of African descent in Brazil, Belize, and the United States. In so doing, the chapter focuses needed attention on an important, but largely unrecognized perspective on globalization and teacher preparation for diversity. The curriculum change examined in the United States involved using a Black Studies intellectual framework to make cultural and heritage knowledge available to teachers and community members (King, 2006, 1992; King & Goodwin, 2007). However, education policy does not reflect a growing body of research that shows positive impacts of culturally relevant curriculum content and pedagogy, as well as racial socialization for Black students' learning and identity development (Chavous et al., 2003; Lee, 2008; Murrell, 2009). In Brazil, a national policy directive that requires incorporating African and Afro-Brazilian culture and history at all levels has been supported by strategic research partnerships that include a state-university Afro-Brazilian Studies Group, a municipal Cultural Center and Affirmative Action and Diversity programs supported by the Black Movement (Gonçalves e Silva, 2005; Htun, 2004). Higher education practices, curriculum, teacher education and graduate student research training have all been impacted.

Instituted in 1994, Belize's National Identity Policy required that all students be taught about their individual ethnicities as well as Belizean identity. This policy not only reformed the social studies curriculum, but also transformed teacher education programs (Thompson & Crossley, 1999). A review of teacher training programs and reforms before and after the policy reveals the increased importance placed on education as Belize establishes its global presence. This comparative cross-national discussion of educational policies for diversity and teacher preparation illustrates transformative curriculum that supports both group identity and national identity development in three contexts (Banks, 2008).

In tenets of Chapter 13, "Teaching and Administrative Development in Southern Africa: Illustrations from Mozambique and Angola," Mouzinho Mario and Beverly Lindsay maintain that higher education systems are experiencing changes, especially since the early 1990s. In most cases, these changes are closely associated with rapid expansion of enrollments in primary and secondary schools that translate into increased public universities' growing student bodies. Amid these changes are the regional geopolitical and economic conditions of the SADC, a regional bloc formed to ameliorate a range of social conditions and institutions throughout the region. An acute problem within SADC is the severe shortage of qualified and skilled professional educators. This chapter examines the emerging patterns and trends of initial preparation, in-service and continuous development of teachers and other professional educators in two Portuguese-speaking nations, Angola and Mozambique, within the SADC community. Special attention is devoted to the preparation of education administrators for the academy and other public service sectors who must constantly interact with a range of professionals and constituents within their respective nations, the region, and the large African and global communities.

Taking into account the differences in the historical, political, and economic contexts of each nation, they view how universities prepare (or do not prepare) professional educators to address the current and future challenges posed by their ever changing and diverse global environments. With some notable exceptions, the roles of universities in the preparation of teachers and other professional educators for different levels of education, seeking to address sociocultural diversity and ease ethnic tensions, have not been clearly articulated. Often where clear policies, strategies, and responsibilities have been established, there are unresolved tensions between different implementation agencies and stakeholders based upon years of professional experience in teacher training colleges and universities in Southern Africa and their direct involvement with Ford Foundation Commissions, United States' Agency for International Development (USAID) programs, and Fulbright Fellowships. The authors posit that in some ways articulation and implementation can be meshed in order to enhance individual options and those for professionals and students in Mozambique and Angola.

Global Environments and Diversity

In Chapter 14, "Universities and Global Diversity: Movement Towards Tomorrow," Wanda Blanchett and Beverly Lindsay synthesize the major themes that emerged from the various chapters and posit some unique and "global" aspects of globalization and diversity in light of "best practices and modes" that may enhance country-specific and/or cross-national lessons and paradigms. In doing so, they articulate four overarching motifs: 1) the recognitions of varying definitions and conceptualizations of globalization, diversity, and global diversity; 2) the impacts on the practices of higher education; 3) the impacts on unique colleges and universities; and 4) implications and conclusions pertaining to global diversity. They articulate how conceptual clarification and understanding of the abundant components of diversity and globalization can foster global diversity in higher education in myriad environments thereby contributing to equity, fairness, and social justice for everyone.

Bibliography

Adeyemi, Michael B. & Hopkin, Anthony G. (1997). University affiliation and the role of the university in the moderation of teaching practice in Botswana. *Higher Education, 33*, 415–431.

Altbach, Philip. (2004). Globalization and the university: Myths and realities in an unequal world. *Tertiary Education and Management, 10*(1), 1–20 (online print).

Altbach, Philip. (2001). The American academic model in comparative perspective. In P. G. Altbach, P. J. Gumport, & D. B. Johnstone, (Eds.), *Defense of American higher education* (pp. 11–37). Baltimore, MD: The Johns Hopkins University Press.

Altbach, Philip, & Peterson, Patti. (2008). *Higher education in the new century*. Boston, MA: Sense Publishers.

American Association of State Colleges and Universities (AASCU) State Relations and Policy Analysis Research Team. (2008, January). *Top 10 State Policy Issues for Higher Education in 2008. A Higher Education Policy Brief*. Washington DC: Author.

American Council on Education. (2009). *Center for international initiatives.* Retrieved March 15, 2009, from http://www.acenet.edu/Content/Navigation-Menu/ProgramsServices/cii/index.htm

Anderson, James. (1988). *The education of blacks in the South 1860–1935.* Chapel Hill: University of North Carolina Press.

Arnot, Madeleine, & Dillabough, Joann (Eds.). (2000). *Challenging democracy: International perspectives on gender, education and citizenship.* New York: RoutledgeFalmer.

Association of Public and Land-Grant Universities. (2009). *Commission on international programs.* Retrieved March 15, 2009, from http://www.aplu.org/NetCommunity/Page.aspx?pid=264

Ball, A. (2006). *Multicultural strategies for education and social change.* New York: Teachers College Press.

Banco Mundial. (2008) *Qualificação e Emprego de Professores em Angola.* Versão para Comentários. July 2008.

Banks, James A. (Ed.). (2007). *Diversity and citizenship education: Global perspectives.* San Francisco: Jossey–Bass.

Banks, James A. (2008). Diversity, group identity, and citizenship in a global age. *Educational Researcher, 37*(3), 129–139.

Banks, James, & Banks, Cheryl. (Eds.). (2006*). Multicultural education: Issues and perspectives* (6th ed.). Indianapolis: Wiley.

Bates, Richard. (2008). Teacher education in a global context: Towards a defensible theory of teacher education. *Journal of Education for Teaching, 34*(4), 277–293.

Battiste, Marie and Henderson, J. (Sa'ke'j) Youngblood. (2000). *Protecting indigenous knowledge and heritage: A global challenge.* Saskatoon, Canada: Purich Publishing.

BBC News. (2008a, November 27). *Mumbai rocked by deadly attacks.* Retrieved May 21, 2009, from http://news.bbc.co.uk/2/hi/south_asia/7751160.stm

BBC News. (2008b, November 29). *As it happened: Mumbai attacks—28 Nov.* Retrieved May 21, 2009, from http://news.bbc.co.uk/2/hi/south_asia/7753639.stm.

BBC News. (2008c, December 1). *Mumbai victims from all walks of life.* Retrieved May 26, 2009, from http://news.bbc.co.uk/2/hi/south_asia/7758430.stm

Bhagwati, J. (2005). *In defense of globalization.* Oxford, England: Oxford University Press.

Bobo, Lawrence, & Fox, Cybelle. (2003). Race, racism, and discrimination: Bridging problems, methods, and theory in social psychological research. Special Issue: Race, racism, and discrimination. *Social Psychology Quarterly, 66*(4), 319–332.

Bookman, Jay. (2008, November 28). The nightmare in Mumbai continues. *The Atlanta Journal Constitution.* Retrieved March 20, 2009, from http://www.ajc.com/blogs/content/shared–blogs/ajc/bookman/entries/2008/11/28/the_nightmare_in_mumbai_contin.html

Boyer, Ernest. (1989). *Tribal colleges: Shaping the future of Native America.* The Carnegie Foundation. Princeton, NJ: Princeton University Press.

Brown, Gordon. (2008). *Meeting the new global challenge* [Video]. New York: Council on Foreign Relations. Retrieved February 20, 2009, from www.cfr/publications/17765/meeting

Calette, Gregory. (2006, Winter). It is time for Indian people to define indigenous education on our own terms. *Tribal College Journal of American Indian Higher Education, 18*(2), 56–57.

Calhoun, Craig. (2003). "Belonging" in the cosmopolitan imaginary. *Ethnicities, 3*(4), 531–568.

Caribbean Community (CARICOM) Secretariat. (2009). *The Caribbean community*. Retrieved March 20, 2009, from http://www.caricom.org/jsp/community/community_index.jsp?menu=community

Castiano, José P. (2007). *Reconstruction of the education system in Angola: Improving the quality of teacher education.* Midterm Evaluation Report, Luanda.

Champagne, Duane. (2004, Winter). Education for nation-building. *Cultural Survival Quarterly, 27*(4). Retrieved October 29, 2007, from ProQuest, http://www.culturalsurvival.org/publications/cultural-survival-quarterly/274-winter-2003-indigenous-education-and-prospects-cultural

Chavous, Tabbye M, Debra Hilkene Bernat, Karen Schmeelk-Cone, Cleopatra H. Caldwell, Laura Kohn-Wood, and Marc A. Zimmerman. (2003). Racial identity and academic attainment among African American adolescents. *Child Development, 74*(4), 1076–1090

CNN.com/Asia. (2008, November 28). *What is known about the Mumbai attacks.* Retrieved May 26, 2009, from http://www.cnn.com/2008/WORLD/asiapcf/11/28/mumbai.investigation/index.html?iref=newssearch#cnnSTCText

Coalition of Urban Serving Universities. (2008). *Quick facts.* Retrieved December 1, 2008, from http://www.usucoalition.org/about/quickfacts.html

Cowen, Robert. (2000). Comparing futures or comparing pasts? *Comparative Education, 36*(3), 333–342.

Davies, Lynn. (2006). Global citizenship: Abstraction or framework for action? *Educational Review, 58*(1), 5–25.

Davis, James. (1998). Cultural capital and the role of historically black colleges and universities in educational reproduction. In K. Freeman (Ed.), *African American culture and heritage in higher education research and practice* (pp. 143–154). Westport, CT: Praeger.

Department of Education. (2006). *The National Policy Framework for Teacher Education.* Pretoria: Department of Education.

Department of Education. (2005). *Report of the Ministerial Committee on Teacher Education: A national framework for teacher education.* Department of Education, Pretoria.

Department of Homeland Security. (2007). *Yearbook of immigration statistics, 2007.* Retrieved March 15, 2009, from http://www.dhs.gov/ximgtn/statistics/publications/LPR07.shtm

Dodds, Anneliese. (2008). How does globalisation interact with higher education? The continuing lack of consensus. *Comparative Education, 44*(4), 505–517.

ELRC (Education Labor Relations Council). (2006). *Improving education quality through implementation policies for public educators.* International Research and Study Visits Report. Pretoria: ELRC in association with HSRC.

Etzioni, Amitai. (2004). *From empire to community: A new approach to international relations.* New York: Palgrave.

Europa. (2009). *The history of the European Union.* Retrieved March 20, 2009, from http://europa.eu/abc/history/index_en.htm

Faircloth, Susan C., & Tippeconnic, John W., III. (Forthcoming). Tribally controlled colleges and universities: Impacting indigenous communities locally and globally. In K. A. Schafft & A. Jackson (Eds.), *Rural education for the twenty-first century: Identity, place, and community in a globalizing world.* University Park, PA: Penn State University Press (Rural Studies Series)

Fisher, Sydney, & Ochsenwald, William. (1990). *The Middle East: A history. Vol II* (5th ed.). New York: McGraw Hill.

Fogarty, Mark. (2007, Spring). Commitment to building prosperous nations: Tribal colleges take aim against poverty. *Tribal College Journal of American Indian Higher Education, 18*(3), 208–212.

Fox, Everall. (2006, November). Indian education for all: A tribal college perspective. *Phi Delta Kappan, 88*(3), 208–212.

Friedman, T. (2007). *The world is flat.* London: Picador.

Friedman, T. (2000). *The Lexus and the Olive Tree: Understanding globalization.* New York: Farrar, Straus and Giroux.

Fujikane, Hiroko. (2003). Approaches to global education in the United States, the United Kingdom and Japan. *International Review of Education, 49*(1/2), 133–152.

Gentzkow, Matthew, & Shapiro, Jesse. (2004). Media, education, and anti-Americanism in the Muslim world. *The Journal of Economic Perspectives, 18*(3), 117–133.

Gonçalves e Silva, Petronilha B. (2005). A new millennium research agenda in black education: Some points to be considered for discussion and decision. In Joyce E. King (Ed.), *Black education: A transformative research and action agenda for the new century* (pp. 301–308). Mahwah, NJ: Erlbaum.

Gurin, Patricia, Dey, Eric L., Hurtado, Sylvia, & Gurin, Gerald. (2002). Diversity and higher education: Theory and impact on educational outcomes. *Harvard Educational Review, 72*, 330–366.

Gurin, Patricia, & Epps, Edgar. G. (1975). *Black consciousness, identity, and achievement: A study of students in historically black colleges.* New York: John Wiley & Sons.

Hahn, Carole. (2005). Diversity and human rights learning in England and the United States. In A. Oslen (Ed.), *Teachers, human rights and diversity* (pp. 23–40). London: Trenthan Books.

Henry, Charles P. (2008). Revisiting a world view of race. In B. Lindsay (Ed.), *Ralph Johnson Bunche: Public intellectual and Nobel Peace Laureate* (pp. 45–59). Urbana: University of Illinois Press.

Herrera, Linda. (2007). Higher education in the Arab world. In J. Forest & P. Altbach (Eds.), *International handbook of higher education* (pp. 409–421). Boston: Springer.

Htun, Mala. (2004). Affirmative action: Changing state policy on race in Brazil. *Latin American Research Review, 39*(1), 60–89.

Ihm, Chon Sun. (2006). Internationalization of higher education and workplace competencies: Implications for policy in Korea, *Asian Women, 22*(1), 45–68.

Jessop, David. (2008, June 29). Caribbean tourism—unplanned and in crisis. *Jamaica Gleaner.* Retrieved March 15, 2009, from http://www.jamaica-gleaner.com/gleaner/20080629/business/business5.html

Kelly, Anthony. (2009). Globalisation. *Society & Education*, 7(1), 51–68.

Khouri, Fred. (1976). Review of Bahrain, Qatar and the United Arab Emirates: Colonial past, present problems, and future prospects by Sadik, M. and Snavely, W. *The American Political Science Review*, 70(1), 259–260.

Kim, Pil-Dong. (2004). A comparative study of university reforms: Toward 21st century in Korea, Japan, and China-Focusing on organization reforms, *Journal of Korean Sociological Association*, 38(3), 1–37.

King, Joyce E. (2006). "If justice is our objective": Diaspora literacy, heritage knowledge and the praxis of critical studyin' for human freedom. In A. Ball (Ed.), *With more deliberate speed: Achieving equity and excellence in education—Realizing the Full Potential of Brown v. Board of Education* (pp. 337–360). National Society for the Study of Education 105th Yearbook, Part 2. New York: Ballenger.

King, Joyce E. (1992). Diaspora literacy and consciousness in the struggle against mis-education in the Black community. *Journal of Negro Education*, 61(3), 317–340.

King, Joyce E,. & Goodwin, Susan. (2007). *Criterion standards for contextualized teaching and learning about people of African descent*. Rochester, NY: Rochester Teacher Center and New York: National Urban League.

Knight, Jane. (2008). *Higher education in turmoil: The changing world of internationalization*. Rotterdam: Sense Publishers

Lakshmi, Rama. (2008, November 27). Dozens Die in Mumbai Attacks; Hotels Under Siege; Gunmen Said to Target Americans, Britons. *The Washington Post*. Retrieved March 20, 2009 from http://pqasb.pqarchiver.com/washingtonpost/access/1602638211.html?dids=1602638211:1602638211&FMT=ABS&FMTS=ABS:FT&date=Nov+27%2C+2008&author=Rama+Lakshmi++Washington+Post+Foreign+Service&pub=The+Washington+Post&edition=&startpage=A.1&desc=Dozens+Die+in+Mumbai+Attacks%3B+Hotels+Under+Siege%3B+Gunmen+Said+to+Target+Americans%2C+Britons

Lee, Carol D. (2008). Synthesis of research on the role of culture in learning among African American youth: The contributions of Asa G. Hilliard, III. *Review of Educational Research*, 78(4), 797–827.

Leventhal, Mitch, & Zimpher, Nancy L. (2007). Changing international constructs: How metropolitan universities must engage globally. *Metropolitan Universities: An International Forum*, 18(3), 102–108.

Lewin, Tamar. (2008, February 11). In oil-rich Mideast, shades of the Ivy League. *The New York Times*.

Lindsay, Beverly (2010). *Development and enhancement of global skills for professional educators for The Whole World Over: Educators preparation gone global—A national webinar*. Washington DC: Association of Colleges for Teacher Education. Retrieved from http://aacte.org/index/php?/component/option,com_events/Itemid,28/agid,51/day,04/month,03/task,view_detail/year,2010/

Lindsay, Beverly. (Ed.). (2008a). *Ralph Johnson Bunche: A Nobel peace laureate influencing public intellectualism and diplomacy*. Champaign, IL: University of Illinois Press.

Lindsay, Beverly. (2008b, March). *Cosmopolitan perspectives of challenges in Commonwealth countries: Toward alternative educational administrative paradigms*. Paper presented at American Educational Research Association Conference, New York, NY.

Lindsay, Beverly. (2004). Transforming African and African American sociopolitical and educational realities: Possibilities or pipe dreams? *African Studies Quarterly, 7*(4), 41–47.

Little, Angela, W., & Green, Andy. (2009). Successful globalisation, education, and sustainable development. *International Journal of Educational Development, 29*(2), 166–174.

Longview Foundation. (2008). *Teacher preparation for the global age: The imperative for change.* Retrieved May 26, 2009, from http://www.longviewfdn.org/files/44.pdf

Loomis, Steven, Rodriguez, Jacob, & Tillman, Rachel. (2008). Developing into similarity: Global teacher education in the twenty-first century. *European Journal of Teacher Education, 31*(3), 233–45.

Madany, Ismail, Ali, S., and Akhter, M. (1988). Note on the expansion of higher education in Bahrain. *Higher Education, 17*(4), 411–415.

Makwinja-Morara, Veronica M. (2008, May). *Pre-service teacher training program: What it takes to train student teachers at the university of Botswana.* Paper presented at a Conference on Teacher Education in Mozambique, organized by Universidade Pedagógica, Maputo, Mozambique.

Mansilla, Veronica B., & Gardner, Howard. (2007). From teaching globalization to nurturing global consciousness. In M. M. Suárez-Orozco (Ed.), *Learning in the global era: International perspectives on global education* (pp. 47–66). Berkeley: University of California Press.

Mario, Mouzinho. (2008, March). *Educational administration and teachers in Portuguese–speaking Nations: Emerging strategies, structures and models.* Paper prepared for the Annual Meeting of the American Educational Research Association, New York, NY.

Mario, Mouzinho. (2006, June). *Models of teacher preparation in post–conflict Mozambique: A critical assessment.* Presentation to Doctoral Students of the University of Pretoria Faculty of Education, within the framework of Module 6: Comparative Dimensions of Education Policy and Policy Implementation, in Maputo, Mozambique

Martin, Michaela. (1999). *The Role of the university in initial teacher training: Trends, current problems and strategies for improvement.* IIEP Contributions No. 32.

McCarthy, Cameron, Giardina, Michael D., & Harewood, Susan J. (2003). Afterword. Contesting culture: Identity and curriculum dilemmas in the age of globalization, postcolonialism, and multiplicity. *Harvard Educational Review, 73*(3), 449–465.

McCarthy, Cameron, Rezai-Rashti, Goli M., &Teasley, Cathryn. (2009). Race, diversity, and curriculum in the era of globalization. *Curriculum Inquiry, 39*(1), 75–96.

Ministério da Educação. (2004). *Estratégia para a formação de professores 2004–2015.* Maputo: Author.

Ministério da Educação. (2005). *Plano nacional de educação para todos, 2001–2015: Educação de qualidade para todos.* Luanda: Author.

Ministry of Education and Culture. (2005). *Evaluation of the impact of technical and financial support to the implementation of initial, in-service and continuing professional development of teachers including the crescer system.* Draft Report. Maputo: Author.

Ministry of Health. (2006). *National HIV/STI prevention & control program facts and figures: HIV/AIDS Epidemic Update, January to December 2006.* Kingston, Jamaica.

Morey, Ann I. (2000). Changing higher education curricula for a global and multicultural world. *Higher Education in Europe, 25*(1), 25–39.

Murrell, Peter C. (2009). Identity, agency, and culture: Black achievement and educational attainment. In Linda C. Tillman (Ed.), *The Sage handbook of African American Education* (pp. 89–106). Thousand Oaks, CA: Sage.

Murty, Komanduri S., & Roebuck, Julian B. (1993). *Historically black colleges and universities: Their place in American higher education.* Westport, CT: Praeger.

Mwiria, Kilemi, N'gethe, Njuguna, Ngome, Charles, Ouma-Odero, Douglas, Wawire, Violet, & Wesonga, Daniel. (2007). *Public and private universities in Kenya: New challenges, issues and achievements.* Oxford: James Curry & Nairobi: East African Educational Publishers.

Myers, Linda. (2003). *CU immigration law expert looks at changes in U.S. actions since 9/11.* Retrieved March 15, 2009, from http://www.news.cornell.edu/chronicle/03/7.24.03/immigration_9-11.html

NAFEO (National Association for Equal Opportunity in Higher Education). (2009). *International programs.* Retrieved March 15, 2009 from http://www.nafeo.org/community/index.php?option=com_content&view=article&id=24:international-programs&catid=7:international-programs&Itemid=4

NASULGC (National Association of State Universities and Land-Grant Colleges). (2007, October). *A national action agenda for internationalizing higher education.* Retrieved May 26, 2009, from http://www.aplu.org/NetCommunity/Document.Doc?id=471

National Association of State Universities and Land-Grant Colleges (NASULGC). (2004). *A call to leadership: The presidential role in internationalizing the university.* Retrieved July 26, 2007 from http://www.nasulgc.org/CIP/Task%20Force/Call_to_leadership.pdf

National Association of State Universities and Land-Grant Colleges (NASULGC). (2000, May). *Expanding the international scope of universities: A strategic vision statement for learning, scholarship and engagement in the new century.* Retrieved May 26, 2009, from http://www.aplu.org/NetCommunity/Document.Doc?id=67

Neave, Guy. (Ed.). (2000). *The universities' responsibilities to society: International perspectives.* Amsterdam: Pergammon/Elsevier.

Nye, J. (2005). *Soft Power: The Means to Success in World Politics.* New York: Public Affairs.

Okuni, Akim. (2007). Decentralization and revitalizing school-based teacher support and continuous professional development at primary-school level: Why it has failed in East Africa. *Southern African Review of Education, 13*(2), 107–123.

OECD (Organization for Economic Cooperation and Development). (2008). *Reviews of National Policies for Education: South Africa.* Paris: Author.

Osseiran, Ghia. (2007, November 30). Arab universities kick off bottom-up approach to quality education. *The Daily Star.* Retrieved November 30, 2007, from http://www.dailystar.com.lb/article.asp?edition_id=10&categ_id=2&article_id=87117

Paterson, David A. (2009). *New York state and the global financial crisis.* Retrieved December 20, 2009 from http://www.cfr.org/publication/18456/new_york_state_and_the_global_financial_crisis.html

Pavel, D. Michael, Inglebret, Ella, & Banks, Susan Rae. (2001). Tribal colleges and universities in an era of dynamic development. *Peabody Journal of Education, 76*(1), 50–72.

Price, Michael W. (2005, Spring). Seeds of educational sovereignty—Sisseton Wahpeton cultivating culturally-centered learning. *Tribal College Journal of American Indian Higher Education, 16*(4), 19–20.

Qatar Foundation. (2009). *Who we are: About Qatar foundation.* Retrieved June 15, 2009 from http://www.qf.org.qa/output/page10.asp

Rathmell, Andrew, & Schulze, Kirsten. (2000). Political reform in the Gulf: The case of Qatar. *Middle Eastern Studies, 36*(4) 47–62.

Rhoads, Robert A., Saenz, Victor, & Carducci, Rozana. (2005). Higher education reform as a social movement: The case of affirmative action. *The Review of Higher Education, 28*(2), 191–220.

Rhoads, Robert A., & Torres, Carlos A. (Eds.). (2006). *The university, state, and market: The political economy of globalization in the Americas.* Stanford, CA: Stanford University Press.

Richards, P. (2005, July 20). *Health-Caribbean: AIDS could kill quarter million by 2010.* Retrieved July 21, 2005, from http://www.ipsnews.net/dominologin.asp?Db=ips\eng.nsfandwView=vwWebMainViewand DocID=6295179AD1E4403DC1257044005C0A89

Rizvi, Fazal. (2008). Epistemic Virtues and Cosmopolitan Learning. *Australian Educational Researcher, 35*(1), 17–35.

Rizvi, Fazal. (2004). Debating globalization and education after September 11. *Comparative Education, 40*(2), 157–171.

Robertson, Jamie. (2001, August). Voice of the presidents: The hidden perils of globalization. *Tribal College Journal of American Indian Higher Education, 12*(4), 40–41.

Robertson, Susan L., & Keeling, Ruth. (2008). Stirring the lions: Strategy and tactics in global higher education. *Globalisation, Societies, and Education, 6*(3), 221–240.

Roman, Leslie G. (2004). States of insecurity: Cold war memory, "global citizenship," and its discontents. *Discourse: Studies in the cultural politics of education, 25*(2), 231–239.

Rondinelli, Dennis A., Johnson, James H., & Kasarda, John D. (1998). The changing forces of urban economic development: Globalization and city competitiveness in the 21st century. *Cityscape: A Journal of Policy Development and Research, 3*(3), 71–105.

Roth, Klas, & Burbules, Nicholas C. (Eds.). (2007). *Changing notions of citizenship education in contemporary nation-states.* Rotterdam: Sense Publishers.

Salzman, Harold. (2007). Globalization of R&D and innovation: Implications for U.S. STEM workforce and policy. Washington DC: The Urban Institute. Retrieved December 20, 2008, from http://www.urban.org/UploadedPDF/901129_salzman_stem_workforce.pdf

Smith, Daryl (2009). *Diversity's promise for higher education: Making it work.* Baltimore: Johns Hopkins University Press.

South African Development Community. (2009). *SADC profile*. Retrieved March 20, 2009, from http://www.sadc.int/

Spring, Joel (2008). Research on globalization and education. *Review of Educational Research* 78(2), 330–363.

Stake, Robert. (2005). Qualitative case studies. In Denzin, Norman & Lincoln, Yvonna (eds.), *The Sage handbook of qualitative research*, pp 443–466. Thousand Oaks, CA: Sage Publications.

Stein, Wayne J. (1992). *Tribally controlled colleges: Making good medicine*. New York: Peter Lang Publishing.

Stewart, Vivien (2007). Becoming Citizens of the World. *Educational Leadership*, 64(7), 8–14.

Strand, Kerry, Marullo, Sam, Cutforth, Nicholas, Stoecker, Randy, & Donohue, Patrick. (2003). *Community-based research and higher education: Principles and practices*. San Francisco, CA: Jossey-Bass.

Stromquist, Nelly. (Ed.). (2007). *The professoriate in the age of globalization*. Rotterdam: Sense Publishers.

Stromquist, Nelly. (2002). *Education in a globalized world*. Lanham, MD: Rowan and Littlefield Publishers.

Tenti, Emilio. (2008). Diversidad cultural, universalismo y ciudadanía: Consideraciones sociológicas. In E. Soriano Ayala (Ed.), *Educar para la ciudadanía intercultural y democrática* (pp. 21–48). Madrid, Spain: La Muralla.

The National Center for Public Policy and Higher Education. (2008, April). *Partnerships for Public Purposes: Engaging Higher Education in Societal Challenges for the 21st Century*. Washington DC: The National Center for Public Policy and Higher Education.

The University of the West Indies at Mona. (2007a). *Department of educational studies*. Retrieved February 1, 2008, from http://www.mona.uwi.edu/des/pages/eadmin2.htm

The University of the West Indies at Mona. (2007b). *Mission statement*. Retrieved February 17, 2008, from http://www.mona.uwi.edu/soe/links/mission.htm

Thompson, Cynthia, & Crossley, Michael. (1999). Reforming teacher education in a small state: Problems and potential for distance education in Belize. In Teame Mebrahtu, Michael Crossley & David Johnson (Eds.), *Globalization, education reconstruction and societies in transition* (pp. 137–156). Oxford: Symposium Books.

Torres, Carlos Alberto. (2009). *Globalizations and education*. New York: Teachers College Press.

Toynbee, Arnold. (1948). *Civilization on trial*. Oxford: Oxford University Press.

United Kingdom 2009. (2009). *What is the G20?* Retrieved March 28, 2009, from http://www.g20.org/about_what_is_g20.aspx

USAID. (2008). *Jamaica HIV/AIDS Health Profile*. Kingston, Jamaica: USAID.

U.S. Census Bureau. (2006). *Selected population profile in the United States: Jamaican, 308–309*. Retrieved March 15, 2009, from http://factfinder.census.gov/servlet/IPTable?_bm=y&-reg=ACS_2006_EST_G00_S0201:582;ACS_2006_EST_G00_S0201PR:582;ACS_2006_EST_G00_S0201T:582;ACS_2006_EST_G00_S0201TPR:582&-qr_name=ACS_2006_EST_G00_S0201&-qr_name=ACS_2006_EST_G00_S0201PR&-qr_name=ACS_2006_EST_G00_S0201T&-qr_name=ACS_2006_EST_G00_S0201TPR&-ds_name=ACS_2006_EST_G00_&-TABLE_NAMEX=&-ci_type=A&-redoLog=false&-

charIterations=454&-geo_id=01000US&-geo_id=NBSP&-format=&-_lang= en

Van den Berghe, Pierre L. (1967). *Race and racism: A comparative perspective.* New York: John Wiley and Sons.

Vichit-Vadakan, Juree. (2007). Reflections on university and urban public university. *Metropolitan Universities: An International Forum, 18*(3), 109–18.

Warner, Linda Sue. (2006). Native ways of knowing: Let me count the ways. *Canadian Journal of Native Education, 29*(2), 149–64.

Waterbury, John. (2003). Hate your policies, love your institutions. *Foreign Affairs, 82*(1), 58–68.

Watson, David. (2007). *Managing Civic and Community Engagement.* England, Open University Press.

Welch, Anthony. (2003). The discourse of discourse analysis: A response to Ninnes and Burnett. *Comparative Education, 39*(3), 303–306.

Wilson, David. (2003). The future of comparative and international education in a globalised world. *International Review of Education, 49*(1–2), 15–33.

Wilson, Reginald. (1994). The participation of African Americans in American higher education. In M. J. Justiz, R. Wilson, & L. G. Bjork (Eds.), *Minorities in higher education* (pp. 195–211). Phoenix, AZ: Oryx Press.

Wilson, William Julius. (1978). *The declining significance of race: Blacks and changing American institutions.* Chicago: University of Chicago Press.

Yang, Rui. (2002). University internationalisation: Its meanings, rationales and implications. *Intercultural Education, 13*(1), 81–95.

Hopson, Rodney, Yeakey Carol, & Boakari, Francis (Eds.). (2008). *Power, voice and the public good: Schooling and education in global societies.* Chennai, India: Emerald Publishers.

Zajda, Joseph. (Ed.). (2007). *International handbook of globalization, education and policy research.* Norwell, MA: Kluwer Academic Publishers.

Zogby, James, and Zogby, John. (2004). *Impressions of America: How Arabs view America, how Arabs learn about America.* Study commissioned by the Arab-American Institute. Retrieved from http://www.aaiusa.org/page/file/ 229fc3112466dc002f_wvm6bhed9.pdf/ 2004_Impressions_of_America_Poll

Part I

Geopolitical and Regional Matters in Higher Education

2 The University in Turbulent Times: A Comparative Study of the United States and Russia

Nelly P. Stromquist and Anna Smolentseva

Steady growth in the forces of globalization, led particularly by those of an economic and technological nature, has drawn in and greatly influenced other aspects of society. The notion of a "knowledge society" now permeates many social spaces, positioning the university as a key institution both in the creation of the new knowledge and in the transformation of this knowledge into marketable products. In this chapter we compare two countries that have occupied polar positions in the past: the United States as the epitome of free market principles and thus decentralized action, and Russia as a country mostly guided by centralized planning in higher education.

The U.S. data derives from primary sources from two research universities (one private, the other public) as illustrative studies rather than broad generalizations and from the extensive research literature on contemporary trends in higher education. The Russian data is based on a survey of 703 faculty members in seven Russian regions; this survey focused on three of the most established types of institutions in Russia: classical universities, technical universities, and pedagogical universities (former institutes). The sample involves faculty in eight fields: four in the natural and physical sciences and four in social sciences/humanities.

Globalization has brought pervasive changes to the university environment. In this chapter we focus on what we identify as trends closely linked to globalization: (1) the expansion of higher education, (2) the cult of efficiency, (3) the search for excellence, and (4) internationalization. We then link these trends to implications for the university's social mission.

The Massive Expansion of Higher Education

As with most countries in the world, the United States and Russia have seen a rapid expansion of their higher education systems in recent decades. By 2007, the American system comprised 18 million students, the Russian system an enrollment of 7.5 million. An important impetus for the substantial growth at this level of educational is an increased competition for high-paying jobs, which tend to rely on larger knowledge components and more formal certification than in the past. In the United States, the enrollment growth was left to market forces, leading to a profusion of higher education institutions with very differentiated statuses, from research universities to community colleges—a diversity firmly institutionalized in the categories set up by the Carnegie Foundation. This classification, however, does not capture the significant segmentation of higher education, which according to a number of informed observers also include "diploma mills" and "accreditation factories." As Altbach (2006) notes, stratification of institutions has become more pronounced in recent years. The expansion of education in Russia began in the Soviet era, when universities were subject to federal planning and were unfamiliar with the market. As the Soviet Union collapsed, Russian universities were left almost without governmental support and had to learn rapidly how to meet the challenges of the market. Later in the 2000s, universities received more federal support as well as stronger governmental regulation. Higher education has expanded over time, and now 19% of young adults aged 20 to 29 are currently enrolled in such institutions in Russia; the equivalent figure for the United States is 23% (OECD, 2007), thus producing a large number of students to be served and a sizable population segment to prepare for social and labor integration.

The Cult of Efficiency

The expansion process has been characterized by efforts to create more marketable degrees and to reduce those degree programs perceived to attract few students and thus not to generate substantial profits. In the United States, fields such as business administration, international law, neurosciences, and communications have expanded while offerings in disciplines such as philosophy, history, and European languages have seen resources curtailed. The spirit of efficiency has also generated more managerialist leadership and decision making, including a greater role by central administrative staff in decisions affecting the university (Gumport, 2000; Gaffikin & Perry, 2009).

Undoubtedly, one of the most tangible imports from the business world into the American academy is the strategic plan.[1] Gaffikin and Perry (2009) call it "the most important brand statement of the research university" as it "embraces its full range of institutional/structural initiatives" (p. 129). Strategic planning is defined as "a process operating in an extended time-frame (three to five years) which translates vision and values into significant, measurable and practical outcomes" (West-Burnham, 1994, cited in Bush & Coleman, 2000, p. 15). Strategic planning is different from day-to-day operations in three dimensions: its longer time horizon, the range of issues considered, and its broad scope of action (Caldwell & Spinks, 1992, cited in Bush & Coleman, 2000).

While university presidents and deans are said to have little coercive authority because they "cannot order professors to teach better courses, or pay more attention to students, or labor longer at their research" (Bok, 2003, p. 114), strategic plans are able to move colleges, departments, and faculty members into directions they cannot avoid.[2] Strategic plans are especially influential because they are enforced by the Provost Office, which was the first determinant of the plan's content. Further, the Provost Office has at its disposal the tools of taxation and deans' evaluation to secure compliance. Strategic plans are presented as the product of institutional consensus in which faculty members have had ample participation. In fact, these plans proceed through the creation of task forces, which are described as "an ideal way to solve problems and generate policies" (Bush & Coleman, 2000, p. 69). The composition of these task forces occurs through provost appointment rather than formal representation or election. Reflecting the intense diffusion of globalized economic and technological influences upon the university, strategic plans aim at positioning their respective university among the leading universities in the country, if not the world. They attach strong importance to research, links with industry, internationalization, and the use of technologies to expand distance education offerings. Surprisingly, the U.S. strategic plans of today resemble the Soviet models of the past.

Since one of the key features of strategic planning is to move institutions toward greater efficiency, the implementation of such plans usually results in the downsizing or elimination of programs unable to raise "sufficient" revenues. Fields and disciplines that do not attract large numbers of students risk being declared "stagnant" and thus eliminated. In the American private university under study, the Department of German was closed without the prior knowledge of its own faculty. In the College of Education of the same university, such areas as reading and literacy, teacher training of primary school teachers, and comparative education were eliminated in favor of programs with greater enrollment. In the American public university, because of its mandate to serve the state, the elimination of fields of study is under greater scrutiny; consequently, decisions center mostly on downsizing through a merging of departments to lower expenditures via the reduction in the number of chairs and clerical personnel.

The most important and controversial measure in Russia has been the shift in higher education admissions. Noting that the United States and other countries use nationwide tests for university admissions, Russian educational policymakers recently have adopted this procedure. By 2009 national testing had become the main form of gaining access to higher education. Although some institutions fought for the right to alternative admission rules and succeeded in using the results of national and regional subject competitions, the nationwide testing prevails. In the Russian context, preparation for the nationwide entrance examination has become a profitable business and involves private tutors from universities and even bribes.

Efficiency issues are also being invoked in Russia in an attempt to reclassify institutions of higher learning from those oriented toward providing baccalaureates and primarily teaching activities to those providing mostly graduate education and top quality research. On the Russian agenda there is a list of approximately a dozen research universities at the national level that will receive additional governmental funding. This may lead to a deterioration and decline of a number of regional institutions of higher learning. It remains unclear which criteria will be used to select the top strata among institutions and to estimate their performance during the realization of the project. The social mission of higher education is often underestimated, despite the fact that in an age of rapid technological and cultural change higher education becomes vital in preparing future generations for social and professional adaptation.

Not having the instruments and freedoms adopted by Western institutions (such as endowments and some intellectual property rights) and having limited opportunities to operate as independent market players, Russian institutions of higher learning most frequently rely on tuition fees as a main source of non-governmental financing. Thus, they do as much as possible to attract more students. Typically, that entails establishing new departments and new degree or non-degree programs in popular fields (e.g., economics, law, social sciences). For instance, at Moscow State University the number of schools has almost doubled during the past decade through the addition of new specializations such as business, public auditing, television, and translation and interpretation. In the United States, although there is substantial support coming particularly from research contracts with the federal government, universities—both public and private—see themselves relying increasingly on student tuition and fees for their operational expenditures (Eckel & King, c. 2004).

The Search for Excellence

Only two decades ago U.S. universities inhabited environments of predictable funding and student enrollment with little competition among institutions (Gioia & Thomas, 2000). Today, with the reduction of state support for public universities and increased competition for tuition revenues among both public and private universities, there is a perennial concern for revenues. The two main financial resources are research contracts and student tuition fees. In the American public university under study, "research dollars" are greatly sought and welcome; this university today depends on research by a factor of three compared to the support it receives from the state in the form of faculty and administrative salaries. In the private university, research support is also avidly pursued, but since it depends on student tuition for 83% of its revenues, there are intense efforts to increase student enrollment through the provision of certificates and online degrees.

Under the competitive climate that permeates universities, there is a powerful drive for excellence. Many U.S. universities seek to position themselves among the 10 to 25 top ranking institutions—clearly a mathematical impossibility that intensifies the competition and, which being a zero game, causes many universities to embark constantly on new ventures. In other parts of the world, including Russia, global and international forces make institutions of tertiary education reflect on their international standing and adopt measures to improve it, particularly among those that are or aspire to become research universities.

The pursuit of excellence, far from preparing faculty to develop norms promoting a global citizenship and solidarity, positions universities as sites of intense inter- and intra-institutional competition. Competition for students and resources is at the core of this goal, which means that for many universities excellence and marketing the university go hand in hand. The knowledge provided, then, becomes a product for which a market exists. Seeking to present one's university as unique in a particular way, or "branding," is common in the U.S. Fields such as engineering and the hard sciences, law, medicine, and business administration do address societal problems, but they loom rather as hot issues from the marketing perspective. The "soft sciences" and the humanities, considered less saleable than the hard sciences, receive less attention. A case in point reflecting current trends is the establishment of a Homeland Security Center at the private university under study. This major $12 million R&D effort, to last three years, has not a single faculty member from the social sciences (with the exception of a few from Policy, Planning, and Development) or the humanities, and not a single woman. It is difficult to believe that a nation can address security (and thus peace) without having an understanding of history, ethnic identity, nationalism, and social exclusion.

To assess their performance, a common practice today among American universities is to compare themselves to "peer institutions." These are institutions considered similar to one's own in terms of mission, quality, and size and thus worthy of emulation. However, the institution that one university holds to be its peer may have a different view of itself and thus select other peer institutions as its frame of reference. "Peer institutions," in practice, does not mean developing a community of universities.

While the official discourse of higher education institutions endorses the concept of excellence, in practice there are signs this actually reduces attention to quality. In Russia, student enrollments have grown very fast, supported by the establishment of new institutions and programs, but little attention was given to quality assurance. Federal procedures of accreditation, licensing, and degree requirements ensure the quality of higher education, but these procedures have been weakly enforced and non-governmental agencies of accreditation do not exist in the country.

Lately, the Russian government has tried to strengthen its control over the quality of education, and some institutions have lost their licenses. Mergers were initiated by the government to achieve another goal: the establishment of world-class research universities in various parts of the country, which is achievable only by accumulation of financial, human, and other resources. Thus, the Southern Federal University in Rostov and the Siberian Federal University in Krasnoyarsk were founded in 2006 by presidential decree. It is expected that federal universities will follow research priorities defined by government; that they will combine education, research, and business components, and that they will be among the world top 100 universities by 2020 (Ministry of Education and Science, 2007).

The Public Chamber of the Russian Federation, a body comprising elements of civil society and assigned the task of examining federal legislation and its implementation, issued in 2007 a report on the education situation in the country. It highlights two important issues: inequality of access and educational quality. The authors approach the quality of tertiary education largely from the international perspective employing such indicators as the low position of Russian universities in international rankings and the decreasing number of international students (discussed hereafter). They also consider socio-economical indicators such as the absence of higher compensation for tertiary level education faculty and the opinion of employers on the quality of graduates. Interestingly, the inter- and intra-institutional competition is not mentioned as an important factor in achieving excellence.

In Russia, the massive enrollment expansion and the want of additional income for faculty have had a negative impact on the academic profession and the quality of faculty work. Being forced to look for additional income; academics allocate most of their time not for research, reading literature, writing, keeping themselves current with recent developments in their fields, but in seeking supplemental jobs, mainly teaching (Smolentseva, 2003). During 1991–2003, the student body doubled, while the higher education faculty increased by only 30%, thus raising the student-faculty ratio at public institutions from 12:1 to 18:1 over the same period. Similar trends can be observed in the non-state (private) sector. Coupled with the brain drain of the professions in the 1990s and low supply of new faculty over the post-Soviet period, the pressure on the existing professoriate has increased considerably. In the survey mentioned earlier, when estimating the changes in their personal work over the past five years, almost half of the faculty reported that the teaching load at their full-time job had increased and one-third of the respondents noted that they had to spend more time at other jobs. On recent changes in their professional activities, faculty most often reported those related to teaching: they renovated courses more often (55%), engaged in new teaching methods (46 percent), and used computer technologies in teaching (39 percent).

About a half (47%) noted they experienced a heavier teaching load for their full-time positions. Faculty members also indicated higher accountability (43%).

A particular feature of Russia is that most of the part-time academics have a stable full-time academic employment in other institutions. The Russian academic labor market is not that large; usually, regular academics in one institution also work as part-time and hourly-paid faculty at public and non-public institutions. Insufficient salaries in higher education have undermined the prestige of the academic profession and forced many faculty members to look for additional jobs. Today, according to our survey data, about 50% of Russia's faculty has supplemental jobs and every tenth faculty member has three or more additional jobs.

In the United States, academics in prestigious universities as a rule do not seek supplemental employment as in Russia, although it is well known that faculty in liberal arts and community colleges tend to work part-time and thus have employment in multiple institutions. In recent years, there has been a substantial growth in contingent faculty—professors hold short-term contracts and/or are hired on a part-time basis. While 20 years ago, 85% of faculty in U.S. universities were full-time and most were on "tenure track," that is, "scholars who can hope for a career in higher education" (Altbach, 2009, p. 16), today two-thirds of the faculty is off tenure track and half work part-time. In the private research university under study, the College of Education went in less than 10 years from 100% tenured/tenure-track faculty to less than 50%. Now a new class of full-time contract instructors can be found at most universities. Although ostensibly this creates a more flexible staff that can be easily allocated to courses, it is also the case that these instructors can be paid between half and one-third of regular faculty. A crucial consequence of the increased contingent faculty in the United States is that these individuals do not participate in university or departmental decisions; thus, administrative leadership is becoming all the more dominant. In the case of Russia, academics have always had less autonomy and opportunities to influence governance due to the high centralization of the system. An outburst of faculty participation in governance took place between the late 1980s and early 1990s after the dissolution of the Soviet Union, but at present the realities of academic life are increasingly producing a declining interest in governance, deteriorating opportunities for such participation, a growth of individualism, and an atomization of academic life.

One of the phenomena of globalization is the increasing role of universities in producing knowledge for the postindustrial economy. In Russia, knowledge production was concentrated in the Academy of Sciences, while higher education institutions traditionally trained the pool of professionals for the national economy. On average, leading research staff and facilities were concentrated outside universities. Statistics show that in Organization for Economic Cooperation and Development (OECD) countries higher education produces 18% of their entire R&D (OECD, 2006). This indicator differs notably across countries; in the United States it amounts to 14% in comparison to 6% in Russia. At the institutional level, research expenditures in Russian universities comprise an insignificant part of university budgets. On average, the larger proportion of the budget (86%) goes to provision of education, while about 5% is spent on R&D (Ekonomika, 2004). In top research institutions that number might be higher, as in St. Petersburg State University, where it reaches 12%. It is important to note that the budgets of Russian and world-class institutions in other nations are not comparable. As Ward estimates (cited in Mohrman, Ma, & Baker, 2007), the budget of a top American research university with a medical center reaches $1.5 billion on average and about 30% to 40% of that amount comes from competitive research grants. In the United States about 30 institutions with such budgets can be found, while in Europe no university has comparable resources. However, no single model of a university might be successful.

With excellence defined mostly in terms of rankings, a tension emerges between excellence and equity. Measures that could distribute social capital and highlight such values as solidarity and social justice find themselves in an increasingly reduced space; moreover, they are seen as initiatives that divert universities from primary objectives. Frequent references to diversity can be found in official documents such as strategic plans, but this notion is not about affirmative action or increasing the participation of marginalized minorities but rather seeking the enrollment of international students and hiring professors from other countries who might have the talent necessary for the university to increase its international prestige. University leaders—both administrators and faculty members—are confronted with a dilemma; unfortunately, the prevailing position forges ahead in the direction of greater university recognition and prestige rather than the quiet work of examining society and its current direction (Bok, 2003; Tierney, 2008).

In their desire to achieve high rankings in the *US News and World Report*—a non-academic journal that nonetheless has become the predominant source of institutional rankings in the United States—several universities are seeking to reduce the time needed for Ph.D. completion. To accomplish this objective, administrators are opting for the model of the full-time student who is fully funded by the university. This model demands full dedication to one's program of studies and builds on the concept of research apprenticeship; however, its implementation eliminates the enrollment of potential students with experience who presently have jobs and families and cannot live with stipends that are sufficient only for single individuals. The full-time student requirement also effectively eliminates women with young children who need access to childcare. Moreover, to the extent that this model favors young students, it may act against the utilization of experience and wisdom that is so crucial in the social sciences Do we want future professionals who have no profound acquaintances with the real world? For its part, the fully funded student model results in small Ph.D. cohorts, which means that specialized courses may not be provided due to the very small class sizes that often result; an unintended effect is the generation of a highly competitive Ph.D. program yet one based on rather generic courses.

Internationalization

Internationalization is a concept in widespread use among most universities in the world. At the same time, several meanings can be attached to this word. Bond and Lemasson (1999) argue that one purpose of internationalization should be to prepare students to become internationally knowledgeable and interculturally competent. From a perspective of global solidarity, internationalization could be interpreted as the process that brings to the fore the problems of other, mostly developing, countries and tries to incorporate in the curriculum the knowledge needed to address those problems as well as to raise social awareness. Under this definition, regions such as Sub-Saharan Africa and Western Asia would receive attention. However, a de facto definition of internationalization in U.S. universities emphasizes the development of contacts with prestigious universities and research centers abroad, the promotion of study-abroad programs for their students, and the recruitment of international students who are able to pay their tuition or who come with strong scientific backgrounds. Few of these universities are engaged in such practices as infusing an international dimension throughout the curriculum, using an interdisciplinary approach, developing comparative approaches, broadening American knowledge of other countries, or increasing self-reflection on American culture (Bond & Lemasson, 1999; see also NASULGC, 2004). Given the emphasis on the generation of resources and the capturing of human capital, internationalization tends to center on East Asian and European regions.

To manage internationalization initiatives, many American universities are creating high-level administrative positions and appointing to these positions persons with strong business and interpersonal skills. Internationalization responsibilities call for a constant scanning of the external environment, contacting potential partners, establishing institutional networks, recruiting international students, and recruiting stellar faculty who can transfer their fame and resources to their new university. In many internationalization efforts, faculty views are solicited to secure endorsement rather than to propose alternatives. The two U.S. research universities under study are pursuing constant internationalization efforts. The private university has established offices in five countries to facilitate its various tasks and presently seeks to become the "first global university," which its provost defines as being built on an international network of 20,000 alumni thus moving from being a world-*class* university to becoming a world-*sized* university. The public university has just reorganized its former Office of International Programs to create instead a Center for Global Initiatives with a more proactive leader assigned to the position of associate provost.

The internationalization strategy has become one of the most influential factors in the development of Russian higher education. Historically, the Soviet model of tertiary education involved a major international component that was targeted at dissemination of Soviet values among other nations. With the fall of the USSR, international enrollments have dramatically decreased as has the entire system that prioritized international recruitment and governmental financial support for overseas students. The past decade demonstrates a stable growth of international enrollments. In 2007, this enrollment reached 95,000 students, still short of the previous 126,000 during the Soviet era. In the United States, because of its unbroken trajectory in appealing to international students and the use of English as the language of instruction, the number of international students has always been larger. At the time of the demise of the Soviet Union (1989), international student enrollment in the United States was 386,850; by 2007 it was 623,805 (representing 3% of the total enrollment) (National Center for Education Statistics, 2009).

Innovation from the West has notably changed the educational terrain in Russia: Ideas from the West have introduced new models that, while not always implemented, have been discussed, have altered the discourse, have created a competition among alternative ideas, and have provided a push for further development. On the other hand, the realization of Western ideas restricted, to a certain extent, the development of national ideas and directions. For instance, financial support from the Western agencies provided development only for certain areas in the social sciences and the humanities and specific themes that might be a priority only from the sponsors' point of view. At the same time, not every Western pattern has been borrowed. Despite introducing and implementing many patterns related to the market economy, such as the notion of educational services, marketing of educational services, strategic planning, university mission, and degrees and credits, the key structures remained unchanged. Generally speaking, the instrumental values, that is, the means of goal achievement, have been transformed, while terminal values have proven to be more enduring. Priorities set by the Russian state for national development and education prevails. The state defines educational goals (e.g., the training of cadres for the national economy) and educational content (through educational standards approved by the state); likewise, the state keeps strict control over the whole tertiary education system (through licensing, accreditation, graduation requirements, financing, institutional management, and enrollment targets, among others).

This control goes beyond the public sector of education, affecting private education as well. As in many other parts of the world, the private sector of higher education has grown in Russia since its emergence in 1993. It does not have the longstanding history and traditions as the one in the United States, and is rather small, serving about 17% of students in 2007. (In the United States, however, about two-thirds of the students enroll in public institutions, in large part because of the lower tuition costs in those institutions. In fact, the American Association of State Colleges and Universities (2008) identifies "affordability" as the most critical policy issues for higher education). Russian private universities are usually small institutions offering training in social sciences, humanities, business, and law and are funded mostly by tuition fees. The situation of the private sector is complicated by demographic trends (the number of secondary school graduates nearly equals the number of places in public higher educational institutions) and the current economic crisis, which push families into reducing expenditures on education. According to some estimates, that could negatively affect private educational institutions (Belyi, 2009).

For Russian universities, the opportunity to enroll international students has become a notable source of non-governmental funding and thus serves as an important incentive for the development of internationalization. At the federal level, internationalization is also considered an important step toward transforming Russia into a serious player in the international education market and exporting education as a commodity like gas and oil. However, there are obstacles restricting the expansion of international education within the country. Some of these are the Russian language (which is much less used in the world than English and thus requires teaching in English or providing Russian language training prior to enrollment), the insufficient infrastructure of universities (the quantity and quality of dormitories, etc.), and security issues for overseas students. Also, the quality of education and comparability of Russian degrees is an important factor in considering internationalization issues.

Partly to increase internationalization, Russia joined the Bologna declaration in 2003. This involves transition to the European bachelor-master (four plus one-two years) (in contrast to the Soviet five-year specialist model), introducing thus a new model of credit transfer and accumulation system. Although currently only about one-tenth of all higher education graduates earn degrees in the Bologna mode, the new system will expand in the next years, according to recent policy guidelines. Policymakers declare that the European model, following Bologna principles, will enable the country to optimize educational costs and returns by avoiding the five-year "over-education," unnecessary for most of positions now in demand in the labor market. The policy also implies a more selective access to the master's degree as well as a potential shrinking of free education at this level, which is a source of concern for families and the higher education community. While the Russian government is quite committed to the new two-tier (bachelor-master) approach, this system has not been entirely understood and legitimized in society as distinct from the five-year specialist diploma and seems not to be as fully beneficial not only to students and families but also to employers.

Adaptation of the European educational model in Russia is one of the examples of policy borrowing. In search of new approaches to education at the time of transformation from Soviet society to a postindustrial one, Russian policymakers have continuously appealed to Western experience. At the beginning of post-Soviet reforms, neoliberal values were brought into Russian education by overseas experts, the World Bank, Western foundations, and other Western actors. As a result, there were changes in university admissions (discussed earlier), the development of new fields in social sciences, new curricula and textbooks, and experiments with the "money-follows-the student" principle, among others. Globalization has influenced the adoption of internationalization practices at national, regional, institutional, and individual levels through such norms as international students, international contacts, joint projects, and exchanges. However, only a small number of Russian professors are involved in this activity (Smolentseva, 2007).

Conclusions

Although Russia and the United States are at very different points in their position in the capitalist economy and have traversed contrasting historical trajectories, our study seeks to show that many contemporary changes are moving their universities into patterns of significant convergence, despite some elements that still reflect particular national contexts.

The increased competition for financial resources is prodding both U.S. and Russian universities into marketing strategies that give priority to fields explicitly linked to the economy. The social sciences and the humanities are eclipsed by science and technology in the United States, while the same trend is only now emerging in Russia. This is happening despite economic and cultural changes that require the preparation of new generations for social and professional adaptation. With the decreased importance of the social sciences and humanities, the ability of the university to provide a critical voice is being diminished.

The growing emphasis on research is creating a stark separation between research and teaching, which suggests that there will be less involvement in counseling and otherwise working with students, precisely at a moment when the expansion of higher education is increasing the number of individuals who represent their family's first generation to attend college. It is likely that universities may not be providing sufficient attention to students from ethnic and linguistic minorities or to those who are economically disadvantaged. While in the U.S. context there are frequent references in institutional discourse to the concept of diversity, it is often framed as a demographic variable,that is, incorporating international students, rather than as becoming sensitive to needs and cultural differences of the new domestic students entering the higher education system.

As administrators gain greater salience in the decision making of universities, faculty members as professionals and autonomous intellectuals are left behind. Professors are becoming contingent workers, which forecasts that their voices in shaping higher education institutions will diminish and their role as societal observers will be devalued.

The experience of the United States and Russia points to several recommendations: First, faculty members and students should take advantage of the positive elements of globalization: Access to knowledge, knowledge production and dissemination facilitated by new technologies, greater opportunities for new contacts and collaboration, more opportunities to meet different cultures and enrich their professional and personal experience. Second, future faculty should be aware of the stratification and differentiation in higher education, which can be found in any system of higher education and which is intensifying in the global era (Stromquist, 2007). This diversification will produce more pressure on faculty, shape their identities into winners (researchers) and losers (teachers), and affect the conditions and rewards in their place of work. Third, the confluence of crucial forces such as the growing inter-institutional competition, the accelerated search for markets, and the rapid pace of technological innovations requires new forms of university governance which will rely, for example, on the ability to constantly scan the competitive environment and make quick decisions. In this new context, university leaders—both administrators and faculty members—are confronted with a dilemma. As administrators—full-time personnel with technical expertise in certain areas—assume greater dominance over university affairs, a crucial question will be how to redesign the governance roles for faculty so that they maintain some degree of influence and autonomy in guiding the university's mission.

We argue here for the safeguarding of several values which require faculty engagement: the priority of quality over revenue generation in the creation and provision of educational programs, preservation of the importance of teaching as a major aspect of the academy, the defense of academic endeavors as a full-time profession, maintenance of disciplines that do not directly link to science and technology but that constitute part of human civilization, a serious effort to include disadvantaged groups of society, achievement of a balance between managerial leadership and responsibility for social well-being and cohesion, and the defense of a critical stance in academic work rather than a mechanical endorsement of goods and services requested by dominant external groups. Blackmore challenges us to "reclaim education as a site of advocacy and social and political action both within and in relations to communities of practice, and . . . to revitalize a sense of collectivity, no matter how temporary or transitory" (2005, p. 191). These values, shown here to be in danger of disappearing, must be preserved, not only in the United States and Russia, but in all institutions of higher education in order to assess and guide the human condition, its history and its prospects, as we develop materially and intellectually into the coming decades.

Notes

1 Strategic plans are distinct from other plans, such as academic plans or institutional fund raising plans, which tend to have a shorter time horizon and a more limited focus.
2 Some initiatives seek to address the environment, energy, global health—issues that certainly will benefit most of society. At the same time, the greatest deployment of research activities is spent in problems identified by the private sector, which may or may not coincide with problems of great social importance.

References

Altbach, Philip. (2006). Globalization and the University. In James Forest & Philip Altbach (Eds.), *International handbook of higher education* (pp. 121–139). Dordrecht: Kluwer.

Altbach, Philip. (2009). It's the Faculty, Stupid! The Centrality of the Academic Profession. *International Higher Education, 55*, 15–17.

American Association of State Colleges and Universities. (2008). Top 10 State Policy Issues for Higher Education in 2008. Washington DC: American Association of State Colleges and Universities.

Belyi, Mikhail. (2009, May 20). Probel v obrazovanii [A Blank Spot in Education]. Gudok, Russia.

Blackmore, Jill. (2005). "The Emperor has No Clothes": Professionalism, Performativity and Educational Leadership in High-risk Postmodern Times. In John Collard & Celia Reynolds (Eds.), *Leadership, gender & culture in education. Male & female perspectives* (pp. 173–194). Berkshire, UK: Open University Press.

Bok, Derek. (2003). *Universities in the marketplace. The commercialization of higher education.* Princeton: Princeton University Press.

Bond, Sheryl, & Lemasson, Jean-Pierre (Eds.). (1999). *A new world of knowledge: Canadian universities and globalization.* Ottawa: International Development Research Centre.

Bush, Tony, & Coleman, Marianne. (2000). *Leadership and Strategic Management in Education.* London: Paul Chapman Publishing.

Eckel, Peter & King, Jacqueline. (*c.* 2004). *An Overview of Higher Education in the United States. Diversity, Access, and the Role of the Marketplace.* Washington DC: American Council on Education.

Ekonomika Obrazovania v Zerkale Statistiki. Informatsionny Biulleten. (2004). *Moscow: Higher School of Economics, 1*(3).

Gaffikin, Frank & Perry, David. (2009). Discourses and Strategic Visions: The

U.S. Research University as an Institutional Manifestation of Neoliberalism in a Global Era. *American Educational Research Journal, 46*(1), 115–44.

Gioia, Dennis & Thomas, James. (2000). Sensemaking During Strategic Change in Academia. In M. Chris Brown II (Ed.). *Organization & Governance in Higher Education,* (5th ed., pp. 352–378). Boston: Pearson Custom Publishing.

Gumport, Patricia. 2000. Academic Restructuring: Organizational Change and Institutional Imperatives. *Higher Education, 39,* 67–91.

Ministry of Education and Science. (2007). *Establishing new universities in South and Siberian federal districts.* Retrieved May 1, 2009, from http://mon.gov. ru/pro/pnpo/fed/

Mohrman, Kathyrn, Ma, Wanhua, & Baker, David. (2007). The Emerging Global Model of the Research University. In Philip G. Altbach & Patti McGill Peterson (Eds.), *Higher education in the new century: Global challenges and innovative ideas (*pp. 145–177). Rotterdam: Sense Publishers.

NASULGC (National Association of State Universities and Land-Grant Colleges). (2004, October). *A call to leadership. The presidential role in internationalizing the university. A report of the NASULGC task force on international education.* Washington DC: NASULGC.

National Center for Education Statistics. (2009). *Contexts of postsecondary education. Characteristics of postsecondary students.* Washington DC: National Center for Education Statistics, U.S. Department of Education.

OECD. (2007). *Education at a Glance 2007—Home.* Retrieved November 10, 2007, from www.oecd.org/edu/eag2007

OECD. (2006). *Main science and technology indicators. Key figures* (2006). OECD. Retrieved November 10, 2006, from http://www.oecd.org/dataoecd/ 49/45/24236156.pdf

Smolentseva, Anna. (2003). Challenges to the Russian Academic Profession. *Higher Education, 45*(4), 391–424.

Smolentseva, Anna. (2007). Emerging Inequality in the Academic Profession in Russia. In Nelly P. Stromquist (Ed.). *The Professoriate in the Age of Globalization* (pp. 153–179). Rotterdam/Taipei: Sense Publishers.

Stromquist, Nelly P. (2007). (Ed.). *The Professoriate in the Age of Globalization.* Rotterdam Taipei: Sense Publishers.

Tierney, William. (2008). *The impact of culture on organizational decision making.* Sterling, VA: Stylus Publishing.

3 Beyond Globalization: Possibilities and Challenges in Korea and China

Kiwan Sung

This chapter presents significant changes being made in Higher Education Institutions (HEIs) in Asia, especially, the Republic of Korea and the People's Republic of China, in order to meet the new world order of globalization and internationalization (Altbach & Peterson, 2008). More specifically, this chapter examines to what extent Western countries such as the United States have influenced the reform of HEIs in both countries (Altbach, 2001; Kim, 2004) and how the world crises such as the International Monetary Fund (IMF) crisis in the 1990s and the subprime mortgage crisis have impacted HEIs in both countries through merging their administrative offices, improving budgetary efficiency, and enforcing more rigorous accountability in administrative, academic, and research performances in hopes of producing better educators and professionals in various disciplines.

Accordingly, this chapter considers and identifies key changes on both national and institutional levels in view of various political, sociocultural, and economical factors which are shaping current efforts to restructure and revitalize HEIs in both Korea and China. More specifically, this chapter highlights prime examples of such changes as curricular revisions to serve students from other countries, mandatory offerings of English courses, funding young scholars and graduates, the influx of foreign institutes and teachers, and the necessity of sending their students overseas to enhance their international competitiveness (Ihm, 2006; Kim, 2004).

As the world enters a new era after the market-oriented globalization which resulted in the current economic crisis due to the subprime mortgage shock (Krugman, 2008), there are more challenges for HEIs in Asian countries. For example, both Japan and the Republic of Korea have limited natural resources but plenty of human resources. As for the People's Republic of China, it has enjoyed a relatively fast and steady economic development with the world's largest population; it still faces the long-lasting problems of ensuring both social and educational development for its people who are a great asset in terms of providing cheap labor. Especially, as the members of G-20, both Korea and China should deal with the domestic challenges of restructuring their social and educational programs to continue to utilize human resources while also meeting the expectations of their neighboring Asian countries as well as the world. For example, Korea is expected to contribute more to resolve world and regional problems such as food, water, and energy shortages; environmental threats including global warming; as well as regional conflicts due to internal and external tensions in countries such as Afghanistan, Iraq, and South Asian countries such as Pakistan and Sri Lanka (UNDESA, 2009; UNESCO, 2009).

In order to cope with fast and unpredictable changes occurring in the post-market-oriented and glocalized era, both Korea and China have made intensive efforts to streamline and enhance their educational systems to achieve innate complementary relationships with their social and economical development. Accordingly, this chapter focuses primarily on some of the most important efforts being made to develop HEIs in Korea and China and examines particular policies and changes to make those with graduate degrees as well as those with only bachelor's degrees competitive human resources. Concrete examples and cases compiled from diverse sources are included along with the author's extensive administrative and teaching experiences in HEIs in order to further illustrate key change efforts in the two countries.

In other words, this chapter, in particular, utilizes scholarly and policy literature, research studies, documents related to educational policies and changes from the fields of higher and comparative international education in order to highlight some characteristics of changes along with key challenges occurring in the two countries in the Far East region. Furthermore, the results of a case study (Stake, 2005) of one of the top 10 Korean universities and one of the key 211 Project Chinese universities are reported because they exemplify rather concerted efforts to globalize their campuses, programs, and personnel.

Current State and Direction of Reforms in Korea

Kim (2004) reports that educational reforms in East Asian countries such as China, Japan, and Korea have followed the United States and manifest more openness; for example, via diverse policies toward immigrants and foreigners, and through the enhancement and marketeering of their academic and research programs. However, it is also noted that despite such common features, there are some key differences between China and Korea due to the different conceptualizations of the reform, historical and organizational particularities, or conditions of HEIs such as government regulations or the extent of decentralization.

On the one hand, China's education has grown rapidly during the last decade and is engaging in vigorous reforms by merging its universities to serve the student enrollment of more than 15% of those who finish secondary schools and are eligible for university enrollment (MOEPRC,

2009). On the other hand, Korea, interestingly, has a remarkable growth in student enrollment surpassing that of Japan in 2001, which had a stable state of student enrollment with 72% of those who finished secondary education.

According to the Organization for Economic Cooperation and Development (OECD, 2008), South Korea has the highest rate in terms of the percentage of secondary students going to colleges or universities, which is close to more than 82%. As of 2008, there were 1,943,437 students among the youth aged 18 to 25 who were enrolled in regular four-year HEIs and 1,330,080 who were active in such institutes of higher education. Active students refers to those who are actually taking courses without taking leave of absence due to the mandatory military service for male students or for study abroad or other reasons such as taking time off to earn tuition or to prepare for national examinations such as the bar examination, higher civil service or foreign service exams, or exams for government employees such as police or other public officers, which are thought of as high-paying or stable jobs with the guarantee of life-long employment.

According to the Korean Educational Development Institute (KEDI, 2009), there are a total of 174 universities. Among them, there are 23 national universities run by the central government and 2 public universities run by provincial or large municipal offices. The rest of the 149 private universities are run by educational foundations or funded by large or local businesses. KEDI also reports that there has been a steady increase in the number of the graduate programs.

As of 2008 among the 1,055 graduate programs, there were 158 general programs offering traditional subject matters in liberal arts, social sciences, or engineering while 150 professional programs were offered dealing with highly specialized areas such as law or medical fields. In addition, there were 747 special graduate programs offering rather practical or vocational courses in the areas of business, public administration and tax, language, art, or technology. Relatedly, there were more than 300,000 graduate students in both master's (General: 84,562; Professional: 21,472; Special: 145,976; Total: 252,010) and doctoral programs (General: 45,107; Professional: 4,295; Total: 49,402).

Despite such fast growth, however, many educational policies and restructuring efforts that have been initiated seem to be at a halt due to the diverse interests of its stakeholders as well as economic crises of IMF and recent subprime mortgage default. That is, whereas the government and media have boasted the unprecedented fastest recovery from the IMF crisis, many students have suffered due to the decrease of family income or sudden laying off of their parents due to the bankruptcy of small and mid-sized companies and massive restructuring of big conglomerates. Adding insult to injury, the economic crisis caused by the subprime mortgage since 2007 has resulted in a sudden crash in stock price and drop in the exchange rate. As a result, the competitive edge of exporting goods to the world market has disappeared, and it is expected that the economic growth rate of Korea in 2009 will be around 0.2%, the lowest in the last 30 years (Korea Development Institute, 2009). Such economic downturn has put many students into the desperate situation of prolonging their study or leaving schools for part-time jobs to earn tuition for at least a year or more.

In addition, the real estate bubble has popped resulting in the loss of the homes of the poor or middle-class families while the decrease in full-time jobs deteriorates job prospects for the young more than ever. However, interestingly, despite facing such ensuing difficulties, many families in Korea continue to send their children to HEIs or to study abroad as mentioned earlier.

Accordingly, in order to meet these parents' and students' high expectations, it is imperative for HEIs in Korea to upgrade their programs. Kim (2006) emphasizes that, in the age of globalization, the HEIs in Korea offer programs which help Korean students to understand their own identities in the global context through reflective and logical thinking and decision making in selecting and utilizing information that is necessary for them. That is, Kim views that it is important for Korean HEIs to nurture their students in order for them to appropriate science and technology in an ethical and desirable manner by being democratic citizens.

Furthermore, Kim strongly argues that revising foreign language programs is one of the key factors in enhancing students' language skills, especially, English. As a matter of fact, English has become the global *lingua franca* for most non-English speaking Asian countries as well as those in G-20 countries (Jenkins, 2007; McKay, 2003). Given that the current mobilization of materials and information is only possible through technology and the use of the English language, both Korea and China invest tremendous efforts and resources to teaching the English language to their students (Kim & Jeon, 2005).

In line with the key interest in language and advanced fields, a large number of Korean postsecondary students go to the United States to study. In the school year of 2008/2009, more than 75,000 Korean postsecondary students went to the United States to study, which is the third largest number after China (103,260) and India (98,235) (Open Doors, 2009a). However, despite the increase of the number of students studying abroad in a number of English-speaking countries, more than 40% of the South Korean students studying abroad in postsecondary programs are studying only English rather than earning degrees in important subject areas (Weidman, 2007). For example, Weidman reported that in 2006, among more than 190,000 students who studied abroad, about 36,220 were studying for graduate degrees and more than 77,500 students for undergraduate degrees. However, according to him, there were more than 76,600 students who were taking a variety of English courses. Weidman reasoned that more students leave Korea, which is a highly economically and educationally advanced country, because they now have the financial means to do so.

There is also fierce competition for students to enter top-notch universities in Korea comparable to that in Japan during the 1980s. In fact, such competition forces some families to use up all financial means to send their children abroad to study English or enroll them in advanced disciplinary courses in foreign universities. So much so that the term "goose father" is used to refer to fathers who stay alone while using up all financial means to send their children abroad to study English or enroll them in advanced disciplinary courses; English is considered the "golden tongue" for many Korean parents who send their children to local private institutes or to study abroad (Cho, 2007). Korea is also considered a new haven, dubbed as "gold rush" in teaching, for English-speaking foreigners to easily find teaching jobs regardless of their qualifications (Huer, 2009).

According to Weidman (2007), the claim made by Korean parents and media that they send their children to study abroad due to Korean education's inefficiency and the lack of creative and critical thinking in curricular and instructional methods or systems is not necessarily true. First, Korean students were among the top in the Program for International Student Assessment (PISA), second only to Finland in terms of average scores. Second, Korean students ranked first in problem-solving ability, which is considered one aspect of creativity. Therefore, Korea's educational system and curriculum appear to be as good as those in the countries in which most South Korean students study (Weidman, 2007).

In addition, despite the claim of economic loss due to many study-abroad students, just under 5% of the postsecondary students, whose parents can afford such investment, study abroad (Weidman, 2007). Accordingly, the current and popular phenomena of studying abroad and learning English in Korea have occurred due to Korea's unique valuing of education as extremely important, as manifested in the term, "education or English fever" (Kang, 2008; Park, 2009; Weidman, 2007). As a matter of fact, education is often praised for providing a main impetus and quality human resources for the unprecedented economic development of the nation in 1980s. Such a firm belief in education is so historical and cultural that many consider education the primary pathway for social and individual mobility, especially in today's globalized society.

With little natural resources and a long history of export-driven industries, Korea has to keep up with global change as in the popular rhetoric of "educating their students and workforce to compete in the global market posed by most universities as well as media and business sectors" (Weidman, 2007). As a matter of fact, the Gross Domestic Product (GDP) of South Korea in 2006 was $897.4 billion (exports—$326 billion, imports—$309.3 billion), which means more than 70% of Korea's GDP is generated through foreign trade. Accordingly, with the upcoming plans of Free Trade Agreements with the United States, the European Union (EU), Mexico, and its neighboring countries, Korea will have to rely more on international markets in which there is fierce competition from Japan, China, India, and other economically emerging countries.

In such a context, it seems that the ever-increasing and strong emphasis on language abilities, especially English, and understanding of other cultures through global education or multicultural education seems a natural and reasonable trend in the world (Banks, 2002; Kim, 2007). However, given the excessive spending for language learning abroad, which is estimated to be $15.8 billion (Samsung Economic Research Institute, 2006), rather than postsecondary education, the government is eager to act fast in implementing more English-oriented policies or programs while some parents spare no effort or money in sending their children to study abroad first or to better schools for their children to have a competitive edge in their career advancement in the global marketplace.

In other words, the current phenomena of sending students abroad and the emphasis on English and technological advancement in Korea offer many challenges for the HEIs in the country. Due to the expensive labor cost and relocating major manufacturing Korean companies to countries with cheaper labor cost such as China, Vietnam, or other Asian countries, full-time jobs are scarce even for domestically educated and qualified youth let alone those who study abroad. Accordingly, it becomes imperative for the Korean government and educational institutes to restructure and upgrade their academic programs to provide quality education especially when major media and businesses (mis)lead the public to believe their educational system is poor compared to those in the United States and the United Kingdom.

Such urgency is now being addressed by the Korean government and universities, which are implementing some key measures to bolster their national and academic competence and excellence through new human resource development plans and curricular revisions to serve domestic students better while drawing more foreign students, as in the university structural reform plan (MOEHRD, 2004). First, more collaborative research is encouraged between corporations and universities, and, more urgently, with foreign research centers in major companies and universities rather than establishing superficial paper relationships with no substantial engagements or operating in their own locked system. For example, the government encourages HEIs to establish and operate more research institutes while existing research institutes do their best to seek out collaborative research and joint projects with international and private counterparts. In an effort to bring about such a change, the three key government-funded research foundations—Korea Research Foundation, Korea Science and Engineering Foundation, and Korea Foundation for International Cooperation of Science and Technology—merged into the National Research Foundation of Korea (NRFOK) as of June, 2009. The

NRFOK continues to fund existing programs such as World Class Universities (WCU), Brain Korea (BK) 21, and the New University for Regional Innovation projects while also inviting foreign scholars or establishing joint research centers with the United States, the EU, and other neighboring countries (NRFOK, 2009).

However, there should be more consistent systemic and financial support by the governmental organizations and academic and business sectors to make such efforts fruitful so that excellent foreign scholars or leaders and students from highly developed and developing countries can come to Korea and contribute to the nation's development as a global and educational leader.

Second, one of the main reasons for the public perception of the lack of competitive educational programs in Korean schools is due to the impracticality of language education, especially English. It is mostly due to the test-oriented curriculum and instruction, which forces teachers to prepare their students to be accepted into good universities or offered positions in good companies (Sung, 2002). That is, rather than teaching English for communicative purposes as stipulated in the National Foreign Language Curriculums since 1992 (MOEHRD, 2006), many schools and teachers still engage in rigid instructional practices while both parents and students are only interested in short-term goals of getting good scores for entering a university or finding a job. Thus, it is often reported that Korean graduates are not communicatively competent in English compared to their counterparts in Malaysia, Singapore, or Hong Kong for which one of the official languages is English. As a matter of fact, Korean students' average TOEFL (Test of English as a Foreign Language) score of 78 points out of 120 was the 89th percentile, but the mean score for the speaking was 136th among 161 countries (Cho, 2007). However, though Korean schools should do better in teaching foreign languages (English) more effectively and practically, such a claim should be viewed with caution given that these countries do not force or mandate these tests to all levels of students regardless of their age as a requirement for entrance examinations for schools or job interviews as in Korea.

Major HEIs in Korea utilize a special admission process of selecting their students, mostly based on their English proficiency. For example, those who are English proficient living abroad or have high scores in English proficiency tests such as TOEFL or TEPS (Test of English Proficiency developed by Seoul National University) are admitted in many major fields at universities as "English or Globally Competent Students" regardless of their GPAs in high school or scores in the National College Entrance Examination. For example, a new national university, Ulsan National University of Science and Technology, now offers all the courses in English beginning their first year in 2009. In other words, without the development of personal English proficiency, it is very difficult for many Korean students to attend one of the top-notch universities, or their admission may be denied due to the lack of English abilities required by these universities regardless of other good qualifications.

Many HEIs in Korea also make tremendous efforts for their faculty to offer courses in English while mandating their students to take a certain number of classes taught in English as a graduation requirement. For instance, Korea Advanced Institute of Science and Technology has increased the number of courses offered in English and, at Korea University, more than 35% of their courses are offered in English (Hankyoreh, 2007). In fact, the proportion of courses offered in English is another landmark standard in the evaluation of the university's internationalization as judged by major domestic and foreign institutes and companies such as *Chosun Daily* and Quacquarelli Symonds (QS) in the United Kingdom. Especially, the top tier universities are keen on these evaluations and do their best to improve their rankings each year by offering more courses in English. In fact, these universities require the faculty in majors such as liberal arts or business programs to offer English-only classes and also new incoming faculty are required to teach at least one course in English or design an evaluation practice which puts strong weight on English. However, the increase of English-only courses is said to be problematic due to the faculty's and students' lack of proficiency and the difficulty of the content in some majors, which may cause degradation in the learning of subject matter (Hankyoreh, 2007). There is also a concern that such requirements may lead both faculty and students to think of English as a panacea while the HEIs do not make enough effort to address many problems in the administration and management and curricular and instructional matters (Kim, 2006).

There is no doubt that English should be taught to Korean students as part of enhancing their communicative abilities and global competence. However, the current system of recruiting foreign teachers as conversation teachers regardless of majors when they have a BA should be improved, and more efforts are necessary to include them in curricular and instructional activities rather than disenfranchising them with no rights or duties after their classes (Sung, 2002). In fact, in order to upgrade university English curricular and instructional programs, more native English-speaking teachers should be recruited as tenured faculty who can teach and conduct research rather than as a temporary non-tenured supplementary faculty through such programs as English Program in Korea (EPIK) or Teach and Learn in Korea (TaLK) led by the National Institute for International Education or the national or provincial offices of education. HEIs in Korea also should do their best to provide consistent support for the foreign faculty to engage in collaborative research and teaching with domestic faculty and researchers instead of treating them as mere lecturers or expatriates to cover basic English skills temporarily. In addition, more immersion programs such as English for academic or specific purposes or content-based English teaching should be implemented through a concerted effort by both Korean and foreign faculty in order to meet the needs of an increasing number of foreign students as well as domestic students. That is, the overemphasis of technical and economical aspects of English or the view of English as a mere communication tool ignores the importance of language as the manifestation of one's identity. As a result, English may become a tool of linguicism (Phillipson, 1992), as in the era of colonialism and imperialism at the turn of the 20th century rather than a liberating and empowering tool for Korean speakers of English (Gandhi, 1998; McLaren, 2006).

Third, though Korea is truly a knowledge-based and technology-advanced society in which universities play an important role in developing its economic and social power, some universities with low enrollment are struggling to secure enough students to keep their academic programs (Weidman, 2007). As a matter of fact, in addition to many problems innate in any HEI such as defining their missions and goals, setting up better curricular standards, recruiting better faculty and students, and enduring academic accountability (Lucas, 1996), many Korean HEIs have faced financial problems due to the current economic crisis and the expected drop in school-aged children for the next two or three decades due to the lowest birth rate of 1.13% among the OECD nations (OECD, 2009).

Thus, in order to resolve problems due to a short-sighted policy of allowing the excessive number of colleges and universities established in the late 1980s and 1990s, low enrollment due to the exodus of study-abroad students, and the lowest birth rate in the world, the Ministry of Education, Science, and Technology (MEST) has strongly driven the policy of merging small-sized national colleges and universities into corporate universities using a carrot and stick policy of providing special funding and tough regulations to the universities at the same time (Y. Kim, 2009). For instance, it is reported that MEST will announce the list of the private universities to be liquidated, which is dubbed as a "Big Bang Reform," due to the low enrollment and financial and management problems (B. Kim, 2009). Such a drastic measure is sure to affect mostly the universities in rural and provincial areas in the southern region in Korea.

Therefore, a consortium, if it is to be formed in the future, among the universities in the same region or provinces can streamline stronger and more competitive programs in each university, assign particular roles for universities to compete against other domestic and foreign institutes, and even establish joint degree programs and exchange faculty and students while sharing the facilities among the member universities (Kang, 2005).

Fourth, it is currently a norm that universities with low enrollment do their best to recruit foreign students to improve their financial situation and ultimately their chances of survival. In fact, these universities may have no choice but to restructure their own programs by merging with other universities or tapping into a different resource base, that is, to recruit more foreign students to survive. As of 2007, there are only slightly more than 49,000 foreign students in Korea, mostly from China, Vietnam, Japan, Mongolia, Taiwan, and a few European countries. Yet many universities are still doing their best to recruit more foreign students for internationalization, on the one hand, and for enough enrollment, on the other hand.

The Korean government also announced an ambitious plan for increasing the number of foreign students to 100,000 by the year 2012 (Joon-gAng Daily, 2008). However, more than 90% of these students come from a few Asian countries while the number of students from America and Europe is less than 3% and only1% from Africa. Accordingly, the mere increase of the number of foreign students without the effort of ensuring regional diversity and quality education should be avoided. Furthermore, given that there is a growing concern over the ill-prepared foreign students, universities should regularly update their programs and learning environments by offering foreigner-track courses and level-specific curricular subjects as in the case of Kyung Hee University where I work (JoongAng Daily, 2008). These programs help foreign students overcome the initial difficulty of academic courses that deal with content-specific and context-reduced subject matter offered in English or Korean. In addition, the government or provincial offices can designate a university in each region and special scholarships to offer quality academic and support programs for foreign students from diverse countries. Last, but not least, private sectors such as conglomerates and legal foundations, in my opinion, should provide more funding for foreign students since they are great human resources that will contribute to secure the benefits for Korea in the future internationalized world.

As a way of enhancing their academic competitiveness globally, HEIs in Korea have made an effort to develop credit transfer and dual degree programs as well as student exchanges by collaborating with foreign HEIs, especially in the North American, European and Asian countries. For example, some major Korean universities have developed internationally competitive academic programs such as joint degree or partial study-abroad programs. With the opening of market and reforms in various sectors as the result of the IMF crisis and global competition, the top-notch universities such as Korea University and Yonsei University offer their business courses not only in English, but also in collaboration with schools in the United States, Europe, and in Asian countries such as China, Hong Kong, and Singapore, whose programs are accredited by the Association to Advance Collegiate Schools of Business and the Brussels-based European Foundation for Management Development (Moon, 2009).

Thus, it may be no longer necessary for Korean universities to look only into ways to send their students abroad as they are actively developing their own competitive programs by benchmarking the good elements of other programs and integrating them to meet regional needs to serve a diverse student population both domestically and internationally. Such an effort to globalize academic programs will continuously occur in the highly sought out fields such as business, education, technology, and other areas of mutual interest between Korean and foreign institutions, which may provide a great impetus to enhance the quality of global and international education in Korea. However, there is a criticism that some of these joint or collaboratively developed programs with some leading foreign universities do not help much because they are basically to prepare domestic students to study abroad (Weidman, 2007).

Another strong impetus for changes in education and research is the annual evaluation of universities by domestic agencies and institutes which engage in joint development of evaluation criteria with foreign institutes. That is, the major organizations performing the evaluation of colleges and universities—such as the Korean Council for University Education and *Chosun, Dong-A*, and *JoongAng Daily* newspapers—all consider internationalization in which the proportions of foreign faculty and the number of courses offered in English along with the numbers of incoming foreign students and outgoing domestic students are examined and compared nationwide. As a matter of fact, it is now typical for most universities in the upper tier to require new faculty to publish an article internationally as well as to teach at least one class in English in order partly to internationalize their program and partly to meet these evaluation requirements in order to enhance their standings in (inter)national rankings of universities.

The universities' keen interest in meeting the evaluation criteria of these agencies has a sort of double-edged sword of positive and negative impacts. On the one hand, it can provide a positive momentum to regularly review their own administrative, academic, and research capacities as well as various instructional and facility services for students and restructure the areas which need improvement based on the comparative results against other (inter)national universities. On the other hand, it also precipitates a growing concern that universities are becoming more market-oriented than academic and research-based following the logic of efficiency in administration and management in the era when market-oriented neoliberalism is considered more of a cause for current global economic failure.

In other words, though in need of structuring adjustments and innovation to prepare students for the new glocalized world, universities should not be a temporary venue or niche market for these efficiency and profit-minded proponents who still believe in autonomy of market rather than the importance of globally concerted and consistent efforts to meet diverse needs of various stakeholders in different parts of the world (Giroux, 2008). Therefore, in order to lead their nation as an advanced knowledge- and technology-based society to the world playing field, HEIs in Korea should not succumb to unreasonable demands by outside agencies such as businesses or industries without looking inward scrupulously and meticulously to restructure internal programs by collaborating with and even competing against these external agencies.

That is, it is my view that both flexibility to take into account various demands by social members in various communities and autonomy to decide on what changes each university should prioritize or pursue are necessary because it is the university that has to ensure full accountability and transparency with whatever it sets out to do to meet global challenges for the society and students.

Another important issue in preparing Korean graduates for the future is to uphold the ideal for quality education for all. It is true that Korea is at a crossroads in its relentless march toward competition due to globalization, and is in need of continuing current educational success by helping the gifted youth and those who have high potential to maintain and enhance the knowledge-based and effective society to another level (Seol, 2004). However, it is also imperative for Korean universities to serve the poor and female students who are equal in terms of numbers in enrollment, but not on an equal basis with their counterpart in terms of advanced degree acquisition and job security (KEDI, 2009). That is, while students from poor families have difficulty in pursuing advanced degrees and drop out in the middle of the course, it is not easy for the advanced-degree seeking female students, whose enrollment has now reached 620,000 (46.6%), to find employment after graduation.

Seol (2004) proposes the possibility of globalization from below rather than from above. More specifically, he proposes an issue-centered global multicultural education in which transnational issues such as human rights, war prevention, peace, and environment are dealt with. Such a suggestion results from the drawbacks of the globalization led by few elites or superpowers, multinational corporations, or international associations such as IMF or World Trade Organization (WTO).

The efforts and changes described earlier occur in many different ways according to the case study (Stake, 2005) of my university, which was ranked 8th in the nation in 2009. For example, the university where I work changed the name of one of the three campuses to "Global Campus" few years ago and dropped its regional city name used for more than 25 years. Then, benchmarking the leading universities in the United States, United Kingdom, Japan, China, and Australia, the University established residential college programs for all incoming freshmen to take extra credit courses or other human development courses such as freshmen leadership seminars, foreign languages, and other culture-based programs as well as athletic programs. Both undergraduate and graduate students work as mentors for both freshmen and foreign students in the international zone to help them adjust to the new school environment and academic fields of study.

In addition, the Global Studio Networks program is being implemented to enable students to easily access academic content and research related to their fields through the provision of academic online courses and special lectures delivered through synchronous and asynchronous broadcasting via the Internet or telecommunications tool from various regions such as New York, Paris, and Beijing.

There is also a consistent effort to offer a more interdisciplinary program based on the concept of "consilience" (Wilson, 1998) in which global civic education takes a prime position in the midst of practical and technology-based curriculums that are emphasized for marketability or students' future job search in the industrial or technological fields. In addition, my university also initiated a World Civic Forum as part of its 60th anniversary in collaboration with the United Nations Department of Economic and Social Affairs under the theme of "Building Our Humanitarian Planet." This event resulted from the ongoing efforts by the University to enhance students' leadership and awareness on important world issues to achieve its goal of global eminence by bringing in the scholars and experts on civic engagements for world issues such as social justice, climate change, corruption, democracy and peace, and development and implementation of Millennium Development Goals for youth (World Civic Forum, 2009).

Such an effort is crucial in that the universality imposed by the globalization from above is not acceptable to everybody, but rather depends on the context where different sociocultural expectations operate in a unique way (Noh, 2004). Therefore, as Noh suggests, it may be that radical pluralism, where cultural diversity is more valued, is more viable for global citizenship education or multicultural education for HEIs in Korea.

Current State and Direction of Reforms in China

Immediately after the communist party took over in 1949, all the universities in China were nationalized following the then U.S.S.R. model. Accordingly, due to such restructuring during the political turmoil and struggle, the number of universities had dwindled to the extent that the number of liberal arts, law, and management and finance was down to 6.8% by 1962 (Jin & Nan, 2005). Worse yet, the Cultural Revolution from 1966 to 1977 further precipitated the reduction of the number of the universities and students. Beginning in 1977 the open policy led by Deng Xiao Ping restored the educational zeal in China by increasing the number of HEIs to 1,054 in 1986 from the mere 392 in 1976. However, such an unexpected increase of HEIs, which were supported nationally in the 1980s, worsened the national financial status and valuable resources were wasted due to bureaucratic inefficiency (Jin & Nan, 2005).

According to the report by the Ministry of Education of the People's Republic of China (MOEPRC, 2009), since the implementation of the

8th 5-Year Plan for Educational Development in the 1990s, it is reported that as of 1995 there were 2,210 HEIs in China with 1,054 regular 4 year HEIS for graduates of secondary schools and 1,156 adult HEIs which offer vocational programs or continuing education programs for older people.

During that period, the Chinese government funded the establishment of 101 national key and 58 disciplinary laboratories in order to bolster both advanced research bases and educational bases. In addition, postgraduate programs developed rapidly with more degree programs and by the end of 1995, 219 HEIs were authorized to award doctoral degrees while 471 HEIs awarded master degrees through 4,000 doctoral and 7,400 MA programs. The number of postgraduate students enrolled had also reached 145,000, which is a 55.7% increase compared to that in 1990, indicating an average annual growth rate of 9.3% (Jin & Nan, 2005).

Jin and Nan (2005) reported that along with the espousal of socialists' market economy theory in the 1990s, there has been a steady increase in the numbers of undergraduate and graduate students, especially after year 2000 when higher education in China began to engage in systematic changes. That is, the promulgation of "Directions of Chinese Educational Development and Progress" in 1993 and joining the WTO in 1999 spurred China to better educate their students.

According to the *China Statistical Yearbook* (2008), the number of 4-year colleges and universities has increased more than four times from 950 in 2000 to 4,478 in 2007. As of 2007, there are 795 institutions providing postgraduate programs (479 regular institutions of HEIs and 316 research institutions) run by central ministries and agencies, MOEPRC, local departments, and departments of education and non-education. No private educational organizations offer a postgraduate program or research institutes in HEIs while the Ministry of Education (MOE) does not operate its own research institute. However, there are 1,908 regular HEIs with full undergraduate or specialized courses and vocational and technical colleges while there are 413 adult programs and 906 private institutes.

During the period between 2000 and 2007, the number of students in HEIs increased more than three times from 5,560,000 to 18,849,000 (*China Statistical Yearbook*, 2008). Among them were 1,195,047 postgraduates (doctor's degree 222,508 and master's degree 972,539) and 5,659,194 regular university or discipline-specific college or institute degrees. That is, 2,820,971 students were enrolled in full-time undergraduate courses at universities and 2,838,223 students in colleges where specialized discipline programs and courses were offered. The latter were enrolled in adult undergraduate and college programs, in Internet-based courses, in graduate programs leading to advanced degrees for employees, or in postgraduate courses for advanced study.

During the 8th and 9th 5-year plans, China focused on reforming the management system and education provision system of HEIs by promoting the joint education provision mechanism between central and local governments in order to improve the fragmented administrative and management system in the past (Kim, 2002; MOEPRC, 2009). For instance, the central and local governments established cooperatively-run schools, which social and business sectors were also allowed to join, or to privately run schools. Such a multi-channel funding system is clearly due to the socialistic market economy and has provided great impetus for the internal reform within educational institutions in China. In addition, during the last two decades, China expanded its educational capacity and potential through more international cooperation and exchanges along with the legal establishment and enactment of various laws for education (MOEPRC, 2009).

According to MOEPRC (2009), there have been consistent efforts to change HEIs during the 9th 5-Year Plan for China's Educational Development and the Development Outline by 2010, which is set by the 5th Plenary Session of the 14th National Congress. The efforts include the universalization of 9-year compulsory education and illiteracy eradication among young and middle-aged groups, development of vocational and adult education, development of higher education, optimization of the educational structure, improvement of education quality and efficiency, and establishment of a socialistic education system framework with Chinese characteristics to prepare for the 21st century (MOEPRC, 2009). Some specific changes occurring in HEIs are highlighted as follows:

1)   Education is prioritized as a strategically important factor in developing a cohesive relationship between education, economy, and society. Accordingly, proactive plans to achieve economic and social progress and develop human resources in science, technology and education are supported by the Law on Education, the Outline for Educational Reform and Development in China, and the spirit of the 5th Plenary Session of the 14th National Congress.

2)   Being aware of the necessity of adapting education to diverse social and economic needs, the "Three Orientation (that is, modernization, the whole world, and the future)" principle is used as the landmark standard for the systematic structure and the development scale and speed of education so as to "meet the needs of future social progress." In addition, the Three Orientation principle is also used to carry out in-depth reforms on the curriculum system, teaching contents, and methodologies for program enhancements at HEIs.

3)   Engaging in the reform of educational systems in order to accelerate their development is considered a key for the socialistic market economy. Therefore, all HEIs are to follow the Outline for Educational Reform and Development promulgated by the State Council

and the Central Committee of the Communist Party of China (CPC) to reform their education provision, management, and educational investment systems and also improve recruitment and employment of students as well as tuition-charging.

4) Although the Outline proposes a balance between quantity and speed and between quality and efficiency, more emphasis is placed on the improvement of quality and efficiency. In other words, China's HEIs are now moving into the stage of ensuring quality and efficiency in its restructuring efforts while continuing with the enlargement of its size and speedy development in order to meet current challenges from inside and outside.

5) Given the socialistic direction of the education in China, the CPC's educational policies take prime positions in any effort in localizing and diversifying education and research in HEIs. Along with such a political structure and the uniqueness of China as the most populated country in the world, total decentralization of educational governance, seems difficult as in many developed and industrially advanced countries. Therefore, most HEIs supported by the government are still under the direction of the Party officers and serve to produce quality labor force in industry and agriculture.

(MOEPRC, 2009)

In addition, the Outline also requires HEIs to strengthen the moral and value education of its nation and people by focusing on the state, patriotism, collectivism, socialism, national unity, and civilized behaviors through understanding their own culture, discipline, and idealism.

Based on the aforementioned direction, China has effected four distinct changes in HEIs: Reform of administration and management, establishment of more HEIs in collaboration with local governments and private sectors, diversification of financial resources, and upgrading academic and research abilities through human resources development as expounded in detail hereafter (Kim, 2002; MOEPRC, 2009).

Reform in Management and Administration

The administration of HEIs has been reformed by allowing each municipality to open and manage its own schools, which is now close to 30% of all universities. More private universities have been established with the number having reached 175 along with 810,000 students, and 69 joint universities that were established in collaboration with foreign institutes as the result of the WTO membership in 1999 (Jin & Nan, 2005). In fact, the official website of the MOEPRC (2009) states that:

By 2010, only few typical key HEIs and some HEIs with strong professional background which are not convenient for local governments to manage will be administered directly by central government. For many other HEIs, their administration will change to local governments or rely on local governments as the main administrative body.

Accordingly, while the central government directs overall reform with national policies, both local governments and HEIs are to play more active roles for regional development by engaging in university macro management activities such as legislating, planning, funding, information provision, and other necessary administrative measures. As a result, it is expected that HEIs in China will develop a more advanced educational system by engaging in effective management and operation in providing better consultation, information and evaluation measures, as well as legal support in collaboration with the central, local, and social sectors.

Restructuring HEIs through Joint Establishment and Management

The MOEPRC announced that during the 9th 5-Year Plan, the "Joint Establishment" and "Joint Education Provision" will become the main format in order to diversify the funding channels and service groups to involve both the State and the provincial governments in HEI reforms (Jin & Nan, 2005; Kim, 2002). Accordingly, the restructuring effort and management of universities involve expanding the ownership of administration to universities by allowing them to restructure majors, revise curriculums or modify teaching materials, collaborate with outside agencies or companies, and redistribute the basic investment or expense provided by the central government. HEIs in China are also allowed joint program establishment and management in collaboration with the bureaus or agencies in the central and local governments in order to improve the inefficiency of the centralized management.

More importantly, through the "211 Project" in the 1990s, China restructured and integrated universities into 100 key schools which exclusively received government or provincial support in order to make them comprehensive and enhance their qualities following the U.S. model (Altbach, 2001; Altbach, Berdahl, & Gumport, 2005; MOEPRC, 2009). The name of the 211 Project stems from the policy of rigorous selection and exclusive support for 100 schools to prepare for the 21st century, and as of 2005, 107 universities have been selected to participate in this 211 Project (Jin & Nan, 2005). For instance, the five universities in Beijing and six universities in Guangzhou now cooperate in their programs and management to eliminate their weakness in teaching and research by sharing their strengths.

In another case, I have visited and engaged in numerous discussions with the faculty at the business management programs and administrative staff at the international offices at Chang'An University in order to develop collaborative academic and cultural programs for the last few years. Chang'An University, which is one of the universities among the 100 key HEIs based on the 211 Project, is a good case of how the reform efforts described earlier are materialized. Located in Xian, the oldest and first capital city of the first United China and the following dynasties, this national university has two campuses after merging the transportation, mechanical engineering, and architectural universities nearby as directed by the Chinese government in 2000.

As a result, it became the top university in transportation, especially in large vehicles such as buses or trucks and has a good reputation in economics and management such as logistics, finance and accounts, business administration, statistics, MIS, and e-commerce, and international economics and trading. Accordingly, it houses a number of the government-led research institutes and centers where its graduates work during and after graduation. As a result of the merger, its national ranking rose from 76th to 64th in 2009. The university is very comprehensive having 20 schools; which are similar to colleges in the West but can be a little smaller than a college but larger than a department, with more than 30,000 undergraduates, 5,000 master's, and 1,000 doctoral students. Among them, 500 students are studying abroad as exchange students in foreign countries such as the United States, Korea, Russia, and the like, in an effort to enhance their students' language abilities and job prospects.

Diversification of Funding Sources

With the increasing number of students and its fast economic development, the central government has also engaged in the reform of investment and funding by allowing universities to charge tuition in 1994 and forcing all universities to follow suit in 1997 and to also engage in profit making ventures or businesses (Jin & Nan, 2005). For instance, during the 9th 5-Year Plan, it is expected that all students pay some fees or expenses even though the government fund is still provided for the poor through scholarships, student loans, part-time job provisions, and the remission of tuitions and stipends.

As a socialistic country, China still uses a unique system for student employment. Both employers and students are directed to have regular meetings so that they can choose their workers and jobs rather than follow the national guidance. However, those students who studied with scholarships from the State or province are still subjected to previously agreed-upon commitments or contracts. Furthermore, in order to provide equal education for the poor, there is more effort to reform student recruitment by using both nation-wide and university-led plans to allow universities to secure more students through the "homecoming policy" of recruiting the students from the less developed regions and sending them back to their hometowns while also allowing graduates to choose their own jobs based on social demands (Jin & Nan, 2005).

Reform in Internal Personnel Management to Enhance Teaching

Reform in internal management is being made by revising personnel management and distribution by implementing rigorous merit systems despite a rather stable tenure system as a socialist country. That is, instead of upholding life-long employment up to the age of 63 and equal pay and treatment policies, the government now puts strong restrictions on the promotion of the faculty based on their research and teaching records, and even encourages universities to elect vice presidents or deans through voting (Jin & Nan, 2005).

More specifically, it is emphasized that new teaching philosophy and reform of teaching materials and methodologies are necessary to contribute to economic and social progress, which clearly reflect the State's effort to modernize and incorporate the latest developments in science, technology, and culture. As a matter of fact, China's reform of HEIs strongly encourages postgraduates to participate in various research institutes or centers run by the HEIs or government organizations (Kim, 2002). This is to systematically channel postgraduates to various advanced programs in liberal arts, social and natural sciences, and technology and also to produce important knowledge or scientific research outcomes for the enhancement of teaching and quality improvement of HEIs in the long run.

There is also a continuous effort to reform the National Entrance Examination for HEIs to relieve students of the heavy burden of preparing for the test and ensure the maintenance of a balance in their overall development in intelligence, morale, and physical aspects. In addition, HEIs are asked to expand their service profile for disciplines through teacher training, which help teachers and students apply what they had learned through diverse internships. Such emphasis on the integration of teaching, research, and social application will help enhance students' abilities in analyzing and solving problems. As a matter of fact, as a socialistic country, China's education puts a strong emphasis on producing good teachers to educate their students based on the Party's directives and researchers who can serve national modernization and its future (MOEPRC, 2009).

Last, but not least, as in Korea and most Asian countries, HEIs in China put a heavy emphasis on English by aligning its curriculum to meet students' communicative needs as well as offering basic courses to help them pass the College English Test mandated to all HEIs in China (Kim & Jeon, 2005; Sohn, 2003; Zhao & Coniam, 2008). In addition, many universities are now looking into ways to internationalize its program by hiring more faculty from foreign countries and developing academic agreements and exchange programs with universities which offer similar majors and institutes such as in the United States, India, Japan, and Korea.

Discussion and Conclusion

From this investigation into how HEIs in Korea and China are preparing their postgraduates for the competitiveness in a globalized international context, some commonalities and differences have been found. First, while the HEIs in Korea are moving toward a relatively stable stage in their education of students as did Japan in the late 1980s and 1990s, they are suffering from the new challenges posed by globalization, the current economic crisis, and the decreasing enrollment due to both the excessive number of colleges and universities established in the 1990s, and due to the low birth rate among Korean families. China, which is the fastest growing economy in the world, has done its best to improve the quality of education as well as the expansion of its education to the public. In doing so, China's MOE is at the helm of merging its universities into 100 key comprehensive universities through the 211 Project and an ongoing structural readjustment of their administration and management.

Second, whereas both Korea and China have sent many domestic students to study abroad in Western English-speaking countries such as the United States, Canada, and the United Kingdom, Korea's HEIs seem to struggle more internally than China's HEIs due to the exodus of Korean students to these countries. Consequently, in order to meet the enrollment quota, many universities in the provincial areas are accepting more foreign students from neighboring countries such as China, Japan, Vietnam, and Mongolia. The universities in Seoul and its satellite cities do their best to internationalize or globalize their academic programs by establishing joint degree or exchange programs with foreign institutes, offering more English-only classes, and recruiting foreign students to enhance their reputation and ranking in the nation and the world.

In the meantime, China is going through the stage of aligning its administration and management of the universities to establish a more developed educational system that strives to achieve a decentralized operation and privatization through tuition charges as well as the collaboration of local governments and private organizations.

Third, the effort to merge universities in both countries is also driven by different reasons. That is, though it is true that the MOEs and governments in both Korea and China have a strong influence in directing current reforms, Korea does so to reduce the number of its HEIs by merging two or three national or private universities into a corporate university to lessen the financial burden on the central government and the universities involved in such mergers. China has, however, merged both small and mid-sized universities to provide comprehensive academic and research programs with more efficient administration and management. In addition, China has implemented the policy of a tuition charge for all students and has also allowed the establishment of universities or research institutes by local government organizations or research agencies in collaboration with the central government or private social sectors.

Fourth, with the start of WTO in 1995, both Korea and China have opened their education markets. In Korea, there are now more foreign institutes or agencies which collaborate with local and industrial institutes in order to establish joint academic and professional programs. Accordingly, with the dwindling number of students in the future, Korea has emphasized the readjustment of university enrollment, improvement of educational environments, and program specialization. In so doing, despite strong criticism and resistance from universities and colleges, the government has encouraged national universities to merge with struggling private universities or two-year junior colleges and is actually forcing financially struggling ones to merge with others to avoid closing them within a few years.

China, however it appears will expand its educational services to more students through mergers and privatization for years to come despite the current world economic crisis. Therefore, it is more likely that, despite the concern and measures to ensure quality of teaching and research in HEIs, the quantitative development of teaching and relevant policies in China will continue as long as its economy can afford to do so.

Fifth, as export-oriented countries with the traditional Confucius view of respecting education, both Korea and China put a strong emphasis on learning foreign languages as well as learning and researching in various fields. As a matter of fact, Both China and Korea are the second and third largest senders of their students to the United States (Open Doors, 2009b). Accordingly, the HEIs in both countries consider English as an indispensible tool for their students as manifested in an excessive zeal for studying abroad in English-speaking countries, a proliferation of private English teaching institutes, an increasing number of courses taught in English, and test-driven English teaching for jobs and promotions in Korea. China also mandates the College English Test as a graduation requirement nationwide and sent 81,127 students to the United States in the academic year of 2007/2008, second only to India (Open Doors, 2009b).

Last, but not least, both China and Korea have been restructuring their educational systems for better academic and research performances through both centralizing and decentralizing their governance. However, they also face difficulties in meeting students' needs and enhancing global competitiveness due to a rapid increase in student enrollment during the last two decades, the lack of systemic efforts to catch up with the top-down change efforts, and an excessive focus on efficiency, privatization, and technology rather than educational software.

As for Korea, its educational system and policies are more decentralized, which allow universities to seek foreign funding to restructure or establish new programs especially in the economic free zones such as Incheon and Jeju Island. However, the government and MEST also are strongly pushing Korea's HEIs to enhance their programs both to keep domestic students from going abroad and to recruit more foreign students for the universities with low enrollment in the provincial areas. Furthermore, they also drive a policy of "merge or perish" to reduce the number of universities, especially in the provincial areas in Korea.

In the meantime, China's HEIs can enhance their administration and management and both academic and research programs through continuous efforts of restructuring universities, decentralized policies, and more privatization of education in collaboration with social sectors. Accordingly, it remains to be seen whether Korea will be successful in regenerating its educational zeal to meet new challenges in the knowledge-based globalization period by glocalizing its HEIs based on their needs and visions. In the same vein, China will have to prepare for more quality-based restructuring of its HEIs to ensure the soft-landing of the current structural adjustment through merging, decentralizing and privatizing, and reforming administrative and academic management.

References

Altbach, Philip. (2001). The American academic model in comparative perspective. In P. G. Altbach, P. J. Gumport, & D. B. Johnstone, (Eds.), *Defense of American higher education* (pp. 11–37). Baltimore, MD: The Johns Hopkins University Press.

Altbach, Philip, & Peterson, Patti. (2008). *Higher education in the new century.* Boston, MA: Sense Publishers

Altbach, Philip, Berdahl, Robert, & Gumport, Patricia. (2005). *American higher education in the twenty-first century: Social, political, and economic challenges.* Baltimore, MD: The Johns Hopkins University Press.

Banks, James. (2002). *An introduction to multicultural education.* Boston: Allyn & Bacon.

China Statistical Yearbook. (2008). Retrieved April 20, 2009 from http://www.stats.gov.cn/tjsj/ndsj/2008/indexeh.htm.

Cho, Joohee. (2007, July 2). English is the golden tongue for South Koreans. *The Washington Post*, p. A16. Retrieved March 30, 2009 from http://www.washingtonpost.com/wp-dyn/content/article/2007/07/01/AR2007070101259.html

Gandhi, Leela. (1998). *Postcolonial theory.* New York: Columbia University Press.

Giroux, Henry. (2008). *Against the terror of neoliberalism: Politics beyond the age of greed.* Boulder, CO: Paradigm Publishers.

Hankyoreh (2007). *Editorial: Excessive emphasis on English only classes in universities.* Retrieved March 15, 2009 from http://www.hani.co.kr/arti/opinion/editorial/231245.html.

Huer, J. (2009). *Is English teaching here 'gold rush'?* Retrieved May 28, 2009, from http://www.koreatimes.co.kr/, http://www/news/opinion/2009/05/272_44577.html

Ihm, Chon Sun. (2006). Internationalization of higher education and workplace competencies: Implications for policy in Korea, *Asian Women*, 22, 1, 45–68.

Jenkins, Jennifer. (2007). *English as a lingua franca: Attitude and identity.* Oxford: Oxford University Press.

Jin, Shizhu, & Nan, Xuefeng. (2005). Recent reform of Chinese university and Yanbian university. *Journal of Korea Regional Geography*, 11(5), 488–499.

JoongAng Daily. (2008). *Editorial: Inducement of foreign students: Quality before quantity.* Retrieved March 10, 2009 from http://article.joins.com/article/article.asp?total_id = 3248236, 2008.08.05

Kang, Byung Woon. (2005). Policy suggestions for university structure reforming plan of the government. *The Journal of Educational Administration*, 23(2), 421–46.

Kang, Shin-who. (2008). *Korean English fever betrayed by test scores.* Retrieved March 22, 2009 from http://www.koreatimes.co.kr/www/news/nation/2008/06/117_25279.html

KEDI (Korea Educational Development Institute). (2009). *Statistics on universities.* Center for Educational Statistics. Retrieved May 5, 2009 from http://std.kedi.re.kr/index.jsp

Kim, Bong Eok. (2009, May 25). Special report: Restructuring of universities-closing down insolvent private universities: Are they only responsible for the insolvency with no substantial support over the years? *Kyosu Newspaper*, p. 5.

Kim, Eun-Ju, & Jeon, Jihyeon. (2005). A comparative study of national English curricula of Korea, China and Japan: Educational policies and practices in the teaching of English. *English Teaching*, 60(3), 27–48.

Kim, Hyunduk. (2007). A comparative study of multicultural education and global education in the U.S. *Korea Journal of Comparative Education*, 17(4), 1–23.

Kim, Ji-Eun. (2006). Globalization and education in Korea: A critical comparison with Japan. *Korea Journal of Comparative Education*, 75, 107.

Kim, Pil-Dong. (2004). A comparative study of university reforms: Toward 21st century in Korea, Japan, and China-Focusing on organization reforms, *Journal of Korean Sociological Association*, 38(3) 1–37.

Kim, Pil-Dong. (2002). The development of Chinese higher education and directions of recent reforms in universities. *Studies of Social Sciences*, 13, 83–110.

Kim, Yu Jeong. (2009, May 25). Where will the Big Bang start? *Kyosu Newspaper*, p. 2.

Korea Development Institute. (2009). *Economic bulletin.* Retrieved April 30, 2009 from http://www.kdi.re.kr/kdi_eng/trends/economic_trends_back.jsp

Krugman, Paul. (2008). *The return of depression economics and the crisis of 2008.* New York: W. W. Norton & Company.

Lucas, Christopher. (1996). *Crisis in the academy: Rethinking higher education in America.* New York: St. Martin's Press.

McKay, Sandra. (2003). *Teaching English overseas: An introduction.* Oxford: Oxford University Press.

McLaren, Peter. (2006). *Race and hope: Interviews with Peter McLaren on war, imperialism, and critical pedagogy.* New York: Peter Lang.

MOEHRD. (2006). *The revised national foreign language curriculum.* Ministry of Education and Human Resources Development. Seoul: Korea.

MOEHRD. (2004). *A university structuring reform plan for the enhancement of its competitiveness*. Ministry of Education and Human Resources Development. Seoul: Korea.

MOEPRC (Ministry of Education of the People's Republic of China). (2009). *National outline for medium and long-term education reform and development*. Retrieved October 23, 2010, from http://www.moe.gov.cn/publicfiles/business/htmlfiles/moe/moe_2792/index.html

Moon, Ihlwan. (2009, May 8). Asia seeks its own brand of business schools. *Business Week*. Retrieved September 9, 2009 from http://www.businessweek. com/globalbiz/content/may2009/gb2009057_031418.htm?chan = top+news_ top+news+index+-+temp_global+business

Noh, Chan Ok. (2004). Global citizenship education in the age of pluralism. *Social Studies Education*, 43(4), 207–224.

OECD. (2008). *Education at a glance 2008: OECD indicators*. Paris: OECD Publishing.

OECD. (2009). *Society at a glance 2009—OECD social indicators*. Retrieved March 21, 2009, from Organization for Economic Co-operation and Development. Retrieved from http://www.oecd.org/els/social/indicators/SAG

Open Doors (2009a). *Leading countries of origin: Open Doors 2009 report on international educational exchange*. Retrieved October 23, 2010 from http://opendoors.iienetwork.org/

Open Doors. (2009b). *International students on U.S. Campuses at all-time high*. Retrieved April 23, 2009 from http://opendoors.iienetwork.org/?p = 131590

Park, Jin-Kyu. (2009). English fever in South Korea: Its history and symptoms. *English Today 97*, 25(1), 50–57. Retrieved January 10, 2010 from http://journals.cambridge.org/action/displayFulltext?type = 1&fid = 4614536&jid = ENG&volumeId = 25&issueId = 01&aid = 4614532

Phillipson, Robert. (1992). *Linguistic imperialism*. Oxford: Oxford University Press.

Samsung Economic Research Institute. (2006). *The economics of English*. CEO Information, 578. 2006. 11. 15

Seol, Kyujoo. (2004). The rise of global civil society and the orientation of multicultural citizenship education. *Social Studies Education*, 43(3), 31–54.

Sohn, Sun Young. (2003). College English teaching in China. *The Journal of Teaching English Literature*, 7(1), 270–273.

Stake, Robert. (2005). Qualitative case studies. In Denzin, Norman, & Lincoln, Yvonna (Eds.), *The Sage handbook of qualitative research*, pp. 443–466. Thousand Oaks, CA: Sage Publications.

Sung, Kiwan. (2002). Critical theory and pedagogy: Remapping English teaching in Korea. *English Teaching*, 57(2), 65–89.

UNDESA. (2009). *United Nations Department of Economic and Social Affairs*. Retrieved May 25, 2009 from http://www.un.org/esa/desa/

UNESCO. (2009). United Nations educational, scientific, cultural organizations: Retrieved May 20, 2009 from http://portal.unesco.org/en/ev.php-URL_ID = 29008&URL_DO = DO_TOPIC&URL_SECTION = 201.html

Weidman, John. (2007). Insight into Korea (20): Globalization of Korean higher education: A turn for better? Retrieved April 3, 2009, from http://www.koreaherald.com/specialreport/Detail.jsp?newsMLId=20070730000008

Wilson, Edward (1998). *Consilience: The unity of knowledge.* New York: Vintage.

World Civic Forum. (2009). *Building our humanitarian planet. Proceedings.* May 5–8, 2009. Retrieved May 28, 2009 from http://www.wcf2009.org

Zhao, Wen, & Coniam, David. (2008). Rethinking the college English curriculum in China. In Y. H. Choi, & B. Spolsky (Eds.), *ELT curriculum innovation and implementation in Asia* (pp. 39–70). Seoul: Korea.

4 Globalization and Higher Education in the Middle East*

Issam E. Khoury and Beverly Lindsay

[A]ll of us must recognize that education and innovation will be the currency of the 21st century."
> President Barack Obama, Speech at Cairo University, June 4,
> 2009 (Office of the Press Secretary, 2009, para. 72)

The sharing of knowledge, ideas and values is the noblest way to transcend barriers. In this sense, globalization is the architect, which constructs academic bridges across cultural and geographical landscapes.
> Her Highness Sheikha Mozah Bint Nasser Al-Missned, First Lady
> of the State of Qatar, 1995 (quoted in Qatar Foundation, 2009b)

As presented in chapter one, the volume seeks to answer some important questions regarding the relationship between universities and globalization and the role that the former play in the process of the latter. Some critical questions were posed in chapter 1 about how universities prepare professional educators for changing global diversity, and how these universities translate macro-level global issues into viable policies, practices, and programs at respective sites. Taking three countries from the Arabian (Persian) Gulf region as a case study, this chapter seeks to explicate these matters by focusing on specific institutional policies that demonstrate how globalization is shaping the preparation of professional educators, and how these universities are translating macro-level global issues into policies and practices.

We begin by articulating a theoretical and conceptual framework of globalization that is informed by the works of Dodds (2008), Yang (2003), and Mazawi (2008). Dodds (2008) offers a synthesis of much of the literature on globalization, placing that literature in three categories, each of which offers a different lens on the process and theory of globalization. Yang (2003) is particularly concerned with the negative effects of globalization on institutions of higher education, claiming that globalization in the arena of higher education is primarily a Western imposition

* The research for this chapter was sponsored, in part, by a Qatar University Administrative and Research Grant for the co-authors.

that eradicates the national in favor of the Western. Mazawi (2008) posits that globalization of higher education in the Gulf States is not so simple as to indicate the imposition of the West, but instead is "the outcome of multifaceted processes situated at the juncture of global, geo-regional and national dynamics that intersect in various and complex ways" (p. 60).

With this framework in place, we proceed to explore two phenomena in the Gulf region. The first is the case of Education City, an ambitious project in Qatar that has brought six American universities onto one campus to offer American-style education in the region. "Education City" was established in Qatar in 1995 as the cornerstone of the Qatar Foundation's project to transform mineral wealth into human capital (Qatar Foundation, 2009). The City brings together the branch campuses of six American institutions: Texas A&M, Georgetown, Carnegie Mellon, Virginia Commonwealth, Northwestern University, and the Weil Medical College of Cornell University. Each campus specializes in one or two majors, with a liberal arts education undergirding each of those programs. Examining "Education City" as one block, we seek to ascertain how students and nationals in the region have received American-style education, and how Education City has transformed and is transforming the nature of education in Qatar.

The second focus of this chapter will be how globalization has, in turn, affected the curricula of Arab universities in the region. The curricular content and programmatic initiatives of major universities in the Arabian Gulf, namely Qatar University, Zayed University (UAE), and Sultan Qaboos University (Oman) are analyzed in an effort to ascertain the effect of globalization on shaping future generations. These universities represent three of the six countries of the Arab Gulf Cooperation Council (GCC) and, in the interest of space, will serve as a sample of national universities in the region that are engaged heavily in processes of globalization.[1]

To accomplish these tasks, content and web analyses of various university websites and news sources are employed, along with participant observation and personal interviews conducted by the senior author. Various communications also occurred with professional educators in Qatar and/or those associated with Education City who are also in the United States.

Theoretical and Conceptual Framework

Dodds (2008) offers a broad review of recent literature on globalization and starts with a quote from Amin (1997): "The more we read about globalization . . . the less clear we seem to be about what it means and what it implies" (p. 506). In some articles, globalization is referred to as global flows of information, technology, knowledge, culture, and even identity (Dion, 2005; Scott, 2005; Muhammad, 2005). Similarly, Van Vught, Van der Wende, and Westerheijden (2002) describe the recruitment of international students as "the globalization game" (p. 112), although little of the literature discusses the global flow of students. While the Institute of International Education (IIE) publishes an annual statistical report on international students and study abroad, this is focused largely on American students studying abroad and international students studying in the United States (Institute of International Education, 2009). There has been limited analysis of the role these students play in the multiple processes of globalization from economic, social, cultural, and political perspectives.

The second trend within the literature on globalization discusses the phenomenon as marketization (Dodds, 2008, p. 508). In this strand of the literature, the market is central as is the competition that is intrinsic to capitalist ideology. Thus, the literature in this strand examines, on the one hand, competition between domestic institutions of higher education and those from other countries (Mok & Tan, 2004). Thus, we see universities that are or aspire to be featured on the *Times Supplement of Higher Education's* "Top 200 World Universities" list as an example of this trend. On the other hand, globalization-as-marketization literature can also refer to national university systems that work to increase their standards in order to seek to improve national economic effectiveness (Dodds, 2008; The Times Higher Education, 2009).

The final strand within Dodd's article is the relationship of globalization to particular policy objectives. In this strand of the literature, globalization is understood as an ideology that is innately linked to policy objectives that disadvantage the majority. This strand of literature is filled with negative references to globalization as leading to "an erosion of human values" (Narsee, 2005), and even as "an ideological justification for neo-imperialist" policies (Imam, 2005, p. 472).

Strongly related to this strand of the literature is the article by Rui Yang (2003) that offers a harsh attack on the effects of globalization on higher education. He starts by defending the claim that globalization leads to homogenization and as such must be taken seriously (Yang, 2003). Citing works by Back et al. (1997) and Knight and De Wit (1997), he argues that globalization leads to "the homogenization of national identities and cultures" (Yang, 2003, p. 270) since the "origins of globalization are . . . largely Western and Western political and economic institutions are reproduced as part of the process" (p. 284). He essentially contends that globalization originates in the West and, therefore, its outcomes are nothing more than Western models imposed in developing countries.

Yang articulates a very important point that is directly related to one of the foci of this chapter as he asserts that "Education as investment in human capital has become a key plank of educational policy platforms in many countries. This reductive and functionalist view has never been successful in promoting educational achievement" (Yang, 2003, p. 278). This statement would be challenged by the rulers of Qatar who have invested sizeable financial resources in the development of educational institutions (for example, at Qatar University, and through the development of Education City), and in providing opportunities for Qatari students (for example, through the offering of scholarships for Qatari students to study in Qatar, the Arab World, Australia, Europe, Canada, and the United States) (Supreme Education Council, 2010; Stasz et al., 2007).

Yang remains critical of the effects of globalization on higher education, while Mazawi (2008) seems to temper his approach as globalization relates to higher education in the Arabian Gulf region. He posits that the influence of the United States on Gulf educational systems has been strong and that the imperative to adhere to American standards in curriculum and accreditation are quite evident (Mazawi, 2008). However, it is important to note that the educational initiatives, being discussed in this chapter, are neither governed (by) nor spearheaded by any official American government agency. The partnerships and relationships that are being developed are not meant to achieve a precisely voiced American State Department-funded goal (although other initiatives such as the Middle East Partnership Initiative of the United States Department of State are meant for those purposes). The European Union has put forth policy objectives specifically designed to link the European Union and the GCC states in concrete policy matters through the establishment of European universities in each of the Gulf States (Luciani & Neugart, 2005). We will maintain that the relationship between the United States and Gulf academic institutions appears to be a symbiotic one, benefitting both sides of the partnership. The structures and practices that brought about these relationships indicate that globalization is not always a top-down flow from the powerful to the emergent, but instead a partnership that is redefining the nature of globalization in the arena of higher education (Lindsay, 2010).

Education City

Education City is part of the Qatar Foundation for Education, Science, and Community Development, an ambitious, one-of-a-kind project in the region, that is the brainchild of the Emir of Qatar, His Highness Sheikh Hamad bin Khalifa Al-Thani, and is chaired by the first lady, Sheikha Mozah bint Nasser Al-Missned. The Foundation includes a number of non-profit organizations that work in the fields of community development, education, and scientific research (Qatar Foundation, 2009c). However, the hallmark of the Foundation is Education City, a project so ambitious that it has been described as "one of the most spectacular partnerships" (Waterbury, 2003, p. 65). In deciding which universities would comprise Education City, the Emir and the First Lady toured a number of institutions around the world before deciding on American institutions (Mendenhall, 2005). The strong relationship between the United States and GCC countries has been well-documented and it is likely this reason that American institutions were selected over those from Europe, Canada, and Australia (Herrera, 2007; Mazawi, 2008).

In the early explorations of American universities, a number were contacted such as those in the Consortium for Institutional Cooperation (CIC) that is composed of the major research universities in the Midwest and the Pennsylvania State University. The CIC members, for the most part, were also members of the Midwest Universities Consortium for International Activities, Inc. (MUCIA) that engaged in international activities especially in developing or emerging nations. At the time of the initial explorations, MUCIA was located at the Ohio State University and headed by a professor of agricultural sciences with extensive international experiences. Each of the university representatives to MUCIA, including one of the authors who was the Dean of International Programs at Pennsylvania State University, shared preliminary plans with their presidents and/or provosts. For a host of reasons, there was limited interest by various university senior executives, such as those at Pennsylvania State University, to develop programs in Qatar. Perceptions existed about the relative importance of Qatar and the Middle East, along with fiscal considerations, as voiced at sites such as Pennsylvania State University. Simultaneously, Qatari leaders engaged in discussions with the University of Virginia, Texas A&M University, and others. While some University of Virginia officials were receptive to programs in Qatar, the Virginia Legislature was not supportive. Hence other universities were contacted, they expressed receptiveness, and moved forward in the development of the programs now offered in Education City.[2]

There are currently six American campuses that offer complete Bachelor's degrees at Education City, and all are based on the strong liberal arts tradition (although two universities, Cornell and Texas A&M universities do offer graduate and professional degrees). The question that arises in this context is whether the move to bring American-style education to the Arabian Gulf region is part of a trend of globalization.

The case of Education City, situated in the capital of Doha, can be examined from a number of perspectives in relation to the literature on globalization. On the one hand, it is easy to place it as an example of the flow of goods from one country to another. Indeed there is a clear flow of goods, services, knowledge, culture, information, technology, faculty, and staff from one area of the world to another. The six universities in Education City were funded by the government of Qatar to bring their American educational systems, professors, and curricula to the state of Qatar. By bringing American education to Qatar, the government provides students from the region viable alternatives to 1) national universities in the region; 2) other American universities in the Middle East (such as the American universities in Lebanon and Egypt); and 3) the necessity of going to North America, Europe, or Australia to obtain a Western education.

Similarly, Education City also serves as an example of the marketization trend in globalization (Dodds, 2008). As per this strand of the literature, competition drives innovation, and that competition exists between domestic and international institutions of higher education (Dodds, 2008). The establishment of Education City in Doha does not serve to increase directly the quality or effectiveness of Qatar's national higher education system since the universities are all American institutions. However, it might be understood that Education City indirectly serves to improve the effectiveness of Qatar's national education system by serving as competition.

It is easy to view Education City in yet another perspective within the literature on globalization and that is globalization is intrinsically linked to an ideology. Dodds (2008) samples the literature and sees that much of it links globalization with particular policy objectives. Seen in this light, Education City might be viewed as a homogenizing tool that will serve to diminish Qatar's national identity and culture (Yang, 2003). Gender serves as a salient example of how Qatar's national identity and culture is being watered down at Education City. Supporters of this point of view will point to the fact that all American campuses in Education City are co-educational whereas traditional institutions of education (at all levels) in Qatar employ separate-gender education. They might also argue that these American institutions are designed primarily to endear the Arab and Muslim worlds to an American-centric perspective that is inherently antithetical to a Muslim-centric one. Sheikha Mozah might respond by saying that "by bringing the education to Qatar, the country [Qatar] respects its [own] traditions and builds its future" (Mendenhall, 2005). Similarly, the dean at Georgetown University affirms that the goal is not indoctrination but instead "cross-cultural understanding and . . . educating citizen leaders" (Hanley, 2007, p. 31).

Nevertheless, it is not difficult to see why the perspective of Education City as an ideological outpost has some merit since John Waterbury, former president of the American University of Beirut, states that "today's crisis is not one of values, let alone civilizations, but one of interests . . . [and] the United States now dominates the world militarily and economically" (2003, p. 60). What is unique about Education City is the fine line that is drawn between American institutions and its foreign policies. These institutions stand as hallmarks of what many consider to be the strongest higher education system in the world. In the words of a recent alumna from Carnegie Mellon University in Qatar:

> I think you can be against American policies, and you can be against a lot of the policies coming out of the west towards the Arab world right now. But by accepting an American education, and by equipping yourself with an American education, you're opening doors to

negotiations and dialogues in the future that can help to resolve those issues.

(Brancaccio, 2009)

This perspective is echoed and refined by a senior academic affairs administrator at one of the institutions in Education City. In an interview with the first author, an Associate Dean of Academic Affairs affirmed that they were invited to Qatar. Carnegie Mellon accepted the offer to establish a campus in Qatar because it was consistent with their international and global initiatives, rather than imposing themselves on Qatar in an attempt to expand American influence (personal communication, June 16, 2009). The Dean of Carnegie Mellon University in Qatar, Charles E. Thorpe, emphasized, "We're teaching our Qatari students how to deal with the Western world, without forcing them into acting like Westerners or changing their personal values" (Unknown, 2008). This was echoed by the Associate Dean who asserted that in addition to coming to Qatar, Carnegie Mellon are expanding their reach by taking students on service-learning trips to Kenya, Malaysia, and Pittsburgh (I.E. Khoury, June 16, 2009).

The experiment that is Education City cannot be neatly categorized in any of the categories of globalization literature that were identified by Dodds (2008). Indeed, those who vehemently oppose Education City will point to the obvious examples of how local and Islamic cultures are being overshadowed in favor of an American worldview. Yang's (2003) assertion that globalization is inextricably intertwined with homogenization serves as the foundation of that argument. Those who favor American education will assert that the quality of an American education and the possibilities for intercultural understanding supersede any implications of an imperialist agenda. What has yet to be researched regarding to Education City is the quality of academic rigor that exists at these branch campuses as compared to the rigor at the home campuses of these universities. As most of these universities have only graduated one or two classes so far, that has yet to be ascertained.

Local Universities

In addition to the ambitious project that is Education City, and projects such as New York University setting up a campus in Abu Dhabi, and Rochester Institute of Technology and Michigan State University setting up branch campuses in Dubai, local universities have existed in the Middle East for a considerable time. The earliest institutions of higher education (though they took different forms than now observed) existed in the Middle East for centuries since education in the Middle East can be traced back to Islamic training schools (*madrasas*) in the 7th century (Massialas, 1991). Such training schools are somewhat analogous to the normal schools in the colonial United States that evolved into universities. These *madrasas* taught Arabic language and Islamic religion (revealed sciences) and mathematics and logic (rational sciences) where instruction focused on memorization and writing. In this informal milieu, the position and authority of professor-scholar was unquestioned (Massialas, 1991). Even with the establishment of a formal institution of higher education in Baghdad in 1067, instruction concentrated on a system of teaching "logic and rhetoric, so as to know how to avoid ambiguity of thought and language" (Massialas, 1991, p. 982). The curriculum of this period centered on the words and actions of the Prophet Muhammad, and the interpretation of these by his companions and followers, and subsequently by Islamic jurists.

At the zenith of the Muslim Empire in the 14th century, prominent institutions of higher education existed in the metropolises of Baghdad, Damascus, and Cairo. All higher learning was structured in similar fashion (Massialas, 1991) wherein the forms of knowledge and information were based on an authority-scholar who delivered unquestioned material to students. According to Eickelman (1989), "Mosque-universities had no sharply defined body of students or faculty, administration, entrance or course examinations, curriculum, or in most cases unified sources of funds" (p. 312). The content matter at this time was heavily influenced by the two-fold sciences approach: revealed and rational. However, according to Massialas (1991), "the cultural heritage of the Arab Islamic world has not, on the whole, contributed much to the identities of modern universities in the Arab world" (p. 983). Esposito (1998) maintains that Islamic civilization has contributed philosophy, science, and political thought to the West, and Makdisi (1990) would contend that such "common features of the contemporary university—such as the conferring of master's and doctoral degrees, protections for academic freedom, inaugural lectures, the wearing of robes and holding of 'chairs'—originated with the *madrasa*" (cited in Herrera, 2007, p. 20).

Between the 14th and the 19th centuries, the development of higher education in the Arab world was fairly stagnant. The resurgence of higher education in the Arab world would occur during the second half of the 19th century when the Ottoman Empire would look to Europe and Russia for higher educational models that could be locally implemented to advance in a new world order (Herrera, 2007). At roughly the same time, the British and Americans would be sending missionaries to the region, not for the purposes of conversion as this is against Islamic teachings and punishable by law, but primarily "focused on concerns of service and example" (Murphy, 1987, p. 4). It is within this context that we see the establishment of the American University of Beirut (1866) and the American University in Cairo (1919). According to Massialas (1991), there were only eight Arab universities in the Middle East in 1940, and that number had increased to 72 in 1986. Herrera (2007) notes that that number has swelled to over 200 institutions of postsecondary education in recent years.

In the Arabian Gulf region, higher education is a relatively new phenomenon. King Abdullah University in Saudi Arabia was the first institution founded in the region in 1957 (Alkhozai, 2008). A number of national universities have been established since then, among them Qatar University (1973), Zayed University (1988), and Sultan Qaboos University (1986). These national universities represent three of the six countries of the Arab Gulf Cooperation Council (Qatar, the United Arab Emirates, and Oman respectively) and will serve as a sample for understanding the development of higher education in the region.

Before continuing, it helps to offer a brief historical synopsis of these countries. The histories of these three countries follow a similar trajectory. They were all controlled or substantially influenced by Great Britain for a substantive part of the 20th century. Both Qatar and the United Arab Emirates became independent in 1971, the latter composed of the union between seven small states (formerly known as the Trucial States). Oman had been independent for a few centuries before the 1970s, but with the rise in 1970 of the current ruler, Sultan Qaboos bin Said Al Said, the nation would enter a new era of its history. All three states have maintained balanced diplomatic relations regionally and internationally, and have garnered much investment and support from governments, businesses, educational institutions, and non-profit organizations around the world. They are all home to extensive reserves of oil and/or gas, and have used the finances generated from these resources to embark on impressive large-scale development projects, such as the man-made islands of The Pearl in Qatar, and the Palms in Dubai. Furthermore, "close economic and geopolitical alliances with the United States contributed to the choice of the American model . . . as the prevailing higher education model in the Gulf" (Herrera, 2007, p. 413). This will become increasingly evident as the following cases are presented.

A feature common to the three countries in question is the large number of expatriates that live within each of these states. According to the latest available statistics, Omanis, Qataris, and Emiratis only constitute 17%, 18%, and 20%, respectively, of the population of each of those countries (CIA The World Factbook—Oman, 2009; Qatar Statistics Authority, 2007; UAE Interact, 2009). In order to counteract such large expatriate populations in their boundaries, these states have adopted Omanization, Qatarization, and Emiratization policies. These nationalization policies seek to educate nationals and place them in key positions (to replace foreign workers) that will, in turn, contribute to national and economic development (Wallin, 2005). These nationalization policies affect various aspects of the economy, and are particularly salient when discussing the trend of globalization in education at three national universities in the Gulf.

Qatar University, founded in 1973 as the College of Education, became the country's national university in only four years. It currently enrolls approximately 7,200 students (Qatar University, 2009a) divided into seven academic colleges: Arts and Sciences, Engineering, Business and Economics, Law, Shari'a (Islamic studies), Pharmacy, and Education. In addition, there is a remedial program for college first-year students called the "Foundation Program" which seeks to improve students' skills in Arabic, English, mathematics, and computer literacy. According to Rugh (2002), "as much as 35–40 percent of instructional resources in higher education are spent on remediation of skill deficiencies of college entrants" (p. 412). At Qatar University, this is certainly the case, as 34.4% of its 7,889 students in fall 2007 were enrolled in the Foundation Program (Qatar University, 2008). Approximately 5,000 students are regularly enrolled in degree-granting programs, and of that number, 40% are enrolled in the Colleges of Engineering (823), Education (515), and Business and Economics (732). This seems to be directly correlated to Qatarization policies that seek to employ Qataris in the ever-increasing industries of oil and natural gas, ensuring future business success, and improving the quality of teachers at K-12 levels, (Stasz et al., 2007). The remaining students are enrolled in the Colleges of Arts and Sciences, Law, and Shari'a and Islamic Studies, which all serve the nation in different ways.

During the summer of 2009, the first author spent an intensive period of time undertaking a practicum at Qatar University, and was able to observe how an Arab university maintains its own identity while interacting with global forces. Qatar University is embarking on a series of projects that they envision and hope will culminate in Qatar University being placed on the world stage as a global university. As the only national four-year institution of higher education in the State of Qatar, the university is seeking to prepare its graduates for a globalized world in which they can easily interact. A number of their academic programs are accredited by international accrediting bodies from the United States, such as ABET (the accreditation body for computer science, engineering, and technology programs) and the National Accrediting Agency for Clinical Laboratory Sciences, and Canada, such as the Canadian Society of Chemistry and the Canadian Society for Accreditation of Pharmacy Programs (Qatar University, 2009b). These strategic actions fall in line with the trend of globalization that is occurring in Qatar. Dodds (2008) would categorize this as falling within the trend of globalization-as-marketization in that Qatar is seeking to improve the quality of its national university in the hopes of making it competitive on a global stage.

In addition, Qatar University has embarked on a university-wide reassessment of its teaching and learning philosophy. As mentioned earlier in the chapter, Arab educational institutions were focused on limited subjects and these were based on a learning philosophy that was instructor-

and information-centered. What Qatar University is doing is adapting its teaching philosophies to ensure that it is student-centered, with the ultimate goal of becoming accredited by the American regional Commission on Colleges of the Southern Association of Colleges and Schools (SACS). The model of the university in Qatar is no longer the static, information-centered university that provides students with extensive information, some knowledge, and few skills. Instead, Qatar University is seeking to position itself as an international university (indeed, it is already international by virtue of its student make-up which is 31% non-Qatari and the fact that it belongs to a number of international associations, such as the Union of Arab Universities and the International Association of Universities) (Qatar University, 2008; Qatar University, 2009b). While Education City represents a flow of information into the country, Qatar University is seeking to make significant strides in order to ensure that a uniquely Qatari brand of higher education is available to the citizens of Qatar. Furthermore, by working toward the goal of American university accreditation, it is ensuring that its graduates are academically at par with their international counterparts and thus have the flexibility of pursuing advanced education abroad.

In the mid-2000s, Qatar embarked upon the implementation of a Core Curriculum based on the American liberal arts education model where a range of liberal arts, science, and communications courses are required. Qatar is implementing this curriculum, while ensuring that Arab and Islamic values remain at the core. Indeed, the first learning outcome of the Core Curriculum is to develop a strong sense of and commitment to an Arab and Islamic identity. This outcome is in contrast to Yang's (2003) assertion that globalization equals homogenization. The philosophy of the Core Curriculum program is to develop the skills and attitudes that are required by the marketplace in Qatar, which is increasingly globalized and in need of qualified graduates.

Qatar's neighbor to the south is the United Arab Emirates, which is probably best known internationally for the economic boom, and recently recession, that has affected the city of Dubai. However, not often heard in the news is the state of higher education in these emirates. Zayed University was founded in 1998 to "inspire, encourage, educate, and lead a powerful generation of students" (Zayed University, 2009). Zayed University currently enrolls more than 3,000 male and female students on separate campuses in Dubai and Abu Dhabi. It also stands as one of only six universities founded and based in the Arab Middle East that are fully accredited by one of the six American regional college and university accrediting bodies. In 2008, the Middle States Commission on Higher Education accredited Zayed University. Middle States accredited The American University in Cairo in 1982, and the American Universities of Beirut and Sharjah in 2004 (Middle States Commission on Higher Education, 2009). In 2007, the Southern Association of Colleges and

Schools accredited the American University in Dubai, and the Lebanese American University was awarded candidate status by the New England Association of Schools and Colleges (NEASC-CIHE, 2009; SACS, 2009)

Zayed University offers ten undergraduate and ten graduate degree programs in five academic colleges (Qatar University, 2009c). It is significant that Zayed University sought American accreditation shortly after its inception, in not just some its programs but for the entire institution. It is the only institution that is not explicitly "American" that has currently received full institutional accreditation in the Arabian (Persian) Gulf region.

Zayed's initiatives are quite similar to those at Qatar University—a strong core curriculum program (that is quite structured to help ensure that students are provided a common educational experience), a learning outcomes-based curricular model, and standards to help meet those of the American accrediting body. Although aligned with the Middle States Commission accrediting standards, the university's Colloquy on Integrated Learning (general education program) incorporates Arabic language and Islamic studies, as well as Global Studies courses, as required courses for all students (Zayed University, 2007). By ensuring a strong foundation in the national language and in the religion and culture of the United Arab Emirates, the university is ensuring that its students are grounded in the national culture and are adept to living in a globalized world.

The last university, discussed in this chapter, is Sultan Qaboos University in Oman. Chartered by a decree of the Sultan in 1982, the university is the Sultanate's national university, located in the capital Muscat, and comprises eight academic colleges that enroll close to 15,000 students in foundation, undergraduate, and post-graduate degree programs (Sultan Qaboos University, 2009b).

When examining the literature on globalization, Sultan Qaboos University stands as an example of a trend of globalization-as-marketization as the nation tries to serve as the primary vehicle in the "Omanization" of the country. The University has sought ABET accreditation for its engineering programs. Sultan Qaboos is clearly seeking to position itself as a regional and international leader in the areas of biotechnology; earthquake monitoring (a problem that Oman faces given its geographical location); environmental studies; oil, gas, and water research; remote sensing; and geographic information systems by setting up and funding research centers in these areas. Furthermore, the university is preparing its workforce to serve the nation in highly specialized areas such as agricultural economics, marine sciences, and mechatronics engineering (Sultan Qaboos University, 2009a).

However, Sultan Qaboos University's initiatives are not completely insular. Their Omani Studies Center (OSC) attracts scholars and researchers from around the world to engage in the study of Omani culture, history, society, literature, economy, geography, and politics (Sultan Qaboos University, 2009c). It is interesting to note that with this seemingly welcoming attitude to scholars learning about and engaging with Oman, the director's welcome letter on the OSC's website states that "In a globally changing world, preserving one's identity and culture becomes an utmost priority" (Sultan Qaboos University, 2009c). Indeed globalization is seen as both a positive and a threatening force that needs to be both welcomed and challenged. A highly globalized world is one that benefits Oman by bringing Oman to the world and the world to Oman.

It is perhaps this sentence that best summarizes the interplay of globalization and higher education in the Middle East. The reality appears to be both welcoming and threatening; both engaging and encroaching; and both enhancing and negating. Nevertheless, globalization is always ever-present and inescapable.

Synthesis

Globalization is a complex process involving the interplay of many factors— social, political, cultural, and economic. In the Arabian Gulf region, contemporary higher education began in 1957 with the establishment of the King Abdullah University and has since exponentially expanded. In Qatar, the royal family embarked on establishing Education City as a unique enterprise in bringing American campuses to the Gulf region. While Yang (2003) would argue that this project will inevitably lead to the homogenization of Qatari culture, those directly involved in the project appear committed to the ideal that the culture will not be homogenized as much as it will inevitably change in response to ever-changing global forces (Lindsay 2010). At national universities in Qatar, Oman, and the United Arab Emirates, curricula and programs have been established to help ensure that local identities and cultures are maintained in an environment that seeks to promote the skills and knowledge necessary for the development of the nation-state. While these projects are closely linked with American academic standards, the content of these programs continues to maintain a national focus, and thus it seems that globalization is not so much an imposition as much as it a symbiotic relationship between indigenous features of the Arab world and the United States.

How to maintain authentic symbiotic and cooperative partnerships will be a tremendous challenge for the Gulf States and their universities while moving into the next decades of the 21st century that may be beset by shifting formal and informal global alliances among diverse regions. With such external shifts, the universities must be both proactive and reactive to ensure mutual benefits to the nations via internationalization and while tapping into aspects of globalization. That is, to paraphrase

President Barack Obama and Sheika Al-Missned, globalization means recognizing that education is the currency of this century that encompasses the infusion of diverse cultures and people and can epitomize architectures of academic bridges.

Notes

1 We recognize there are limitations to the selection of the three universities in terms of size, history, location, country conditions, and the like. Nevertheless, they serve as illustrations of the phenomena being examined in this chapter.
2 The contents of this paragraph are based upon one of the author's notes from her position as Dean of International Programs at The Pennsylvania State University.

Bibliography

AACTE. (2010, March 4). Development and enhancement of global skills for professional educators: The roles of Colleges and Universities. In *The Whole World Over: Educator Preparation Gone Global*—A national webinar. Retrieved March 4, 2010, from http://aacte.org/index.php?/component/option,com_events/Itemid,28/agid,51/day,04/month,03/task,view_detail/year,2010/

Abdulla, Abdulkhaleq. (2006). The impact of globalization on Arab Gulf States. In J. W. Fox, N. Mourtada-Sabbah, & M. A. Mutawa (Eds.), *Globalization and the Gulf* (pp. 180–188). New York: Routledge.

Alkhozai, Mohammed. (2008). The challenges of vocational training: BIBF, an institute of higher education. In Christopher Davidson, & Peter Mackezie Smith (Eds.). (2008). *Higher education in the Gulf states: Shaping economies, politics and culture.* London, Berkeley, and Beirut: London Middle East Institute at SOAS and SAQI.

American Council on Education. (2009). Center for International Initiatives. Retrieved February 1, 2009, from http://www.acenet.edu/Content/NavigationMenu/ProgramsServices/cii/index.htm

AMIDEAST. (2008). Special Initiatives: AMIDEAST 50th Anniversary Conference Summary Report. Higher Education in the Arab World: Preparing for the Global Marketplace. Retrieved June 9, 2009, from http://www.amideast.org/success_stories/special_initiatives/conference/default.htm

Appiah, Kwame. A. (2006). *Cosmopolitanism: Ethics in a world of strangers.* New York & London: W.W. Norton & Co.

Amin, Ash. (1997). Placing globalization. *Theory, Culture and Society, 14*(2), 123–127.

Association of American Colleges and Universities. (2009). *Liberal education.* Retrieved February 1, 2009, from http://www.aacu.org/resources/liberaleducation/index.cfm

Association of Public and Land-grant Universities. (2009). Commssion on International Programs. Retrieved February 1, 2009, from http://www.aplu.org/NetCommunity/Page.aspx?pid=264

Brancaccio, David. (Writer). (2009). *Education City.* In B. Breslauer (Producer), NOW on PBS. Retrieved June 1, 2009, from http://www.pbs.org/now/shows/420/

CIA The World Factbook-Oman. (2009). Retrieved June 17, 2009, from https://www.cia.gov/library/publications/the-world-factbook/geos/mu.html

Crystal, Jill. (1989). Coalitions in oil monarchies: Kuwait and Qatar. *Comparative Politics, 21*(4), 427–443.

Dion, David-Pascal. (2005). The Lisbon process: A European odyssey. *European Journal of Education, 40*(3), 295–313.

Dodds, Anneliese. (2008). How does globalisation interact with higher education? The continuing lack of consensus. *Comparative Education, 44*(4), 505–517.

Eickelman, Dale. (1989). *The Middle East: An anthropological approach.* (2nd ed.). Englewood Cliffs, NJ: Prentice Hall.

El-Khawas, Elaine. (2007). Accountability and quality assurance: New issues for academic inquiry. In J. J. F. Forest, & P. G. Altbach (Eds.), *Internatinoal Handbook of Higher Education* (pp. 23–37). Boston: Springer.

Esposito, John. (1998). *Islam: The straight path.* New York and Oxford: Oxford University Press.

Fisher, Sydney. N., & Ochsenwald, William. (1996). *The Middle East: A history* (5th ed. Vol. 2). New York: McGraw Hill.

Gentzkow, Matthew, & Shapiro, Jessie. (2004). Media, education, and anti-Americanism in the Muslim world. *The Journal of Economic Perspectives, 18*(3), 117–133.

Georgetown University. (2007). *Annual Report 2007.* Retrieved May 25, 2009, from https://guqshare.qatar.georgetown.edu/PublicRelations/AnnualReport/reports/report2007.pdf

Hanley, Delinda. (2007). Qatar's Education City is building bridges to a better future [Electronic Version]. *Washington Report on Middle East Affairs,* 30–31. Retrieved June 1, 2009, from http://www.wrmea.com/archives/August_2007/0708030.html

Herrera, Linda. (2007). Higher education in the Arab World. In J. J. F. Forest, & P. G. Altbach (Eds.), *International Handbook of Higher Education* (pp. 409–421). Boston: Springer.

Imam, Syeda Rumnaz. (2005). English as a global language and the question of nation-building education in Bangladesh. *Comparative Education, 41*(4), 471–486.

Institute of International Education (2009). *Open doors: Report on international education exchange.* New York: Institute of International Education.

Khouri, Fred. (1976). Review of Bahrain, Qatar, and the United Arab Emirates: Colonial past, present problems, and future prospects by Muhammad Sadik and William Snavely. *The American Political Science Review, 70*(1), 259–260.

Lewin, Tamar. (2008a, Sunday, February 10). U.S. universities rush to set up outposts abroad. *The New York Times.* Retrieved from http://www.nytimes.com/2008/02/10/education/10global.html

Lewin, Tamar. (2008b, Monday, February 11). In oil-rich Mideast, shades of the Ivy League. *The New York Times.* Retrieved from http://www.nytimes.com/2008/02/11/education/11global.html?_r=1

Lindsay, Beverly (2010). *Development and enhancement of global skills for professional educators for The Whole World Over: Educators Preparation Gone Global.* Washington DC: Association of Colleges for Teacher Education.

Luciani, Giacomo, & Neugart, Felix. (Eds). (2005). *The EU and the GCC: A new partnership*. Munich: Bertelsmann Foundation.

Makdisi, George. (1990). *The rise of humanism in classical Islam and the Christian West*. Edinburgh, Scotland: Edinburgh University Press.

Massialas, Byron. (1991). The Arab World. In P. Altbach, (Ed.). *International higher education: An encyclopedia* (Vol. 2). New York and London: Garland Publishing, Inc.

Mazawi, Andre. (2008). Policy politics of higher education in the Gulf Cooperation Council member states: intersections of globality, regionalism and locality. In Christopher Davidson, & Peter Mackezie Smith (Eds). (2008). *Higher education in the Gulf states: Shaping economies, politics and culture*. London Middle East Institute at SOAS and Saqi: London, Berkeley, and Beirut.

McGlennon, David. (2006). *Building research capacity in the Gulf Cooperation Council countries: Strategy, funding, and engagement*. Paper presented at the UNESCO Colloquium on Research and Higher Education Policy, Paris, France.

Mendenhall, Peter. (2005). U.S. style education emerging in Qatar, *MSNBC.com*. Retrieved June 10, 2009, from http://www.msnbc.msn.com/id/6870667/print/1/displaymode/1098

Middle States Commission on Higher Education. (2009). Institution Directory. Retrieved June 11, 2009, from http://www.msche.org/Institutions_Directory.asp

Mok, Ka-Ho, & Tan, Jason. (2004). *Globalization and marketization in education: A comparative analysis of Hong Kong and Singapore*. Cheltenham: Edward Elgar.

Muhammad, Rukiya. (2005). Promoting intercultural communication. *Higher Education Policy, 18*(4), 353–359.

Murphy, L.R. (1987). *The American University in Cairo*. Cairo, Egypt: AUC Press.

Myers, Linda. (2003). CU immigration law expert looks at changes in U.S. actions since 9/11. Retrieved October 10, 2008, from http://www.news.cornell.edu/chronicle/03/7.24.03/immigration_9-11.html

Narsee, Sheila. (2005). Navigating unchartered waters: Peace within hearts, hands, and minds. *Higher Education Policy, 18*(4), 341–351.

National Association for Equal Opportunity in Higher Education. (2009). International Programs. Retrieved March 4, 2009, from http://www.nafeo.org/community/index.php?option=com_content&view=article&id=24:international-programs&catid=7:international-programs&Itemid=4

NEASC-CIHE (New England Association of Schools and Colleges Commission on Institutions of Higher Education). (2009). Roster of Institutions. Retrieved June 17, 2009, from http://cihe.neasc.org/about_our_institutions/roster_of_institutions/#Overseas

Office of the Press Secretary. (2009). Remarks by the President on a New Beginning. Retrieved from http://www.whitehouse.gov/the_press_office/Remarks-by-the-President-at-Cairo-University-6-04-09/

Osseiran, Ghia. (2007, Friday, November 30). Arab universities kick off bottom-up approach to quality education. *The Daily Star*. Retrieved June 1, 2009, from http://www.dailystar.com.lb/article.asp?edition_id=10&categ_id=2&article_id=87117

Qatar Foundation. (2009a, April). About Qatar Foundation. Retrieved June 10, 2009, from http://www.qf.org.qa/output/page10.asp

Qatar Foundation. (2009b, April). Timeline. Retrieved June 10, 2009, from http://www.qf.org.qa/files/QFR_timeline_V6.swf

Qatar Foundation. (2009c, April). Who we are. Retrieved June 10, 2009, from http://www.qf.org.qa

Qatar Statistics Authority. (2007). Annual Abstract. Retrieved June 10, 2009 from http://www.qsa.gov.qa/Eng/publication/Annabs2008.htm

Qatar University. (2008). Book of Trends. Retrieved June 10, 2009, from http://www.qu.edu.qa/offices/oipd/documents/Book_of_Trends_07_08.pdf

Qatar University. (2009a). Our Students. Retrieved June 10, 2009, from http://www.qu.edu.qa/theuniversity/students.php

Qatar University. (2009b). International Accreditation. Retrieved June 10, 2009, from http://www.qu.edu.qa/theuniversity/accreditation.php

Qatar University. (2009c). Colleges. Retrieved August 10, 2010, from http://www.qu.edu.

Rathmell, Andrew, & Schulze, Kirsten. (2000). Political reform in the gulf: The case of Qatar. *Middle Eastern Studies, 36*(4), 47–62.

Rugh, William. (2002). Arab education: Tradition, growth and reform. *Middle East Journal, 56*(3), 396–414.

Scott, Peter. (2005). Essay review: Universities and the knowledge economy. *Minerva, 43*, 297–309.

Southern Association of Colleges and Schools. (2009). Commission on Colleges. Retrieved from http://www.sacscoc.org/details.asp?instid=12755

Stasz, Cathleen, Eide, Eric, Martorell, Francisco, Constant, Louay, Goldman, Charles, Moini, Joy, et al. (2007). *Post-secondary education in Qatar: Employer demand, student choice, and options for policy.* Santa, Monica, CA, Arlington, VA & Pittsburgh, PA: RAND-Qatar Policy Institute. (R. Corporation o. Document Number)

Sultan Qaboos University. (2009a). *Academic Programs.* Retrieved June 10, 2009 from http://www.squ.edu.om/tabid/76/language/en-US/Default.aspx

Sultan Qaboos University. (2009b). *Glance at SQU.* Retrieved June 10, 2009 from http://www.squ.edu.om/tabid/61/language/en-US/Default.aspx

Sultan Qaboos University. (2009c). *Omani Studies Center.* Retrieved June 10, 2009 from http://www.squ.edu.om/Default.aspx?alias=www.squ.edu.om/osc

Supreme Education Council. (2010). Scholarship Programs. Retrieved June 10, 2009 from http://www.english.education.gov.qa/section/sec/hei/sco/

The Times Higher Education. (2009). QS world university rankings 2009. *Top 200 World Universities.* Retrieved May 25, 2009 from http://www.timeshighereducation.co.uk/Rankings2009-Top200.html

UAE Interact. (2009, November 23). Expat numbers rise rapidly as UAE population touches 6m. Retrieved June 1, 2009 from http://uaeinteract.com/docs/Expat_numbers_rise_rapidly_as_UAE_population_touches_6m_/38510.htm

Unknown. (2008). Answers from Charles E. Thorpe. Retrieved June 11, 2009 from http://news.blogs.nytimes.com/2008/02/11/answers-from-charles-e-thorpe/.

Van Vught, F., Van der Wende, M., & Westerheijden, D. (2002). Globalization and internationalization: Policy agendas compared. In J. Enders, & O. Fulton (Eds.) *Higher education in a globalizing world: international trends and mutual observations: A Festschrift in honour of Ulrich Teichler* (pp. 103–120). London: Kluwer Academic.

Wallin, Michelle. (2005, September 19). United Arab Emirates work hard to increase local hiring. *The New York Times*. Retrieved May 25, 2009 from http://www.nytimes.com/2005/09/19/business/worldbusiness/20emiratescnd. html?pagewanted=1&_r=1&fta=y

Waterbury, John. (2003). Hate your policies, Love your institutions. *Foreign Affairs, 82*(1), 58–68.

Yang, Rai. (2003). Globalisation and higher education development: A critical analysis. *International Review of Education, 49*(3/4), 269–291.

Zayed University. (2009). About Zayed University. Retrieved June 8, 2009 from http://www.zu.ac.ae/main/explore.asp

Zayed University. (2007). Colloquy on Integrated Learning. Retrieved June 1, 2009 from http://www.zu.ac.ae/colloquy/

5 Shifting Tides in Jamaican Higher Education

Beverly Lindsay

Can't get me out this race . . .
(Bob Marley, lyrics of "Bad Card," 1980)

We are at a critical juncture in our university's existence, and recent developments at the national level underscore the need for dialogue regarding the exceedingly challenging global, regional and national economic environment

(Shirley, 2008a, p. 1)

Little could I have anticipated that the lyrics of the late Reggae singer, Bob Marley, would permeate part of my field research in Jamaica, sponsored by an American national professional organization. The grant focused on globalization and diversity and entailed field research at four colleges and universities in Kingston wherein one of the administrators, whom I interviewed, frequently quoted various Bob Marley, concluding with the lyrics portrayed earlier. Other interviewees echoed his ruminations. Perhaps I should have remembered my initial visits to Jamaica during the late 1970s and 1980s when Marley's lyrics could be heard virtually everywhere, and his life was constantly exposed in the media as part of a global phenomenon; a phenomenon that is, in many ways, distinct from how we examine globalization and diversity at the end of the first decade of the 21st century. It has often been stated that music is a universal language; but all music is not equal in terms of global dissemination that is infused with diverse cultures from Jamaica, other Caribbean nations, and North Africa as were Marley's melodies. The lyrics often juxtaposed the life of the economically poor in Trenchtown (an area in Western Kingston) with the contrasting British culture and lifestyles that were waning—yet still represented notable sociocultural disparities (Goldman, 2006; Niaah & Niaah, 2008). Nevertheless, a new epoch (suggested in various Marley lyrics) could be emerging that might begin to bear visible fruits a generation later in universities that seek to address and respond to contemporary global economic and sociopolitical conditions that echo promises and also lessen disparities that stifled cultural diversity.

It is the contemporary conditions that set the stage for this chapter, as conveyed in the quote by the Principal (equivalent to an American university president or chancellor) of the University of the West Indies, Mona, who espouses the need for university dialogues regarding global challenges within the national and regional context. Acute economic downturns are a critical challenge. While economic conditions change expectedly over decades (for example, about seven Jamaican dollars equaled one American dollar in the 1970s), rapid changes can be devastating. In early October 2008, about 68 Jamaican dollars equaled one American dollar. Only weeks later, about 100 Jamaican dollars equaled one American dollar (United States Department of State, 2009a). Certainly, universities are immediately challenged by this economic reality as they seek to fulfill their *raison d etre* of proving quality education while remaining attuned to external socioeconomic and cultural conditions—as highlighted in the Marley and Shirley quotes.

How are global conditions translated into the preparation of professionals in Jamaican higher education? To begin answering the central query, this chapter seeks to: 1) present an overview of fluid global and national circumstances affecting Jamaica; 2) articulate select conceptual frameworks in relation to factors external to higher education; 3) explicate the perspectives of higher education administrators regarding globalization and diversity in conjunction with mission statements, strategic plans, academic programs, and the like; and 4) synthesize the perspectives via global and diverse conditions as emerging models are posited.

Global and National Conditions Impacting Jamaica

During the past generation emigration from Jamaica to Great Britain, the United States, and Canada—the three main receiving countries—has decreased. The Planning Institute of Jamaica (PIOJ) indicates a 34% decline in legal migration from Jamaica from 1995 to 2006 based upon the number of immigrant visas issues by embassies in Jamaica (Brooks, 2007). This has been especially the situation to the United Kingdom since it curtailed immigration beginning in the late 1960s (United States Department of State, 2009a). Figures should also include visas issued in other nations; however, a manager of the State Department's Population Unit estimates that overseas statistics would be similar to domestic ones. In March 2003, British legislation required Jamaicans to obtain visas in their home country rather than the United Kingdom (Brooks, 2007).

Nevertheless, Jamaica is among the top 20 countries sending emigrants to the United States. From 1990 through 1999, over 177,140 individuals, who listed Jamaica as their last country of residence, obtained permanent residence status in the United States. From 2000 to 2007, 136,579 acquired permanent status, with 24,976 becoming permanent residents in 2006 and 19,375 in 2007 (Immigration Statistics, 2007). In 2007, just over 13,600 Jamaicans admitted to the United States were sponsored by immediate relatives with American citizenship, while unrelated and/or distant relative families sponsored almost another 5,000 and over 730 were sponsored by employers (Immigration Statistics, 2007). While the number directly sponsored by employers is small compared to other categories (all categories are not listed), once in the United States, some form of employment is pursued by adults.

Such individual and family employment, along with financial corporate arrangements, provides notable sources of remittances (that is, transmission of funds) that are vital to the Jamaican economy. About US$1.6 billion in remittances were submitted in the late 2000s, compared to approximately US$658,300,000 in the early 2000s, with the largest amount coming from the United States, Canada, and the United Kingdom. Similarly, the Bank of Jamaica states that about US$1.66 billion were remitted in 2007 and approximately US$1.71 billion in 2008. Over US$1 billion was expected for 2009, although notably less than in the previous years (U.S. Department of State, 2009a; Bank of Jamaica, 2009) given the economic downturn. The higher education sector, like others, is immediately affected by changes in the economy.

Along with economic challenges are the continuing problems of HIV/ AIDS and youth violence. The HIV/AIDS crisis curtails the matriculation of students to universities and professionals to their careers, particularly those 16 to 45 years of age. For example, the Caribbean Commission on Health and Development estimates that over 500,000 Caribbeans are living with the disease. By the end of 2009, the figure was expected to increase to nearly 700,000. About 250,000 will likely die within five years if the pandemic is not halted (Richards, 2005). A disruption in Jamaican national development—stemming from a depletion of skilled citizens (especially young men) lost to the pandemic and violence—poses multiple urgent concerns for educational institutions. For instance, a World Bank study documented that about 20% of Caribbean youth, including Jamaicans, carried a weapon to school within a month. Equally telling, about 20% of male students and 12% of female students were members of gangs (World Bank, 2003 cited in Jules 2008).

While the aforementioned problems are present, Jamaicans have contributed positively to global conditions as observed through their Nobel Laureates and research. For example, in 1979 former University of West Indies (UWI) Vice Chancellor, Arthur Lewis, was awarded the Nobel Prize in economics. Similarly, in 2007, UWI, Mona full professor, Anthony Chen, was part of the Intergovernmental Panel on Climate Change (IPCC) that shared the Nobel Peace Prize with former American Vice President Al Gore. In 2007–2008, about Jamaican $405 million was received in external grants, representing double the amount of the previous year, focusing on HIV/AIDs, diabetes, Caribbean climate diversity, and other areas of special note in Jamaica and the Caribbean (Shirley, 2008b).

Although there are mixed perspectives of CARICOM (Caribbean Community) and the CSME (Caribbean Single Market and Economy), this regional bloc (composed of 12 Caribbean nations) focuses on economic, cultural, and political issues of the West Indies specifically and simultaneously in relation to global conditions. Given the appearance of blocs such as the European Union (EU) and Southern African Development Community (SADC) that focus on geopolitical relations designed to enhance their global positions, CARICOM and CSME similarly emerge and are in response to global economic and sociocultural matters. Ensuring individual national economic development while concurrently promoting Caribbean regional growth, in light of generic and distinct features of diversity, are overarching aims. Specifically, prominent features of the CSME include the free movement of goods and services; free movement of labor; and free movement of capital (CARICOM Secretariat, 2009).

Conceptual Frameworks and Higher Education

The aforementioned discussion of external factors impacting higher education leads us to explicate alternative models and re-examine standard frameworks that often concentrate primarily on higher education. In terms of alternative frameworks, those from international relations, political science, and sociology appear apropos—including those that focus on what may be termed geopolitical macro-level influences, New World Order, global governance, and public or civic engagement.

Jules (2008) advocates a rethinking of educational models by considering Caribbean nations as individual countries and as part of the geopolitical arena of the Caribbean. In essence, Jules' analysis is part of what Slaughter (2005) and Zakaria (2009) contend is a New World Order that emerged after the postcolonial period with the waning of British sociopolitical and cultural dominance and notably after the devolution of the Soviet Union. Large and small nations were affected as new alliances emerged; and each nation had to be attuned to the geopolitical and economic initiatives and constraints of the other. An examination of the new order involves the articulation of a range of comprehensive conditions expanding beyond national boundaries to permeate global matters (Jules, 2008), such as those cited in the preceding subsection.

Jules (2008) contends further that Anglophone or English-speaking Caribbean education evolves from the metropole model of Great Britain, including both the postcolonial era and the current intact remnants. In order to remove the vestiges of flawed socioeconomic and educational systems that do not address macro-level conditions, some reform agendas were established as new governments were elected. For instance, with the election of Prime Minister Michael Manley in the 1970s, mass literary and adult education campaigns were initiated. With the advent of another government following the Manley administration, foci shifted so that various educational endeavors were halted or stagnated, thus comprehensive problems and relics linger. Hence related sociopolitical conditions remain or are exacerbated, contributing to ongoing semi-literacy among select demographic groups thus making it difficult for them to obtain viable vocational or professional employment. Semi-literacy is preset since examinations have been administered (somewhat similar to those in England) at the end of primary school that limit secondary school options.

The geopolitical conditions of under or unemployment move beyond the shores of one Caribbean nation leading to the need to address employment at a regional level (Jules, 2008; Jules, 2006). Variables within the region, the emergence of shifting global economic conditions, and resulting political and trade alliances outside the Caribbean led to the formation of CARICOM. The challenge of balancing individual state and multi-Caribbean needs is present when, for instance, professionals move within the region.

Building further upon the literature from international relations linked to education, Mundy (2007) discusses the concepts and applications of global governance that she asserts move beyond the frameworks of a world order. Certainly, there are debates within disciplines concerning when conceptual and paradigmatic shifts occur as noted when Mundy (2007) maintains that a shift to "global governance" occurred after 1990; yet Slaughter's and Zakaria's works, published in 2005 and 2009, still expound the New World Order framework in the 2000s. Overlapping dimensions, programs, and organizations are included in the world order and global governance.

According to Mundy (2007),

> Global governance typically captures the fact that the global polity is an evolving set of processes and interactions (rather than a fixed rule system and administrative hierarchy) that involves heterogeneous private and public actors or scales of action: local, national, international, and transnational.
>
> (p. 343)

Global governance, according to some policymakers and political scientists, concentrates on specific pragmatic reforms. To political activists, the global public domain of global governance entails social movements and other visible public actions. Still some postmodern scholars are leery of global governance since they envisioned it as a continuation of adverse capital differentials of modernity (Mundy, 2007). The relative roles and import of multinational organizations such as the World Bank and the United Nations (UN) and its related entities like UNESCO (United National Educational and Scientific and Cultural Organizations), regional blocs such as CARICOM and the European Union, and the G-8 and G-20 become de facto forms of governance since their policies often prescribe what can occur within nation-states. A range of policies and programs directly affect colleges and universities as witnessed when the World Bank allocated US$15 million for a national strategic plan for early childhood programs that involves professionals from teacher education colleges (World Bank, 2009).

Finally, frameworks associated with public or civic engagement assume prominence. During significant junctures of the 20th century, perspectives emerged concerning the public service roles of universities that help us comprehend the foundations for 21st century roles. Such views are witnessed as components of university mission statements and writings of renowned scholars and policy executives. The initiatives of James Conant, an eminent Harvard University president, introduced a general education curriculum to provide comprehensive perspectives to incorporate an awareness of public service roles (Conant, 1945). Later, Professor and Nobel Peace Laureate Ralph Bunche articulated public service roles for universities to prepare students to challenge societal conditions and address concrete problems (Bunche, 1940; Lindsay, 2008). Conant's and Bunche's understanding of universities and public service roles are echoed as we fast-forward to the early 2000s wherein a terminological shift changes to public engagement. Various professional associations—ranging from the National Association of State Universities and Land-Grant Colleges (2007), the National Center for Public Policy and Higher Education (2008) to the American Sociological Association (2004)—discuss the concept and need for university public engagement. For example, American Sociological Association (ASA) maintained that, "public sociology should transcend the academy and engage wider audiences to be inclusive and democratic" by building bridges that connect multiple communities (American Sociological Association, 2004).

Scholars and university policymakers such as Jacoby and Associates (2009), Kezar, Chambers, and Burkhardt (2005), Watson (2004), and Neave (2000) articulate universities' public involvement with communities. Various international scholars and policymakers, such as former UN Commissioner Mary Robinson, posit key roles for universities and scholars to change conditions by direct engagement in endeavors contributing to democratic societies by grooming students and professionals for leadership, scholarship, and new technological development and administration (Robinson, 2004). While such broad statements are expressed, how might the concepts and practices of public engagement be manifested in Jamaican higher education?

Ascertaining, linking, or altering of the several conceptual frameworks may be observed via an examination of the perspectives (of) and program implementation by Jamaican higher education administrators. Further we may move beyond educational paradigms and incorporate a multidisciplinary approach by positing nexuses and paradigms for public engagement in view of the macro-level frameworks.

Perspectives of Higher Education Administrators

When undertaking field research in Jamaica in 2008–09, I engaged in participant observations of seminars, meetings, conferences, and informal dialogues; interviewed administrators, faculty, students, and staff; and examined mission statements, strategic plans, curricular programs, and similar documents. The research occurred at four higher education sites in Kingston: the UWI, Mona; the University of Technology; Mico University College, and Shortwood College. The University of the West Indies, Mona is the original campus of the UWI that was established in 1948 as an overseas College of the University of London. There are also campuses in Trinidad and Tobago, Barbados, and an Open Campus serving students from 15 Caribbean nations and other countries. Collectively, the campuses enroll approximately 40,000 students with about 14,570 at Mona, historically viewed as the premier campus in the Caribbean. A comprehensive range of programs are offered in undergraduate, diploma, master's, professional, and doctoral concentrations (University of the West Indies, 2008; Shirley, 2008b).

The University of Technology, established in 1958 as the Jamaica Institute of Technology with just over 50 students, became the College of Arts and Science, and Technology (CAST) that continued to offer certificates and diplomas. In 1986, CAST began offering degrees and was granted full university status in 1995. In 2008/2009, approximately 9,725 students were enrolled with 60% being full-time matriculants in undergraduate and graduate programs in technical and professional areas such as built environment (for example, architecture and land management), business, computer science, education, engineering, health and applied sciences, and law (University of Technology, 2008a; University of Technology, 2008b).

Mico University College traces its origins to 1835 when it was established as a non-denominational Christian teacher training school. Reportedly the oldest teacher education institution in the Western Hemisphere, its co-educational programs originally trained British volunteers to teach in Jamaican schools (Mico University College, 2008b). Currently, 1,500 students pursue undergraduate and master's degrees in a range of educational fields on campus and in conjunction with other Jamaican higher education sites such as the University of Technology, the Edna Manley College of the Performing Arts, and the Vocational Training and Development Institute. Often referred to as the "poor man's university," it is known for programs in special education and a diploma in police sciences that is also offered via an arrangement with the police department (Mico University College, 2008a).

Founded in 1885 as an institute to train women teachers, Shortwood College prepares students in a range of elementary and secondary school subjects and counseling. It is known especially for its programs in preparing French and Spanish teachers. In the 2008–09 academic year, approximately 925 students were enrolled at the College (Office of the Principal, personal communication, July 22, 2009). After opening admission to men in 2001, it broadened the curriculum to include cooperative endeavors with the University of South Florida in the offering of its first master's degrees along with the existing diploma and emerging baccalaureate programs (Shortwood Teachers' College, 2008a; Shortwood Teachers' College, 2008b).

While participant observations and interviews occurred with a range of programs and students, faculty, professional staff, and administrators, this analysis focuses primarily on higher education administrators (including a few who had just transitioned within the past year), given current analytical frameworks and page limitations. Included in the administrative categories are: principals, deputy principals or vice presidents for academic affairs, deans, deputy deans, department heads (for example, social sciences, communications, language arts, and natural and physical sciences), and program directors (for instance, online diploma and degree programs, medical specialties, and volunteer and service learning). All 16 administrators exercised line and/or budget authority in their respective positions. To ensure anonymity, individual administrative positions and statements will not be linked to particular higher education institutions except when they are cited in the media, a published piece, or some other mode of non-private material.

The protocol questions (though all are not analyzed in this chapter) are portrayed on the Pennsylvania State University website (Note: Waiting for page to be published.) from which several motifs emerged that reflect positive aspects of globalization and diversity as well as ongoing challenges.

The Motifs

Globalization

Globalization is presented in the mission statements, strategic plans, and statements of individuals. For example, the UWI asserts that its "enduring mission is to propel the economic, social, political and cultural development of West Indian society through teaching, research, innovation, advisory and community services and intellectual leadership" (Office of Planning and Development, 2007, p. 6). The mission statements of the University of Technology, Mico University College, and Shortwood College focus on the specialized nature of their institutions such as enhancing entrepreneurial endeavors of the technical professions, fostering scholarship for educational leadership, and designing and implementing courses and programs to help students acquire sound knowledge, useful skills, and good leadership, respectively (Morrison, 2008; Mico University College, 2008b; Shortwood Teachers' College, 2008a; Shortwood Teachers' College, 2008b).

While mission statements are essential, strategic plans are more informative since they articulate steps to achieve changes. The UWI's strategic plans seek to initiate programs and projects to:

> Situate self and society in a changing world order and provide a sound basis for public policy formulation and decision making; help the region to comprehend the nature and significance of contemporary issues and emerging global influences; and strive to be a significant contributor to global intellectual growth and human development by active scholarship that harnesses the creative energies, cultural diversity, social experiences, biodiversity and other aspects of the region.
> (Office of Planning and Development, 2007, pp. 6–7)

The University of Technology summary of strategic objectives maintains that "academic reform [is] to embrace [sic] concept of education for citizenship, and relevance" (Morrison, 2008, p. 4), which appears to emphasize the public engagement role that will result in globally competent, well rounded and entrepreneurial graduates (Morrison, 2008). Similar explicit statements are not readily observable in written documentation from Mico and Shortwood.

Basically, several administrators elaborated upon select university mission statements and/or strategic plans in citing globalization and international factors as areas to which higher education needed to respond and/or to initiate changes. Foremost among these are macro-level economic variables like trade and remittances and fiscal factors such as the downturn in the economy, according to one principal. The former contributes to national debts so that the university campus cannot expect increased funding from the government, while the latter causes increased financial strains for students and limited resources for the university endeavors. Nevertheless, the economic constraints are coupled within an era of increased competition when new offshore universities are establishing programs or relatively new campuses are being founded and/or growing. In 2004, the University College of the Caribbean emerged from an amalgamation of the Institute of Management Sciences and the Institute of Management and Production offering degrees already provided by the UWI and the University of Technology.

Several administrators cited the dominance of major Western superpowers and lingering colonialism so that powerful nations or blocs of nations decide certain rules, impose culture, and languages of their choices, regardless of the authenticity of the world citizens' original countries and cultures. The case of Jamaican 2008 Olympic multiple Gold medal winner, Usain Bolt's, spirited dances and maneuvers just before and after winning medals was an illustration. Perhaps a slight paraphrase of Marley's, "You can't get [beat] me out of this race . . . I'm in your place" might have been exemplified in Bolt's boisterous behavior. Yet such locally celebrated movements were criticized and some even hinted that his medals should be revoked (CBC Sports, 2008; O'Connor, 2008) for what various administrators viewed as positive cultural sharing, rather than cultural imperialism or annihilation of indigenous norms (Carnoy, 1974; Freeman, 2005).

Still other administrators asserted the positive features of Bolt's and the Jamaican women University of Technology students' winning Olympic medals. Moving from postcolonial university status to producing the best, world-class athletes cast favorable light on Jamaican universities and students. Thus, international organizations and governments might fund academic sports programs and provide funds for capital sports constructions. A cadre of professional sports managers, trainers, and educators could emerge and serve Jamaica and the larger world.

Societal needs of Jamaica and the Caribbean, according to several administrators, are closely related to the world community. One woman contends that while Jamaica is concerned with violence and HIV/AIDS, relatively little attention is given to the physical environment. The greening of the campus and surrounding community should be an important concern in terms of the preservation of resources and related economic stewardship since conserving the natural environment saves financial resources. In citing this illustration she paraphrased Jamaican radio host and media personality, Wilmont Perkins, who claims that colleges and universities are not doing enough to transform the society. This perspective contrasts with that of an administrator, from another university, who maintained that their counseling programs included global issues such as global warming, healthy environments, and eco-environmental issues for small island states. Interestingly, the former administrator was not at the UWI, although she included the works by 2007 Nobel Peace Laureate Al Gore and the input by the UWI professor who was part of the Nobel Prize team.

Cable television from Florida and select cities such as New York and Chicago bombard the majority of Jamaican homes. Many of the poorest homes, despite not having basic necessities, would nevertheless have cable television since it is a form of recreation. In short, some North American culture may be replacing that of the British, thus portending new global concepts and the diversity (or lack thereof) in the transference to Jamaica. One local program depicts a Jamaican counselor's journey to Chicago to ascertain how some successful programs for gang violence might have transferable features to Jamaica. The challenge is having a variety of such multi-national programs seen by millions in Jamaica, rather than the various superficial programs that characterize much of the current cable programming.

Diversity

A very senior professor and program director asserted that the technicalities of fields like engineering, medicine, and computer science should not allow one to hide from diversity. Rather, "deal with it." For example, a senior Jamaican medical doctor during his youth seemed to believe that his academic talents and physical appearance would permit entry into various English medical colleges and other professional venues. His proper English name did not reveal his Jamaican identity. Upon appearing for a medical school interview in England, the interview panel was surprised to see a Jamaican young man. A senior English doctor exclaimed, "Oh, no! This is a mistake, not for you lad, for *our* (emphasis added) lad!" According to the interviewee, this was a normalizing moment for the then young Jamaican, his epiphany that contributed to the now senior Jamaican medical doctor demonstrating a profound concern with diversity.

A university executive voiced some jarring views of her experience of diversity while in the United States during her graduate study. She maintained that "people look through you or they are seeing something exotic, just a nigger. Or they speak slowly as if you can't understand since the Jamaican accent is different from the [Midwestern] American one." To her, being a minority, after being in a majority status all her life, is especially raucous. Given that there are teacher shortages in the southern part of the United States, a significant numbers of her university graduates migrate and earn American credentials. Such graduate migrants need to be prepared for diverse, sometimes inhospitable, professional environments.

Several senior university executives maintained that volunteer or service activities are graduation requirements. Exposure to diversity seems to be the benefit, rather than global exposure, as students volunteer in hospitals and health clinics, community sports programs, physical and mental rehabilitation centers, and social service organizations. In essence, the universities and college are encouraging civic or public engagement.

Remedies Through Globalization and Diversity

Online programs

At all four sites the development and continuation of online programs for Jamaican and Caribbean students was emphasized as means to address national and global needs. This is especially the situation for working adults or those who reside in areas that do not have easy access to campuses. Students from throughout the Caribbean and select ones from Asian and North American nations matriculate online. Since Jamaica and other Caribbean nations are moving toward undergraduate degrees for all levels of primary and secondary teachers, some current teachers are upgrading via online courses. Simultaneously, public school administrators, government staff and professionals, business employees, health care providers, and the like are continuing their education and/or earning degrees and diplomas online. Master's degrees in several areas of education and business such as early childhood, administration, higher education, counseling, human resource management, and planning are being offered. Some course content covers aspects of globalization and diversity similar to residential instruction and incorporates perspectives from some various Caribbean nations. One administrator claimed that such online instruction is integral to CARICOM as it seeks to facilitate movement among professionals within the Caribbean. Because there are varying levels of gross domestic production (GDP) (for example, US$12.2 billion in Jamaica and US$408.1 million in Grenada in the mid-2000s, (U.S. Department of State, 2009b), a common online diploma or degree will help produce credible credentials (among CARICOM) so that professional migrants will earn appropriate salaries.

Endeavors are also being undertaken, as part of globalization and diversity, to introduce simultaneously video modes of instruction with universities in other nations so that students are the recipients of global interactions thereby benefiting students in multiple locales. One administrator declared, "A healthy respect is developed between people for their differences and insularity is broken-down."

The Open Campus, the fourth campus of the UWI is designed for students throughout the Caribbean and is one of the best illustrations of globalization within a regional context. The Principal of UWI stated that the Open Campus can be a "means of access to the university" and simultaneously provide education to those who cannot financially afford to be resident students. An administrator claimed that school principals (from various parishes in Jamaica and other countries) are eager to converse with their counterparts in online courses to glean insight into practical administrative issues, curriculum implementation, and teachers' questions to administrators. In the absence of online courses, this communication could not occur.

Diversity and the Curriculum

The curriculum at all universities incorporates modules or courses in ethics and foundations of education (or similar titles) that include diversity components such as race, nationality, gender, and sometimes age, religion, and disability. Counseling and administrative curriculum certainly included diversity and globalization. Undergraduate and graduate degree students in the social sciences and humanities covered diversity and globalization. To what extent the students actually internalized the material was a question voiced by several administrators.

Although the vast majority of Jamaicans understand English, not all can speak, read, and write standard British or American English. Hence several Language Arts and Humanities administrators stated that English is a means to understand diversity as the global *lingua franca*, although spoken and written differently. So, the works of diverse writers from Canada, Africa, the United States, India, and Great Britain are used, ranging from Margaret Atwood, to Wole Soyinka, to Toni Morrison, to Salman Rushdie, and Zora Neael Hurston. However, it is imperative to communicate in standard English to ensure effective communication as developed through the analysis of diverse global English-speaking authors.

Synthesizing for Creative Models

As this chapter began, we juxtaposed quotes from two vastly different Jamaicans—a world-renowned reggae singer and the principal of the foremost university in the Caribbean—that portrayed stages of Jamaican society from the 1970s and 1980s into the first decade of the 21st century. During the ensuing decades, the essence of diversity and globalization remained, yet simultaneously shifted. The shifts necessitate Jamaican higher education to take into account the multiple components of globalization, in part, via select conceptual frameworks ranging from geopolitical macro-level influences, New World Order, global governance, and public or civic engagement.

Converging vectors may be observed from the several conceptual frameworks as explicated (from) and examined in mission statements, strategic plans, program implementation, and the like as voiced by 16 administrators from four higher education institutions in Kingston. Diversity and globalization are intertwined. While the meshing occurs, there are unique research and scholarly opportunities for Jamaican higher education. In the initial part of this chapter, the annual report of the Principal of the UWI, discussed the increase of external research funding for areas such as HIV/AIDS and diabetes. During conversations, we pondered how research on such diseases, having a disproportionate effect on people of African ancestry, could be researched in a "controlled" environment where the daily influences of discrimination and racism are absent. Hence university faculty and their professional graduates might identify environmental and dietary conditions preventing the ravages of such diseases and develop medicines to lessen their effects. As successful solutions are discovered, they could be transported to diverse global populations thereby demonstrating public engagement in national and global arenas.

Principals and vice presidents stressed that deans and faculty will have to respond to external market changes that are part of the macro-level globalization equations. Viable programs need to be initiated and/or expanded, such as the hospitality and tourism concentrations that simultaneously take into account eco-tourism with the latter helping to ensure that current immediate economic gains do not contribute to long-term economic declines. This realization means linking economic markets that the national government supports along with the preparation of graduates who will support new initiatives. It means, for instance, that the new UWI, Montego Bay campus provides access to diverse Jamaicans while preparing them for viable careers that may address global environmental factors. The inclusion of other Caribbean students would demonstrate how Jamaican sites train professionals that would be part of the movement of labor espoused by CARICOM—that is, aspects of geopolitical macro-level entities and global governance.

Successful programs could be disseminated via online and residential modes to Africa, Asia, and other Caribbean nations. For instance, focused online programs in light of special needs such as those in the School of Nursing could be structured for nurses and health care professionals. Similarly, the relatively new UWI program for medical students from Gaborone, Botswana in residence in Jamaica and Jamaican faculty in Botswana represent cooperative global endeavors for diverse regions.

Perhaps the ultimate questions are: To what extent can the UWI, Mona and the University of Technology initiate and respond to globally diverse conditions? To what extent can Mico University College and Shortwood College introduce new prototypes for educators; since preparing educators, in the strict sense of the term, is their overarching mission? As the four sites ponder and respond to such questions, new models can emerge from evolving conceptual frameworks that reflect shifting national and global tides.

References

American Sociological Association. (2004). *2005 ASA Conference Theme.* Retrieved March 1, 2009, from http://www.asanet.org

Bank of Jamaica. (2009). *The balance of payments: Remittance update.* Retrieved July 14, 2009, from http://www.boj.org.jm/uploads/pdf/rem_updates/rem_updates_jan2009.pdf

Brooks, L. (2007). Jamaicans shut out abroad. *Jamaica Gleaner.* Retrieved February 18, 2008, from http://www.jamaicagleaner.com/gleaner/20070701/lead/lead4.html

Bunche, Ralph J. (1940). The role of the university in the political orientation of Negro youth. *Journal of Negro Education,* 9.

Caribbean Community (CARICOM) Secretariat. (2009). *The Caribbean single market and economy.* Retrieved July 14, 2009, from http://www.caricom.org/jsp/single_market/single_market_index.jsp?menu=scsme

Carnoy, Martin. (1974). *Education as cultural imperialism.* New York: David McKay.

CBC Sports. (2008). Bolt earns sprint double, breaks world record. *CBC.CA.* Retrieved June 23, 2009, from http://www.cbc.ca/olympics/athletics/story/2008/08/20/mens-200-finl.html

Conant, James. (Ed.). (1945). *General Education in a free society: Report of the Harvard committee.* Cambridge, MA: Harvard University Press.

Freeman, Kassie. (2005). Black populations globally: The costs of the underutilization of Blacks in education. In Joyce King (Ed.), *Black education: A transformative research and action agenda for the new century* (pp. 135–156). Mahwah, New Jersey: Lawrence Erlbaum Associates, Inc.

Goldman, Vivien. (2006). *The book of exodus: The making and meaning of Bob Marley and The Wailers' album of the century.* New York: Three Rivers Press.

Immigration Statistics. (2007). *Office of Immigration Statistics.* Washington DC: Homeland Security.

Jacoby, Barbara and Associates. (2009). *Civic engagement in higher education: Concepts and practices.* San Francisco: Jossey-Bass.

Jules, Didacus. (2008). Rethinking education for the Caribbean: A radical approach. *Comparative Education, 44*(2), 203–214.

Jules, Didacus. (2006). Power and educational development: Small states and the labors of Sisyphus. In M.O. Afolayan, D. Browne, & D. Jules (Eds.), *Current discourse on education in developing nations: Essays in honor of B. Robert Tanachnick and Robert Koehl* (pp. 17–29). New York: Nova Science Publishers.

Kezar, Adrianna J., Chambers, Tony C., Burkhardt, John C., & Associates. (2005). *Higher education for the public good: Emerging voices from a national movement.* San Francisco: Jossey-Bass.

Lindsay, Beverly. (Ed.). (2008). *Ralph Johnson Bunche: Public Intellectual and Nobel Peace Laureate.* Urbana: University of Illinois Press.

Lindsay, Beverly, & Scales, Tara. (2010). *Working protocol for research on Jamaica.* Retrieved from **NOTE: Waiting for page to be published.**

Marley, Bob. (1980). *Bad card lyrics.* Retrieved June 27, 2009, from http://www.elyrics.net/read/b/bob-marley-lyrics/bad-card-lyrics.html

Mico University College. (2008a). *About Us.* Retrieved June 29, 2009, from http://www.themicouniversitycollege.edu.jm/AboutUs/tabid/57Default.aspx

Mico University College. (2008b). *Mico University College: Changing to preserve its legacy—Handbook 2008.* Kingston, Jamaica: The Mico University College.

Morrison, Errol. (2008*). A golden future: Innovation, technology & entrepreneurship.* Retrieved October 29, 2008, from http://www.utech.edu.jm/UTECH50.swf

Mundy, Karen. (2007). Global governance, educational change. *Comparative Education, 43*(3), 325–357.

National Association of State Universities and Land-Grant Colleges. (2007). *A national action agenda for internationalizing higher education.* Retrieved February 23, 2009, from http://www.aplu.org/NetCommunity/Document. Doc?id=471

National Center for Public Policy and Higher Education. (2008). *Partnerships for public purposes: Engaging higher education in societal challenges for 21st century.* Washington DC: The National Center for Public Policy and Higher Education.

Neave, Guy. (Ed.). (2000*). The universities' responsibilities to society: International perspectives.* Amsterdam: Elsevier Science.

Niaah, Jalani, & Niaah, Sonjah Stanley. (2008). Bob Marley rastafari and the Jamaican tourism product. In Marcella Daye, Donna Chambers, & Sherma Roberts (Eds.), *New perspectives in Caribbean tourism* (pp. 40–64). London: Routledge.

O'Connor, Ashling. (2008). Usain Bolt has the right to showboat, says Frankie Fredericks. *Times Online.* Retrieved June 24, 2009, from http://www.timeson-line.co.uk/tol/sport/olympics/article4587895.ece

Office of Planning and Development. (2007). *The University of the West Indies: Strategic Plan 2007–2012.* Kingston: University of West Indies.

Richards, Peter. (2005, July 20). *Health-Caribbean: AIDS could kill quarter million by 2010.* Retrieved July 21, 2005, from http://www.ipsnews.net/dominologin.asp?Db=ips\eng.nsfandwView=vwWebMainViewand DocID=6295179AD1E4403DC1257044005C0A89

Robinson, Mary. (2004, December). *Human rights and ethical globalization.* Retrieved January 15, 2005, from www.asanet.org

Shirley, Gordon. (2008a). *Principal's message.* Retrieved June 21, 2009, from http://myspot.mona.uwi.edu/principal/principals-message

Shirley, Gordon (2008b). Principal's report 2007–2008: Principal's overview. Retrieved June, 21, 2009, from http://myspot.mona.uwi.edu/principal/principals-report

Shortwood Teachers' College. (2008a). *About us.* Retrieved June 29, 2008, from http://www.stcoll.edu.jm/about.html

Shortwood Teachers' College. (2008b). *Mission statement.* Retrieved June 29, 2008, from http://www.stcoll.edu.jm/mission.html

Slaughter, Anne-Marie. (2005). *A new world order.* Princeton: Princeton University Press.

United States Department of State. (2009a). *Background note: Jamaica.* Retrieved June 28, 2009, from http://www.state.gov/r/pa/ei/bgn/2032.htm

United States Department of State. (2009b). *Background notes: Grenada.* Retrieved July 9, 2009, from http://www.state.gov/r/pa/ei/bgn/2335.htm

University of Technology (2008a). *About UTech.* Retrieved June 29, 2008, from http://www.utechjamaica.edu.jm/index.htm

University of Technology (2008b). *Colleges & faculties.* Retrieved June 29, 2008, from http://www.utechjamaica.edu.jm/Academic/Coll_Fac.htm

University of the West Indies. (2008). *About UWI, Mona.* Retrieved June 26, 2009, from http://www.mona.uwi.edu/about/history.php

Watson, David. (2004). *The university and civic engagement.* London: Association of Commonwealth Universities—The ACU Benchmarking Programme.

World Bank. (2009). *Jamaica early childhood development project.* Retrieved July 13, 2009, from http://web.worldbank.org/external/projects/main?Project id=P095673&theSitePK=40941&pagePK=64283627&menuPK=228424&pi PK=73230

World Bank. (2003). *Caribbean youth development: Issues and policy directions.* Washington DC: Word Bank.

Zakaria, Fareed. (2009). *The post-American world.* New York: W.W. Norton & Company.

Part II

Unique Colleges and Universities and Global Influences

6 Historically Black Colleges and Universities in New Orleans: Domestic and Global Engagement in the Post-Katrina Era

Beverly Lindsay and Tara Scales Williams

A hurricane . . . the wind howls . . . stormy weather . . .
("It Feels Like Rain," lyrics by John Hiatt, sung by Aaron Neville)

Six years ago in August 2005, the worst natural disaster in the United States devastated the Dillard University campus where all buildings were engulfed in six to ten feet of water. Fortunately, prior to the impact of Katrina, the Dillard President and senior executives executed the decision to evacuate the campus so that students were safely ensconced from a few days to a couple of weeks at another campus in Louisiana or in the homes of their parents, friends, relatives, and even friendly strangers. During the Fall Semester of the 2005/2006 academic year, students enrolled temporarily, that in some cases became permanent, at universities throughout the nation. The central administrative offices of Dillard University were situated in Atlanta amid the nationally known Clark Atlanta University complex, where W. E. B. DuBois commenced several seminal sociological studies, including those focusing on the displacement and migration of African Americans (Jones, 2006; U.S. Department of Education, 2007).

In May 2009, the first full four-year Katrina class graduated from Dillard University. Happiness permeated the campus as evinced by the warm and encouraging words of commencement speakers—actress, Cicely Tyson and Georgetown University Professor, Michael Eric Dyson (Dillard University, 2009). While happiness ensued, long-lasting challenges prevail for a first-rate liberal arts college that happens to be among the top five Historically Black Colleges and Universities (HBCUs) that produces the most national graduates who go forward to earn doctoral and professional degrees (United Negro College Fund, 2010; U.S. Department of Education, Office for Civil Rights, 1991). How might this phenomenon continue while Dillard strives to rebuild and engage in the New Orleans metropolitan area and Gulf Coast region trounced by Katrina? In short, an innovative type of university engagement will be vital. Similar matters surface for two other HBCUs in New Orleans—Southern University at New Orleans (SUNO) and Xavier University.

Special note must be made of the changing demographics in the metropolitan area and the region, in the wake of Katrina, as diverse workers from other parts of the United States and, indeed, other nations migrate to New Orleans and the region seeking work. Their efforts are as important, though not as visible as those of world-famous actor Brad Pitt who has continually thrust national visibility upon rebuilding New Orleans as a green environment (Eggler, 2007; Make it Right, 2009). Simultaneously, the socioeconomic and cultural bases of the region must be reestablished while recognizing the comprehensive changes ranging from new economic enterprises derived from the culinary tastes of new migrants for Salsa juxtaposed with the world-renowned New Orleans Blues and Jazz. Such factors seem to highlight alterations necessitating university engagement like the establishment of new university policies and applied research centers and institutes.

For this chapter, we address salient questions that encompass *inter alia*: 1) Will (or how might) original missions and roles for preeminent HBCUs be altered in light of historical enrollment and degree completions? 2) Will (or how might) original roles encompass or expand to include globalization? 3) How might HBCUs respond to different migration patterns and new diverse populations in the region with different educational and sociocultural needs? 4) Will there be alternative University administrative structures, positions, and/or programs to facilitate engagement? 5) What may be the interrelations with elected New Orleans, Louisiana, and Congresspeople and Senators? 6) What are the roles of philanthropic organizations in the process of rebuilding?

Historical Missions and Roles of HBCUs

HBCUs are academic institutions that were established before 1964. Their primary mission was, and remains, the education of African Americans at a time when many institutions did not admit African American students (Brown II & Freeman, 2002; Garibaldi, 1984; Ricard & Brown II, 2008; Roebuck & Murty, 1993). Representing 3% of the nation's higher education institutions, HBCUs graduate approximately 20% of African Americans who earn undergraduate degrees (United Negro College Fund, 2010). In an examination of the mission of HBCUs from the view of the institutions' presidents, Ricard and Brown II's (2008) findings support the literature that HBCUs continue to serve a unique purpose; however, they also assert that HBCUs do not necessarily serve a mission that is unique. Rather "their mission *matters* because they cater to a special population of student learners who continue to need services and assistance that other types of institutions fail to make available to them" (p. 105) and must move beyond traditional roles and missions as we observe in the current missions and purposes of the three New Orleans HBCUs.

Dillard University is a private, four-year liberal arts HBCU, founded in 1869, and is affiliated with the United Church of Christ and the United Methodist Church. The mission and vision of Dillard University is

> To produce graduates who excel, become world leaders, are broadly educated, culturally aware, and concerned with improving the human condition. Through a highly personalized and learning-centered approach Dillard's students are able to meet the competitive demands of a diverse, global and technologically advanced society.
>
> (Dillard University, 2008)

In addition to the mission and vision, Dillard has several strategic pillars. Among these pillars, three are of particular interest as they relate to globalization, changing demographics, and the university's response to these changes. First, "Dillard University will infuse globalization into its curriculum so that it expands its reach to other languages, cultures and countries;" second, "Dillard University will be engaged in the revitalization of its home, New Orleans;" and third, "Dillard University will develop a Gulf Coast Public Policy Center" (Dillard University, 2008). The student handbook also discusses what it calls the "New Dillard" stating that graduates of the New Dillard "will be global citizens excelling in a competitive world and committed to the improvement of the human condition."

Xavier University of Louisiana, a private four-year HBCU founded by Saint Katherine Drexel and the Sisters of the Blessed Sacrament, was established as a high school in 1915 and in 1925 became a university. As the only historically Black, Catholic University, its mission is "to contribute to the promotion of a more just and humane society by preparing its students to assume roles of leadership and service in a global society" (Xavier University of Louisiana, 2010a).

SUNO,[1] a public, four-year university, is a part of the Southern University system that is the only HBCU university system in the United States. SUNO was established in 1956 "as a branch of Southern University and Agricultural & Mechanical College (Southern University) in Baton Rouge by Act 28 of the Extraordinary Session of the Louisiana Legislature of September 4, 1956" and opened its doors in 1959 in Pontchartrain Park (Southern University at New Orleans, 2010a). SUNO's mission is

> To create and maintain an environment conducive to learning and growth, to promote the upward mobility of diverse populations by preparing them to enter into new as well as traditional careers, and to equip them to function optimally in the mainstream of the global society.
>
> (Southern University at New Orleans, 2010a)

Conceptual Landscapes

With over one million people leaving New Orleans due to Hurricane Katrina (300,000 African Americans), this was the "largest rapid movement of individuals in history due to a natural disaster" (Freeman, 2007). In essence, the natural disaster served as the most critical illustration of push factors causing the immediate rapid migration (Donner & Rodriguez, 2008; Lindsay, 1986). Emigrants were pushed out due to the collapse of the physical, social, economic, and educational infrastructures. The Brookings Institute conducted an analysis of the 2006 American in Community Survey of the population shift in New Orleans post-Katrina. According to their analysis, those who were pushed from New Orleans ("out-migrants") compared to those who stayed ("stayers") were more likely to be Black, younger and poorer, and more likely to have children. In addition, "in-migrants" were more likely to be White, childless, and have more education (Donner & Rodriguez, 2008; Lindsay, 1986). There was also a higher percentage of Hispanics who were in-migrants compared to stayers (Frey, Singer, & Park, 2007). For example, Hispanics from border states such as Texas and those from Central and South America, who arrived after Hurricane Katrina to help with rebuilding, were attracted to the city due to a most prevalent pull factor (Donner & Rodriguez, 2008; Lindsay, 1986), that is, employment options pulled workers to the area because there were more viable opportunities in New Orleans than those in their original locales.

The Greater New Orleans Community Data Center (Plyer & Ortiz, 2009) conducted an analysis of the U.S. Census Bureau's 2008 American Community Survey and contrasted demographic profiles to those of the Census 2000. They found that in the late 2000s the New Orleans Metropolitan was

> less poor with fewer adults lacking a high school diploma, fewer households with children, more one or two-person households, fewer households lacking vehicles, a larger share of the population that is foreign-born, a higher homeownership rate, and more homeowners without mortgages.
>
> (Plyer & Ortiz, 2009, p. 2).

In short, it appears that a substantial number of the very poor who migrated elsewhere may not have returned; and as we shall observe shortly, the population composition of the city shifted due to an increase of different demographic groups.

In 2000, the population of New Orleans was 484,674, with the majority of the residents being African American (67.3%). There were also 28.1% White residents, 0.2% American Indian and Alaska Native, 2.3% Asian, 0% Native Hawaiian and Other Pacific Islander, 3.1% residents of Hispanic or Latino origin, and 4.2% foreign born. In addition, 1.3%

identified as two or more races (U.S. Census Bureau, 2000). Markedly different from the 2000 Census was the population estimate for 2006 (New Orleans post-Katrina) of 223,388, reflecting a −53.9 decline from April 1, 2000 to July 2006 as reflected in Table 6.1.

As depicted in the 2006–2008 American Community Survey, the three-year population estimate (2006–2008) for New Orleans, observed in Table 6.1, was 270,245 (U.S. Census Bureau, 2008). Of that, 60.5% were African American, 34.4% White, 0.1% American Indian or Alaskan Native, 2.9% Asian, 0% Native Hawaiian and Other Pacific Islander, 4.5% Hispanic or Latino (of any race), and 5.8% foreign born. In addition, 0.9% were estimated to be two or more races.

Of particular interest is the decrease in African Americans (from 67.3% to 60.5%), the increase in Asians (from 2.3% to 2.9%), Hispanics (3.1% to 4.5%), and foreign-born (4.2% to 5.8%). There is also an increase in Whites by about 6%, which offsets a 6% decrease in African Americans. These demographic shifts per se likely prove to impact the culture of New Orleans. However, because the African American population remains the majority, a major cultural shift may be somewhat limited in the immediate future. While some of the data are estimates, it will be interesting to scrutinize the actual shift in the population as the 2010 census is completed. We would surmise that while New Orleans will remain predominately Black, the numbers of Whites, Hispanic, and Asian residents would increase beyond that of approximately 16% of total population derived from the statistics in Table 6.1. A 16% different population composition in less than a decade certainly portends notable cultural, educational, and social shifts.

As a result of Hurricane Katrina and the subsequent migration of residents to surrounding states and the emigration of non-residents to New Orleans, often hired to help rebuild the city, the demographics of the city have altered. However, is this alteration reflected in the enrollment

Table 6.1 2000 U.S. Census Data and 2006–2008 American Community Survey Estimates

	2000 Census	*2006–2008 American Community Survey Three-year Estimates*
Population	484,674	270,245
African American	67.3%	60.5%
White	28.1%	34.4%
American Indian and Alaska Native	0.2%	0.1%
Asian	2.3%	2.9%
Native Hawaiian and Other Pacific Islander	0%	0%
Hispanic or Latino origin	3.1%	4.5%
Foreign born	4.2%	5.8%
Two or more races	1.3%	0.9%

Source: U.S. Census Bureau

patterns at the three New Orleans HBCUs? If so, how will this impact the academic majors offered as well as the support services provided? Will there be an increased need for English as a Second Language (ESL) services or migrant programs? It appears that facets of globalism are now at the doorstep of the region and many of the adults and/or their children may now attend HBCUs or utilize some of their programs. If such evolvements occur, we suggest that the future viability of HBCUs is to embrace an integrated domestic and global model.

Katrina's Impact on HBCUs in New Orleans

As a result of Hurricane Katrina and the subsequent breach of the levees in the ninth ward, the ensuing floods seriously impacted New Orleans universities. Those that sustained the most significant damage were the three HBCUs: Dillard, Xavier, and SUNO. All three universities sustained substantial hurricane damages. The damage estimates were: Dillard, $350 million to $400 million; Xavier, $35 million to $40 million; and SUNO, $350 million (*The Chronicle of Higher Education*, 2006). Damages cannot only be estimated in a dollar amount based on physical damage, but in terms of loss of human capital, resources, and structural shifts. As we shall see from the following statistics, the hurricane and subsequent flooding affected enrollment, graduation, and academic programs at these three universities, and the long-term impact on enrollment and graduation of students and the number of faculty remains to be seen.

Over the last 30 years, enrollment at HBCUs has steadily increased. According to the National Center for Education Statistics (NCES) (Provasnik & Shafer, 2004), in fall 1980, there were 233,557 students enrolled in degree-granting HBCUs (of that 218,009 at four-year institutions). The racial/ethnic composition based on fall enrollment in degree-granting HBCUs was as follows: White: 10.4%; African American: 81.8%; Hispanic: 1.6%: Asian or Pacific Islander: 0.6%; American Indian: 0.2%; and non-resident alien: 5.4%.

In 1990, there were 257,152 students enrolled in degree-granting HBCUs, with 240,497 enrolled at four-year institutions. Of the total number of students enrolled, 13.4% were White, 81.2% were African American, 1.5% were Hispanic, 0.7% were Asian or Pacific Islander, 0.1% were American Indian, and 3.1% were non-resident aliens. In 2000, there were 275,680 students enrolled (250,710 at four-year institutions). Of the total students enrolled, 11.9% were White, 82.4% were African American, 2.3% were Hispanic, 0.8% were Asian or Pacific Islander, 0.2% were American Indian, and 2.4% were non-resident aliens (Provasnik & Shafer, 2004). The most recent data provided by NCES at the time of this printing was for fall 2006, when 308,774 students were enrolled at HBCUs of that, approximately 83% (255,150) were African American (Snyder, Dillow, & Hoffman, 2009).[2]

NCES data indicate that over the last ten years the number of degrees conferred (including associate, bachelor, master, doctor, and first professional degrees) has steadily increased along with enrollment at HBCUs. In 2000/2001, there were 40,830 degrees conferred at HBCUs and in 2004/2005, there were 42,984 degrees conferred (the last class prior to Hurricane Katrina) (Provasnik & Shafer, 2004; Snyder, Dillow, & Hoffman, 2007). In 2005/2006, there were 43,312 degrees conferred at HBCUs (Snyder, Dillow, & Hoffman, 2008) and in 2006/2007, there were 43,858 degrees conferred (Snyder et al., 2009).

Enrollment at Dillard, Xavier, and SUNO

Historical data shows that in fall 2000, Dillard University enrolled 1,953 students and in 2001, 2,137 students(Provasnik & Shafer, 2004). In 2004, there were 2,155 students (2,140 African American) at Dillard (Snyder et al, 2007). In fall 2009, Dillard enrolled 1,011 students, approximately 95% African American (963 students) and the remaining non-resident alien, Hispanic, Asian, White, and other) (Dillard University, 2010c).

In fall 2000, Xavier University of Louisiana enrolled 3,797 students (3,284 undergraduate, 285 graduate, and 228 professional students) and in fall 2001, there were 3,912 students enrolled (3,340 undergraduate, 346 graduate, 226 first professional students) (Provasnik & Shafer, 2004). In fall 2004, there were 4,121 students enrolled at Xavier and approximately 86% were African American (3,556) (Snyder et al., 2007). In fall 2009, Xavier enrolled 3,338 students (70.3% African American, 29.7% Asian/Asian American, White, Hispanic or other) (Xavier University of Louisiana, 2009).

SUNO enrolled 3,999 students in fall 2000 (3,573 undergraduates and 426 graduates) and in fall 2001, there were 3,741 students enrolled (3,084 undergraduates and 657 graduates). In fall 2004, there were 3,647 students enrolled at SUNO and approximately 96% were African American (3,504) (Snyder et al., 2007). In fall 2009, SUNO enrolled 3,140 students (Southern University at New Orleans, 2010a).

According the *Chronicle of Higher Education* (2006), as expected, estimated undergraduate enrollment at all three HBCUs declined after Hurricane Katrina. Dillard's estimated enrollment, pre-Katrina, was 2,200 and post-Katrina (2006) was 1,100; Xavier's estimated undergraduate enrollment pre- and post-Katrina was 4,200 and 3,100 respectively; and SUNO enrolled 3,400 undergraduate students pre-Katrina and 1,500 post-Katrina.

Degrees Conferred at Dillard, Xavier, and SUNO

NCES also provides data about degrees conferred at the three institutions that the chapter focuses on, providing the total number of degrees conferred and the number of degrees conferred to African American students. In 2001/2002, Dillard conferred 330 bachelor degrees (324 to African American students); and Xavier conferred 488 bachelor degrees (483 to African American students), 71 master (26 to African Americans), and 107 first professional degrees (69 to African Americans) (Provasnik & Shafer, 2004). In 2001/2002, SUNO conferred 6 associate degrees (all to African American students), 350 bachelor degrees (321 to African American students), and 147 master degrees (114 to African American students). In 2004/2005, Dillard awarded 340 bachelor degrees; Xavier awarded 441 bachelor, 80 master, and 96 first professional degrees; and SUNO awarded 31 associate, 440 bachelor, and 166 master degrees (Snyder et al., 2007).

In 2008/09, known as the Katrina class, Dillard awarded 171 degrees (Dillard University, 2010c); Xavier awarded 535 degrees (undergraduate and graduate) (Xavier University of Louisiana, 2009); and SUNO awarded 391 degrees (undergraduate and graduate) (Southern University at New Orleans, 2009a).

Faculty at Dillard, Xavier, and SUNO

According to the *Chronicle of Higher Education*, students were not the only population impacted at the universities, as there were notable reductions in the number of faculty as well (2006). Estimates indicated that at Dillard, faculty numbers reduced from 132 to 91 pre- and post-Katrina, respectively; at Xavier from 238 to 154; and at SUNO from 160 to 70.

Academic Programs at Dillard, Xavier, and SUNO

Dillard offers majors in six divisions: Business; Educational and Psychological Studies; Humanities; Natural Sciences and Public Health; Nursing; and Social Sciences (Dillard University, 2010c). Xavier offers majors in the following academic units: College of Arts and Sciences; College of Pharmacy; and Graduate program (Xavier University of Louisiana, 2010b). SUNO offers associates, bachelor's, and master's degrees in five academic units: Arts and Sciences; Business and Public Administration; Education; Graduate Studies; and Social Work (Southern University at New Orleans, 2010b).

Engagement and Perspectives from Administrators

According to the Kellogg Commission (1999) engagement is "redesigned teaching, research, and extension and service functions that are sympathetically and productively involved with the communities universities serve, however community is defined" (p. 27). Thus, engagement involves all parties at a university participating in a symbiotic relationship with the community served (broadly defined). In the case of the three New Orleans HBCUs, we see that they are engaged in the areas of teaching, research, and service; and they are involved in the rebuilding of the community in which they are housed, thereby enhancing the experiences of the students and assisting in changing the culture of the campus (Association of Public and Land-Grant Universities, 2010a).

As it relates to faculty, engagement is most often seen in the areas of research, teaching, and service. Specifically, engagement manifests itself in terms of "community-based research, service learning and forms of professional service with a public good outcome" (Wade & Demb, 2009, p. 8). Universities have, in some cases, implemented new (and in other cases revamped) structures, positions, and/or programs to facilitate the engagement of their students as we document shortly. Student engagement

> has two key components that contribute to student success. The first is the amount of time and effort students put into their studies and other activities that leads to the experiences and outcomes that constitute student success. The second is the ways the institution allocates resources and organizes learning opportunities and services to induce students to participate in and benefit from such activities.
> (Kuh, Kinzie, Schuh, Whitt, & Associates, 2005)

Simply put, it is "participation in educationally effective practices, both inside and outside the classroom, which leads to a range of measurable outcomes" (Harper & Quaye, 2009).

As the nation's demographics shift and expand into global markets, it becomes imperative that universities seek to engage in research and problem solving that incorporate various disciplines, address public concerns, and are cognizant and sensitive to diverse communities (Campus Compact, 2007). To that end, there are universities who have elected to complete the steps to receive the Community Engagement Classification through the Carnegie Foundation for the Advancement of Teaching. Established in 2006, this classification defines community engagement as "the collaboration between institutions of higher education and their larger communities (local, regional/state, national, global) for the mutually beneficial exchange of knowledge and resources in a context of partnership and reciprocity" (Carnegie Foundation for the Advancement of Teaching, 2010).

In the case of the three New Orleans HBCUs, engagement occurs across the board in various ways, from institutional policies to individual faculty/ staff involvement. Notable is how these universities are engaging students, faculty/staff, and the community. To gain an understanding of how the three HBCUs in New Orleans are engaging students, faculty, administrators, and professional staff, interviews were conducted with senior administrators, student affairs professionals, and faculty at Dillard, Xavier, and

SUNO, along with an examination of mission statements, curricular programs, and the like. To retain anonymity of those interviewed, names and positions are not linked to specific statements. After careful analysis of interviews and documents, several themes emerged reflecting engagement and globalization. The interview protocol is located online (http://www.ed.psu.edu/educ/cshe/people/Lindsay%20Documents/Protocol).

Curriculum

Post-Katrina, SUNO discontinued several academic programs as unviable. Although this was the case, the university was able to gain academic programs that fit within the process of rebuilding. According to the Board of Regents Minutes from January 5, 2006, 19 programs were eliminated, the majority at the secondary education level, as well as some in the STEM (science, technology, engineering, mathematics) disciplines such as Mathematics, Chemistry, Physics, and Physics/Engineering and some in the humanities, social sciences, and business such as History, Art, Political Science, English, Spanish, and Accounting. These were primarily "low-completer programs" and the programs in secondary education that were duplicated at the University of New Orleans located only blocks away. While the majority of these programs were to be eliminated, according to SUNO's website several programs listed for elimination are still in existence, such as English, Mathematics, History, and Political Science (Southern University at New Orleans, 2010b).

Of particular concern is ensuring quality academic program offering at SUNO, according to a tenured full-time education professor and senior executive who was called out of pre-Katrina retirement to help strengthen the education programs. The notion of streamlining due to a *force majeure*—downsizing or eliminating programs or administrative structures due to acts of nature such as hurricanes, floods, or other natural disasters—was a constant theme at SUNO due to the necessary mandate from the University System and/or the Louisiana State Department of Education. This senior professor and executive indicated that she would stay indefinitely to help with the transition, to include challenges such as the trailers still being used for instructional, student, and other services. Another professor in the STEM disciplines also commented on the several academic programs that were downsized, including various secondary programs. He was especially concerned with the low completion rates for African Americans in STEM programs.

Post-Katrina, SUNO sought to engage students through different instructional means such as increasing online courses (Mangan, 2008). As students who were displaced looked to continue their education, the "e-learning component" at SUNO was strengthened. In addition to online learning, SUNO added programs (in the midst of dissolving 19 programs) including Public Administration, Child Development and

Family Studies and alternative certifications in Early Childhood Education because these may provide immediate student community practicums and professional career avenues upon graduation. SUNO also displayed a commitment to rebuilding the city with the Business Entrepreneurship program as well as the Small Business Development and Management Institute available for future business owners (Southern University at New Orleans, 2010a).

According to an administrator in Academic Affairs, Dillard is concerned with ensuring that faculty are able to cover global and multicultural issues and that students are prepared to work in diverse settings. There is a keen interest in ensuring that various syllabi, beyond liberal arts, include global and diverse issues. Several social science faculty (for example, Psychology and Sociology) discussed the physical hardships of Hurricane Katrina since several did not have regular/permanent places to live in the wake of Katrina. They believe their workloads are very heavy; but they will plow through since they are concerned with students having quality education and being able to graduate. They are very pleased that students who were first-year students, when Katrina hit, just graduated in May 2009. Some faculty maintain that Katrina students, having survived the hurricane and its lingering aftermath, can survive in New Orleans or anywhere in the world. For instance, student nurses were directly engaged in select community health endeavors post-Katrina. Some faculty pointedly used the hurricane to teach globalization and diversity in the social science classes since Katrina became a global media phenomena.

"Going Green"

In conjunction with post-Katrina efforts, Dillard has focused on construction via the Leadership in Energy and Environmental Design (LEED) certification that is internationally recognized. The focus is on building sustainable structures or green buildings "by recognizing performance in five key areas of human and environmental health: sustainable site development, water savings, energy efficiency, materials selection and indoor environmental quality" (U.S. Green Building Council, 2010b). LEED certification was developed by the U.S. Green Building Council (USGBC), whose mission is to "transform the way buildings and communities are designed, built and operated, enabling an environmentally and socially responsible, healthy, and prosperous environment that improves the quality of life" (U.S. Green Building Council, 2010a).

Dillard maintains that "the Katrina legacy" has helped focus on new campus construction such as the 55,000 square feet Student Union and Recreation, Health and Wellness Center, scheduled to open in 2010. Housing a movie theater, bowling alley, retail space, and a place for artists (local, students, staff) to showcase their work, the center will be the "first health center to serve the Gentilly community [where Dillard sits] since Hurricane Katrina" (Dillard University, 2010b). This building, along with the 160,000 square feet 21st-Century Professional Schools and Science Building built in 2007, are "green" buildings and LEED certified. These buildings will provide a place for engagement such as health and wellness programs for students and Gentilly residents.

Community Programs

Xavier University was interested in serving the Hispanic community, especially since it has grown (as depicted in Table 6.1) since Hurricane Katrina. Hence, Project Buena Vista was implemented as a program that prepares bilingual speech pathologists. "This program offers bilingual education and community engagement. It will increase the number of highly trained, degreed and state licensed speech-language pathology assistants" (Xavier University of Louisiana, 2008).

Dillard houses the Community Development Corporation (CDC), a non-profit entity, whose charge is to "improve housing conditions and courting [sic] major stores and shops to the area" in order to revitalize the Gentilly neighborhood where Dillard is located. For example, in 2008, the CDC hosted the largest free health fair in New Orleans, using its resources to assist in the rebuilding of the community, particularly since many in the area have not had a personal physician since the hurricane. Held on the Dillard campus, the sponsors and co-sponsors included the University's Divisions of Nursing and Student Success, as well as Blue Cross/Blue Shield of Louisiana; WBOK Radio; EXCELth, Inc.; Primary Care Network; and United Way of Greater New Orleans (Newsome, 2008).

Students

At SUNO, student affairs professionals maintained that their mission includes becoming leading agents in organizational development, helping students to feel at home, and facilitating students' development in acquiring life and leadership skills. Offices that have helped support students are counseling and psychological services, community outreach, service learning (60 hours community service), and ad hoc special programs. To aid in the students' transition back to the campus, the university introduced a Serenity Room post-Katrina and made massage chairs available. In addition, students will be engaged through residential living. Southern has never had residential halls in the past, and after Katrina, the university began building a residence hall scheduled to open 2010 (Southern University at New Orleans, 2010c).

According to an undergraduate student body president at SUNO, he did not leave New Orleans due to the hurricane. He remained since it was a family decision to stay (although his father is a SUNO professional), rather than that of SUNO. He believed that the university was responsive during the hurricane, but hampered by the conditions in New Orleans caused by the mayor and the federal government's lack of response. He stated that many students transferred to Southern University at Baton Rouge; but they would not have the same urban experience as those at SUNO. After some students returned, he contended that the SUNO administration was slow in responding, based upon his conversations and interactions with other students as he elicited feedback on ways to address post-Katrina problems. Because he hoped to graduate within one year or so, he wanted to "put things in place to benefit future students." In the immediate realm, he, other students, and professionals created a temporary outdoor student union in the absence of a dedicated building. A disc jockey played music, people sold barbeque, and students assembled. It became important to envision and implement events for students to congregate and have a sense of community with SUNO.

Structural Changes

SUNO has traditionally operated with an open admissions policy; however, effective fall 2010 this will change. This policy shift might impact enrollment patterns at SUNO, particularly as the university struggles to enhance select majors that will help revitalize the metropolitan area and help students and faculty become attuned to and embrace facets of regional development in relation to global conditions.

One of the university presidents is very interested in globalization, an interest that began with her previous presidency in California and Vice President positions in Minnesota and Arizona. She believes that students and faculty need to be prepared for diversity throughout the United States and the world; of particular interest is the peaceful and negotiated solution to challenges and problems, rather than violence and war. She would like more faculty activity in globalization and in world affairs of the 21st Century.

One of the strategic pillars of Dillard University is the implementation of a Gulf Coast Public Policy Center to include U.S, Gulf Coast States and major cities such as New Orleans. The institute could also include the Caribbean and parts of Central American affected by similar geopolitical conditions and climate. There is a desire to secure external funding for the Center and in some ways cooperate with other Predominately White Institutes (PWIs) and HBCUs in the metropolitan area (Dillard University, 2008).

Philanthropy

Many HBCUs lack substantial financial resources (Ricard & Brown II, 2008) and this was the case at these three institutions post-Katrina. The funds, received by Dillard, Xavier, and SUNO after the hurricane have been derived from assorted sources such as university campaigns,

philanthropic organizations, alumni, friends, and corporate entities especially contributing various amounts to the private universities. For example, Dillard University's Advantage Dillard! raised $41 million toward a
campaign goal of $70 million since the hurricane to be used for student
scholarship, teaching and learning, facilities, technology, general program
support, and endowment (Dillard University, 2010a).

The Teagle Foundation awarded Dillard $500,000 to help students
return and resume their studies (Teagle Foundation, 2005); and in 2007 the
foundation allocated Dillard a $250,000 grant for student scholarships and
faculty development. Further, the Teagle Foundation allotted Xavier University a $100,000 grant for their campus master plan (a $100,000 grant
was also given to Tulane University for the Consortium Scholars Fund)
(Teagle Foundation, 2007). Dillard University also received $200,000
from Lumina Foundation to increase student and alumni involvement with
recruitment, retention, and fundraising efforts (Lumina Foundation, 2007).
The Mott Foundation of Flint, Michigan, gave a $500,000 grant to both
Dillard and Xavier (for a total of $1 million) to assist with scholarships and
rebuilding the campus (Ascribe Newswire, 2006). Xavier received $4 mil-
lion and Dillard received $2 million of a $12 million grant from the Carnegie Corporation (Tulane receiving $5 million; Teach for America receiving
$1 million to increase the number of teachers serving the New Orleans
area) (Carnegie Corporation of New York, 2007).

The President of Xavier University, who remained beyond his planned
retirement in order to help stabilize Xavier, recruited a former Dean to
become Provost. The two have been actively engaged in fund-raising
that is beginning to bear additional fruit. The Provost's experience as an
executive with the Louisiana University system should help him transfer
administrative experience to Xavier where he can creatively help pinpoint
external funds targeted for private HBCUs impacted by crisis in the New
Orleans and Gulf Coast region.

Relationships with Government

According to the American President's Board of Advisors on Historically
Black Colleges and Universities Annual Report 2004–2005 (U.S. Department of Education, 2007), four recommendations were made to the
president that focused on restoring the affected HBCUs not only to their
pre-Katrina state, but to ensure their survival. These recommendations
were made after consultation with the National Association for Equal
Opportunity in Higher Education (NAFEO), the United Negro College
Fund (UNCF), and presidents of the institutions that were affected by the
hurricane. They were as follows:

> 1) Provide funds to allow for the maintenance of key faculty and
> administrative staff salaries and benefits; 2) Provide funds to pay

transition costs, including temporary housing, clothing, transportation, etc., for faculty and staff; 3) Provide funds for campus facilities reconstruction, renovation and restoration, and replacement of
instrumentation; and 4) Provide funds for miscellaneous expenses to
facilitate temporary access, retention and return to the home institution for students and key faculty.

(U.S. Department of Education, 2007, p. 17)

In addition, the President's Board of Advisors on HBCUs suggest that
university executives "make effort(s) to secure, from the Congress, funds
to ensure that Dillard . . ., SUNO, and Xavier . . . can return to their
pre-Katrina state, especially as it relates to the . . . instrumentation and
infrastructure required to carry out their pre-Katrina academic missions"
(U.S. Department of Education, 2007, p. 24).

While such endeavors were articulated through federal advisory
boards, state-elected leaders were also voicing their concern and support
for HBCUs in the New Orleans area. Local HBCU faculty and administrators were attuned to some of the Louisiana Legislative Black Caucus's
initiatives such as their call to rebuild SUNO "not [as] an option, but a
necessity" (Louisiana Legislative Black Caucus, 2005).

Safety concerns became paramount in the wake of Katrina and the
university executives pressured the mayor and city council to ensure
safety precautions around the campuses and surrounding areas. While
such apprehensions were being expressed, it was interesting to note
that "SUNO was ranked #1 in Louisiana and 20th in the United States
in campus safety according to StateUniversity.com's Safe Schools
report in November, 2009" (Southern University at New Orleans, 2009b).
In August 2007, Dillard's CDC, along with several neighborhoods,
held the Gentilly "Night Out Against Crime" as a safeguard (Dillard,
2007).

In addition to safety, health care remains a paramount concern. Louisiana has a vested interest in the 2009 variations of the health care bills,
particularly since they have a desperate need for medical care since Hurricane Katrina.

> Louisiana has one of the poorest populations in the country, with
> all of the problems that generally entails. It has a high percentage of
> uninsured adults, high rates of chronic disease and an acute shortage
> of doctors. In most state-by-state measurements, Louisiana regularly
> ranks at or near the bottom for the health of its residents.
>
> (Robertson, 2009)

Congressman Anh Cao, of New Orleans, was the only Republican to
vote for the health care bill in the House in November 2009 (Congressman Anh "Joseph" Cao, 2009). In addition, Senator Mary Landrieu

(a Democrat) cast a key vote, in December 2009 supporting the Senate version of the health care bill that resulted in $300 million in Medicaid for the state (Robertson, 2009).

Synthesizing Motifs for Future Policy Directions

At the beginning of our chapter, we articulated six fundamental questions that were examined in the four sections: historical missions and roles; conceptual landscapes; Katrina's impact on New Orleans's HBCUs; and engagement and perspectives from administrators. From the explications and examinations, we synthesize policy motifs that may serve as global positioning systems (GPS) for future directions at the New Orleans HBCUs and others moving forward in an era of globalization.

One, it is almost axiomatic to state that a wholistic approach is vital to rebuilding and striving to engage university communities in the wake of an extreme natural disaster. The challenge is to decide what factors are of immediate critical importance; those that can be delayed for short time intervals; and those requiring strategic and academic planning that can be implemented within a few years or even a decade. For example, safety and housing were immediate concerns, yet they linger due to the absence of permanent university and metropolitan physical infrastructures. This effort has been somewhat abated by the successful endeavors of Congressman Anh Cao (the first Vietnamese-American member of Congress) (Congressman Anh "Joseph" Cao, 2009). For example, the Congressman secured $350,000 for Xavier University to expand their College of Pharmacy facilities, as well as securing $300,000 for Dillard University for a community health center (Congressman Anh "Joseph" Cao, 2010).

Two, the ever-present missions and roles of HBCUs in shifting socioeconomic and global environments necessitates careful crafting and redesigning in light of cultural, demographic, and educational shifts. If the overall population of the New Orleans area declines (due to push variables), enrollments at the universities will be affected since many students reside in the area. Simultaneously, the composition has changed so there appears to be a 16-percent increase in non-African American residents (due to pull variables) who have different sociocultural lifestyles and norms that would suggest the call for curriculum modifications as new profile matriculants enter the halls of the HBCUs.

Three, while the HBCUs are critically adjusting to metropolitan, state, and regional concerns, attuning to global geopolitical phenomena must be meshed with the local. To paraphrase the late U.S. House of Representatives Speaker Thomas "Tip" O'Neill, all global matters are local. In 2009, British Prime Minister Gordon Brown conversed with the Principal of King's College London and requested the formation of a study group to undertake a series of discussions between British and American higher education leaders on collaborative programs (UK/US Study Group,

2009). Each group would bring British and American university matters for examination within the context of regional, national, and global phenomena. In essence, the several facets are inseparable as explicated in this chapter. Interestingly, the study group did not include any American or HBCU executives who are African American and/or of color; thus indicating that attempts to address global matters should not overlook local demographic groups.

Four, while *force majeure* exists, it is essential that HBCUs (that graduate over 20% of students who later earn professional and doctoral degrees) continue to prepare students in critical STEM fields. Indeed, in January 2010, almost 80 presidents of the Association of Public and Land-Grant Universities (APLGU) penned a letter to President Barack Obama pledging their universities' commitment to the Science and Mathematics Teacher Imperative (SMTI) whereby additional teachers would be introduced in these critical shortage fields. By 2015, it is envisioned that 10,000 new teachers would be produced via SMTI in light of domestic and global challenges in scientific and technological arenas (Association of Public and Land-Grant Universities, 2010b). It appears that no Louisiana HBCU signed the letter.

Five, the New Orleans HBCUs have undertaken a number of initiatives to enhance university engagement while addressing diverse domestic demographic shifts and respond to global phenomena. Coupling these realities with the fact that New Orleans is a major port city, facets of globalization are further evident as witnessed by the influx of goods and related services from throughout the world. In short, the domestic and global mesh in New Orleans. Thus, universities' plans for applied research centers and institutes appear apropos. Dillard University, for example, envisions a Gulf Coast Public Policy Center that might serve to guide the University's leadership efforts to build responsive and peaceful sociocultural and physical environmental programs to be guiding forces in the post-Katrina era. Such a center could further develop collegial and diplomatic relations with the newly diverse New Orleans populace and those in other nations as domestic and global phenomena are integrated.

Several years ago, the senior author wrote that the characteristics of "competence, comfort, and confidence" should be the foundations from which university students, faculty, staff and administrators operate when addressing the dynamic changes occurring throughout the world (Lindsay, 1998). Competence in academic disciplines, comfort in raising penetrating questions, and confidence in the ability of the universities and those of global colleagues to explore and devise solutions to profound issues that challenge us in the cultural, economic, educational, political, scientific, and technological spheres. The triumvirate of "C's" *(competence, comfort, and confidence)*, through university endeavors, can extend to New Orleans and elsewhere in efforts to provide viable options to global challenges. Hence, while winds may howl, amid stormy weather, globally diverse bridges can be reached and crossed.

Notes

1 Though not new, but perhaps in light of Hurricanes Katrina and Rita, there have been discussions about the merger of SUNO with the University of New Orleans (Fischer, 2006).
2 At the time the volume went to press, more complete demographic profiles of student bodies were not available.

References

Akbar, Renee, & Sims, Michele J. (2008). Surviving Katrina and keeping our eyes on the prize: The strength of legacy and tradition in New Orleans's HBCU teacher preparation programs. *Urban Education, 43*(4), 445–462.

Ascribe Newswire. (2006). *$1 million in Mott Grants Aid Katrina-Ravaged Black Colleges.* Retrieved March 26, 2010, from http://newswire.ascribe.org/cgi-bin/behold.pl?ascribeid=20060928.141007&time=14%2018%20PDT&year=2006&public=0

Association of Public and Land-Grant Universities. (2010a). *University engagement.* Retrieved March 26, 2010, from http://www.aplu.org/NetCommunity/Page.aspx?pid=224

Association of Public and Land-Grant Universities (2010b). 79 University leaders sign letter to President Obama pledging to address national shortage of science and mathematics teachers. *APLU's Online Newsletter.* Retrieved March 26, 2010, from www.aplu.org/NetCommunity

Brown II, M. Christopher, & Freeman, Kassie (Eds.). (2002). Research on Historically Black Colleges. *Review of Higher Education, 25*(3), 237–368.

Campus Compact. (2007). *New times demand new scholarship: Research universities and civic engagement.* Retrieved March 26, 2010, from http://www.compact.org/initiatives/research_universities/conference_report.pdf

Carnegie Corporation of New York. (2007). *Carnegie corporation commits $14 million to revitalize New Orleans' intellectual infrastructure in wake of hurricane Katrina.* Retrieved March 26, 2010, from http://www.carnegie.org/sub/news/new_orleans.html

Carnegie Foundation for the Advancement of Teaching. (2010). *Community engagement elective classification.* Retrieved March 26, 2010, from http://classifications.carnegiefoundation.org/descriptions/community_engagement.php

Congressman Anh "Joseph" Cao. (2010). *Healthcare.* Retrieved March 26, 2010, from http://josephcao.house.gov/Issues/Issue/?IssueID=496Congressman Anh "Joseph" Cao. (2009). *Exclusive: GOPer Cao: Health vote may end career.* Retrieved March 26, 2010, from http://josephcao.house.gov/News/DocumentSingle.aspx?DocumentID=15742240

Dillard University. (2010a). Advantage Dillard! Retrieved March 26, 2010, from http://www.dillard.edu/index.php?option=com_content&view=article&id=248&Itemid=150).

Dillard University. (2010b). Katrina Legacy. Retrieved March 26, 2010, from http://dillard.edu/index.php?option=com_content&view=article&id=246&Itemid=176

Dillard University. (2010c). Quick Facts. Retrieved March 26, 2010, from http://dillard.edu/index.php?option=com_content&view=article&id=57&Itemid=71

Dillard University. (2009). *Cicely Tyson and Michael Eric Dyson to deliver special commencement address to Dillard University's Hurricane Katrina graduating class*. Retrieved March 26, 2010, from http://www.dillard.edu/index.php?option=com_content&view=article&id=677%3Acicely-tyson-and-michael-eric-dyson-to-deliver-special-commencement-address-to-dillard-universitys-hurricane-katrina-graduating-class&catid=130%3Adillard-university-presidents-online-news-apr-09&Itemid=53

Dillard University. (2008). *Mission and vision*. Retrieved March 30, 2010 from http://dillard.edu/index.php?option=com_content&view=article&id=56&Itemid=7

Dillard University. (2007). Dillard/Gentilly takes night out against crime. *The Dillard University Community Development Corporation Newsletter*. Retrieved March 30, 2010 from http://www.dillard.edu/pdfs/cdcnewsletterweb.pdf

Donner, William, & Rodriguez, Havidan. (2008). Population composition, migration and inequality: The influence of demographic changes on disaster risk and vulnerability. *Social Forces, 87*(2), 1089–1114.

Eggler, Bruce. (2007). Brad Pitt is helping rebuild Lower 9th Ward, but residents have leading role. *The Times-Picayune*. Retrieved March 26, 2010, from http://blog.nola.com/times-picayune/2007/09/brad_pitt_is_helping_rebuild_l.html

Fischer, Karin. (2006). Finding promise in pain. *The Chronicle of Higher Education*, p. A21.

Freeman, Kassie. (2007). Crossing waters: Katrina and the other great migration-Lessons from African American K-12 students' education. In Sharon P. Robinson, & M. Christopher Brown II (Eds.), *The children Hurricane Katrina left behind* (pp. 3–13). New York: Peter Lang Publishing, Inc.

Frey, William H., Singer, Audrey, & Park, David. (2007). *Resettling New Orleans: The first full picture from the census*. Washington DC: The Brookings Institution Special Analysis in Metropolitan Policy.

Fussell, Elizabeth. (2009). Hurricane chasers in New Orleans: Latino immigrants as a source of rapid response labor force. *Hispanic Journal of Behavioral Sciences, 31*(3), 375–394.

Garibaldi, Antoine M. (1984). *Black colleges and universities: Challenges for the future*. New York: Praeger.

Harper, Shaun R., & Quaye, Stephen J. (Eds.). (2009). *Student engagement in higher education: Theoretical perspectives and practical approaches for diverse populations*. New York: Routledge.

Hiatt, John (2008). *It Feels Like Rain* [Recorded by Aaron Neville]. Retrieved March 26, 2010, from http://www.lyrics.com/it-feels-like-rain-lyrics-aaron-neville.html

Jones, Robert A. (2006). *Dillard's dire straits: Historically Black college struggles to survive amid New Orleans' post-hurricane diaspora*. Retrieved March 30, 2010 from http://www.highereducation.org/crosstalk/ct0106/news0106-dillard.shtml

Kellogg Commission on the Future of State and Land-Grant Universities. (1999). *Returning to our roots: The engaged institution*. Retrieved March 30, 2010 from http://www.aplu.org/NetCommunity/Document.Doc?id=183

Kuh, George D., Kinzie, Jilllian, Schuh, John H., Whitt, Elizabeth J., & Associates. (2005). *Student success in college: Creating conditions that matter*. San Francisco: Jossey-Bass.

Lindsay, Beverly. (1998). Of competence, comfort and confidence. *International Mosaic*, 2(2), 5.

Lindsay, Beverly (Ed.). (1986). *African migration and national development*. University Park, PA: Penn State University Press.

Lindsay, Beverly, & Williams, Tara Scales. (2010). *Working Protocol for Research on New Orleans HBCUs*. Retrieved March 26, 2010, from http://www.ed.psu. edu/educ/cshe/people/Lindsay%20Documents/Protocol

Louisiana Legislative Black Caucus. (2005). *News Release: Why rebuild SUNO*. Retrieved March 26, 2010, from http://llbc.louisiana.gov/press/WhyRebuild-SUNO.pdf

Lumina Foundation. (2007). Lumina foundation announces fourth-quarter grants. Retrieved March 26, 2010, from http://www.luminafoundation.org/ newsroom/news_releases/2007-02-01.html

Make it right. (2009). *Helping to rebuild New Orleans' lower 9th ward*. Retrieved March 30, 2010 from http://www.makeitrightnola.org/

Mangan, Katherine. (2008). New Orleans colleges slog toward recovery from Katrina. *The Chronicle of Higher Education*, p. A1.

Newsome, Janella. (2008). *Dillard University Press Release: Dillard university host largest free health fair in New Orleans*. Retrieved March 26, 2010, from http://www.dillard.edu/index.php?option=com_content&view=article&id=4 00:dillard-university-host-largest-free-health-fair-in-new-orleans&catid=111: arhived-press-releases&Itemid=505

Plyer, Allison, & Ortiz, Elaine. (2009). *Who lives in New Orleans and metro area now?* Retrieved March 30, 2010 from www.gnocdc.org

Provasnik, Stephan, & Shafer, Linda L. (2004). Historically Black Colleges and Universities, 1976–2001. *(NCES 2004–062) U.S. Department of Education, National Center for Education Statistics*. Washington DC. Retrieved March 26, 2010, from http://nces.ed.gov/pubs2004/2004062.pdf

Ricard, Ronyelle Bertand, & Brown II, M. Christopher. (2008). *Ebony towers in higher education*. Sterling, VA: Stylus Publishing.

Robertson, Campbell. (2009). Louisiana has much at stake in health care debate. *The New York Times*. Retrieved March 26, 2010, from http://www.nytimes. com/2009/12/20/health/policy/20louisiana.html

Roebuck, Julian B., & Murty, Komanduri S. (1993). *Historically Black colleges: Their place in American higher education*. Westport, CT: Praeger Publishers.

Snyder, Thomas D., Dillow, Sally A., & Hoffman, Charlene M. (2007). Digest of education statistics 2006. (NCES 2007–017). *National Center for Education Statistics, Institute of Education Sciences, U.S. Department of Education*. Washington DC. Retrieved March 26, 2010, from http://nces.ed.gov/ pubs2007/2007017.pdf

Snyder, Thomas D., Dillow, Sally A., & Hoffman, Charlene M. (2008). Digest of education statistics 2007. *(NCES 2008–022). National Center for Education Statistics, Institute of Education Sciences, U.S. Department of Education*. Washington DC. Retrieved March 26, 2010, from http://nces.ed.gov/ pubs2008/2008022.pdf

Snyder, Thomas D., Dillow, Sally A., & Hoffman, Charlene M. (2009). Digest of education statistics 2008. *(NCES 2009–020) National Center for Education Statistics, Institute of Education Sciences, U.S. Department of Education*. Washington DC. Retrieved March 26, 2010, from http://nces.ed.gov/pubs2009/2009020.pdf

South, Scott J., Crowder, Kyle, & Chavez, Erick. (2005). Exiting and entering high-poverty neighborhoods: Latinos, Blacks and Anglos compared. *Social Forces, 84*(2), 873–900.

Southern University at New Orleans. (2010a). *About SUNO.* Retrieved March 30, 2010 from http://www.suno.edu/About_SUNO/history.html

Southern University at New Orleans. (2010b). *Academics.* Retrieved March 30, 2010 from http://www.suno.edu/Academics/index.html

Southern University at New Orleans. (2010c). *Student Affairs.* Retrieved March 30, 2010 from http://www.suno.edu/Student_Affairs/housing.html

Southern University at New Orleans. (2009a). *News Release: SUNO 2009 Commencement features three summa cum laude graduates.* Retrieved March 30, 2010 from http://www.suno.edu/News/docs/SUNO-2009_Commencement.pdf

Southern University at New Orleans. (2009b). *News Release: Web site ranks SUNO #1 in campus safety.* Retrieved March 30, 2010 from http://www.suno.edu/News/docs/SUNO_no.1_campus_safety.pdf

Teagle Foundation. (2007). *New Orleans colleges and universities are still working to re-build in the aftermath of Hurricane Katrina.* Retrieved March 30, 2010 from http://www.teaglefoundation.org/grantmaking/grantees.aspx

Teagle Foundation. (2005). *Teagle foundation announces $600,000 grant for hurricane relief efforts at Dillard and Tulane.* Retrieved March 30, 2010 from http://teagle.bmm-nyc.com/about/news/press/20051205.aspx

The Chronicle of Higher Education, (2006, January 20).How many came back? *The Chronicle of Higher Education,* p. A 13

Tolnay, Stewart E., & Eichenlaub, Suzanne C. (2006). Southerners in the west: The relative well-being of direct and onward migrants. *Social Forces, 84*(3), 1639–1663.

U.S. Census Bureau. (2008). *2006–2008 American community survey, data profile highlights, New Orleans City, Louisiana.*

U.S. Census Bureau. (2000). Census *2000 demographic highlights, New Orleans City, Louisiana.*

U.S. Department of Education, Office for Civil Rights. (1991). Historically Black colleges and universities in higher education. Retrieved March 30, 2010 from http://www.ed.gov/about/offices/list/ocr/docs/hq9511.html

U.S. Department of Education. (2007). *Fulfilling the covenant? The way forward: 2004–05 annual report to the president on the results of participation of historically Black colleges and universities in federal programs.* Washington DC: White House Initiative on Historically Black Colleges and Universities.

U.S. Green Building Council. (2010a). About USGBC. Retrieved March 30, 2010 from http://www.usgbc.org/DisplayPage.aspx?CMSPageID=124

U.S. Green Building Council. (2010b). What LEED is. Retrieved March 30, 2010 from http://www.usgbc.org/DisplayPage.aspx?CMSPageID=1988

UK/US Study Group: A Private Report to Prime Minister Gordon Brown. (2009). *Higher education and collaboration in global context: Building a global civil society.* London.

United Negro College Fund. (2010). Our member colleges: About HBCUs. Retrieved March 30, 2010 from http://www.uncf.org/members/aboutHBCU.asp

Wade, Amy, & Demb, Ada. (2009). A conceptual model to explore faculty community engagement. *Michigan Journal of Community Service Learning, 15*(2), 5–16.

Xavier University of Louisiana. (2008). Programs to Prepare Bilingual Speech Pathologists. Retrieved March 30, 2010 from http://www.xula.edu/mediarelations/TMAX/tmax_dec08.php

Xavier University of Louisiana. (2010a). *About Xavier*. Retrieved March 30, 2010 from http://www.xula.edu/about-xavier/index.php

Xavier University of Louisiana. (2010b). *Academics*. Retrieved March 30, 2010 from http://www.xula.edu/academics/index.php

Xavier University of Louisiana. (2009). *XU quick facts*. Retrieved March 30, 2010 from http://www.xula.edu/mediarelations/quickfacts.php

7 Native American Tribal Colleges and Universities: Utilizing Indigenous Knowledges and Ways of Knowing to Prepare Native Peoples to Meet the Demands of an Increasingly Globalized Community

John Tippeconnic III and Susan Faircloth

> We have brothers and sisters just like ourselves in the four directions around the world. . . . [T]ry to be involved with them because that is our calling—to share with those who are also in need of hope and opportunity; to promote and share our spirituality, our culture, and our education; and to pursue economic opportunities together in our struggle to strengthen ourselves globally as a family of tribal nations.
>
> Lionel Bordeaux[1]

Native American tribal colleges and universities are making connections with Indigenous peoples in other parts of the world; these connections broaden the education of students beyond their own local environments, increasing their awareness and understanding of the larger world. From the first tribally controlled college established on the Navajo reservation in 1968 to the newest tribal colleges established in Oklahoma in the 2000s, the Tribal College and University (TCU) movement has gained strength, recognition, and credibility, and has proven successful in providing educational opportunities, grounded in tribal cultures and values, for youth and adults. The challenges have been many; however, the TCUs' use of Indigenous knowledges and ways of knowing has enabled the provision of educational services that are relevant to individual tribes and communities. This approach is locally based yet enables students and educators to view and respond to issues both within and beyond the bounds of the colleges and their surrounding communities.

In this chapter, we draw upon the extant literature, data from the American Indian Higher Education Consortium (AIHEC), websites of the individual colleges, and our personal and professional experiences with the tribal college movement. The first author served as the vice president of the first tribal college, Navajo Community College, later renamed

Diné College. He currently serves on the board of directors of Comanche Nation College, one of the newest tribally controlled colleges. The second author served as the director of Research and Policy Analysis for the AIHEC, a non-profit organization advocating on behalf of the nation's tribal colleges and universities.[2] The purpose of this chapter is to discuss the role of tribal colleges in preparing American Indian and Alaska Natives to meet the challenges and opportunities of an increasingly globalized world. In doing so, it is important to note that globalization is not a new phenomenon for the Indigenous peoples of the Americas, but one that has been evolving for more than 500 years; bringing with it the threat of extinction through the loss of land, language, and life.

Local Tribal Control

Any discussion of the role of tribal colleges in an increasingly globalized world must take into consideration the unique relationship tribal nations have with the government of the United States. Tribes who have attained federal recognition status are considered sovereign nations. This nation to nation relationship sets them apart from any other racial or ethnic group in the United States. This sovereign status is complicated by the fact that these nations are geopolitically situated within the larger borders of the United States. As such, tribal nations have the authority to govern individuals and entities residing or operating within the boundaries of their tribal nations; however, they remain subject, in many ways to the laws and regulations governing residents of the United States.

In the 1960s, tribes began to assert their sovereign status. This movement was prominently demonstrated as they worked to reclaim their right to control education at the local level. For many Indigenous peoples and communities, education has historically served as a means of assimilation, as well as a vehicle through which tribal languages and cultures may be reclaimed, preserved, and strengthened (U.S. Senate, 1969). As such, the importance of local tribal control of education cannot be emphasized enough.

As demonstrated in this chapter, the principle of tribal sovereignty and the policy of tribal self-determination affirm the right of tribes to establish and operate secondary and postsecondary education programs. This includes the legal authority to establish Tribally Controlled Colleges and Universities and the right to make all decisions concerning the affairs of these institutions. Local tribal control means that American Indians are the decision makers within tribal colleges; serving on the governing boards, college administrations, and in faculty and staff positions. Other key decision areas include the development of the college philosophy, vision, mission, fiscal resources, facilities, academic and student service programs, and the hiring of faculty and staff. As Cornell (2001) writes,

In the Indian case, the issue is sovereignty: the right of Indian nations to control their own strategic decisions, resources, internal affairs, relationships with other sovereigns, and so on——in short, to govern themselves. This is a matter, at one and the same time, of law (the legal right to self-rule), of policy (active federal support of that right), and of practice (tribal assertions of self-rule).

(p. 91)

The result is that TCUs provide an education that is more accessible and culturally appropriate than mainstream institutions or those public and private colleges and universities in the United States that provide educational opportunities to the general public. A major difference is that TCUs promote the growth and use of tribal languages and cultures while providing educational programs designed to meet local needs. Although local community building is a priority, the tribal college movement has grown to include the larger regional, national, and international community (Barden, 2003).

The Current Status of Tribal Colleges and Universities

Today, there are more than 40 tribal colleges across the United States and Canada. Tribal colleges are typically located on or near reservations and tribal areas and are chartered by tribes or groups of tribes. Many of them are small, geographically isolated, and struggle from year to year with issues of infrastructure, capacity building, sustainability, and funding. Tribal colleges have often been described as "underfunded miracles" (e.g., Houser, 1991) since the minimum level of funding in the federal authorizing legislation has never been achieved through appropriations. Primary funding for tribal colleges comes from the federal government, and is based on the Indian student count, the number of American Indian student full-time equivalent enrollment. In effect, tribal colleges do not receive funding from the federal government for non-Indian students. A limited amount of funding comes from public and private sources, including local tribal governments.

Tribal colleges provide educational opportunities to students who might otherwise not have access to these opportunities due to geographical and financial factors (Systemic Research, Inc., 2006). Tribal colleges enroll approximately 17,000 certificate- and degree-seeking students, the majority of which are American Indian (80%), many of them nontraditional students and female (66%). Tribal colleges also serve non-Indians; however, the American Indian student enrollment must be at least 51% to receive federal government funding. The largest number of students attend Diné College (1,728), followed by Oglala Lakota College (1,486), Salish Kootenai College (1,080), and Haskell Indian Nations University (889). A listing of tribal colleges is provided in Table 7.1.

Table 7.1 Tribal Colleges

Name of College	Location	Year Chartered	Enrollment[4] Fall 2006
Bay Mills Community College	Michigan	1984	559
Blackfeet Community College	Montana	1974	450
Cankdeska Cikana Community College	North Dakota	1974	232
Chief Dull Knife College	Montana	1975	359
College of Menominee Nation	Wisconsin	1993	511
College of the Muscogee Nation	Oklahoma	2004	**
Comanche Nation College	Oklahoma	2002	271
Diné College	Arizona	1968	1,728
Fond du Lac Tribal and Community College	Minnesota	1987[5]	440
Fort Belknap College	Montana	1984	161
Fort Berthold Community College	North Dakota	1973	203
Fort Peck Community College	Montana	1978	438
Haskell Indian Nations University	Kansas	1993[6]	889
Ilisagvik College	Alaska	1995	253
Institute of American Indian Arts[7]	New Mexico	1962	193
Keweenaw Bay Ojibwa Community College	Michigan	1975	60
Lac Courte Oreilles Ojibwa	Wisconsin	1982	552
Leech Lake Tribal College	Minnesota	1990	198
Little Big Horn College	Montana	1980	317
Little Priest Tribal College	Nebraska	1996	95
Navajo Technical College[8]	New Mexico	1979	390
Nebraska Indian Community College	Nebraska	1979	113
Northwest Indian College	Washington	1983	623
Oglala Lakota College	South Dakota	1971	1,486
Saginaw Chippewa Tribal College	Michigan	1998	97
Salish Kootenai College	Montana	1977	1,080
Sinte Gleska University	South Dakota	1971	917
Sisseton Wahpeton College	South Dakota	1979	279
Sitting Bull College	North Dakota	1973	286
Southwestern Indian Polytechnic Institute	New Mexico	1971	629
Stone Child College	Montana	1984	262
Tohono O'odham Community College	Arizona	1998	195
Turtle Mountain Community College	North Dakota	1972	849
United Tribes Technical College	North Dakota	1968	525
White Earth Tribal and Community College	Minnesota	1997	116
Wind River Tribal College	Wyoming	1997	39

Source: www.aihec.org.

Note: Enrollment was not available for the College of the Muscogee Nation as it is a new college

Demographic Profile of American Indians attending Tribal Colleges and Universities[9]

According to the 2000 Census, there are more than 4 million American Indians in the United States when counted in combination with one or more races. This constitutes approximately 1.5% of the total U.S. population. The largest percentage (48%) lives in Western states. More than one-third live on reservations. American Indians continue to lag behind their peers in terms of college attendance. Six percent of American Indian students attend private colleges compared to 14% of their peers. American Indians earn approximately 1% of all bachelor's degrees granted each year. During the 2005/2006 academic year, approximately 11,000 American Indian students earned bachelor's degrees. American Indians are among the poorest racial and ethnic groups in the United States. "Deep poverty" is particularly evident among American Indians living on reservations (IHEP, AIHEC, & AICF, 2007). The average family income of tribal college students is $13,998, 27% below the national poverty level.

Among students attending TCUs, the most popular area of study is Liberal Arts, followed by the social sciences, vocational and career programs, business, education, and nursing/health. Six tribal colleges offer baccalaureate degrees while two—Oglala Lakota College and Sinte Gleska University—offer master's degrees. In addition to degree granting programs, a number of vocational and certificate programs are also offered by these colleges (Systemic Research Inc., 2006).

Benefits Provided by Tribal Colleges and Universities

Ultimately, TCU students earn degrees or receive training that is culturally based yet provides the necessary knowledge and skills in an academic discipline or workforce area for them to successfully function as a citizen of the community. Preparation to secure employment is a key benefit of tribal colleges. Not only do tribal colleges focus on tribal languages and cultures and their prior relationship between education and economic development, they also make real life connections to health, social, legal, and other areas, enabling students to make connections with communities outside the local tribal area. Recently, the tribal colleges have broadened their outreach to include connections to other Indigenous peoples of the world.

Local Design, Global Impact

In addressing the relationship between tribal colleges and globalization, we argue that tribal colleges operate globally in three primary ways: First, they are more than educational institutions—they are comprehensive or holistic in their approach to provide educational programs to meet the social, economic, health, and culture-related needs of tribal members and the surrounding communities. Second, they are global in the more traditional aspect in that they prepare students to be successful in the world outside the community in which they operate. Finally, the tribal college movement has had a long-lasting impact on Indigenous communities around the world as they have helped to spawn Indigenous higher education movements around the world, including New Zealand and Canada.

The ability to make and sustain global connections is facilitated, in part, by tribal college membership in the AIHEC, which was established in 1972 as a means of collective support. AIHEC has supported and facilitated a broader perspective, including a global view:

> AIHEC is the collective spirit and unifying voice of our nation's Tribal Colleges and Universities (TCUs). AIHEC provides leadership and influences public policy on American Indian higher education issues through advocacy, research, and program initiatives; promotes and strengthens Indigenous languages, cultures, communities, and tribal nations; and through its unique position, serves member institutions and emerging TCUs.
>
> (http://www.aihec.org/)

In addition to AIHEC, tribal college international connections are fostered by the World Indigenous Higher Education Consortium (WINHEC).[10] established during the 2002 meeting of the World Indigenous Peoples Conference on Education in Calgary, Alberta, Canada. WINHEC ". . . provides [an] international forum and support for Indigenous Peoples to pursue common goals through higher education" (win-hec.org). WINHEC's goals are to:

1) Accelerate the articulation of Indigenous epistemology (ways of knowing, education, philosophy, and research);
2) Protect and enhance Indigenous spiritual beliefs, culture and languages through higher education;
3) Advance the social, economical, and political status of Indigenous Peoples that contribute to the well-being of Indigenous communities through higher education;
4) Create an accreditation body for Indigenous education initiatives and systems that identify common criteria, practices and principles by which Indigenous peoples live;
5) Recognize the significance of Indigenous education;
6) Create a global network for sharing knowledge through exchange forums and state of the art technology; and
7) Recognize the educational rights of Indigenous peoples.

(win-hec.org)

Stein (2008) cites the TCUs' international connections with the Maori's Wānanga (places of learning) as one example of the TCUs' willingness and ability to engage Indigenous peoples across the globe in regaining local control of the design and delivery of educational programs and services for Indigenous peoples and communities. Similar to tribal colleges in the United States, Wānangas incorporate the principles and values of New Zealand's Indigenous people, the Māori.[11] These institutions have been instrumental in the preservation and maintenance of Māori language and culture (Ambler, 2005), as well as providing academic and career-related training. In 2001, representatives of the Wānangas were invited to attend a meeting of the AIHEC, an organization working on behalf of tribal colleges and universities. The purpose of this meeting was to establish relationships and to learn from each other. In turn, a group of tribal college faculty and staff traveled to New Zealand in 2001. This process of relationship building helped to facilitate the establishment of WINHEC and also serves as a model for how Indigenous peoples and communities across the world can work together to advance their common interests and goals (see http://www.win-hec.org/?q=node/3).

Valuing Indigenous Knowledges and Ways of Knowing

The founders of the tribal college movement ". . . recognized that they could not just prepare tribal students to be proficient in their own cultures but must also prepare them to be proficient in the non-Indian world that surrounds the tribal communities" (Stein, Shanley, & Sanchez, 2002, p. 77). According to Dr Cheryl Crazy Bull, President of both the AIHEC and Northwest Indian College, "Tribal Colleges and Universities are uniquely positioned to serve as a linkage between our traditional understanding and contemporary life" (Systemic Research, Inc., 2006, p. 1). This is critical to both the continued survival and growth of tribal colleges and universities, as well as Indigenous peoples, tribes, and communities. Inupiaq scholar, Leona Okakok (1989) argues that ". . . educating a child means equipping him or her with the capability to succeed in the world he or she will live in" (p. 253). She continues writing "Education is more than book learning, it is also value-learning" (p. 254). Deloria and Wildcat (2001) reinforced this argument when they wrote,

> Indeed, the educational journey of modern Indian people is one spanning two distinct value systems and worldviews. It is an adventure in which the Native American sacred view must *inevitably* encounter the material and pragmatic focus of the larger American society.
>
> (p. v)[12]

Tribal colleges expose students to the values and ways of knowing of individual tribal peoples and communities through experiential learning, community engagement, and interactions with tribal elders both within and beyond the physical confines of the colleges. In the classroom, curricula tends to incorporate Indigenous-based content as evidenced by a 2006 study by Cole, which found that tribal colleges are ten times more likely than mainstream institutions to offer what he termed "ethnocentric" courses. The term ethnocentric is used in Cole's study to describe the privileging of Indian- or Indigenous-specific content and curricula as opposed to the more historically dominant Western-focused content and curricula. He attributes this finding in large part to the sovereign status of the tribes, which have worked to charter and establish these colleges, as well as their mission statements, which most often include special attention to the maintenance and preservation of tribal languages and cultures. Although Cole argues that the use of such ethnocentric curricula serves to prepare tribal college students only for the local, tribal community, we argue that the training these students receive prepares them to be successful in both the local and global worlds (Cole, 2006). Without a strong grounding in who one is linguistically, culturally, and tribally, there is little chance that tribal peoples and their communities will survive the pressures associated with increasing globalization.

Effects of Globalization of American Indian Peoples and Communities

As we have argued in our earlier work (Faircloth & Tippeconnic, In Press), globalization is not a new phenomenon for Indigenous peoples. For Indigenous peoples of the Americas, globalization began with our first encounters with those who would claim to have discovered us. With this discovery, came the onslaught of disease, forced relocation, large-scale death, and loss of land and liberties (e.g., Faircloth & Tippeconnic, In Press; IHEP et al., 2007). Tribal colleges and universities are uniquely positioned to mediate the effects of modern-day globalization on Indigenous peoples and communities.

Thriving in the Face of Increasing Globalization

In discussing, the relationship between globalization and resistance, Fenelon and Hall (2008), write, "Many indigenous communities attempt to maintain their values and social practices while they adopt and adapt aspects of modernity" (p. 1877). Fenelon and Hall go on to write,

> One observation remains true as it has for more than 500 years—Indigenous peoples will resist and survive because of their ability to maintain community, find leadership, distribute resources fairly among their people, and above all keep our respect for the land, the earth as our grandmother from which we are born and to which we will return.
>
> (p. 1895)

According to Boyer (2003), ". . . the function of Tribal Colleges is to help ensure the survival of indigenous peoples in America" (p. 138). In testimony submitted to the Indian Nation's at Risk Task Force, an administrator from the College of William & Mary wrote,

> The [Task Force] needs to understand the ambivalence with which American Indians view Western education. Historically, it has separated children from their tribes and culture, and left them unable to succeed in either world. Western education did not teach any of the skills needed to survive as an Indian; prejudice against Indians prevented them from surviving in the Western world, even with an education. Therefore, Western education was worse than useless, it was destructive. While this is less true than 300 years ago, the legacy remains.
>
> (Houser, 1991, p. 1)

Throughout history, Western-based models of education have been used as tools of assimilation (Tippeconnic, 1999). In contrast, tribal colleges serve as a means of fighting against those aspects of globalization that are potentially devastating to tribal peoples, communities, and nations (Hall & Fenelon, 2003).

Tribal College Missions

A sampling of tribal college mission statements clearly demonstrates the importance of local control, language, and culture. However, these mission statements also demonstrate ways in which tribal colleges recognize and respond to the world outside the tribal lands on which the colleges are situated. For example, Wind River Tribal College (http://www.wrtribalcollege.com/) is dedicated to preserving and protecting tribal self-determination, language, and culture. Bay Mills Community College (www.bmcc.org) strives to ". . . provide quality educational opportunities, promote research, and facilitate individual development in an accessible, community-based, and culturally diverse environment that supports and maintains . . . culture and language". Comanche Nation College (http://www.cnc.cc.ok.us) prepares students to meet economic and social demands while maintaining their cultural heritage and values. As with the majority of the tribal colleges, Comanche National College serves as a conduit through which students are better prepared to transfer to and be successful in mainstream institutions of higher education, while working to increase awareness of American Indian tribes and communities. Tribal colleges are also cognizant of and responsive to economic trends at the local, as well as the state and national levels (e.g., Little Big Horn College).[13]

Tribal College and University Teacher Training Initiatives

One way tribal colleges have attempted to meet community needs while broadening their outreach and impact, is to build relationships with local elementary and secondary schools by offering teacher education programs. This is in response to a growing need for highly qualified American Indian teachers; a need found in most tribal communities. The preparation of teachers is seen as a way to improve student success in schools and to address the high rate of teacher-turnover found in many schools. Tribal college representatives (American Indian College Fund, 1999) involved in teacher training programs have identified the following strategies as critical to the successful graduation, recruitment, and retention of American Indian teachers:

1) Student-centered program design and instructional approaches;
2) Use of traditional (Native) based curricula and the preparation of teachers who can teach from a Native perspective;
3) Promotion of Native languages and cultures in teaching methods and content;
4) Collaboration with tribal elders;
5) Use of authentic forms of assessments (e.g., portfolios and performance-based academic work);
6) Emphasis on service learning;
7) Opportunities for extensive practicum-based experiences with local schools early in the teacher preparation programs;
8) Opportunities for extended student teaching experiences;
9) Provision of extensive student support services (e.g., mentoring, tutoring, financial aid, advisement, assistance with childcare, housing, transportation);
10) Collaborative partnerships in which Native students are viewed as equals;
11) Joint development of curriculum; and
12) Use of technology (e.g., distance learning).

TCUs are uniquely situated to deliver teacher and administrator preparation programs (e.g., Pavel, Larimore, & VanAlstine, 2003) utilizing many of the principles noted earlier. In 2008, three tribal colleges received awards from the U.S. Department of Education to develop teacher training programs for American Indian and Alaska Native students. The three colleges are: Oglala Lakota College (OLC), Stone Child College, and Salish Kootenai College. What is different about the teacher preparation programs at tribal colleges and universities is best described by the individual missions, goals, and values of these programs. The goals of the OLC teacher preparation program are as follows:

Tribal Goals: Our goal is to improve the quality of education for interns, teachers, and students through consistent awareness, consideration, and integration of Lakota values and culture within reservation schools or schools with a significant number of Native American learners.

Cultural Goals: Our goal is for Oglala Lakota College's teacher candidates to familiarize their students with Lakota virtues and culture and assisting in integrating Lakota ways within instructional materials and curricula.

Community Goals: Community refers to the Lakota belief of *mitakuye oyasin*—we are all related. Our goal is for teacher candidates to become integral role models and effective leaders within the communities in which they serve. This belief encompasses the wide range of diversity that may exist in any community.

Academic Goals: The ultimate goal of the teacher preparation programs is to develop a model of excellence through a collaborative effort that includes formulating, utilizing and evaluating instructional outcomes, methodologies, pedagogy, professionalism, and instructional approaches suitable for all learners.

(http://www.olc.edu/local_links/education/docs/)[14]

While similar in some ways to the goals of mainstream teacher preparation programs, the goals of OLC and other tribal colleges and universities are unique in that they function holistically, building upon and incorporating the values, needs, and strengths of local tribes and communities, while working to equip students to be successful in whatever locale or environment they choose to live and work. In contrast, what is absent in most mainstream colleges and universities is recognition, incorporation, and respect of and for Indigenous values and beliefs.

Challenges and Opportunities

For more than 40 years, TCUs have found themselves uniquely positioned to function in an increasingly globalized world. In doing so, they encounter a number of challenges as well as opportunities. The following sections outline examples of each.

Challenges

1) To focus on the bigger/broader world view while maintaining a strong focus on local educational, economic, and health needs. Often the immediate and local situations do not allow time to focus on the world view or to develop meaningful and productive relationships outside the community within which they operate.

2) To focus on education—recognizing that other issues or areas (e.g., economic, political, health, social) tend to push education to the

background. In response, tribal colleges are challenged to maintain education as a priority.

3) Lack of resources (time, money, leadership) to develop and maintain connections with other Indigenous groups/institutions. Unfortunately, continued emphasis on day-to-day survival of the colleges may limit future opportunities for growth.

4) The need for leaders who have a broader perspective of education, who can make necessary connections with other Indigenous groups, and who have a global view.

5) To conduct research that will add to the knowledge base in Indigenous studies/Native Ways of Knowing and Being, and to share that knowledge especially through mainstream publications that are recognized in the Western research community. The challenge here is to share such knowledge in ways that are acceptable to individual tribes and communities while recognizing that some knowledge is not to be shared beyond the confines of tribes or tribal members.

Opportunities

1) To build networks that span beyond the TCUs and mainstream institutions in the United States.

2) To gain strength by connecting with Indigenous groups/institutions around the world.

3) To share Native Ways of Knowing and Being with others and to see commonalities and differences in cultures, languages, histories, research, etc.

4) To clearly demonstrate that Indigenous knowledges and ways of knowing and being are strong, complex and have a place in both the Western and Indigenous worlds.

5) To assume a stronger presence at national meetings and conferences such as the American Educational Research Association.

6) To develop cross-nation leadership and to engage in faculty and student exchanges with other colleges and universities.

7) To conduct joint/collaborative research studies.

8) To use technology to communicate and build relationships and share ways to deliver courses.

9) To exchange strategies and ways in which to renew tribal/Indigenous languages around the world.

Conclusion

Since their inception, TCUs have played an important role in the education of American Indians and Alaska Natives. Increasingly they are recognized as a critical part of the larger higher education community serving Native peoples in the United States and beyond. If TCUs are to continue to thrive, the policy of tribal self-determination, based on the principle of tribal sovereignty, must be fully respected and applied aggressively by policymakers and fiscal appropriators. Congressional acts and presidential executive orders also need to be fully implemented; however, competing needs and forces in the larger picture of education, as well as local, tribal needs, often result in lower priority for tribal colleges.

In spite of minimal funding at the state and federal levels, tribal colleges continue to serve as a viable alternative to traditional public and private institutions for many individuals, including older adults and Non-Native students, to earn an education, to improve their quality of life, and to compliment the educational opportunities available at public and private colleges and universities. The education students receive through TCUs is tribally based, meaning it is based on the local context, yet broad enough in perspective to facilitate connections and relationships to larger regional, national, and international communities (Barden, 2003). Tribal colleges also help to maintain, renew, and grow tribal languages and cultures, which is a critical function in today's world.

TCUs serve multiple roles. They are unique in that they utilize Indigenous knowledges and ways of knowing as foundational elements of the teaching and learning process. Although tribal colleges experience a number of tensions and challenges (e.g., Nichols & Monette, 2003), including competing with mainstream colleges and universities for funding and other resources (Nichols & Monette, 2003), many of them have established working relationships with mainstream colleges and universities through the development of articulation agreements, co-authorship of research and training efforts, study abroad programs and other collaborative initiatives. The lessons learned from the tribal colleges have much to offer to Indigenous and non-Indigenous communities around the globe.

Notes

1 This quote is taken from the *Tribal College Journal of American Indian Higher Education, 14(2)* where Dr Bordeaux, President of Sinte Gleska University, cites advice he received from tribal elders in 1972.

2 For more information on the American Indian Higher Education Consortium (AIHEC), see www.aihec.org

4 Fall 2006 enrollment. Source: Systemic Research, Inc. (2009).

5 Fond du Lac was established by the state of Minnesota and chartered by the Fond du Lac reservation. In 2003 Fond du Lac became the only community college in the state of Minnesota eligible to offer a four-year degree in elementary education.

6 Haskell was originally established in 1884 as a boarding school for American Indian and Alaska Native students.

7 Congressionally chartered

8 Formerly Crownpoint Institute of Technology

9 Source: Key statistics: American Indians and Alaska Natives (June 4, 2008).

Graduate Management Admission Council. Retrieved April 8, 2009, from http://www.gmac.com/NR/rdonlyres/3B683F19–18D9–4620-A73A-96F9CF0FF19E/0/HO_NativeAmericanIndiansData.pdf

10 WINHEC was officially launched at Delta Lodge, Kananaskis, Calgary in Alberta Canada during the World Indigenous Peoples Conference on Education (WIPCE), August 4–10, 2002. The founding members present were Australia, the states of Hawai'i and Alaska and the American Indian Higher Education Consortium of the United States, Canada, the Wänanga of Aotearoa (New Zealand), and Saamiland (North Norway).

11 For more information, see http://www.tec.govt.nz/Learners-Organisations/Wananga/

12 Originally cited in Castagno, Angelina E., & Brayboy, Bryan M.J. (2008). Culturally responsive schooling for Indigenous youth: A review of the literature. *Review of Educational Research, 78,* 941–993.

13 Little Big Horn College in Montana is working to increase the marketability of tribal arts and crafts on a global scale; also involved in tourism.

14 Excerpted from the Oglala Lakota College Teacher Preparation Handbook. Retrieved May 14, 2009, from http://www.olc.edu/local_links/education/docs/

References

Ambler, Marjane. (2005). While globalizing their movement, tribal colleges import ideas. *Tribal College Journal of American Indian Higher Education, 16*(4). Retrieved May 9, 2010, from http://www.tribalcollegejournal.org/themag/backissues/summer2005/sum05ambler.htm

American Indian College Fund. (1999). Tribal colleges: Training teachers for today & tomorrow, a call to action. Author: Denver, CO.

Barden, Jack. (2003). Tribal colleges and universities building community: Education, social, cultural, and economic development. In Maenette K. P. Benham, & Wayne J. Stein (Eds.), *The renaissance of American Indian higher education: Capturing the dream* (pp. 99–120). Mahwah, NJ: Lawrence Erlbaum Associates.

Bordeaux, L. (2002, Winter). Where will we be in 30 more years? *Tribal College Journal of American Indian Higher Education, 14*(2), 40.

Boyer, Paul. (2003). Building tribal communities: Defining the mission and measuring the outcomes of tribal colleges. In Maenette K. P. Benham & Wayne J. Stein (Eds.), *The renaissance of American Indian higher education: Capturing the dream* (pp. 137–148). Mahwah, NJ: Lawrence Erlbaum Associates.

Cole, Wade M. (2006, October). Accrediting culture: An analysis of tribal and historically black college curricula. *Sociology of Education, 79*(4), 335–387.

Cornell, Stephen. (2001, January). Enhancing rural leadership and institutions: What can we learn from American Indian nations? *International Regional Science Review, 24*(1), 84–102.

Deloria, Vine, & Wildcat, Dan. (2001). *Power and place: Indian education in America* Golden, CO: Fulcrum.

Faircloth, Susan C., & Tippeconnic, John W., III. (In Press). Tribally controlled colleges and universities: Global influence and local design. In Alecia Jackson & Kai A. Schafft (Eds.), *Rural education for the twenty-first century: Identity, place, and community in a globalizing world*. University Park, PA: Penn State University Press (Rural Studies Series).

Fenelon, James V., & Hall, Thomas D. (2008). Revitalization and Indigenous resistance to globalization and neoliberalism. *American Behavioral Scientist, 51*(12), 1867–1901.

Hall, Thomas D., & Fenelon, James. (2003). Indigenous resistance to globalization. What does the future hold? (pp. 173–183). In Wilma A. Dunaway (Ed.), *Emerging issues in the 21st century world-system* (Vol. I). *Crises and resistance in the 21st century world-system.* Santa Barbara, CA: Greenwood Publishing Group.

Houser, Schuyler. (1991). Underfunded miracles: Tribal colleges. In Indian Nations at Risk Task Force commissioned papers. ERIC Document Reproduction Services No. 343 772.

IHEP (Institute for Higher Education Policy), AIHEC (American Indian Higher Education Consortium), and AICF (American Indian College Fund). (2007). *The path of many journeys: The benefits of higher education for Native people and communities.* Washington DC: Authors.

Nichols, Richard, & Monette, Gerald C. (2003). Linking tribal colleges and mainstream institutions: Fundamental tensions and lessons learned. In Maenette K. P. Benham, & Wayne J. Stein (Eds.), *The renaissance of American Indian higher education: Capturing the dream* (pp. 137–148). Mahwah, NJ: Lawrence Erlbaum Associates.

Okakok, Lenora. (1989). Serving the purpose of education. *Harvard Educational Review, 59*(4), 405–22.

Pavel, D. Michael, Larimore, Colleen, & VanAlstine, Matthew J. (2003). A gift to all children: Native teacher preparation. In Maenette K. P. Benham, & Wayne J. Stein (Eds.), *The renaissance of American Indian higher education: Capturing the dream* (pp. 193–211). Mahwah, NJ: Lawrence Erlbaum Associates.

Stein, Wayne J. (2008). Tribal colleges and universities: Supporting the revitalization in Indian country. In Linda S. Warner, & Gerald E. Gipp (Eds.), *Tradition and culture in the millennium: Tribal colleges and universities* (pp. 17–34). Charlotte, NC: Information Age Press.

Stein, Wayne J., Shanley, James, & Sanchez, Timothy. (2002). The effect of the Native American higher education initiative on strengthening tribal colleges and universities: Focus on governance and finance. In Maenette K. P. Benham & Wayne J. Stein (Eds.), *The renaissance of American Indian higher education: Capturing the dream* (pp. 75–98). Mahwah, NJ: Lawrence Erlbaum Associates.

Systemic Research, Inc. (2009). AIHEC AIMS fact book 2007: Tribal colleges and Universities report. Alexandria, VA: American Indian Higher Education Consortium.

Systemic Research, Inc. (2006). AIHEC AIMS fact book 2005: Tribal colleges and Universities report. Alexandria, VA: American Indian Higher Education Consortium.

Tippeconnic, John W., III. (1999). Tribal control of American Indian education. Observations since the 1960s with implications for the future. In Karen Gayton Swisher, & John W. Tippeconnic, III (Eds.), *Next steps: Research and practice to advance Indian education* (pp. 33–52). Charleston, WV: ERIC Clearinghouse on Rural Education and Small Schools.

U.S. Senate. (1969). *Indian education: A national tragedy-a national challenge.* Washington DC: U.S. Government Printing Office.

8 Urban Support Networks: Commuter Urban Public Universities in Global Times

Jorgelina Abbate-Vaughn and Donna DeGennaro

> Now, civilizations, I believe, come to birth and proceed to grow by successfully responding to successive challenges. They break down and go to pieces if and when a challenge confronts them which they fail to meet.
>
> Arnold Toynbee, 1948

Index

This chapter considers globalization in education from the perspective of commuter urban public universities (CUPUs), paying attention to CUPUs negotiated local roles and global aims, their relationships with urban constituencies, and the role of emerging technologies in mediating but not obliterating their local missions.

Introduction

Urban public universities in general have been long associated with the mission of educating the citizenry of their surrounding areas in a delicate balance between providing quality and affordable education, as well as meeting the needs of the communities in which they are nested (Urban Universities Portfolio Project, n.d.). For a number of reasons, many see them as interconnected with the successes and tribulations of the settings that provide them a home:

> The idea of the urban university rolling up its sleeves and getting involved in urban affairs will spread because it is a tremendous opportunity to deal with real issues—crime, taxes, the economy, and elementary and secondary education—the issues that are on people's minds every day of the year. This will generate public and political support, which will be increasingly necessary in this era of diminishing resources.
>
> (Stukel, 1994, p. 21)

In this chapter, we delve into the specific aims of urban public universities that primarily serve the needs of local, commuter students. We offer three case study composites that allow us to analyze urban support networks and how they may be altered by an excessive emphasis on the global at the expense of the local. In the final section, we wrap up with implications for one of the professions highlighted in the case study composites—early care and education—by looking at specific ways in which a global perspective can enhance the preparation of urban professionals committed to local well-being while still attending to the demands of a rapidly globalizing world.

Commuter Urban Public Universities

In the United States, the term *urban* is often used as a euphemism for people of color and communities of low socioeconomic background (Carlisle, Jackson, & George, 2006). In developing countries, the idea of urbanicity may be associated with socioeconomic power. Abroad, the notion of urban public universities as inherently linked to long-needed sustained economic growth is well established (Moreno-Brid & Ruiz-Napoles, 2007). More specifically in Latin America, examples of CUPUs with multifaceted missions and diverse constituencies, similar to the ones on which this chapter centers, include institutions such as the Universidad Autónoma de Santo Domingo, the Universidad Nacional de Buenos Aires, or the Universidad Nacional Autónoma de México. While the concept of residential student is virtually nonexistent in such large universities and thus commuter students are the norm, in the United States, about 85% of college enrollments (in both 2- and 4-year degree granting institutions, both public and private) are students who live off campus (Horn & Nevill, 2006). Surprisingly, very little studies address the needs of such large groups when compared to the body of research on residential students (Dugan, Garland, Jacoby, & Gasiorski, 2008).

CUPUs are one type of university that meet the educational needs of commuter students—those who live with their parents, in rental housing, or are older students with jobs and/or children. They can be located in small urban enclaves like Athens State University in Athens, Alabama, with 19,000 inhabitants, or in large urban conglomerates like the University of the District of Columbia providing higher education access to its over 591,000 urban inhabitants. Nationwide, there are over 70 universities and colleges, both public and private, that are 100% commuter-attended and hundreds more that serve large percentages of commuters (U.S. News and World Report, 2010a).

CUPUs serve significant percentages of economically diverse and older students, and students from cultural, ethnic, and linguistically diverse backgrounds, as their local constituencies primarily draw from the cities in which they are nested. Data from the 66 urban school districts that compose the Council of Great City Schools (n.d.) assist in estimating urban K-12 demographics as 61% eligible for free or reduced price lunch,

79% of racial and ethnic minority groups, and 17% for whom English is not the native language. Many CUPUs such as Jackson State University, Florida International University, University of Massachusetts Boston, and the University of Houston rank high for economic diversity—which may be measured by the percentage of undergraduate students who are eligible for Pell grants—at 76%, 34%, 32%, and 29%, respectively (U.S. News and World Report, 2009). Other CUPUs' main feature is the population of undergraduates aged 25 or above, such as Athens State University, University of Maryland-College Park, and University of the District of Columbia at 90%, 83%, and 51%, respectively (U.S. News and World Report, 2010b).

As other urban public universities, CUPUs provide a reliable K-16 pipeline for local high school completers and community college transfers, 64% of whom remain in the area (Coalition of Urban Serving Universities, 2008). Urban public universities in general pioneer community engagement efforts as well as health disparity research and health-promoting partnerships. Emphasis on service to one's local community is similarly evident in the mission that CUPUs such as City University of New York, University of the District of Columbia, Florida International University, and the University of Massachusetts Boston exhibit. Some make serving the city their explicit mission:

> CUNY invigorates the city and state through partnerships with public schools, economic development initiatives, immigration and financial advice hotlines, and other outreach . . . [providing] New York with graduates trained for high-demand jobs in the sciences, technology, math, teaching, nursing and other critical and growing fields.
>
> (City University of New York, 2010)

Florida International University boasts of having amongst its degree completers "nearly half of all teachers employed in the Miami-Dade County Public School System," which includes in its payroll over 23,500 teachers (Florida International University, 2010). Athens State University goes even further in establishing its goal of serving local communities for prospective students:

> Whether you work full or part-time or whether you are a full-time student, Athens State offers a course schedule to meet your needs whether it be day, night, weekend or distance courses. Because nearly every student is from North Alabama or Southern Tennessee, you will literally attend class with people you know. Don't find yourself being just another student number.
>
> (Athens State University, 2006)

Such institutions "often do not fit the common definition of more traditional colleges and universities" and are instead engaged in "attacking complex metropolitan problems" (Coalition of Urban Serving Universities, 2008) while contributing to the educational, cultural, and general quality of life of the metropolitan and regional areas in which they strive.

As most urban public universities, CUPUs have begun to increasingly engage in the process of *glocalization* (Robertson, 1995) whereby thinking globally, but primarily acting locally, appear to meet both mission and emerging trends. Noddings (2005) refers to this phenomenon as the "power of the local in building a global perspective" (p. 122). Given that urban public universities secure a significant portion of their funding from state legislatures, they may often negotiate the local as permeated, but not overpowered by the global, as a recent convocation speech at a CUPU suggests:

> The forces of globalization are relentless and unforgiving. Many of our esteemed local private colleges see their mission as providing leaders who can move themselves and the jobs they control anywhere in the world to take advantage of changing markets. Most of them leave this area upon graduation. While some of our graduates may play in that world, most of them are committed to working, living, and raising their families *here*. The return on investment on *our* graduates is real. Once again, we must understand that national security, as well as higher moral imperatives, demands no less.
>
> (Motley, 2008)

Some CUPU mission statements navigate more promising global aims while still focusing on the local:

> . . . The University places education at the highest priority in plans to revitalize the city, without placing limits on what citizens can achieve and how they can contribute . . . [it] shares with the rest of the region the responsibility of building a community of learners, able to access a multitude of educational options, as well as access entry and exit points along the educational pipeline. In this way, the city is assured of a world-class workforce, current in their skills and talents, advancing as rapidly as the industry base demands . . . The University reaffirms its commitment to excellence through service, as it prepares its students for the global, technological challenges of life in the 21st Century.
>
> (University of the District of Columbia, n.d.)

Such commendable local goals and global engagement, however, might not be enough for CUPUs to successfully respond to the 21st century challenges and create financially sustainable structures for the long haul (Leventhal & Zimpher, 2007). All college graduates, some contend, must be able to navigate the increasingly global economies and job markets. Thus, all urban public universities must endeavor to update their programs of study and create new ones (Stearns, 2008). Pioneering programs may in turn attract national and international investments that widen the urban nesting area's job markets, while training a skillful and adaptable workforce that can support the aims of globally competitive employers (Rondinelli, Johnson, & Kasarda, 1998). Given the current recession, enrollment increases composed of people "seating out" unemployment by pursuing a higher degree may prompt public universities to seek out more aggressively private revenue streams to support their growth. This in turn usually leads opening up to market competitive careers (Goodman, 2009). Yet, the tension between desirable institutional changes and historical, unstoppable forces like globalization are not always easy to understand or negotiate (Gardner, 2004). In the next section we discuss some of the basic, ostensibly commonly agreed upon goals of higher education for the 21st century.

Goals for Higher Education in the Global Age

According to the Association of International Educators (NAFSA), an educated citizenry demands perspective-aware individuals who have a grasp of the internal and external consequences of the challenges confronted as a nation. Such awareness, NAFSA claims, is enhanced by quality international experiences that higher education must endeavor to both require and facilitate (NAFSA, 2007). The preponderant role of postsecondary education in short-term and long-term national welfare is echoed by other professional associations such as the National Association of State Universities and Land-Grant Colleges:

> Globally engaged universities are critical to maintaining America's place as a world leader and ensuring its national security. America's colleges and universities must prepare graduates to be active participants in a world in which national boundaries are increasingly permeable. Information, capital, products, labor and individuals cross national borders with ever increasing frequency and speed. America's need to remain competitive in the world requires its educational institutions produce globally competent human capital and cutting-edge research.
>
> (NASULGC, 2007, p. 1)

Experiences studying or providing service abroad and taking part in student exchanges remain extremely valuable academically-oriented efforts universities may emphasize. A recent U.S. News and World Report (2010c) survey indicates that the top 100 universities and colleges which have between 41% to 100% students who participate in international study abroad are all private institutions. CUPUs serving nontraditional populations necessitate alternative venues to master the challenges of global awareness underpinned by study abroad experiences, such as greater and more complex engagement with new technologies (Vichit-Vadakan, 2007). As earlier emphasized, while many of the high-earning career opportunities might include a global component, CUPUs are also charged with balancing profitable employment prospects for their graduates with meeting local needs. Their missions underscore preparing local students for viable careers that lead to palliating urban economic disparities, and also produce a social services workforce—urban teachers, social workers, nurses, day care practitioners, police force, emergency medical response teams—that strengthens the urban support network.

The tensions inherent in the sometimes competing goals of global and local agendas are persistent challenges CUPUs must learn to address. Gaffikin and Perry (2009) echo this concern within the larger mission of research universities by interrogating whether they will "further appropriate the language and culture of business and marketing and seek to 'brand' themselves globally as adaptive to dominant trends, particularly those that yield lucrative commercial return" or remain "faithful to a core educational mission, involving challenge to orthodoxy and the independent pursuit of knowledge, while deploying all the positive potential of transnational and intersectoral networking in the global age" (p. 138). Economic restructuring, spatial segregation, and urban poverty are often unintended urban challenges that are reinforced, rather than minimized, by globalization (Lin & Mele, 2005). To combat such social challenges, CUPUs may seek to counteract the negative outcomes of globalizing processes in their urban homes by engaging students in alternative networks that foster local commitments, without undermining the larger global awareness goal. In the next section, we detail the methodology we used to gain an understanding of those urban support networks for CUPU students.

A Context for Urban Life and Composite Case Studies

In the United States, over 38 million (12.6%) of people are immigrants, over 37 million are African-American, and 37 million (12.5%) live in poverty (U.S. Census Bureau, 2008). Over 58% of African Americans live in urban areas and 35 of the largest 50 cities are turning non-Hispanic whites into minorities (Asthana, 2006). Societal needs in urban areas—where low-income families are overly represented or standard English is not the main communication currency—continue to go unmet. Urban support networks, nonetheless, include specific characteristics necessary for many nontraditional students to succeed in CUPUs. Such characteristics ought to inform CUPUs in preparing future professionals who in turn remain committed to contributing to the urban infrastructure that supports nontraditional students in the completion of their education.

Case Study and Research Questions

Case studies enable researchers to examine in-depth one particular "bounded system" or situation over time. An instrumental case study is that in which researchers might preselect a case to gain insights on a larger issue (Stake, 1995). Often, researchers may select cases that reveal relationships which cannot be studied by other means (Yin, 2008). Given the intimate nature of information that can be documented during interviews and focus groups, a composite narrative grounded on theoretical sensitivity from various cases may be extracted and synthesized for the purpose of shedding light on larger phenomena. Theoretical sensitivity is a research process in which the analysis—meaning making—of the data collected is read through the particular experiences of both, researchers and participants (Strauss & Corbin, 1990). We came to this study not only as researchers but also as beneficiaries of past urban support networks, one Caucasian and one Latino; one who went through her studies as a young, single mother, and the other as an immigrant learning English.

The larger issue under review—how urban support networks may be impacted by CUPUs' impetus to globalize programs of study—was guided by the following research questions: (1) Given participants' previous higher education experiences, which are the support networks they deem most important to succeed in the completion of their degrees; and (2) how are those support networks enhanced or threatened by an emphasis on global outreach?

To shed light on such inquiry, we conducted a qualitative case study over a period of two years with 30 nontraditional, commuter urban students. All participants were pursuing their degrees at a CUPU. The foci of the data collection—through individual interviews and focus groups—were to understand participants' previous work and educational experiences, the supports needed to succeed while pursuing an education, their satisfaction with their programs, and their goals upon graduation.

From the transcripts, codes were identified first and emerging themes were discussed as they appeared. Three composite narrative case studies synthesizing experiences from various participants were delineated. The case study composites illustrated aspects of the work professionals such as early care and education practitioners, nurses, and social workers do on behalf of urban communities, support professions which were repeatedly cited by the study participants as intrinsically linked to their ability to attend college. The case study composites were further discussed and refined with the participants during focus groups, to ascertain their credibility and representativeness. During focus groups, the roles and usages of technology as an alternative to develop and maintain global awareness to enhance local commitments were also group-explored.

Investigator triangulation (that in which researchers with different viewpoints examine the same results) was the selected technique for

inherent good karma of adopting a complicated, likely damaged
g adolescent. After all, one of the kids she must find a permanent
ly for used to live on our block. The notion that the social worker's
can tip the balance in favor of such child helps palliate our neighbor-
od's own sense of guilt for not having been the vigilant community we
ould have been for that kid.

How do these case studies fare when balancing commitment to global
or local communities? From focus groups discussions with the participants, interesting theories regarding the globalization of university preparation emerged. They are summarized in the composite narratives that
follow.

Focus Groups Outcomes

In a globally aware age and with ground-breaking training, the early care
and education practitioner caring for young toddlers may be tempted
to extend the toddlers' naptime so that she can finish blogging to save
Darfur. An extra 30 minutes of toddler sleep will help her contribute to
the better world she now envisions. She has been trained to be a global
citizen, to keep abreast of change and social justice in the world. Why to
spend that precious nap hour sanitizing the toys toddlers salivate on with
a vengeance? The toddlers cannot tell the difference anyway. In some
regions of the globe, it is believed, such exchange promotes healthy anti-
body buildup.

The young male nurse takes part of a volunteers' network that sends
him periodically to train rural nurse aids south of the border. He contributes to helping such communities develop best practices to caring for the
elderly. Meanwhile, the Alzheimer's disease patients he cares for back
home grow both agitated and despondent. Like children, the elderly grow
fond of and dependent upon their caretakers and crave continuity. The
revolving door of the nursing profession eventually takes its toll on the
old man. As grandfather's nurse takes a humanitarian ride on the coils of
globalization for a healthier world, grandfather takes his final ride into
oblivion.

What about a science-fiction forecast on the social worker? Stimulus
funds allow the Department of Health and Human Services to provide
young adolescents under its guard with fancy digital communication
devices. The social worker can finally reduce the number of face-to-face
visits to those with whom now she can communicate daily via digital
means and clean up the case-load backlog on her desk. She now even has
time to design and maintain a wiki. Through the wiki, she shares culturally sensitive strategies to palliate the cycle of generational abuse within
families with social workers in Arab countries, exchanges daily tips with
peers around the world, and finds her role in life as having worldwide
reach. The suburban teen in her care has blossomed in both, an innocent

further scrutinizing the data collected (Den.
by the authors/researchers and an additional
peting theoretical perspectives on the aims o.
friend, "regardless of status or role, is expecte
achieve a critical perspective even though this n
mal assumptions underlying the researcher's wor
&Whitehead, 1996, p. 85). The narrative composites
follow in the next section.

Three Case Study Composites

Case Study I

The early care and education practitioner who cares for my toddl
I work: I want her attentive, child-centered, not burdened by co.
from the outside world. In fact, I yearn for her eyes, mind, and soul s.
implicated in meeting my toddler's needs, aware of which toy and bo
to provide that are developmentally appropriate. I need her sound ped.
gogical knowledge to plan activities that facilitate learning as toddlers
grow in strength, curiosity, dexterity, and social awareness. I cringe at the
thought that most of my toddler's milestones I've missed while at work.
Yet, I vicariously re-live them through the oral reports from the teacher
at pickup time.

Case Study II

The nurse who cares for patients with advanced Alzheimer: That strong
man who once upon a time taught my husband in his early adolescence to
build brick walls. He now waves goodbye, without remembering who my
husband is, gently kept upright and aided in his balance by a much stronger, young male nurse. We need this young male nurse to assist grandpa
in the shower, to ensure his medicines and meals are administered timely
and properly, to intervene skillfully and rapidly should grandpa's many
health problems turn critical. We want him gentle, sensitive, focused in
spite of the repetitiousness of his work, willing to indulge the old man
grand story-telling. Smiling when he tucks grandpa in bed is a plus.

Case Study III

The social worker who monitors the foster-home lives of young, physically abused teenagers: Not only me, but the community as a whole needs
her to pay periodic visits to the teens, to exert that sixth sense for early
identification of expected collateral problems. The community relies on
her working 24/7 to find those children a final destination they can call
a family. We will into her car salesman's skills to convince good families

facial expression in his daily phone video reports, and the art of keeping his mouth shut regarding ill-informed choices that sooner than later will land him in juvenile court.

As the composite narratives reveal, the participants expressed a collective fear of globalization as further marginalizing those with fewer means, and did not take into consideration how globalization also produces transnational elites in those same urban conglomerates (Short, 2002). Students seeking to earn degrees for the kinds of physically, time-intensive, and low-paid careers depicted in the composite case studies are a sizable part of a CUPU's constituency. Confronting their understandings of the potential effects of globalization in their chosen careers—as well as on support networks which allow them to attend college—brings attention to Leipziger and Spence's (2007) argument that "the globalization debate tends to (and sometimes is designed to) draw attention away from domestic policy challenges." CUPUs very survival, particularly when in proximity to private university powerhouses, appears to be linked to their maintenance, enhancement, and reinvigoration of the urban support network.

Global Education's Impact on the Urban Support Network

For space limitation reasons, we center our efforts on further reflecting on one of the case study composites, that of the globally aware early care and education urban teacher. How might she benefit from a global education in ways that add, rather than detract, from her commitments to local, diverse children? Programs in early care teacher education are often limited by a Western perspective on young children's development and needs (Göncü, Özer, & Ahioglu, 2009). Nsamenang (2008) emphasizes how different sets of beliefs worldwide impact the definition of what constitutes childhood, which curricula must be afforded to young children, and how competent citizenship is encouraged within a wide range of varying children's circumstances. Even within the United States, teachers of children aged 3–5 may be exposed to different types of early childhood education depending upon competing agencies and policies that regulate standards for teachers in public schools and non-public school settings (Abbate-Vaughn, Paugh, & Douglass 2011). The notion of quality in early care and education is also contested terrain. As Dahlberg, Moss, and Pence (2007) argue, quality

> cannot be conceptualized to accommodate complexity, values, diversity, subjectivity, multiple perspectives, and other features of a world understood to be both uncertain and diverse. The "problem with quality" cannot be addressed by struggling to reconstruct the concept in ways it was never intended to go.

(p. 105)

While a quality sensory learning experience for young children in a developing country may include digging in soil to discover insects and other little creatures, such experiences may be strictly forbidden by policies in other countries due to health and safety (both culturally informed) concerns.

Given such myriad conceptions of childhood and quality care across cultures, and of policies regulating the field, Super and Harkness (2008) question how the arguably bounded discipline of early care and education can contribute to building a worldwide accepted type of science above cultural boundaries, and ponder where the paradigmatic explosion might lead the field. Yet, a comprehensive exposure to such paradigmatic differences might greatly contribute to developing globally aware urban early care teachers. Such global urban practitioners might utilize technologies in their reach to better understand immigrant children's milestones in the context of their native cultures. For instance, in countries where the price of disposable diapers is prohibitive, children are toilet trained successfully much earlier than their American counterparts (Gonzalez-Mena, 2007). Early childhood teachers might develop a curiosity for familiarizing themselves with the child-rearing beliefs of families whose children are in their charge; or to communicate via Skype with early care professionals from the young children's countries of origin to learn what experiences such children might have had in their previous out-of-home care. Urban early care educators might join one of the many online communities to expand their understanding of diverse children (Education in Developing Countries, or The Global Education Collaborative are examples of Ning online social networks). They might exchange insights on the adaptation of immigrant children with their across-the-world counterparts. In deepening her understanding of early childhood in a global context, the toddlers' teacher in the case study might realize that the problems affecting her workplace related to state policies, transitions and school readiness, and accessibility, are worldwide problems in the field (Neuman, 2005).

While benefiting from global vigilance, such problems truly require committed local activism. The mosaic of histories, cultures, and languages in metropolitan conglomerates presents opportunities to re-conceptualize locality and globalization. CUPUs face a unique opportunity to "shape globalization" (Ruby, 2005) in ways that meet their traditional local roles and their emerging goals as members of larger global communities. To do so, they need to understand the forces already in place that transform the ways people learn and negotiate present and future roles, taking active roles in the processes of homogenization and hybridization of cultures and discipline-based discourses (Zajda, 2006).

Conclusion

CUPUs which offer an array of degrees confront the dichotomies of mastering the ride of the global wave while still meeting the increasingly diverse needs of their very local communities. As with other public universities, CUPUs also face the typical pressures higher education institutions must overcome: decaying financial support from the state coffers and the need for increased enrollments and revenue. By serving nontraditional students, whose attrition rates are high and who take longer to graduate, CUPUs must provide a much wider array of academic, financial, and counseling supports as well as reading and study strategy courses (Abbate-Vaughn, 2009; Astin, 2005–2006; Maehl, 2000).

The promise of quick growth by way of online degrees lurks in every urban university power corner office. The temptation to attract middle and upper-middle class international constituencies who pay higher tuition rates can be a powerful argument for internationalizing curricula and aggressively recruiting abroad, in a move that attracts to the United States well-over 600,000 students per year (Open Doors Online, 2008). While some institutions willingly climb onto the magic carpet of globalization, CUPUs ought to hold tight to their intended local missions.

The 21st century global citizen needs awareness of and empathy for difference, so sustained experiences studying abroad top the popularity list. Yet, if diversity awareness or empathy for difference are the goals, they may successfully be achieved by volunteering a semester at a public school in the South Bronx, East St. Louis, or near the Rio Grande border; or helping to rebuild the neighborhoods ravaged by Katrina in New Orleans, getting to know the dreams and hopes of the surviving displaced citizens of below sea-level. This is just the tradition of engaged, service-learning experiences many CUPUs have long promoted, the know-thy-neighbor approach to global diversity education. In a great balancing act, CUPUs must learn to cope with the unavoidable forces of globalization, without undermining their commitments to the local and regional communities that count on them to improve the lives of America's very diverse social fabric. As Gardner (2004) puts it: "While the gradual change of educational institutions can readily be justified, we must also ask what can, and should, happen to educational institutions when dramatic alterations take place in the ambient society" (p. 2).

References

Abbate-Vaughn, Jorgelina. (2009). Addressing diversity. In Rona Flippo and David Caverly (Eds.), *Handbook of College Reading and Study Strategy*, 2nd Edition (pp. 289–313). New York: Routledge.

Abbate-Vaughn, Jorgelina, Paugh, Patricia, & Douglass, Anne. (2011, in press). Sound bites won't prepare the next generation: Early childhood teacher education policy's public-private divide. *Educational Policy* 25(1).

Asthana, Anushka. (2006, August 21). Changing face of Western cities: Migration within U.S. makes whites a minority in 3 more areas. *The Washington Post*. Retrieved December 29, 2009, from http://www.washingtonpost.com/wp-dyn/content/article/2006/08/20/AR2006082000629.html.

Astin, Alexander W. (2005–2006). Making sense out of degree completion rates. *Journal of College Student Retention: Research, Theory & Practice*, 7(1–2), 5–18.

Athens State University. (2006). *An environment for learning.* Retrieved February 11, 2010, from http://www.athens.edu/about/index.php

Carlisle, Lenore R., Jackson, Bailey W., & George, Allison. (2006). Principles of social justice education: The social justice education in school projects. *Equity and Excellence in Education* 39(1), 55–64.

City University of New York. (2010). *Chancellor's message mission.* Retrieved September 7, 2010, from http://cuny.edu/about/index.html

Council of the Great City Schools. (n.d.). *Fact sheet.* Retrieved December 27, 2009, from http://cgcs.org/about/fact_sheet.aspx

Coalition of Urban Serving Universities. (2008). Quick facts. Retrieved December 1, 2008, from http://www.usucoalition.org/about/quickfacts.html

Dahlberg, Gunilla, Moss, Peter, & Pence, Allan. (2007). *Beyond quality in early education and care: Languages of evaluation,* 2nd edition. London: Falmer Press.

Denzin, Norman. (1984). *The research act.* Englewood Cliffs, NJ: Prentice Hall.

Dugan, John P., Garland, John L., Jacoby, Barbara, & Gasiorski, Anna. (2008). Understanding commuter student self-efficacy for leadership: Within-group analysis. *NASAP Journal, 45*(2), 282–310. Washington DC: National Association of Student Personnel Administrators.

Florida International University. (2010). *About FIU.* Retrieved December 27, 2009, from http://www.fiu.edu/docs/about_fiu.htm.

Gaffikin, Frank, & Perry, David C. (2009). Discourses and strategic visions: The U.S. research university as an institutional manifestation of neoliberalism in a global era. *American Educational Research Journal* 46(1), 115–144.

Gardner, Howard. (2004). How education changes: Considerations of history, science, and values. In M. Suarez-Orozco, & D. Qin-Hilliard (Eds.), *Globalization: Culture and education in the new millennium,* pp. 235–258. Berkeley: University of California Press. Retrieved February 11, 2010, from http://pzweb.harvard.edu/PIs/HG_HowEducationChanges.pdf

Göncü, Artin, Özer, Serap, & Ahioglu, Nihal. (2009). Childhoods in Turkey: Social class and gender differences in schooling, labor, and play. In M. Fleer, M. Hedegaard, & J. Tudge (Eds.), *World Yearbook of Education 2009—Childhood studies and the impact of globalization: Policies and practices at global and local levels.* New York: Routledge.

Gonzalez-Mena, Janet. (2007). *Diversity in early care and Education: Honoring differences.* Columbus, OH: McGraw-Hill.

Goodman, Roger. (2009). Global recession and universities: Funding strains to keep up with rising demand. Special Comment. *Moody's International Public Finance.* Higher Education. Retrieved December 27, 2009, from http://global-highered.files.wordpress.com/2009/07/s-globrecess-univ-6-09.pdf

Horn, Laura, & Nevill, Stephanie. (2006). *Profile of Undergraduates in U.S. Postsecondary Education Institutions: 2003–04: With a Special Analysis of Community College Students* (NCES 2006–184). U.S. Department of Education. Washington DC: National center for Education Statistics.U.S. Department of Education. Washington DC: National Center for Education Statistics. Retrieved December 28, 2009, from http://nces.ed.gov/pubsearch/pubsinfo.asp?pubid = 2006184.

Leipziger, Daniel, & Spence, Michael. (2007, May 15). Globalization's losers need support. *Financial Times*. Retrieved February 11, 2010, from http://www.growthcommission.org/storage/cgdev/documents/articles/FT%20Mike%20and%20Danny.pdf

Leventhal, Mitch, & Zimpher, Nancy. (2007). Changing international constructs: How metropolitan universities must engage globally. *Metropolitan Universities: An International Forum*, 18(3), 102–108.

Lin, Jan and Mele, Christopher. (Eds.) (2005). *The urban sociology reader*. New York: Routledge.

McNiff, J., Lomax, P., & Whitehead, J. (1996). *You and your action research project*. London: Routledge.

Maehl, William H. (2000). *Lifelong learning at its best: Innovative practices in adult credit programs*. San Francisco: Jossey-Bass.

Moreno-Brid, Juan Carlos, & Ruiz-Napoles, Pablo. (2007). *Public research universities in Latin America and their relationship to economic development*. Social Science Research Council-United Nations. Retrieved February 11, 2009, from http://www.ideaswebsite.org/featart/may2007/Latin_America.pdf

Motley, Keith. (2008, September 8). *The public university: Facing challenges as a new frontier*. Retrieved February 11, 2009, from http://www.umb.edu/chancellor/2008_motley/speeches/2008_convocation.html.

NAFSA. (2007). An international education policy for US leadership, competitiveness, and security. Washington DC: Author. Retrieved March 29, 2009, from http://www.nafsa.org/_/File/_/neip_rev.pdf.

NASULGC. (2007). *A national agenda for internationalizing higher education*. Washington, DC: NASULGC-A Public University Association. Retrieved March 30, 2009, from https://www.aplu.org/NetCommunity/Document. Doc?id = 471

Neuman, Michelle J. (2005). Global early care and education: Challenges, responses, and lessons. *Phi Delta Kappan*, 87(3), 188–192.

Noddings, Nel. (2005). What have we learned? In Noddings, N. (Ed.), *Educating citizens for global awareness* (pp. 122–140). New York: Teachers College Press.

Nsamenang, A. Bame. (2008). Culture and human development. *International Journal of Psychology*, 43(2), 73–77.

Open Doors Online. (2008). Report on international educational exchange. Retrieved May 20, 2009, from http://opendoors.iienetwork.org/.

Robertson, Roland. (1995). *Glocalization: Time-space, homogeneity-heterogeneity*. London: Sage.

Rondinelli, Dennis, Johnson, James, & Kasarda, John. (1998). The changing forces of urban economic development: Globalization and city competitiveness in the 21st century. *Cityscape: A Journal of Policy Development and Research*, 3(3), 71–105.

Ruby, Alan. (2005). Reshaping the university in an era of globalization. *Phi Delta Kappan*, 87(3), 233–237.

Short, John R. (2002). Black holes and loose connections in the global urban network. *Research Bulletin 76: Globalization and World Cities Study Group Network*. Alexandria, VA: Metropolitan Institute at Virginia Tech. Retrieved February 11, 2010, from http://www.mi.vt.edu/Research/WorldCities/Analyses/Mega.pdf.

Stake, Robert E. (1995). *The art of case study research.* Thousand Oaks, CA: Sage.

Stearns, Peter N. (2008). *Educating global citizens in colleges and universities: Challenges and opportunities.* New York: Routledge.

Strauss, Anselm, and Corbin, Juliette. (1990). *Basics of qualitative research: Grounded theory procedures and techniques.* Sage Publications.

Super, Charles M., & Harkness, Sara. (2008). Globalization and its discontents: Challenge to developmental theory and practice in Africa. *International Journal of Psychology, 43*(2), 107–113.

Stukel, James J. (1994). The urban university attacks real urban issues. *Government Finance Review, 21,* 19–21.

Toynbee, Arnold. (1948). *Civilization on trial.* Oxford: Oxford University Press.

University of the District of Columbia. (n.d.). Mission: Responsibilities of the university. Retrieved February 11, 2010, from http://www.udc.edu/welcome/mission.htm

Urban Universities Portfolio Project. (n.d.). *Defining characteristics of urban public universities.* Retrieved February 11, 2009 from http://www.imir.iupui.edu/portfolio/characteristics.htm.

U.S. Census Bureau. (2008). Poverty. Retrieved February 11, 2009, from http://www.census.gov/hhes/www/poverty/overview.html

U.S. News & World Report. (2010a). *Best colleges: Most campus commuters.* Retrieved February 11, 2010, from http://colleges.usnews.rankingsandreviews.com/best-colleges/most-off-campus

U.S. News & World Report. (2010b). *Best colleges: Most students over age 25.* Retrieved February 11, 2010, from http://colleges.usnews.rankingsandreviews.com/best-colleges/most-over-25

U.S. News & World Report. (2010c). *Best colleges: Most students studying abroad.* Retrieved February 11, 2010, from http://colleges.usnews.rankingsandreviews.com/best-colleges/most-study-abroad

U.S. News & World Report. (2009). *Best colleges: Economic diversity-national universities.* Retrieved February 11, 2010, from http://colleges.usnews.rankingsandreviews.com/best-colleges/national-economic-diversity

Vichit-Vadakan, Juree. (2007). Reflections on university and urban public university. *Metropolitan Universities: An international forum, 18*(3), 109–118.

Yin, Robert K. (2008). *Case study research: Design and methods* (4th edition). Thousand Oaks, CA: SAGE Publications.

Zajda, Joseph. (Ed.) (2006). *International handbook of globalization, education and policy research.* Norwell, MA: Kluwer Academic Publishers.

9   Australian Universities and the Challenges of Internationalization

Anne Hickling-Hudson and Ravinder Sidhu

Introduction

Recent media reports have drawn attention to demonstrations by Indian students in Australia protesting against acts of violence perceived in their eyes to be motivated by racism. The worldwide dissemination of these mediascapes has galvanized the Australian government to intervene, its actions highlighting the maneuverings of a "competition state" (Cerny, 1997) keen to protect its multi-billion dollar education export industry and Australia's reputation as a safe study destination. A public diplomacy initiative was undertaken to promote a counternarrative of good news stories concerning Indian students in Australia (AEI, 2009). Amidst raging debates as to whether the attacks were unfortunate episodes of urban violence or, as many of the protesters claimed, racial violence, this latest crisis in Australia's international education industry has drawn attention to the issue of international student security and the adequacy of regulatory policies and practices.

In a little over 20 years, Australia has succeeded in developing an industry in international education worth $15.5 billion Australian dollars (ABS, 2009). The case for the education industry's success is usually made with reference to this figure, however, this perspective obscures two key factors; first, that education institutions receive only one-third of this $15.5 billion (ABS, 2009), and second, that the costs of teaching and supporting international students is not insignificant and should be factored in discussions of international education's profitability. Nonetheless, the economic rationale for internationalizing the student body has remained important for Australia's universities to help them cope with the burden of underfunding by the state. The Organization for Economic Cooperation and Development (OECD) estimates that in the decade from 1995 to 2005 public funding per student fell by 28% in real terms (Marginson, 2009). Economic rationales aside, Australian universities are also driven by academic and cultural rationales to build an international profile, to engage with the broader global community of scholars, and to produce graduates with global competencies.

The internationalization of universities is understood as the "integration of an international, intercultural or global dimension into the teaching, research and service functions of the university" (Knight, 2003). Turner and Robson (2008) have identified ten themes that capture internationalization's multidimensionality: international engagement, mobility, revenues, international professionals, communication, knowledge-sharing, language policy and practice, programming and curriculum, academic practices, and reciprocity/"Westernization."

Our chapter examines the internationalization challenges faced by Australia's universities, and explores how two of these themes—curriculum and mobility—are understood by academics that we interviewed in two case study universities. We selected these two universities of the five comprising the Australian Technology Network (ATN) group because of the close involvement of the authors with them and because they are favored by significant numbers of domestic and international students. Together, the ATN universities attract 20% of Australia's domestic student population and 25% of international students (Australian Technology Network of Universities, 2009). Our primary focus in this chapter is on teacher education, although university-wide programs designed to further internationalization will also be discussed.

Our research approach is a qualitative analysis of institutional policy and university marketing discourse and of interviews with academic and administrative staff at the two case study universities, which we refer to as Alpha and Beta. With a small number of interviewees, we do not make claims about the generalizability of their views. Rather, in the manner of qualitative research, the interviews provide useful insights into the universities' internationalization practices and suggest questions that may be relevant to universities more generally.

The chapter is structured as follows: In Section 1, we discuss the rise of the education export industry and the variety of programs which came to constitute international education. Section 2 examines the internationalization of university missions and academic practices in two universities within the ATN, highlighting the strengths and limitations of existing approaches. Section 3 proposes a series of changes that would enable a new model for the international university; one which would play a bigger part in addressing global inequalities; and in doing so, further a more ethical globalization for the 21st century.

We discuss these themes with reference to Bartell's (2003) continuum of internationalization, which ranges from the "symbolic" to the "transformative" (Turner & Robson, 2008). A symbolic orientation to internationalization exists when a university is steeped in the national culture despite having a proportion of overseas students and staff. At the other end of the scale, a transformative orientation characterizes a university which has embedded an international way of thinking in most or all of its dimensions. The device of a continuum allows us to consider the postcolonial query of how far contemporary university education, substantially shaped by its role as a carrier of imperial ideas and introduced to many countries through European colonialism (Hudson, 1977, Scott, 1995), is likely to carry out its globalizing vision.

Section 1. International Education in Australia: Marketization and the Formation of a Higher Education Export Industry

The first significant presence of international students in Australian universities can be traced to the Colombo Plan, an educational aid program formulated during the Cold War era. The Colombo Plan was a "gift" intended to establish affiliations and affinities between Australia and the local elites and burgeoning middle classes in the decolonized world (Alexander & Rizvi, 1993; Sidhu, 2006).

In the latter half of the 1980s, market-driven policies were introduced to transform Australia from a heavily protected economy reliant mainly on mineral and agricultural commodities, to one that embraced knowledge-intensive services. The foundation was thus laid for an education export industry that would respond to a globalizing economy. Australian higher education institutions were assisted by the federal government to develop marketing plans to recruit fee-paying international students, and were allowed to retain a proportion of their income. Public universities, which were attended by over 98% of domestic students (Marginson, 2006), grew increasingly reliant on income from international student fees as their operating budgets were reduced by governments of all political persuasions, part of a broader policy to steer the public sector towards the market.

The marketization of international education is noted for its success in building an export industry for Australia, creating employment, and increasing Australia's visibility particularly in the Asia-Pacific region. Unlike public universities in the United States which do not distinguish between out-of-state American and foreign students in their fee structures, Australian universities levy significantly higher fees on international students compared to domestic students. This has provided much needed income for universities at a time of reduced government support, but it has also led to criticisms about the tendency to view these students as "cash cows."

Market-driven internationalization has also seen a closer and potentially problematic link between higher education and migration. In 2001, to make Australian education more attractive globally, Australia's international education industry was articulated with its skilled migration program. International students, who graduated from Australian higher education institutions, including vocational colleges, could now apply for Permanent Residency under the General Skilled Migration program (Birrell, Hawthorne, & Richardson, 2006). This policy has had several effects, some unintended. One is the proliferation of private higher education institutions supported by student fees. Some of these are of unreliable quality and standing, particularly in the vocational fields (ABC, 2009). Another effect is that the policy has attracted some students for whom education is of secondary importance, their primary goal being to achieve permanent residency. Many students, particularly in the vocational college sector, have borrowed heavily to come to Australia to study and work, with work taking precedence in many cases. Some take poorly paid jobs and live in spaces which are often riven with poverty, racism, and crime. In the bid to gain greater market share in the broader global education market, Australia's transformation of international education from an elite to a mass institution, in a context of limited educational aid and inadequate controls on the quality of private institutions, has exposed many students to conditions that compromise their economic and social welfare.

Even in the relatively high-status university sector, limitations in government funding have steered many institutions to emphasize raising revenue ahead of the pastoral care and education of international students. It is in these contexts that the recent difficulties experienced by some Indian students must be understood; although it should be noted that in a recent survey of 6,000 students from eight countries, including India, Australia was rated by a large margin as the safest country compared to other English-speaking destinations in which to study (Herbert, 2009).

Different Dimensions of International Education in Australian Universities

International Students Onshore

Australian international education, unlike the U.S. model, is dominated by the recruitment of international students in undergraduate campus-based degree programs within Australia. American universities by contrast seek to recruit postgraduate students in order to both secure a low-cost research and teaching workforce and maintain numbers in the Science, Technology, Engineering & Mathematics (STEM) fields, which are undersubscribed by U.S.-born students (NCES, 2009). Although Australia has been successful in capitalizing on the global demand for English language based education, the U.S. "attracts the lion's share of the highest achieving students" (Marginson, 2009). The United States also provides scholarships, fellowships, and teaching assistantships for a quarter of its international students, whereas Australia in 2002 was providing only one scholarship for every 66 full fee-paying students (Marginson, 2006).

Offshore Programs: Twinning, Franchising, and the Overseas Campus

In twinning programs, students complete two years of a preapproved Australian curriculum with the partner institution, and finish the degree at the home campus in Australia. The Australian university controls the curriculum and is responsible for quality assurance. Franchising takes place when an Australian university outsources its curriculum to be delivered by a foreign partner university, which retains control over the programs and assessment.

Not many Australian universities have established overseas branches because of the high costs involved and the difficulties in navigating national regulations. Monash University has branches in Malaysia and South Africa. Of the ATN universities, RMIT University has a campus in Vietnam, and Curtin University of Technology has an East Malaysian branch.

Evaluating these offshore programs would necessitate asking how far this aspect of internationalization is influenced by assumptions of the inevitability of the global spread of Western education content, practices, and beliefs. This assumption obviously cannot imply an equal or negotiated intellectual space, and obscures important geo-political issues of power (Turner & Robson, 2008).

Internationalizing Curriculum Content

Universities in countries of the global "North" are faced with a complex task in internationalizing curriculum content. This would entail restructuring a traditionally white-dominant, Western curriculum in such a way that it is based on global knowledges, philosophies, and ethics (Singh, 1998; Hickling-Hudson, 2004). In Australia, the curriculum would have to meet the overlapping needs of clearly defined groups: Indigenous Australians, Anglo-Australians, migrants from non-British backgrounds (the largest numbers of these come from continental Europe, Asia, and the Pacific), refugees (currently coming largely from the Middle East and Africa), and short-stay international students. Curriculum change has started to move in a direction that addresses these complexities, and most universities have professional development strategies that give some support to academics who choose to embark on such change (Gesche & Makeham, 2008). However, this process is still at an early stage; it is often neither cohesive nor consistent, and not all disciplines have embraced it.

Study Abroad and Exchange Programs

Most Australian universities encourage and administer study abroad and exchange programs, seeing this as part of the internationalization of the curriculum. Students largely fund their overseas experience with only very limited financial assistance from the university. This suggests that universities regard it as a "private good" accruing benefits to individual students. We argue that the overseas study experience should be reconceptualized as a public good that contributes to the education of professionals with global competencies who are able to operate in different cultural and social settings. With the exception of language studies majors, Australian students are more likely to travel to English-speaking countries, particularly the United Kingdom and North America, which limits their opportunity to experience cultures other than British-derived ones. Some universities do encourage and support their international students to carry out at least one work placement in their home countries.

Section 2. Interrogating Internationalist Missions and Academic Practices

In the early 1990s, as part of federal government reform, all of Australia's Institutes of Technology, teachers' colleges, and various other specialist vocational institutions were merged to become universities. Adopting the name Universities of Technology, they focus on teaching those disciplines with a vocational orientation (such as engineering, business, teaching, law, public health, creative industries) and highlight work-relevant learning as an institutional strength. The forerunner institutions of our two case studies, which we refer to as Alpha and Beta Universities, included vocational colleges, most of which were established in the 19th century, and teachers' colleges, established in the 20th century.

Internationalist Missions and Networking

The Australian Technology Network of five universities, a grouping within Australia's 37 universities,[1] carries out benchmarking in several areas of internationalization, including the attrition rates of international students and their language proficiency, recruitment costs, staffing levels in international offices, and quality issues in offshore delivery. It is noteworthy that the type of institutionalized collaboration that takes place between members of the group concerns the administrative aspects of internationalization rather than the academic concerns. The ATN group engages with national bodies concerned with policy development of cross border education. Member universities are also collaborating to market the ATN as a "brand" in North America, Europe, and Southeast and North Asia (Administrator 1, personal communication, July 8, 2009). About 15,500 students are studying Education across the five universities, making the network a key supplier of the nation's teachers (Australian Technology Network of Universities, 2009).

Beta University, with international students comprising some 30% of its student body, frames its internationalist vision in the area of teaching and learning as providing students with a "global passport" to learning and working in an "open-world economy." The passport metaphor is instructive: passports have a differential capacity to facilitate border crossings. The use of this metaphor, along with the university's emphasis on the "global portability" of its degrees, suggests an institutional desire to construct global acceptance of its credentials, thus enhancing their students' cross border employability. Such a globally portable graduate, it can be argued, should possess intercultural adaptabilities, as well as professional skills which take into account the needs of different societies, cultures, communities, and ecologies (Patrick, 1997). Underpinning this promotional message then is an implicit claim that Beta's graduates have experienced an education that engages with diverse and multiple perspectives. However, it must be asked how far and how consistently this occurs. Our discussion on the internationalization of academic practices at Beta suggests that some of Beta's staff see these efforts as fragmented, uneven, and subordinated to commercial imperatives. We cannot assume then, that Beta's globally portable graduates armed with global passports will alleviate the cultural hegemony that continues to informs much of what is claimed to be an "international education" (Bagnall, 2004).

Alpha University, with some 16% international students, describes itself as "an international university based in Australia" and like Beta, straddles the global and national:

> [Alpha] is strongly committed to internationalization. We think of ourselves as an international university based in Australia rather than an Australian university with international students. This is a very important vision for us because it goes to the core of our mission as a university, which is to produce graduates with the skills and abilities to work anywhere in the world.
>
> (Administrator 1, interviewed July 8, 2009)

In this vignette, we see a discursive attempt by Alpha to break from a model of internationalization, which privileges international student recruitment to one that focuses on producing globally portable graduates. However, in a vastly unequal world, where the English-speaking metropolitan countries continue to enjoy hegemonic power, the claim of producing globally portable graduates does not in itself suggest a transformative educational agenda. Similarly, while Alpha portrays international students as "enhancing cultural and social diversity," its public statements do not make it clear how its academic practices and institutional mission engage with this diversity. The institution also highlights the international experience of its staff and their engagement with the broader international community of scholars but is short on details as to how its international engagements might address some of the pressing global problems of decolonizing countries in the Asia-Pacific region. As at Beta, staff interviewed at Alpha suggested that, while progress is being made, they would like to see the university achieve more in all of these areas outlined in the profile statements.

How the Curriculum for Student Teachers Addresses Diversity

Academic interviewees in our case study universities[2] criticized the internationalization of the curriculum for its unevenness, both across the various departments, and within them: "In some programs there are a few academics doing good stuff towards internationalization. In other programs there is no focus. The attitude is that there's no need to change a national or domestic focus" (Academic 4, interviewed June 22, 2009).

Teacher education was regarded as one of the areas in which international studies were not consistently embedded. While teacher education mission statements express a commitment to preparing teachers to teach for cultural diversity, the focus is on diversity within the Australian rather than the global context. Teacher preparation about global and international issues is not embedded in the curriculum as a core aspect of study, but is left at an elective level.

The universities have undoubtedly made some advances compared to teacher education programs they offered in the 1990s where Australian diversity studies were mostly not compulsory, and if offered, were confined to an elective or two (Hickling-Hudson & McMeniman, 1996). Alpha University now requires all student teachers to undertake a first-year compulsory unit concerned with understanding Indigenous educational issues, in particular, the cultural context that gives rise to racism in all its forms. However, without follow-up subjects, students are left with insufficient knowledge and skills to inspire confidence that they can work effectively in the areas of Indigenous and/or multicultural education. Examples like this, and small numbers of students choosing diversity-centered elective subjects, highlight limitations in the Education degree's capacity to prepare teachers for diversity. Claims made by Alpha's Department of Education of successful intercultural and international preparation of teacher education graduates were met with indignation:

> I mean, for our [supervisor] to write in the report that we've embedded Indigenous knowledges, that we've embedded sustainability, we've embedded internationalization—we have not! We have *not!*. . . . Just because people write words on paper doesn't mean a single thing.
>
> (Academic 1, interviewed June 29, 2009)

Reflecting on why so many student teachers could reach their final year with little knowledge of issues of diversity and their links to broader global and national inequalities, both academics interviewed at Alpha University emphasized the fragmentation and lack of cohesion within the teacher education curriculum:

> It's the way our units [subjects] are structured. They are not cohesive. Students are highly impressed and ready to go. . . . to engage with the

concepts taught in Indigenous education [in Year 1]. By their third year, they've forgotten it. . . . They don't get anything else. It's what I'm saying, that it isn't embedded. It's in the literature, it's in [our university's] policy, but no one enforces it.

(Academic 1, interviewed June 29, 2009)

Academic 2 indicated "Diversity education in our undergraduate (B.Ed.) program is minimal. It's unsystematic. It happens in only a few subjects, and most of them are electives" (Academic 2, interviewed July 17, 2009).

At Beta University, our interviewee, a supervisor in the Education department, was more positive about the preparation given to student teachers to enable them to engage with diversity and develop culturally responsive teaching skills. Student teachers are required to complete a compulsory subject on the educational implications of diversity and difference. In addition, the broader Education curriculum is seen to promote social inclusion and respect for diversity. This academic said that in teacher preparation:

Multiculturalism is taken for granted, given the diversity of the community that the university is situated in. The issues arise all the time whether it's in inclusive education, or diversity and difference, or understanding the learner, or orientation to teaching. Whenever those issues are addressed in any subject, the multicultural side of our society is taken into account.

(Academic 3, interviewed July 2, 2009)

However, other academic interviewees at Beta University held the view that its preparation of student teachers was Australia-focused and hardly international. They attributed what they saw as the parochial character of teacher education programs to the localist vision of the state education bureaucracy including an implicit desire to guard against "brain drain":

The traditional role [of teachers] is seen as preparing local students in local schools. But many young people have a wider view of the world than that, and want to study global issues. With changing global times, teacher education should start with a global approach. Students should be told that their qualification will be global. But I think that the State Education department would see this as promoting the threat of a brain drain. They want teachers to stay and work here.

(Academic 4, interviewed June 22, 2009)

There are significant pedagogical challenges associated with engaging with classroom diversity, promoting intercultural learning, and maximizing learning for all students in a respectful and friendly environment. This was highlighted by Academic 2 at Alpha University who spoke about her experiences in the master's program in TESOL (the teaching of English to speakers of other languages), a popular course with Education professionals from overseas. The program has enrolled increasingly fewer Australian students, who find the course too expensive, and the end result is that student composition is skewed in favor of international students who might constitute up to 70% of classes. As one academic observed "It's purely because the university keeps putting the fees up. So domestic students say they can't afford it, and they go online where they can do it cheaper. So we've got a different dynamic. This creates tensions. . . ."(Academic 2, interviewed July 17, 2009).

Some Australian students were impatient with the halting English of international students, and felt too much time was given to addressing their needs. Others responded well, volunteering over two hours a week to help the overseas students improve their English, thus establishing international connections and friendships which usually proved to be of lasting value to both sides.

As regards to curriculum, the TESOL program was seen to be well-conceptualized, taking cultural diversity seriously in terms of pedagogy and content. Intersections between language, culture, and gender were carefully theorized using a socio-linguistics and critical literacy approach.

> We look at issues like global Englishes and English with an accent and tensions between native and non-native speakers. We engage with the politics of it . . . We do a reasonable job in terms of not presenting a one-way transmission model of our version of the world; we go a reasonable way towards building on the students' knowledges and trying to make it dialogic and trying not to always use Eurocentric examples and Western examples of things . . . We have a critical orientation in TESOL, which starts out from the premise of let's theorize culture, and let's theorize language, and let's take an intercultural approach. . . .
>
> (Academic 2, interviewed July 17, 2009).

The TESOL degree program receives high ratings from international students, with students responding very well to the critical approach adopted by the curriculum. Many had been schooled and socialized within a functionalist curriculum of linguistics and grammar-based education. Their undergraduate degrees in language had "never theorized culture or gender and they've never theorized anything from a social stance. They love the new approach . . . they take to it enormously . . . We talk with them about culture and the nature of it, and deconstruct all those monolithic ideas . . ." (Academic 2, interviewed July 17, 2009).

Mobility: Domestic Students and Teaching Practice

Although teaching for diversity is a practice rhetorically encouraged in all Australian primary and high schools, it is often not successfully achieved, even in the few schools where a majority or a large proportion of students are Indigenous or from non-English speaking backgrounds (Hickling-Hudson and Ahlquist, 2004). Few student teachers do their practice teaching in culturally diverse schools and even fewer can do a practicum overseas.

The Education division at Alpha University organizes international practicums on a small scale. Students have the opportunity to practice-teach in international schools in Southeast Asian countries; mainly Singapore, Malaysia, and Hong Kong. These schools, in which English is the language of instruction, cater for the children of expatriate professionals and local elites. Small bursaries are offered to those selecting this practicum, but the costs are largely borne by the students. Only nine or ten Alpha University students a year (out of an annual cohort of around 800) take up the international practicum. At Beta University, some students undertook teaching practice in communities in Thailand, while others went to international schools in Cambodia and Laos. A China-based practicum is also available. Students complete a four-month internship in Beijing, teaching English in private Early Childhood centers, where children are given an hour of English a day from the age of three. Students in this placement kept up with their university studies while abroad, so finishing their degree at the same time as their peers, but with an intensive experience of teaching English in an overseas setting (Academic 3, interviewed June 26, 2009).

At Beta University, our interviewee from Education felt that the teacher education curriculum should require students planning an overseas practicum to study English as a second language in order to develop their fluency in using grammatical and well-written English as they were often required to teach English overseas. In her view, it was "not the cultural side of preparing them that is a problem. It is more the nitty gritty of working with student teachers whose English language skills are so poor" (Academic 3, interviewed June 26, 2009). Our interviewee at Alpha University, Academic 2, felt that a TESOL subject should be compulsory for all student-teachers, since it was an approach increasingly needed in Australian schools.

In contrast to the thousands of international students who study in Australia, only about 1% of all Australian students do study tours or practicum programs overseas. Outgoing student mobility is recognized throughout the Australian university sector as a weakness. According to our interviewees, the logistics of studying overseas on exchange or practicum programs present difficulties for students, as many of them are working to support their university study. Few have the financial means to embark on overseas travel. In this context, most of the students doing Education degrees were not interested in doing an overseas practicum.

Mobility: International Students Studying in Australian Universities

Australian Education degrees attract very small numbers of undergraduate international students, as most teachers are trained in their home countries. The majority of international students in Education are studying for a postgraduate degree at master's or doctoral level or a Graduate Diploma of Education (Grad Dip. Ed), a one-year teacher training course for graduates.

Commenting on the international student cohort doing the Grad Dip. Ed. at Beta University, Academic 3 said that some

> . . . have really struggled on their placements. We are talking about running a winter school for them around English for classroom purposes, just to give them a little bit more support. But a lot of them are reluctant to admit that they have a problem. . . . [Yet] they can't process English fast enough for the sorts of active words in classrooms that we have, rather than the more passive classes they are used to.
> (Academic 3, interviewed July 2, 2009)

In the view of the staff, international students with English as an additional language needed extra help before they could do an effective practicum. A small number of international students viewed the Grad Dip. as a means to secure permanent residency ahead of training for a career as a teacher. Their low levels of commitment and poor performance in the practicum was a source of significant frustration for academic staff who felt the university's reputation was being compromised by enrolling such students.

British, American, and Australian research into intercultural contact in universities has consistently found that international students are keen to make cosmopolitan friendships, but face difficulties (Brown, 2009; Sovic, 2009; Bullen & Kenway, 2003; Smart & Ang, 2000). Although universities laud their international student body in marketing and promoting the international character of their institutions, they have not been very successful in welcoming and embedding international students more effectively into the broader fabric of university social life. Almost inevitably, when they are ready to return home, international students express regret that they were not able to make friends with Australian students. Some attempts have been made by the universities' pastoral care and support services divisions to promote greater intercultural contact between international and domestic students. These endeavors had limited success according to our interviewees:

I think several social factors underlie this. One is that perhaps we haven't cracked the code of different social patterns and expectations between international and domestic students, so the two groups remain at some distance. For example, there's a social drinking culture among some young Australians, while most international students don't drink. Another is that many Aussie students go to uni in their home state. They already have their networks of friends, and there really isn't the motivation to add new friends. Then too, many of them work long hours to support their living costs while they are studying, and they just don't have time for new friends.

(Administrator 2, interviewed June 26, 2009)

For some academic staff, the social, cultural, and intellectual integration of international students into the fabric of university life was impeded by the university's desire to secure revenue ahead of providing adequate funding of support services. TESOL lecturers at Alpha felt that a reasonable portion of student fees should be deployed to improve the academic and campus experience of international students:

[We are] woefully underfunded in terms of centralized academic support for international students. They (the university) won't see the equation in terms of the money that international students bring in through fees, and the money that it costs to make sure that they have a really good academic experience . . . In the old regime, TESOL used to be able to keep much of the money it brought in. Now it all goes to the [university]. When we used to have that money, we gave students a lot of social as well as academic support, opportunities to talk and model and try out new approaches.

(Academic 2, interviewed July 17, 2009)

Academics in Internationalist Teaching and Research

The field of Education requires most of its academics to be immersed in local and national education issues and practice. Relatively few have specialist skills or even an orientation towards internationalist issues in education. This was borne out by our observations and conversations at our two case study universities in which there were only a few academics involved in research projects overseas, or in teaching Education subjects with an international focus. In the past, Beta University had taught an off-shore M.Ed. degree program in two Southeast Asian countries, but that had now come to an end. Alpha University had won contracts, funded by AusAid, to teach their Education degrees in three countries of Asia and the Pacific. In these countries, national governments had negotiated for the university to teach a B.Ed. Early Childhood degree and an M.Ed. degree in Leadership, Policy and Planning (Administrator 4, interviewed July 1, 2009).

Aware that many of the academics asked to incorporate intercultural and international content into their courses lack the skills and knowledge to do so, both our case study universities formulated policies and programs to assist academics to develop their skills of teaching for diversity. Alpha University had, from 2006–2007, supported various teaching projects to assist academic staff to respond to the university's internationalization objectives. A learning and teaching investment fund at Beta University provided financial support for staff projects. Beta also had a policy of encouraging teaching and research collaborations between staff in its Australian and Southeast Asian campus.

At Beta, all new academic staff who do not already have a teaching qualification have to do the Graduate Certificate in Tertiary Teaching and Learning, which helps to prepare them for teaching in a variety of academic disciplines. This course has a compulsory subject on the internationalization of the curriculum. Those who successfully complete the certificate have the option of going to Beta University's offshore campus for a week to participate in joint sessions with staff there and to develop a better understanding of how Beta University can relate to the setting of a developing country. This Graduate Certificate is an unusual requirement and suggests the seriousness of Beta University about providing professional development programs for its academics. Teaching and Learning programs for academics are also available at Alpha University, but they are not compulsory and do not necessarily provide the opportunity to study international issues.

Formal professional development programs like those introduced by Beta to facilitate internationalization of the curriculum can still be met with resistance from individual academic staff. Academic 3, who had senior management responsibilities, noted that staff gave different rationales for resisting the imperative to internationalize; some declared internationalization as irrelevant on the grounds that they did not have international students, or because they did not have students undertaking an overseas practicum. Others felt that because their subject consisted of universalist content, it was unnecessary to include an international or intercultural dimension. "So we do get some prima donnas who resist engaging with what internationalization in higher education can mean. . . ." (Academic 3, interviewed July 2, 2009). However she was sympathetic because she realized that some academics, who might have adopted a more functionalist or positivist approach to their research, may not have had the opportunity to consider the merits of internationalization:

> I've worked in post-structuralist methodologies for the past 15 or so years. The notion of multiple subjectivities and no one true story, opens up immediately to an internationalizing space and the need to value different ways of knowing. But I realize that doesn't come as naturally to people in other areas.
>
> (Academic 3, interviewed July 2, 2009).

Section 3. Rethinking the International University for the 21st Century

Our chapter has highlighted some of the tensions and challenges facing ATN universities as they seek to link their national and local missions with a broader international vision. Our case study universities, like most Australian universities, have had mixed success in their attempts to internationalize their curricula, provide internationalist professional development for their staff, and support study and travel programs for their students.

Our interviewees' accounts suggest that in spite of some creative efforts, the glowing claims about internationalization in their universities' mission statements are more of an aspiration than a reality. Though the issues of concern identified in this research came mainly from academics in teacher education, they have relevance for the entire university. For example, it is likely that most disciplines could point to an unsystematic approach to internationalization across the curriculum with the result that international perspectives are neither coherent nor embedded. University policy encourages curriculum change, but other factors militate against institution-wide change, such as large teaching loads, a performance culture that privileges research over teaching, and short-term, competitive funding policies instead of sustained funds to support internationalization.

It is rare for academics to have professional development assistance in curriculum strategies for internationalization, and when offered, some spurn such initiatives. Top-down directives are often difficult to implement. Ultimately the goal to internationalize depends on convincing the university community, in particular the academic community, of its importance, and establishing sound policies and subsequent conditions that empower and enable staff to make these changes (O'Regan, 2006). The financial cutbacks experienced by many universities have reduced their ability to support staff with resources to engage in a coherent, consistent, and continuing internationalization of curricula. Here, we argue that there is an urgent need for university leaders to lobby politicians and policymakers at the national level to re-engage with an ethical, cultural vision of internationalization.

There is inadequate university support to enable students to study abroad, so this occurs rarely in most degree programs. There is the question of how the university deploys the fees paid by international students, with some academics expressing their view that more ought to be spent on course support and improvement. Some overseas students of English language education are very happy with the tuition they receive in Australia, but at the same time express dissatisfaction with the low level of interaction with Australian students that they experience.

Many Australian universities, like the two ATN Universities we examined, have arguably taken initial and partial steps towards becoming international. Their major focus has been on recruiting international students and earning income from international sources such as student fees and international development programs. Complementing this is their employment of increased numbers of international staff, their encouragement of academics to internationalize curricula and venture into international research, their initiation of engagement projects in selected overseas countries, and their establishment of administrative sections to support some of these processes. These steps should be seen as part of a larger and more difficult challenge. As Turner and Robson (2008) point out,

> If the aim of internationalization is to transform the cultural community, the discourses and the learning environment at higher education institutions, there are challenges to the working practices of all staff across the institution. This may involve a level of discomfort . . .
>
> (p. 67)

Universities need to meet these challenges in order to go beyond a merely symbolic engagement with the global in their teaching, research, and community service functions.

This will not be easy in a situation in which the global educational market has tended to reproduce global inequalities of power. Simon Marginson (2006) aptly analyzes the many dimensions of this situation, pointing out that the current hierarchy of universities:

> . . . maintains the unequal value of education in the developing world compared to the developed world, and sustains asymmetries in student flows, capital flows, cultural engagement and cultural respect. Students from developed nations rarely enroll in developing countries. Economic revenues flow from the developing countries to the export nations, and aid dollars rarely compensate. By spreading English language and Americanised practices, global education markets colonise non-English cultures and identities. . . . Along with global hegemony comes global insularity, a blindness to other languages and the cultures embedded in them, regardless of the immense richness these entail.
>
> (pp. 905 & 907)

International students are implicitly held responsible for the globalization of cultural hegemony perpetuated under the guise of "international education." They are seen as "choosing" an education that gives them advantages, and their choices are taken by universities to be a vote of confidence and the mandate to maintain things as they are (Bagnall, 2004).

What might a revitalized international university look like? We argue that in order for this new university to exercise responsibility and care in its global engagements, it has to break away from the tenacious hold of two sets of influences: the imagination of the nation-building imperial university of the 19th and 20th centuries and the model of the competitive entrepreneurial research university premised on a particular kind of relationship with industry and the state. The power/knowledge cultures fostered by these models have done little to challenge or alleviate widening inequalities at the local, national, and global levels. Michael Singh (2005) speaks of the need for Australian universities to actively displace the thinking associated with "White Australia" politics by giving expression to cosmopolitan multiculturalism, a project that could disrupt traditions that "reserve the centre for Anglo-Australians and the margins for Others" (p. 33). He suggests that university funds might be re-directed to a teaching/research program, operating across multiple disciplines, that created pedagogies for enabling transnational learning communities. This would open opportunities for students and academics wanting to be part of transnational labor markets as much as global /national citizens and multicultural learners. The interdependence and interconnectedness that comes with being part of a globalized world suggests the need for universities to place human development, social justice, and concern for the earth at the center of its actions and logics. "Whatever we choose, we necessarily have to work self-critically with compromised and historically encumbered education policies, pedagogies and politics" (p. 35).

Notes

1 *Australian Universities*. There are four main groupings of Australia's 37 public universities (the three additional private universities are not in these groupings). These have been formed as collaborative professional associations to promote the mutual objectives of the member universities. There are a number of benefits in this, including marketing advantages, practical benefits of collaboration, and the increased lobbying power that comes from being part of a group. The four main groupings currently active are:
Group of Eight (Go8) (which consist of the older universities)
Australian Technology Network (ATN)
Innovative Research Universities Australia (IRU Australia)
New Generation Universities (NGU)
The universities are listed on the website: Australian-universities.com
2 The Interviews, June 28–July 17, 2009
Alpha University
Academic 1: in the Faculty of Education. Interviewed June 29, 2009.
Academic 2: in the Faculty of Education. Interviewed July 17, 2009.
Administrator 1: in a university-wide division. Interviewed July 8, 2009.
Administrator 2: in the Faculty of Education. Interviewed June 26, 2009.
Administrator 3: in the Faculty of Education. Interviewed June 26, 2009.
Administrator 4: in the Faculty of Education. Interviewed July 1, 2009.
Beta University
Academic 3: in the Faculty of Education. Interviewed July 2, 2009.
Academic 4: in the Faculty of Business. Interviewed June 22, 2009.
Academic 5: in the Faculty of Business. Interviewed June 22, 2009.

References

ABC (Australian Broadcasting Corporation) Four Corners. (2009, July 27) Holy cash cows. Full transcript. Reporter Wendy Carlisle. Retrieved July 27, 2009, from http://www.abc.net.au/4corners/content/2009/s2637255.htm

ABS (Australian Bureau of Statistics). (2009). International Trade in Services, Credits, Education Related Travel, by Educational Sector, by Type of Expenditure by Calendar Year. Retrieved October 12, 2009, from http://www.abs.gov.au/AUSSTATS/abs@.nsf/DetailsPage/5368.0.55.0042008?OpenDocument

AEI. (2009). Australian government's response to recent international student issues. Retrieved June 13, 2009, from http://aei.gov.au/AEI/Media/Default.htm.

Australian Technology Network of Universities. (2009). Retrieved October 13, 2009, from http://www.atn.edu.au/docs/Inquiry%20into%20Teacher%20Education.pdf

Alexander Don, & Rizvi, Fazal. (1993). Education, markets and the contradictions of Asia-Australia relations. *Australian Universities Review, 33*(1), 8–13.

Bagnall, Richard. (2004). *Cautionary tales in the ethics of lifelong Learning Policy and Management: A Book of Fables.* The Netherlands: Springer.

Bartell, Martin. (2003). Internationalization of universities: a university culture-based framework. *Higher Education, 45,* 43–70.

Birrell, Bob, Hawthorne, Lesley, & Richardson, Sue. (2006). Evaluation of the general skilled migration categories. Retrieved July 29, 2009, from http://www.immi.gov.au/media/publications/research/gsm-report/index.htm

Brown, Lorraine. (2009). An ethnographic study of the friendship patterns of international students in England: An attempt to recreate home through co-national interaction. *International Journal of Educational Research, 48*(3), 184–193.

Bullen, Elizabeth, & Kenway, Jane. (2003). Real or imagined women: staff representations of international postgraduate women. *Discourse, 24*(1), 35–49.

Cerny, Philip. (1997). Paradoxes of the competition state: the dynamics of political globalization. *Government & Opposition, 32*(2), 251–274.

Gesche, Astrid, & Makeham, Paul. (2008). Creating conditions for intercultural learning and teaching. In Meeri Hellsten and Anne Reid (Eds.), *Researching international pedagogies. Sustainable practice for teaching and learning in higher education.* Singapore: Springer.

Herbert, Bronwyn. (2009, October 13). Study finds students feel safe. Transcript of radio report for *The World Today,* ABC Radio National, Australia.

Hickling-Hudson, Anne. (2004) Educating teachers for cultural diversity and social justice. In G. Hernes (Ed.) with M. Martin, *Planning for diversity: Education in multi-ethnic and multicultural societies* (pp. 270–307). Paris: International Institute for Education Planning (UNESCO).

Hickling-Hudson, Anne, & Ahlquist, Roberta. (2004) The challenge to deculturalisation: Discourses of ethnicity in the schooling of Indigenous children in Australia and the USA. In Anne Hickling-Hudson, Julie Matthews, & Annette Woods (Eds.), *Disrupting preconceptions: Postcolonialism and education* (pp. 39–56). Flaxton, Australia: Post Pressed Publishers.

Hickling-Hudson, Anne, and McMeniman, Marilyn (1996) 'Pluralism and Australian Teacher Education.' In Maurice Craft (Ed.) *Teacher Education in plural societies: An international review* (pp. 16–26). London: Falmer.Hudson, Brian. (1977). The new geography and the new imperialism. *Antipode: A Radical Journal of Geography, 9*(2), 12–19.

Knight, Jane. (2003). Updated internationalization definition. *International Higher Education, 33*, 2–3.

Marginson, Simon. (2009). Is Australia overdependent on international students? *International Higher Education*, no. 54 Winter. Retrieved from http://www.bc.edu/bc_org/avp/soe/cihe/newsletter/Number54/p10_Marginson.html

Marginson, Simon. (2006). National and global competition in Higher Education. In Hugh Lauder, Philip Brown, Jo-Anne Dillabough, & A. H. Hasley. (Eds.), *Education, Globalization and Social Change*. Oxford: Oxford University Press.

NCES (National Center for Education Sciences). (2009). Students who study Science, Technology, Engineering and Mathematics (STEM) in postsecondary education. Retrieved August 15, 2009, from http://nces.ed.gov/pubs2009/2009161.pdf

O'Regan, Justine. (2006). Local Moorings, International Visions: Fabricating Internationalized Practices in Australian Higher Education. Unpublished PhD thesis: Queensland University of Technology.

Patrick, Kate. (1997). *Internationalizing the university: Implications for teaching and learning at RMIT*. Melbourne: RMIT.

Scott, Peter. (1995). *The meanings of mass higher education*. Buckingham: Open University Press.

Sidhu, Ravinder. (2006). *Universities and globalization: To market, to market*. Mahwah, NJ: Lawrence Erlbaum Assoc.

Singh, Michael. (2005). Enabling Transnational Learning Communities: Policies, Pedagogies and Politics of Educational Power. In Peter Ninnes, & Meeri Hellsten (Eds.), *Internationalizing higher education. Critical explorations of pedagogy and policy*. Hong Kong, The University of Hong Kong: Springer.

Singh, Michael. (1998). Globalism, Cultural Diversity and Tertiary Education. *Australian Universities Review, 41*(2), 12–17.

Smart, D., & Ang, G. (2000). *Fostering social cohesion in universities: Bridging the cultural divide*. AEI (Australian Education International): Canberra.

Sovic, Silvia. (2009). Hi-bye friends and the herd instinct: international and home students in the creative arts. *Higher Education, 58*(6), 741–761.

Turner, Yvonne, & Robson, Sue. (2008) *Internationalizing the University*. London & New York: Continuum.

Part III

University Students and Colleges and Schools of Education

10 An International Survey of Higher Education Students' Perceptions of World-Mindedness and Global Citizenship[1]

Luanna H. Meyer, Christine E. Sleeter,
Ken Zeichner, Hyun-Sook Park,
Garry Hoban, and Peter Sorensen

There is growing interest internationally in the dispositions and skills needed by teachers in order to prepare children to be world-minded and global citizens. This chapter describes the results from the *Citizenship and World-Mindedness Survey* to assess the extent to which prospective teachers are prepared to prepare children for a future that requires international understandings and collaboration. A team of teacher education researchers from a dozen major universities in Australia, New Zealand, the United States, and the United Kingdom collaborated in the development and validation of the survey that was administered to approximately 1,200 students at the start of their degree study. Confirmatory factor analysis revealed five dimensions of global-mindedness—social responsibility, skilled dispositions and open-mindedness, personal efficacy, ethnocentrism and nationalism, and global kinship. Teacher education students scored significantly higher on global-mindedness than students majoring in other disciplines. Three entry predispositions and experiences were also related to global-mindedness, including interpersonal skills, ways of thinking, and participation in community work. We discuss the implications of our findings for planning teacher education program components to prepare teachers who have the potential to prepare children to be globally-minded.

Introduction

Today's universities are expected to prepare students for an increasingly interconnected world, and what this means for university curricula is an important issue (Childress, 2009; Dodds, 2008). Fujikane (2003) summarized two pedagogic imperatives based on his analysis of university curricula in Japan, the United Kingdom, and the United States:

(1) calling for new curricula since the world is changing and conventional educational practices based on the previous international

worldviews are no longer appropriate; and (2) creation of new world citizens with proper knowledge of, skills for, and disposition applicable to the globalised world.

(p. 145)

But what are the knowledge, skills, dispositions, and understandings needed for participation in the global community, how do they develop, and what role can universities realistically play in developing them? There are numerous examples of new curricula reflecting the implications of globalization across the disciplines, including business (e.g., Rader & Meggison, 2007), history (Pace, 2007), geography (Ray & Solem, 2009), foreign languages (e.g., Kramsch, Howell, Warner, & Wellmon, 2007), science and technology (e.g., Jordan & Yeomans, 2003), and teacher education (e.g., Merryfield, 2000). Donald (2007), for example, examined critically the complex challenges for conceptualizing and designing humanities curricula that would be more responsive to globalization after reviewing his university's articulation of graduate skills, attributes, and knowledge. Similarly, Feest (2008) analyzed how the undergraduate engineering curricula for globalization might be redesigned as part of his argument that engineering should play a major role in combating poverty and building sustainability.

In addition to discipline-specific initiatives such as these, universities are also defining knowledge, skills, and dispositions at the institutional level to enable graduates who can engage with persons from other countries and cultural contexts (Kennedy, 2004; Marshall, 2005). Dispositions such as intercultural competence, world-mindedness, and global citizenship are widely acknowledged as crucial to international participation (Banks, 2008; Humes, 2008; Spring, 2008). Oxfam (2006), for example, proposes that learning outcomes for global citizenship should include social justice and equity knowledge, critical thinking skills, empathy, and value and respect for diversity. Despite these being evident in higher education graduate profiles, there is limited empirical evidence regarding their assessment and what undergraduate experiences lead to their attainment (Deardorff, 2006; Shephard, 2009).

Cultural Perspectives on Global-Mindedness

Outcomes of global-mindedness must also be scrutinized through diverse cultural lenses towards better understandings of cultural bias. Whose values do the graduate profile and stated outcomes represent? Are they truly "global" or do they reflect particular national values? Stated dimensions of global-mindedness should not themselves be mono-cultural, and there is risk that much of this work in higher education may reflect "western" values and higher social class rather than diverse perspectives (Mellor &

Prior, 2004; Reed, 2004). As an example, Durkin (2008) reported how the western intellectual tradition of "critical argumentation" clashes with East Asian cultures favoring conciliatory accommodation, dialogue, and harmony. She posits the development of a "third way" acknowledging that neither tradition is completely adaptive for today's global society so that both must accommodate new approaches.

Further, the lack of consensus about what is meant by globalization (Dodds, 2008) requires that faculty wrestle conceptually with their assumptions and visions before plunging into curriculum development. Many writers see a distinction between globalist and internationalist missions for higher education (e.g., Cambridge & Thompson, 2004; Yang, 2002), distinguishing among those that focus on concern for greater human rights and global justice versus those that focus on integration of nations into a world economy and learning to succeed within that system. Zeichner and O'Connor (2009) argue that this is a site for ideological battles, proposing "critical global education" as an alternative to neoliberal conceptions that is driven not by economics but by social concerns and the dynamics of transformative change. They promote university curricula that provide students with the knowledge and understanding to challenge existing power hierarchies and

> imagine an alternative vision of globalization where the disparities between rich and poor do not continually grow, where the profits are not privatized and the losses socialized, where security is not preferred to justice, where the ends of financial success do not justify the means of wealth accumulation, where the prerogative to consume rapaciously does not prevail over the planet's health, where the few do not speak for the many.
>
> (p. 9)

Predispositions for Global-Mindedness

Given this robust debate, it is perhaps surprising that there is limited research about student learning leading to knowledge, skills, and dispositions for global-mindedness. There are studies of student learning as a function of international cultural immersion or exchange program participation (Pyvis & Chapman, 2007; Stachowski, Bodle, & Morrin, 2008), perspectives of international students attending universities in other countries (Habu, 2000; Kenway & Bullen, 2003), and how university students interpret specific global issues such as September 11 (Wade, 2002). Absalom and Vadura (2006) surveyed Australian students' perceptions of university initiatives to internationalize by integrating content about other countries into children's literature, sociology, international relations, and languages. Students reported that interacting with people from other countries was far more powerful than learning about them, leading these researchers to conclude that such approaches do not adequately enhance existing views and understandings of globalization.

If higher education is to contribute positively to students' global understandings, baseline information about students' existing predispositions and prior experiences is needed. Just as universities strive to advance disciplinary knowledge, higher education efforts to enhance global awareness should begin with knowledge about what students know and understand.

Undergraduate Conceptions of Global-Mindedness

Late in 2005, researchers from four countries—the United States, England, Australia, and New Zealand—launched an international project to investigate issues surrounding the preparation of university graduates for "global citizenship and world-mindedness." This collaborative project was designed as multi-year, mixed-method research to inform evidence-based practice towards nurturing global consciousness in higher education. In this chapter, we focus on the first phase of our research to survey perspectives of undergraduate students in various disciplines and across national contexts.[2] Survey design was informed by a comprehensive review of the literature in relevant areas to identify constructs, terms, and phrases relevant to global-mindedness. Some of these represent attitudes and skills around diversity, including cultural pluralism, intercultural competence, and religious tolerance. Others refer to how one thinks about challenges and problems such as Dewey's "skilled dispositions," open-mindedness, self-efficacy, personal responsibility, and peaceful resolution of conflict. Still others refer specifically to attitudes such as ethnocentrism and nationalism, in contrast to constructs of interconnectedness, global kinship, and world-mindedness; Mansilla and Gardner (2007) define global-mindedness as "the capacity and the inclination to place our self and the people, objects, and situations with which we come into contact within the broader matrix of our contemporary world" (p. 58). Terms such as citizenship and democracy also appear in discussions of global-mindedness—seen either as universals or as culturally biased. Finally, we reviewed available measures of intrapersonal and experience factors from previous research conducted with university students and adults associated with aspects of global-mindedness (Hett, 1993; Lawthong, 2003; Prior, 1999; Zhai & Scheer, 2004).

The Survey

The *Citizenship and World-Mindedness Survey*[3] includes questions about demographics (for example, gender, age, disability, ethnicity, generation, citizenship, marital status, current program of study), future academic aspirations, type of hometown and high school, prior academic achievement, and experiences living, doing community service, and studying abroad. We also asked about previous intercultural experiences including personal discrimination or bullying experiences based on gender, culture, sexual orientation, religion, and so on.

A "Connections and Perspectives" section assesses attitudes about global-mindedness with potential utility for use as a pre-post measure of change in personal dispositions. An "Experiences" section provides self-reported information about experiences and skills that might be incorporated into interventions.

Connections and Perspectives

This section probes global-mindedness and was conceptually modeled after measures such as the E-Scale developed to measure ethnocentrism (Adorno, Frenkel-Brunswik, Levinson, & Sanford, 1964) and the C-Scale developed to measure conservatism (Lapsley & Enright, 1979; Wilson & Patterson, 1968). Items are constructed to avoid the influences of cognitive level, grammatical complexity, task conflict, and social desirability by posing opinion "catch phrases" reflecting typically repeated opinions. Some items were adapted with permission from Hett (1993) and others influenced by the Sasakawa Peace Foundation (Cogan, 1997), Oxfam (2006), and other sources (Deardorff, 2006; Lawthong, 2003; Zhai & Scheer, 2004). Respondents rated statements from 1 to 4, where 1 equaled strongly disagree and 4, strongly agree. Polarity of "accepting" responses was deliberately varied randomly (and reverse scored accordingly).

Experiences

Students self-rate their strengths and weaknesses in areas such as communication skills, cultural awareness, and leadership ability and their involvement in volunteer work and other activities. Items were influenced by research on various activities to develop global-mindedness and intercultural understandings (Chang, Astin, & Kim, 2004; Hurtado, 2005; Merryfield, 1996).

Participants

The purpose of the survey is to assess student attitudes at the start of different programs in which they had voluntarily enrolled. Students in the first year of study in degree programs at six universities in four countries participated in the survey in 2008, including approximately 500 from the United States, 400 from New Zealand, and 100 each from Australia and England. In all cases, students completed the survey within the first few weeks of study so that responses would be unlikely to be affected by later program components designed to develop perspectives related to the concepts assessed by the survey. We assessed three student cohort groups—teacher education, business, and a third disciplinary area of interest to each university. Most students in the sample were undergraduates, with the exception of some of the teacher education students who were enrolled in a year-long program leading to teacher registration following completion of a subject area degree. Nearly 1,150 students participated, though missing data on some items resulted in reduced numbers for some analyses. Approximately half (N = 506) were enrolled in teacher education, over one-third in business (N = 323), and nearly 100 each in law (N = 85) and humanities (N = 94). The numbers from other disciplines in the sciences and social science are small and so omitted from these analyses. Ethics approval was attained at each university for voluntary, anonymous participation with informed consent.

The sample included 65% women and 35% men, and 75% were aged 24 and under. Respondents reported ethnicity as European Caucasian (65%), African (3%), Asian (14%), Pacific (3%), Indigenous (4%), Latino or Hispanic (7%), and Arab or Middle Eastern (2%) descent; some did not provide this information. Over 15% reported being born in another country, more than one in five had lived in another country, about 8% said they had done community service in another country, and about 15% had studied abroad.

Data Analysis and Findings

Factor analysis identified five dimensions of global-mindedness (see Table 10.1), and analyses of variance (ANOVA) were carried out to analyze for differences across disciplines and countries. High scores on the Ethnocentrism and Nationalism factor indicate negative dispositions towards global-mindedness, whereas high scores on the other four factors reflect positive attitudes. Although factors are inter-correlated, the magnitude of correlations is quite small (none larger than .12) hence it is reasonable to conclude these represent different dimensions. Factor analysis of the Experiences section identified three factors: (1) interpersonal skills, such as communication, social and leadership; (2) ways of thinking, such as religious tolerance, accepting differences, and divergent thinking; and (3) participation in activities such as volunteer work, publications, clubs, and organizations. These experience factors are significantly related to positive scores on the dimensions of global-mindedness measured by the scale, suggesting that interventions with these types of experiences could result in enhanced global-mindedness.

Comparisons Across Disciplines

Table 10.2 reports the results of ANOVA showing differences on dimensions of global-mindedness by discipline. Mean scores over 3 represent

Table 10.1 Survey Dimensions of World-Mindedness

Dimension	Definition	Sample items
Social Responsibility (SR)	Belief that communities, organizations, and universities have a duty to promote intercultural understandings	• I think my country needs to do more to promote the welfare of different racial and ethnic groups • Enhancing a person's ability to be part of a multicultural society and global economy should be part of higher education in today's universities
Skilled Disposition & Open-Mindedness (SD)	Willingness to understand a wide range of perspectives regarding social issues and to tolerate ambivalence and debate	• Democracy thrives on different views • I try to consider different points of view on an issue before making up my own mind, even when I have a strong first impression
Ethnocentrism and Nationalism (EN)	Putting one's own nation's interests first, and belief that conflict, inequality, and exclusion are appropriate and even inevitable	• Some degree of inequality is necessary in a society that wants to be the best in the world • The needs of my own country must continue to be our highest priority in negotiating with other countries
Personal Efficacy (PE)	Personal agency and responsibility to make a difference in a complex social world	• There is little I can do to make the world a better place to live.* • I believe that my personal decisions can affect the welfare of others and what happens on a global level
Global Kinship (GK)	Empathy with the circumstances of others and desire to respond actively to global challenges	• I feel very concerned about the lives of people who live in politically repressive regimes • I think it is fair for some of my taxes to go to help other countries even if everything could be spent in my own country

Source: *Citizenship and World-Mindedness Survey*

Note: The "ethnocentrism and nationalism" dimension is regarded as inversely related to global-mindedness, whereas high scores on the other four factors are regarded as positively related to global-mindedness. Items marked with a * are reverse-scored so that high scores reflect high scores on that dimension.

Table 10.2 Results for the ANOVA comparisons across majors for the five factors

Factor	F test	p–value	Mean BU sample	Mean ED sample	Mean LA sample	Mean HU sample
SR	$F_{3,1004} = 6.91$	<.001	3.10^a	3.25^{a,b}	3.12^a	3.34^b
SD	$F_{3,967} = 14.32$	<.001	3.15	3.31^c	3.44^d	3.35^{c,d}
EN	$F_{3,917} = 28.93$	<.001	2.58	2.25^e	2.39	2.17^e
PE	$F_{3,983} = 9.64$	<.001	2.77	3.01^f	2.97^f	2.99^f
GK	$F_{3,972} = 5.70$	.002	2.69^g	2.85^g	2.85^g	2.79^g

Source: *Citizenship and World-Mindedness Survey*

Note: BU= Business; E = Education; LA = Law; HU = Humanities; superscripts indicate those respective means that are not significantly different from one another ($p < .05$), Student-Newman-Keuls test.

agreement, whereas mean scores under 3 suggest disagreement. No group scored above a mean of 3 on the Global Kinship dimension; all groups scored just under an average of 3, and groups did not differ from one another. On Personal Efficacy, only the Business students' scores differed significantly; they were least likely to believe that personal actions can make a difference compared with students in all other disciplines. With the exception of lower scores from Business, all other group means near 3 reflected agreement (not "strong" agreement). For the negative dimension of Ethnocentrism and Nationalism, Business and Law students scored significantly higher in comparison with Education and Humanities who did not differ from one another. Note, however, that all means are between the "disagree" and "agree" ratings.

All student groups tended to agree with items in the Social Responsibility dimension, with Humanities scoring highest followed by Education. All student ratings for Skilled Dispositions and Open-Mindedness were between the "agree" and "strongly agree" ratings, with Law scoring highest followed closely by Humanities and Education; Business scored lowest with a mean rating just above "agree."

Comparisons Across Countries

Table 10.3 shows student ratings by country. These findings should be viewed as preliminary given that the British and Australian student cohorts comprised only education students, whereas the U.S. and New Zealand samples included other majors as well.[4] Students score similarly to one another internationally at just under a mean value of 3 for agreement on the dimension of Global Kinship. Scores on the Ethnocentrism and Nationalism (negative) dimension are slightly above the "disagree" rating for all countries except for New Zealand, where student ratings are half-way between disagree and agree; New Zealand students are also significantly higher on this negative dimension than those from any other

Table 10.3 Results for the ANOVA comparisons across countries for the five factors

Factor	F test	p–value	Mean AU sample	Mean NZ sample	Mean UK sample	Mean US sample
SR	$F_{3,1032} = 16.37$	<.001	3.30[b]	3.08[a]	3.07[a]	3.33[b]
SD	$F_{3,995} = 8.73$	<.001	3.17[c]	3.21[c,d]	3.29[d,e]	3.35[e]
EN	$F_{3,944} = 13.84$	<.001	2.24[f,g]	2.48	2.17[f]	2.32[g]
PE	$F_{3,1011} = 6.98$	<.001	3.00[i]	2.82[h]	2.93[h,i]	3.01[i]
GK	$F_{3,1000} = 5.10$	.002	2.94[k]	2.73[j]	2.88[k]	2.82[j,k]

Source: *Citizenship and World-Mindedness Survey*

Note: AU = Australia; NZ = New Zealand; UK = United Kingdom; US = USA; superscripts indicate those respective means that are not significantly different from one another ($p < .05$), Student-Newman-Keuls test.

country. Student means are highest overall for the Skilled Dispositions and Open-Mindedness dimension, and student scores on the other two positive dimensions of Social Responsibility and Personal Efficacy are just slightly lower but reflecting agreement with these items as well. Interestingly, on Social Responsibility, students from the United States and Australia score significantly higher than students from New Zealand and the UK.

Discussion

In accordance with findings reported by Absalom and Vadura (2006), we found that students entering universities today in four English-speaking countries—Australia, New Zealand, England, and the United States—are not "blank slates" when it comes to concepts of global-mindedness. In general, the students we surveyed appear to have positive or some-what neutral understandings and dispositions about constructs related to international and intercultural interactions. It is important, of course, to acknowledge some limitations in these data. Not all disciplines were represented in the student samples across universities and countries, and we have chosen not to draw implications based on findings for sub-samples where all students completing the survey were from one country or even one university. For example, all Law students in this sample were from one university in New Zealand, where Law is an undergraduate program, which is different from programs in the United States. Thus, findings that these students were like Business students in showing higher Ethnocentrism and Nationalism scores than students in Education and the Humanities could have been a function of being a New Zealand sample. Results might be quite different for Law students in another country, such as the United States, where Law is a graduate program as well, which could introduce other differences.

Where our sample is more diverse internationally, however, it is appropriate to discuss the disciplinary and national differences we found.

Undergraduates in Business were significantly more negative on different dimensions of global-mindedness in comparison with their student peers, particularly in Personal Efficacy and Skilled Dispositions/Open-Mindedness. Given expectations and demands that today's business graduates operate in a global economy, these findings suggest the need for additional experiences to ensure they develop strong intercultural skills and understandings for global-mindedness (Rader & Meggison, 2007). It is widely assumed that persons choose a teaching career due to altruistic and caring motives, and our data suggest that students in education have significantly more positive attitudes in most areas in comparison with others. While further research is needed to interpret national patterns on global-mindedness, it is interesting that New Zealand students appear to be more insular in comparison with their counterparts in the other three countries, which might be expected in a considerably smaller, island country. Another interesting cross-national finding is that students from both the United States and Australia rated themselves higher than those from either England or New Zealand on Personal Responsibility. Follow-up qualitative research including student interviews will investigate these issues further.

An important lesson to be learned from these findings is that program initiatives to enhance global-mindedness must build further on existing positive attitudes—not risk repetition of what students already know and value. There are inherent challenges in efforts to imbue values and strategies such as critical thinking and open-mindedness that require acceptance of diverse points of view—not telling people what or how to think. How do universities promote divergent thinking without risking further validation of patterns of hate, prejudice, and religious intolerance, which may be defended as freedom of speech and open expression of ideas? Our findings that certain experiences were positively related to global-mindedness also suggest areas for future research to investigate the impact of similar undergraduate experiences on dimensions of global-mindedness.

These are not simple challenges. Higher education has a long and rich history of successful teaching across and within the disciplines, but less is known about our ability to teach those sometimes elusive "graduate attributes" (Shephard, 2009). Durkin's (2008) suggestion that we need to explore alternative, cross-cultural strategies for discussing and debating knowledge and understandings requires that we recognize how existing approaches within particular national contexts risk imposing monocultural values onto international perspectives. Whatever the approach taken by higher education programs and universities, we strongly encourage that educators measure and monitor the impact of what they do.

Notes

1 An earlier version of portions of this chapter was presented at the Annual Meeting of the American Educational Research Association, San Diego, CA,

April 2009. We gratefully acknowledge input during development of the survey from Alfredo Artiles, Elizabeth Kozleski, Zeus Leonardo, John Loughran, Bill McDiarmid, Gisele Ragusa, Rob Rueda, Stan Trent, and Libby Tudball. We also thank Andrea Milligan who assisted in data interpretation, Lynanne McKenzie for managing data entry, and Flaviu Hodis for the data analysis.

2 Our research group is culturally diverse. Nevertheless, it is important to acknowledge that the national and university contexts in which this work was done are "western" hence inevitably reflect some cultural bias. We decided to begin the project focused on these English-speaking, western contexts, and that expansion of the project to other national contexts would require that researchers from those contexts drive the next stage. It did not seem appropriate for us to attempt to "adapt" this survey for those contexts.

3 The survey is available from the authors on request.

4 The survey has been revised based on these results and will be administered in 2009–10 to additional student cohorts involving several new universities and countries as well as additional disciplines across all universities.

References

Absalom, Matthew, & Vadura, Katharine. (2006). Student perceptions of internationalization of the curriculum: An Australian case study. *Arts and Humanities in Higher Education: An International Journal of Theory, Research and Practice 5*(3), 317–334.

Adorno, Theodor W., Frenkel-Brunswik, Else, Levinson, Daniel J., & Sanford, R. Nevitt. (1964). *The authoritarian personality.* New York: John Wiley & Sons,.

Banks, James A. (2008). Citizenship education and diversity: Implications for teacher education. In M. A. Peters, A. Britton, & H. Blee (Eds.), *Global citizenship education: Philosophy, theory and pedagogy* (pp. 317–331). Rotterdam: Sense Publishers.

Cambridge, James & Thompson, Jeff. (2004). Internationalism and globalization as contexts for international education. *Compare: A Journal of Comparative Education, 34*, 161–175.

Chang, Mitchell J., Astin, Alexander W., & Kim, Dongbin. (2004). Cross-racial interaction among undergraduates: Some consequences, causes, and patterns. *Research in Higher Education, 45*, 529–553.

Childress, Lisa K. (2009). Internationalization plans for higher education institutions. *Journal of Studies in International Education, 13*, 289–309.

Cogan, John J. (1997). *Multi-dimensional citizenship: Educational policy for the twenty-first century.* Tokyo: Sasakawa Peace Foundation.

Deardorff, Darla K. (2006). Identification and assessment of intercultural competence as a student outcome of internationalization. *Journal of Studies in International Education, 10*, 241–266.

Dodds, Anneliese. (2008). How does globalisation interact with higher education? The continuing lack of consensus. *Comparative Education 44*(4), 505–517.

Donald, James. (2007). Internationalisation, diversity and the humanities curriculum: cosmopolitanism and multiculturalism revisited. *Journal of Philosophy of Education, 41*(3), 289–308.

Durkin, Kathy. (2008). The Middle Way: East Asian master's students' perceptions of critical argumentation in U.K. universities. *Journal of Studies in International Education, 12*, 38–55.

Feest, Tim. (2008). Engineers: Going global. *Industry and Higher Education, 22*(4), 209–213.

Fujikane, Hiroko. (2003). Approaches to global education in the United States, the United Kingdom and Japan. *International Review of Education, 49*(1/2), 133–152.

Habu, Toshie. (2000). The irony of globalization: The experience of Japanese women in British higher education. *Higher Education, 39*(1), 43–66.

Hett, E. Jane. (1993). *The development of an instrument to measure global mindedness.* Unpublished doctoral dissertation, University of San Diego.

Humes, Walter M. (2008). The discourse of global citizenship. In Michael A. Peters, Alan Britton, & Harry Blee (Eds.), *Global citizenship education: Philosophy, theory and pedagogy* (pp. 41–52). Rotterdam: Sense Publishers.

Hurtado, Sylvia. (2005). The next generation of diversity and intergroup relations research. *Journal of Social Issues, 61*, 595–610.

Jordan, Steven & Yeomans, David. (2003). Meeting the global challenge? Comparing recent initiatives in school science and technology. *Comparative Education, 39*(1), 65–81.

Kennedy, Kerry J. (2004). Searching for citizenship values in an uncertain global environment. In W. O. Lee, David L. Grossman, Kerry J. Kennedy, & Gregory P. Fairbrother (Eds.), *Citizenship education in Asia and the Pacific: Concepts and issues* (pp. 9–24). Hong Kong: Kluwer Academic Publishers.

Kenway, Jane, & Bullen, Elizabeth. (2003). Self-representations of international women postgraduate students in the global university "contact zone." *Gender and Education, 15*(1), 5–20.

Kramsch, Claire, Howell, Tes, Warner, Chantelle, & Wellmon, Chad. (2007). Framing foreign language education in the United States: The case of German. *Critical Inquiry in Language Studies, 4*(2–3), 151–178.

Lapsley, Daniel K., & Enright, Robert D. (1979). The effects of social desirability, intelligence, and milieu on an American validation of the conservatism scale. *The Journal of Social Psychology, 107*, 9–14.

Lawthong, Nuttaporn. (2003). A development of the Global-mindedness scale in Thai socio-cultural context. *Journal of Institutional Research South East Asia (JIRSEA), 1*(2), 57–70.

Mansilla, Veronica B, & Gardner, Howard. (2007). From teaching globalization to nurturing global consciousness. In Marcelo M. Suárez-Orozco (Ed.), *Learning in the global era: International perspectives on global education* (pp. 47–66). Berkeley: University of California Press.

Marshall, Harriet. (2005). Developing the global gaze in citizenship education: Exploring the perspectives of global education NGO workers in England. *International Journal of Citizenship and Teacher Education, 1*(2), 76–92.

Mellor, Suzanne, & Prior, Warren. (2004). Promoting social tolerance and cohesion in the Solomon Islands and Vanuatu. In W. O. Lee, David L. Grossman, Kerry J. Kennedy, & Gregory P. Fairbrother (Eds.), *Citizenship education in Asia and the Pacific: Concepts and issues* (pp. 175–194). Hong Kong: Kluwer Academic Publishers.

Merryfield, Merry M. (2000). Why aren't teachers being prepared to teach for diversity, equity, and global interconnectedness? A study of lived experiences in the making of multicultural and global educators. *Teaching and Teacher Education, 16*(4), 429–443.

Merryfield, Merry M. (1996). *Making connections between multicultural and global education: Teacher educators and teacher education programs.* Washington DC: American Association of Colleges for Teacher Education.

Oxfam. (2006, April 26). *Education for global citizenship.* Oxford, United Kingdom. Retrieved March 15, 2008, from http://www.oxfam.org.uk/education/gc

Pace, David. (2007). The internationalization of history teaching through the scholarship of teaching and learning: Creating institutions to unite the efforts of a discipline. *Arts and Humanities in Higher Education: An International Journal of Theory, Research and Practice, 6*(3), 329–335.

Prior, Warren. (1999). What it means to be a 'good citizen' in Australia: perceptions of teachers, students, and parents. *Theory and Research in Social Education, 27,* 215–247.

Pyvis, David, & Chapman, Anne. (2007). Why university students choose an international education: A case study in Malaysia. *International Journal of Educational Development, 27*(2), 235–246.

Rader, Martha, & Meggison, Peter. (2007). The Business education curriculum. *Delta Pi Epsilon Journal, 49* (1), 26–31.

Ray, Waverly & Solem, Michael. (2009). Gauging disciplinary engagement with internationalization: A survey of geographers in the United States. *Journal of Geography in Higher Education, 33*(1), 103–121.

Reed, Gay Garland. (2004). Multidimensional citizenship, Confucian humanism and the imagined community: South Korea and China. In W. O. Lee, David L. Grossman, Kerry J. Kennedy, & Gregory P. Fairbrother (Eds.), *Citizenship education in Asia and the Pacific: Concepts and Issues* (pp. 239–255). Hong Kong: Kluwer Academic Publishers.

Shephard, Kerry. (2009). Assessing affective attributes at all levels of higher education. In Luanna H. Meyer, Susan Davidson, Helen Anderson, Richard Fletcher, Patricia M. Johnston, & Malcolm Rees (Eds.), *Tertiary Assessment and Higher Education Student Outcomes: Policy, practice, and research* (pp. 143–152). Wellington, NZ: Ako Aotearoa: National Centre of Tertiary Teaching Excellence.

Spring, Joel. (2008). Research on globalization and education. *Review of Educational Research, 78*(2), 330–363.

Stachowski, Laura L., Bodle, Aaron, & Morrin, Michael. (2008). Service learning in overseas and Navajo Reservation communities. *International Education, 38*(1), 40–65.

Wade, Bruce H. (2002). How does racial identity affect Historically Black Colleges and Universities' student perceptions of September 11, 2001? *Journal of Black Studies, 33*(1), 25–43.

Wilson, Glenn, & Patterson, John. (1968). A new measure of conservatism. *British Journal of Social and Clinical Psychology, 8,* 264–269.

Yang, Rui. (2002). University internationalisation: its meanings, rationales and implications. *Intercultural Education, 13*(1), 81–95.

Zeichner, Ken, & O'Connor, Kate. (2009, April). Preparing teachers for critical global education. Paper presented at the Annual Meeting of the American Educational Research Association, San Diego, CA.

Zhai, Lijuan, & Scheer, Scott D. (2004). Global perspectives and attitudes toward cultural diversity among summer agricultural students at the Ohio State University. *Journal of Agricultural Education, 45,* 39–51.

11 European Union Universities and Teacher Preparation

Lani Florian

Introduction

This chapter focuses on developments in teacher education in Europe that are designed to address a diversity agenda that arises from the processes of globalization and the resulting need to prepare teachers to work in schools that are increasingly diverse. The developments are outcomes of European Union (EU) policies that seek "unity in diversity"[1] as the countries of Europe, with their distinctive national, ethnic, cultural, and linguistic diversities work together on common goals. The chapter considers how pan-European reforms promote globalization *in* education by describing education initiatives that respond to its outcomes, such as the changing demographic of schooling brought about by economic migration. It also considers how these reforms have influenced the globalization *of* education through the alignment of education policy across the 27 member countries of the EU. Examples of projects and initiatives that illustrate how the reforms have influenced the preparation of teachers in the countries of the EU are provided.

Harmonization and integration across the countries of Europe have been important themes in Europeanization since the end of the Second World War when the Council of Europe[2] was established to promote unity, social and economic progress, and safeguard the ideals and principles of a common heritage. Indeed, many commentators point to this period as the beginning of the current cycle of globalization (Coatsworth, 2004). Like the Council of Europe, the EU also seeks integration and harmonization, but in addition to similar goals, it has legislative and regulatory powers. The origins of the EU are located in the movement to form a common market, a process that began in 1951 when 6 countries[3] formed the European Coal and Steel Community. It was expanded over the next two decades as more countries joined[4] and began working together to create a "Single Market." The EU was established in 1992 with the signing of the Treaty of Maastricht, and the completion of the Single Market with its "four freedoms" regarding the movement of goods, services, people, and money. As this chapter will argue, these four freedoms and the economic imperative that underpins them are foundational to education policy in the EU. As the European Quality Charter for Mobility makes clear:

> Mobility in education and training is an integral part of the freedom of movement of persons—a fundamental freedom protected by the Treaty—and one of the main objectives of the European Union's action in the field of education and training, based both on common values and on respect for diversity. It is an essential tool for creating a genuine European area of lifelong learning, for promoting employment and reducing poverty, and for helping to promote European citizenship.
>
> Mobility brings citizens closer to one another and improves mutual understanding. It promotes solidarity, the exchange of ideas and a better knowledge of the different cultures which make up Europe; thus mobility furthers economic, social and regional cohesion.
>
> (European Parliament and Council, 2006)

The EU is a supranational body with governance powers[5] that have been transferred to it from its member states. [6] Today, with 27 member states, "the EU is often described as the 'New Europe', characterized by intense localism against a background of cooperative internationalism" (de Blij, 2005, p. 222). The combination of localism and internationalism is an important dynamic in Europeanization. Teachers, for example, tend to be perceived nationally (Zgaga, 2007), and are trained locally for jobs in their home countries. Throughout Europe, education remains an area of national and sub-national jurisdiction. However, the training of teachers also occurs within an important EU movement to *align* the preparation of teachers as part of the drive to harmonize and integrate standards in education at a time when the increasing mobility, migration, and urbanization of people has created new challenges for national systems of education.

Thus, while education remains under the jurisdiction of member states, it is also considered a "specific commitment" within the EU and many education programs are supported under various policy initiatives of its "education area." Cooperation across the EU is a matter of social cohesion, justice, and equity in education. Here, broad concepts of "social inclusion" and "exclusion" are used to express concerns about the challenges of social cohesion, and while these concepts have been criticized (e.g., Levitas, 2005), they are often used in educational discourse to emphasize concern for meaningful participation in community life. As Casba (2007) has noted:

> ... the connection between community involvement, education and social cohesion ... has proved to be especially relevant in educational

centres where children from social groups at risk of exclusion and immigrant families attend. Projects such as the Early Intervention Programs in Scotland, the Learning Communities in Spain, or some of the Second Chance Schools in several European member states, among others, share the component of community involvement, in a wide variety of levels and modalities, from entering the classroom, to school management or after-school programmes. . . . Local community projects working in the field of education can be connected to enhancing social cohesion by empowering community members within schools and developing an active citizenry . . . The European School Charter, aimed at fostering coexistence in society and reducing school conflicts, includes this orientation.

(pp. 16–17)

Persson (2005) identified three major trends of globalization that effect schooling in Europe: the impact of the information society, internationalization and the removal of barriers between labor markets, and the impact of the scientific technical world. Each of these trends is reflected in EU education initiatives that are both responses to, and facilitators of, the globalizing forces of the movement of people, goods, and ideas. There is a consensus that teachers play a key role in meeting the economic, social, cultural, and technological challenges facing member states and the community as a whole as "education policy has increasingly become an integral part of economic and social policy" (Buchberger, Campos, Kallos, & Stephenson, 2000, p. 2). Across Europe, high-quality teachers and high-quality teacher education are seen as playing a key role in fulfilling the aspirations of the EU for economic competitiveness and the social cohesion that is needed to achieve it.

Globalization and Diversity in European Education Systems

The Changing Demographics of Schooling

While the concept of globalization has been defined variously (Dodds, 2008) and is open to different interpretations (Weiner, 2005), having both adherents and detractors (Kelly, 2007), there is little doubt that its effects are reflected in the changing demographics of schools and the concurrent pressures to reform schooling. The EU processes of harmonization and integration have important implications for equitable educational opportunity within national systems of education as the citizens of Europe exercise their freedom of mobility, and schools become more diverse and multicultural in terms of ethnicity, language, and religion. The removal of barriers between labor markets means that today citizens of EU member states can travel more easily to work and study in other member states.

Additionally, an increasing number of refugees have sought asylum in Europe from conflicts elsewhere. While the demographic trends among the countries of Europe are markedly different, there are common issues with regard to multiculturalism and diversity in schools. In Austria, for example, 85.88% of non-Austrian residents are from countries outside of the EU, however, of this number, 45% are from the former Yugoslavia. In France, on the other hand, the majority of immigrants come from the Maghrib[7] countries and Turkey. In both countries, the majority of immigrants reside in urban areas. While Germany and the United Kingdom receive higher numbers of applications from asylum seekers than other EU member states, the relatively large populations in these two countries means that the proportion of the population who are asylum seekers is lower compared with less densely populated countries like Sweden and Norway. However, whatever the size, these groups tend to be concentrated in mostly urban areas, so while numbers may be low, proportions of children from these groups within a school may be high. In addition, the proportion of foreign nationals under the age of 15 within a country, as well as the number of school-aged pupils whose first language is not the language of instruction in a school, are thought to pose particular challenges for national education systems (Eurydice, 2003/2004a and b).

As a result, teachers routinely encounter a wide range of students in classrooms where they are also expected to achieve pre-specified national standards of academic performance, regardless of differences in prior experience, languages spoken, and other factors that may create difficulties in learning for students, leading many teachers feeling unprepared to teach all students. Dealing with differences and diversity is identified as one of the biggest problems faced by schools across Europe, with behavior as well as social and/or emotional problems presenting the biggest challenges (EADSNE, 2006). The view that classroom teachers are unqualified to teach certain groups of students is reinforced in the media where it is not uncommon to find stories about how schools are struggling with an influx of migrant pupils, and/or students with special needs. Such a view perpetuates the idea that schools need teachers with different kinds of qualifications to work with different groups of students, raising questions about how teacher education can best prepare teachers to respond to the challenges of diversity (Florian, 2009).

Moreover, there is also recognition that there are disparities in terms of who gets what with respect to educational provision and opportunity. Children of migrant workers in Germany face different problems to those of Muslim girls in France, Roma children in the Czech Republic, or Albanian immigrants in Italy. However, within the member states these groups of children often face discrimination and attain low levels of educational achievement. And yet, not all immigrant groups have this experience. In some countries, for example England, the children of certain migrant groups, especially those of East Asia and parts of South Asia, are among the highest achieving groups in school. However, more often than not, increasing immigration into the EU is associated with problems of multiculturalism and racism (Buchberger et al., 2000), rather than the solutions to economic problems that are offered by the freedom of mobility. Expectations and achievement levels for some children are still too low in many schools (Gillborn & Youdell, 2000).

Increasingly throughout Europe, a broad concept of inclusive education has begun to emerge as a strategy for achieving social cohesion (Casba, 2007), and as part of the response to the equity issues that are raised in relation to the harmonization and integration processes of the EU, rather than as a response to a particular group of learners, such as students with disabilities. Greater awareness of the exclusionary pressures associated with migration, mobility, language, ethnicity, disability, and intergenerational poverty, and the reciprocal links between these factors and underachievement, has led to an increasing interest in the development of inclusive education as a strategy for improving educational equity within Europe. Although inclusive education is not specifically defined, it is generally considered a process of increasing participation and decreasing exclusion from the culture, community, and curricula of mainstream schools (Booth, Ainscow, Black-Hawkins, Vaughan, & Shaw, 2000). Additionally, there is an increasing awareness that the implementation of inclusive education has implications for teacher education (Florian & Rouse, 2009; UNESCO, 2008).

Globalization in Education

Globalization *in* education refers to the outcomes of globalization: from the increasing diversity of national populations resulting from economic migration and its effect on schools, which are increasingly multicultural and multilingual, to reforms that are driven by a firm conviction that education can be predictive of future well-being and an antidote for inequality (Suárez-Orozco and Qin-Hilliard, 2004). Economic and technological developments also have a globalizing influence in education particularly with regard to curricular decisions. In today's fast-paced world, as information can be exchanged rapidly across boundaries of time and space, so too can the kind of jobs that are needed to fuel the global economy. While people continue to migrate to jobs, jobs also move. As Gardner (2004) noted, there is nowadays a widespread awareness that today's youth will leave school for a different world, raising questions about what and how teachers should teach. Gardner (2004) argues that a curriculum suitable for an "era of globalization" should focus on a limited number of key concepts approached from multiple perspectives and encompass an understanding of the global system; a capacity to think analytically and creatively within the disciplines; an ability to tackle problems and issues that do not respect disciplinary boundaries; knowledge of and ability to interact civilly and productively with individuals from quite different cultural backgrounds, both within one's own society and across the planet; knowledge of and respect for one's own cultural tradition(s); the fostering of hybrid or blended identities; and the fostering of tolerance (pp. 253–255).

An example of this approach is manifest in the Scottish educational system, which like many others, is undergoing a series of changes in response to globalization, migration, economic change, and international comparisons. Attempts to tackle the chronic underachievement of marginalized groups of children are at the core of national initiatives such as the new "Curriculum for Excellence" (Scottish Executive, 2004) with its aim to replace an emphasis on "knowing what" with "knowing how." The new curriculum focuses on the four capacities of education: that schooling should prepare students to become successful learners, confident individuals, responsible citizens, and effective contributors. Further, the Education (Additional Support for Learning) (Scotland) Act (Scottish Executive, 2005) introduced the new concept of "additional support needs" to refer to any child or young person who, for whatever reason, requires additional support for learning. Government funding for two important teacher education projects has followed these policies. One is the Inclusive Practice Project at the University of Aberdeen, which aims to develop a new approach to training primary and secondary teachers to ensure that they have a greater awareness and understanding of the educational and social issues that can affect children's learning; and have developed strategies they can use to support and deal with such difficulties (for a detailed description see Florian & Rouse, 2009). The second involved collaboration between the seven Scottish universities that prepare teachers. Here teams of teacher educators, including those who specialize in initial teacher education and inclusive education from each university, developed a framework outlining the essential knowledge, skills, and values required of teachers in order to further the development of social inclusion in Scotland (Scottish Teacher Education Committee, 2009).

EU Education Initiatives and Examples of Projects

While differences in national contexts may produce variations in how teachers are trained and school systems are organized, the conceptual and philosophical problems of equity and inclusion *in* schooling are shared concerns. Persson (2005) noted that the EU has been active in responding to the challenges of globalization for education through "the gradual construction of an open and dynamic European educational area" (p. 11). Although education remains under the legislative and decision-making jurisdiction of member states, a number of education programs are supported under the auspices of the EU's Lifelong Learning

Programme (LLP). The LLP, which replaced the earlier Socrates program, consists of four education sub-programs (authorized from 2007 to 2013) that support collaborative transnational activities across all sectors and phases of education. These are:

1) Comenius for schools;
2) Erasmus for higher education;
3) Leonardo da Vinci for vocational education and training;
4) Grundtvig for adult education; and
5) Jean Monnet for university-level projects on European integration.

(Europa, 2009b)

A detailed overview of the European education agenda and an overview of the range of programs sponsored by the various EU institutions has been provided by Persson (2005). In the following sections a sample of EU projects aimed at addressing issues of social justice, diversity, and equity are described. The projects provide an indication of the range of activities that are supported by the LLP.

Cultural Diversity

One Socrates[8]-Comenius project (Bartolo et al., 2007), for example, illustrates how issues of social justice, equity, and diversity are part of an inclusive education agenda as it is being developed in the EU. Here a group of teacher educators from seven EU countries (Czech Republic, Germany, Lithuania, Malta, the Netherlands, Sweden, and the United Kingdom) cooperated on a collaborative project to develop materials for responding to student diversity in classrooms. A good example of cooperative internationalism, the members of the research group also had varied backgrounds as educators, for example, some members of the team were specialists in subject areas while others were special educators. While the academic and cultural diversity of the partners meant that a large variety of issues would need to be addressed, the common theme addressed by the partners was a concern for social justice:

> All students are entitled to a quality education and we need to find better ways for enabling each one to be engaged in meaningful learning activities and to make progress. And we understand that in order to achieve this, we need first of all to promote an openness to student diversity, an attitude of appreciation for diversity, an assumption that it is normal to be different and to provide a differentiated curriculum and learning experience. Students are diverse and engage with the curriculum at diverse points and in diverse ways, and good teachers are first of all prepared for responding to student diversity.
>
> (Bartolo et al., 2007, p. xiii)

The materials that were produced focus on activities that support teachers to develop inclusive practices when they feel challenged by the presences of students whose backgrounds and experiences may be different from their own. These differences include language, culture, disability, religion, and so on. The materials also encourage collaborative action research as a professional development tool.

Special Needs Education

The Jean Monnet program provides support to the European Agency for Development in Special Needs Education (EADSNE). The agency is an independent organization maintained by the Ministries of Education in the participating countries, most of whom are members of the EU. While the Agency has a specific focus on students with special educational needs, its mission is to promote their full participation within mainstream education and training. The Agency's project, "Teacher Education for Inclusion" is examining how all teachers (mainstream and specialist/special education teachers) are prepared for inclusive education (EADSNE, 2009).

Language Issues

The EU has policies that protect minority languages. It has funded projects and commissioned studies on the regional and minority languages of Europe (e.g., Gaelic, Catalan, Sami, Romani, etc.) as there is a concern to keep the many languages of Europe alive as well as to support the native language learning of non-native language speakers within member states. The LLP Erasmus program provides support for students to take intensive language courses in the official languages of the EU as well as Icelandic, Norwegian, Turkish, Basque, Catalan, and Galician (Europa, 2009c). Teachers and prospective teachers are supported in training abroad projects funded under the Comenius (student teaching and in-service), Leonardo Da Vinci (vocational education), Erasmus (higher education staff mobility), and Grundtvig (adult education teaching practice) programs.

In addition to language learning, there are projects to support the content learning of bilingual and multilingual learners as well as native and non-native language speakers. For example, the Content and Language Integrated Learning (CLIL) model, a development of bilingual education, is seen as especially responsive to language diversity in Europe where member states and jurisdictions have had to address "the complex specificities of linguistic and cultural diversity" (Coyle, 2002, p. 27). This model, which is used in over 30 countries, relies on foreign language as a tool to support subject learning; for example, German students learning mathematics in Spanish. A wide range of EU initiatives fund programs to support language learning and learning through languages (Coyle, 2008).

Teacher Education

The Thematic Network on Teacher Education in Europe (TNTEE), also funded initially as part of the Socrates/Erasmus program, established a transnational forum for the development of teacher education in Europe (Europa, 2009d). Its membership includes all EU countries, Norway, Iceland, Switzerland, and the United States. The TNTEE is coordinated from Umeå University in Sweden, and serves as a clearinghouse for teacher education research in Europe. It produced the European Commission report on the quality of teacher education in Europe (Commission of the European Communities, 2007), providing an example of how an area within education, such as teacher education, which is organized and controlled nationally, benefits from cooperative internationalism.

Globalization of Education

Globalization *of* education refers to both a process of alignment of national systems for purposes of comparability, collaboration and exchange, and a process of differentiation for the purposes of competition and marketization. Universities, for example, differentiate themselves from each other as they compete for students, but align themselves with each other as they collaborate on research and knowledge exchange activities. The University of Aberdeen's recently approved curriculum reforms are a case in point. As the objectives of the reform project specify: The aim was to make the University's approach "distinctive within the UK and aligned with developments in some of the world's leading universities; to enhance the Aberdeen learning experience; to enhance disciplinary study; and to produce better informed, more rounded and more intellectually flexible graduates." The newly approved programs are intended to be "more attractive to students; more relevant to employers; and more relevant to wider societal needs" (University of Aberdeen, 2008). And yet, while moves to differentiate and align are simultaneous, they occur within national contexts where the role and status of universities vary greatly in terms of how they are funded and supported by the state and in terms of their admission policies. In the United Kingdom, for example, relatively few students go on to university at the end of secondary school, but those that do generally finish in the allotted time of 3 to 4 years. In other countries, such as France, universities are far more accessible, enrolling many more students, but attaining relatively low completion rates.

Alignment of Education in the EU: The Bologna Process

As the member states of the EU have opened their borders, and as the EU has expanded to include more members, there has been an increasing recognition of the essential role that universities play in promoting and ensuring economic prosperity (Commission of the European

Communities, 2007). The Bologna accords, signed in 1999, recognized a European "higher education area" as a necessary strategy "to promote citizens' mobility and employability and the Continent's overall development" (Bologna Declaration, 1999). The original aim was to create a European space for higher education by 2010. Such space was to be created by the convergence of voluntary national reforms of higher education resulting in a system of comparable degrees as well as a system of transferable credits to enable mobility and promote quality assurance. Today more than 40 governments are working to establish common European standards for higher education (Corbett, 2005). A European Credit Transfer and Accumulation System (ECTS) has been agreed upon for higher education degrees at bachelor's, master's, and doctoral levels, and a post-2010 Bologna Process for the consolidation and communication of existing reforms is underway (EUA, 2010).

Teacher Education in European Universities

A TNTEE Green Paper[9] on Teacher Education in Europe (Buchberger et al., 2000), noted that while diversity of programs in terms of their structure is often identified as a salient feature of teacher education in Europe, there are many common patterns and trends across universities in different countries in the preparation of teachers. While teacher education for primary teachers has been influenced by the "normal school" tradition where practical training and teaching practice were historically associated with upper secondary level education (although these have been transferred to postsecondary level non-universities and/or integrated into universities), programs preparing teachers to work in secondary schools were more strongly influenced by an academic tradition and have traditionally been part of university-level education. Over time, the perceived shortcomings of these models of teacher education are thought to have given rise to the contrasting models of "professionalized teacher education" (e.g., Finland, France, or Portugal), which focuses on the development of autonomous and competent teachers, critical intellectuals acting in the interest of their students; or "competency based" models (e.g., England and Wales) similar to those that are widely used in the United States. Still, teacher education has experienced more convergence than divergence over the past 30 years as teacher education has become more formalized.

The European Commission funded Sigma Project (Buchberger et al., 2000) provided a cross-national evaluation of teacher education in the member states in part to enable the coherent integration of knowledge about how teachers might best be prepared, and to facilitate a pan-European network of teacher educators where the conceptual and philosophical problems of equity and inclusion in schooling can be considered as shared concerns. While there are differences in what it means to be a teacher in different countries, there is also a consensus that teacher quality is related to educational outcome. However, the politics of teacher education remains a matter of intense localism and member states control entry into the profession. Even within the countries of the United Kingdom (England, Wales, Scotland, and Northern Ireland), there are national differences in the professional status of teachers as well as differences in how one becomes a teacher and the approach to teacher preparation that is adopted.

International Comparisons of Educational Participation and Achievement

Another form of alignment occurs as a byproduct of international comparisons of how well students within a country perform on standardized tests such as PISA (Programme for International Student Assessment), TIMSS (Trends in International Mathematics and Science Study), and PIRLS (Progress in International Reading Literacy Study). Results of these tests are widely used as international indicators and benchmarks of how well national systems of education are preparing students to live and work in the global economy. As proxy measures, the tests are of "high-stake value" for countries, part of the process of gaining competitive advantage in the marketplace. Preparing students to do well on the tests can have the unintended effect of "homogenizing" curricula.

Given that the original and still fundamental mission of the EU is economic prosperity, with social cohesion acknowledged as a necessary condition, it is not surprising that the economic objectives of schooling, closely linked to a human capital approach to education, dominate the education policies of supranational bodies like the EU. The result, however, is that education for economic purposes is privileged over other purposes of education, as critics of globalization are quick to point out (Kelly, 2007). In addition, marketplace reforms of education have long been associated with various types of inequities in schooling as those with social capital are able to take competitive advantage over those without (e.g., Ball, 1990; Power & Whitty, 1999).

Conclusion

Issues of global diversity are reflected in an increasing multicultural and multilingual student population in both urban and non-urban schools. The movement of people both as a result of economic migration and refugee status has led to new meanings of multiculturalism within the countries of Europe and a new agenda for social inclusion across Europe. Providing a meaningful education to marginalized groups of students within the member countries of the EU poses distinctive challenges for each country as well as to EU policymakers.

The EU recognizes the need to support member states to respond to the challenges of globalization. A 2007 report of the Commission of the European Communities cited a European Council report that found "Education and training are critical factors to develop the EU's long-term potential for competitiveness as well as for social cohesion." It called for reforms "to ensure high quality education systems which are both efficient and equitable." Over the past years, a range of EU programs have provided support for projects to promote the development of teachers' competences, and recently a new Lifelong Learning Programme has increased support for teacher mobility and for cooperation between teacher education institutions. These initiatives are aimed at increasing social cohesion within Europe via cultural exchanges that improve understanding and tolerance of differences. In addition, multinational research projects have been funded by these programs to develop materials and support for teachers in responding to student diversity in schools.

The trend in Europe has been towards the integration of all types of initial teacher education into university faculties. European universities enjoy a long history and substantial legacy as a model of higher education in the modern world, and high-quality university-based teacher education is thought to play an important role in achieving EU objectives (Europa, 2009e). The concept of alignment has a specific meaning in the EU where the Bologna Process has been agreed for the purpose of supporting mobility and exchange.

The four freedoms of the Single Market—the movement of goods, services, people, and money—have, to a large extent narrowly focused EU education policy on economic outcomes. However, the movement of people has also raised equity issues that have focused other policy developments and education projects on issues of social justice, and citizenship. While globalization has its critics, particularly among those who criticize the "human capital" approach to schooling as a form of "prostitution" (Kelly, 2007, p. 54), the increasing diversity of schools cannot be ignored. Responding to this diversity has created a social inclusion agenda within education that calls for the preparation of teachers at all levels who understand from multiple perspectives, and can teach as Gardner (2004) has called for, the fostering of tolerance through a curriculum suited to an era of globalization.

Notes

1 "Unity in diversity" is the official slogan of the European Union
2 The Council of Europe is made up of 47 member states working together to promote the development of a common democratic and legal area across Europe based on common democratic values, human rights, and the rule of law. The Council also seeks cooperation with non-member states (http://www.coe.int/aboutCoe/).

3 Belgium, the Federal Republic of Germany, France, Italy, Luxembourg, and the Netherlands.
4 Denmark, Ireland, and the United Kingdom joined in 1973; in 1981 Greece became the 10th member, followed in 1986 by Spain and Portugal; Austria, Finland, and Sweden joined in 1995. In May 2004 they were joined by the Czech Republic, Cyprus, Estonia, Latvia, Lithuania, Hungary, Malta, Poland, Slovenia, and Slovakia. (Europa, 2009a).
5 These are distributed among three institutions: the European Parliament, the Council of the European Union, and the European Commission.
6 Member states from January 2007 are: Austria, Belgium, Bulgaria, Cyprus, Czech Republic, Denmark, Estonia, Finland, France, Germany, Greece, Hungary, Ireland, Italy, Latvia, Lithuania, Luxembourg, Malta, Poland, Portugal, Romania, Slovakia, Slovenia, Spain, Sweden, the Netherlands and the United Kingdom.
7 Morocco, Algeria, and Tunisia
8 Socrates was replaced by the Lifelong Learning program in 2007.
9 Discussion document.

References

Ball, Stephen (1990). *Politics and policy making in education*, London: Routledge.
Bologna Declaration. (1999). *The Bologna Declaration on the European space for higher education*. Retrieved June 8, 2009, from ec.europa.eu/education/policies/educ/bologna/bologna.pdf
Bartolo, Paul A., Janik, Ivan, Janikova, Vera, Hofsäss, Thomas, Koinzer, Petra, Vilkiene, Vida, Calleja, Colin, Cefai, Carmel, Chetcuti, Ale, Peter, Lous, Annemieke, Mol, Westo, Gun-Marie, & Humphrey, Neil (2007). *Responding to student diversity: Teacher's handbook*. Malta: University of Malta Faculty of Education.
Booth, Tony, Ainscow, Mel, Black-Hawkins, Kristine, Vaughan, Mark, & Shaw, Linda (2000). *The index for inclusion: Developing learning and participation in schools*, Bristol: CSIE.
Buchberger, F., Campos, B. P., Kallos, D., & Stephenson, J. (2000). *Green Paper on teacher education in Europe: High quality teacher education for high quality education and training*. Umeå, Sweden: Thematic Network on Teacher Education in Europe.
Casba, Bánflavy (2007). *The education and the social inclusion of disabled persons in Europe: reforms, theories and policy developments*. Report of Include-ED, Sixth Framework Programme. Brussels: European Commission.
Coatsworth, John H. (2004). Globalization, growth and welfare in history. In Marcelo M. Suárez-Orozco & Desirée Baolian Qin-Hilliard (Eds.), *Globalization: Culture and education in the new millennium* (pp. 38–55). Berkeley: University of California Press.
Commission of the European Communities. (2007). *Improving the quality of teacher education. Communication from the Commission to the Council and the European Parliament*. COM (2007) 392 final. Brussels: Author.
Corbett, Anne (2005). *Universities and the Europe of knowledge: ideas, institutions and policy entrepreneurship in European Community higher education policy, 1955–2005*. Basingstoke, UK: Palgrave Macmillan.

Coyle, Do. (2008). Content and Language Integrated Learning: towards a connected research agenda for CLIL pedagogies.

Coyle, Do. (2002). Relevance of CLIL to the European Commission's Language Learning Objectives. In D. Marsh (Ed.), *CLIL/EMILE-The European dimension: Actions, trends and foresight potential.* Public Services Contract DG EAC: European Commission, Strasbourg.

de Blij, Harm. (2005). *Why Geography matters: Three challenges facing America.* Oxford: Oxford University Press.

Dodds, Anneliesse (2008). How does globalization interact with higher education? The continuing lack of consensus. *Comparative Education, 44*(4), 505–517.

EADSNE. (2009). *Teacher education for inclusive education,* Retrieved November 19, 2009, from http://www.european-agency.org/news/launch-of- the-teacher-education-for-inclusion-project

EADSNE. (2006). *Inclusive education and classroom practice.* Retrieved January 12, 2009, from http://www.european-agency.org/iecp/iecp_intro.htm

EUA (European University Association). (2010). A decade of the Bologna Process. Brussels: European University Association.

Europa. (2009a). *The history of the European Union,* Retrieved June 11, 2009, from http://europa.eu/abc/history/

Europa. (2009b). *European Commission education and training.* Retrieved July 6, 2009, from http://ec.europa.eu/education/lifelong-learning-programme/doc78_en.htm

Europa. (2009c). *Erasmus Programme to finance intensive language courses for Erasmus students in Basque, Catalan and Glacian.* Retrieved July 6, 2009, from http://ec.europa.eu/education/news/news1518_en.htm

Europa. (2009d). *The Thematic Network on Teacher Education (TNTEE).* Retrieved July 6, 2009, from http://tntee.umu.se/index.html

Europa. (2009e). *Toward a Europe of knowledge.* Retrieved July 8, 2009, from http://europa.eu/legislation_summaries/other/c11040_en.htm

European Parliament and Council. (2006). On transnational mobility with the Community for education and training purposes: European Quality Charter for Mobility. *Official Journal of the European Union 30.12.2006 L394/5.* Brussels: European Parliament and Council.

Eurydice. (2003/04a). *Integrating immigrant children into schools in Europe: Country reports, Austria.* Brussels: Author.

Eurydice. (2003/04b). *Integrating immigrant children into schools in Europe: Country reports, France.* Brussels: Author.

Florian, Lani. (2009). Preparing teachers to work in 'schools for all'. *Teaching and Teacher Education, 25*(4), 553–554.

Florian, Lani, & Rouse, Martyn. (2009). The inclusive practice project in Scotland: Teacher education for inclusive education. *Teaching and Teacher Education, 25*(4), 594–601.

Gardner, Howard. (2004). How education changes: Considerations of history, science and values. In Marcelo M. Suárez-Orozco & Desirée Baolian Qin-Hilliard (Eds.), *Globalization: Culture and education in the new millennium* (pp. 235–258). Berkeley: University of California Press.

Gillborn, David, & Youdell, Deborah. (2000). *Rationing education: Policy, practice, reform and equity.* Milton Keynes: Open University Press.

Kelly, Anthony. (2007). *School choice and student well-being: Opportunity and capability in education*. New York: Palgrave Macmillan.

Levitas, Ruth (2005). *The inclusive society? Social exclusion and new Labour* (2nd ed.). London. Palgrave.

Persson, Mangus. (2005). Continuing professional development and networking in Europe. In Alex Alexandrou, Kit Field, & Helen Mitchell (Eds.), *The continuing professional development of educators: Emerging European issues* (pp. 9–24). Oxford: Symposium Books.

Power, Sally, & Whitty, Geoff. (1999). Market forces and school cultures. In J. Prosser (Ed.), *School culture* (pp. 15–29). London: Paul Chapman.

Scottish Executive. (2005). *Supporting Children's Learning: Code of Practice* Edinburgh: Author.

Scottish Executive. (2004). *Curriculum for Excellence*. Edinburgh: Author.

Scottish Teacher Education Committee. (2009). *National framework for inclusion*. Retrieved June 8, 2009, from http://www.frameworkforinclusion.org

Suárez-Orozco, Marcelo M., & Qin-Hilliard, Desirée B. (2004). Globalization: Culture and education in the new millennium In Marcelo M. Suárez-Orozco, & Desirée Baolian Qin-Hilliard (Eds.), *Globalization: Culture and education in the new millennium* (pp. 1–37.). Berkeley: University of California Press.

UNESCO. (2008) *Conclusions and recommendations of the 48th session of the ICE*. Retrieved March 1, 2010, from http://www.ibe.unesco.org/International/ICE48/English/index.html

University of Aberdeen. (2008). *Enhancing Learning: The Aberdeen Approach. The Final Report of the Curriculum Commission*. Retrieved June 9, 2009, from http://www.abdn.ac.uk/curriculum-reform/Aberdeen Scotland: Author

Weiner, Gaby. (2005, November 12–13) The nation strikes back: Recent influences on teacher education in Europe. Paper presented at the symposium Educational Reform and Teachers, Hitotsubashi University, Tokyo, Japan.

Zgaga, Pavel. (2007, February, 9–10). Teacher education, the European dimension and the Bologna Process. Paper presented to the Teacher Education Policy in Europe (TEPE) Network Workshop, University of Tallinn. Retrieved February 9–10, 2009, from http://www.slideshare.net/martlaa/teacher-education-the-european-dimension 27 April 2009

12 Engaged Research/ers, Transformative Curriculum, and Diversity Policy for Teacher Education in the Americas: The United States, Brazil, and Belize

Joyce King, Melissa Speight Vaughn, Petronilha Beatriz Gonçalves e Silva, Regina Conceição, Tatiane Cosentino Rodrigues, and Evaldo Ribeiro Oliveira

> A major problem facing nation-states throughout the world is how to rec-ognize and legitimize difference and yet construct an overarching national identity that incorporates the voices, experiences and hopes of the diverse groups that compose it.
>
> James A. Banks, 2008

Introduction

For nearly two decades Dr Gonçalves e Silva and I, this chapter's two senior authors, have collaborated on various education and action-research activities in our respective universities and communities in Brazil and the United States.[1] In this chapter, written with a team of our cur-rent and former graduate students, who are also educators, we address an important but largely unrecognized perspective on globalization and teacher preparation for diversity. In nations with a shared history of African enslavement as well as different, though arguably similar, lega-cies of anti-black racism, people of African descent globally not only need educational equity, truthful curriculum, and culturally competent teach-ers, we also need to develop our identity and consciousness as African descent people to overcome racial injustice.[2] Banks (2008) argues that in multicultural societies both cultural democracy and cultural citizenship are needed in this global age. In this chapter we share our perspective regarding this view of globalization as engaged researchers seeking to understand and support solutions that we have investigated in education policy, curriculum transformation, and teachers' professional develop-ment in the United States, Brazil, and also Belize.

First, we discuss the U.S. context where curriculum transformation

(King, 1995) has recognized the added value of ethnic identity and racial socialization for group consciousness as a requirement for cultural democracy and human freedom (King, 2005). Next, we consider the Black Movement and the struggle against racism in Brazil that helped to bring about a federal law that mandates teaching African and Afro-Brazilian history and culture at all levels. In our examination of the Brazilian context, where the states and cities maintain public schools (Fishman & Gandin, 2009), we also discuss one municipal government's earlier policies for diversity in partnership with an Afro-Brazilian Cultural Center, as well as emerging affirmative action initiatives in public universities. Last, we discuss diversity policy and teacher preparation in Belize that requires all students learn about their individual ethnicities as well as the Belizean national identity. Each context offers a particular vantage point from which to consider issues of national and racial or ethnic identity, pluralistic education, and teacher preparation for cultural democracy.

The United States: A Textbook Case of Miseducation

> . . . my children are no longer connected emotionally, spiritually, psychologically, or existentially to [Africa] our "motherland."
>
> Carlos E. Russell, 2009

In the United States Black youth are vulnerable to racial animosity, crippling belief structures, economic marginalization, cultural alienation, and self-doubt with regard to their cultural heritage and identity. To reverse this situation teachers need liberating knowledge from beliefs that naturalize the racial/social order—dysconscious racism (King, 1991)—and parents and community members need knowledge of African people's heritage of educational excellence to demand not only high quality teaching, but education that is also liberating versus the limited focus on eliminating the "achievement gap" and increasing students' scores on "high stakes" tests.

The Afrocentric curriculum movement (Asante, 1991) has been all but sidetracked by this high-stakes testing regime. Furthermore, education policy does not reflect a growing body of research that shows positive impacts of culturally relevant curriculum content and pedagogy, as well as racial socialization for Black students' learning, identity development, and resiliency (Chavous et al., 2003; Lee, 2008; Murrell, 2009). Nor does educational policy address the paradox that while U.S. society is culturally diverse, to be "successful" Black youth are more likely to be encouraged to "assimilate." The emphasis is on the pursuit of individualistic educational goals to escape from their communities rather than as a pathway toward accomplishments that can contribute to their sense of belonging as citizens of a cultural democracy *and* to group strength for people of African descent.

Recently, community mobilizations have achieved legislation that requires African American history in Philadelphia schools, taught from a Black Studies perspective, and beginning with the state of New Jersey, Amistad Commissions have also been established in Illinois, Connecticut, and New York to investigate similar curriculum reforms (State of New Jersey, 2010).[3] Susan Goodwin and Joyce King have produced a Model Curriculum Framework, including Criterion Standards for Contextualized Teaching and Learning about People of African Descent, developed in partnership with the Rochester, New York Teacher Center (RTC), and the National Urban League (Goodwin & King, 2007). At the RTC professional development "practice site," an African/African American "living" museum developed by Susan Goodwin, pedagogical/cultural demonstrations and workshops prepare teachers to produce model lessons using criterion standards such as these:

1) African humanity and civilization are anterior in the recorded history of the world. Classical Africa was a primary influence on European growth, development, and civilization;

2) African diasporan histories begin in Africa with human history, not with the period of enslavement . . .;

5) African descent people are one people, continental and diasporic. There is a cultural unity across diasporan communities as well as a common experience of domination, disenfranchisement, and social/political/economic inequalities . . .;

17) Globalization refers to the most recent phase of the worldwide economic system of interlocking interests, power structures, and institutions of domination that transcend national borders . . .

(Goodwin & King, 2007)

Teachers are using these standards, which are informed by a Black Studies intellectual approach, to develop meaningful curricula. One teacher reports, for example:

The criterion standards are a very powerful set of norms, especially for teaching students of color. Not only do the standards support learning and educational development suited for the 21st century, but the overall ontological orientation enables the student to produce knowledge consistent with his/her own cultural tendencies.

(A. Kareem, personal communication, July 10, 2009)

Recommendations of the American Educational Research Association (AERA) Commission on Research in Black Education suggest policy levers that include an important role for Black Studies scholarship in transforming educational practice, including teachers' professional development.[4] For example, in contrast to the standards just discussed, textbooks that continue to separate Egypt culturally and geographically from Africa, and the dominant narrative about African enslavement ("Africans sold their own brothers and sisters into slavery") undermine Black students' identification with Africa and their cultural agency (King, 1992).[5] It is not unusual to hear Black students declare: "I ain't no African," when the subject of our African ancestry comes up at school (King & Williams, in press).

This knowledge problem, which is global (Gonçalves e Silva, 2005; Seck, 2005), highlights the practical importance for teacher and student learning and development when curricula, effective teaching, and academic success are understood to include maintaining a positive identification with one's cultural heritage. This is what the imminent scholar Asa G. Hilliard emphasized as education *and* socialization for incorporation into one's community (Lee, 2008).

Thus, the transformative curriculum task of rewriting partial, hegemonic narratives of enslavement requires African perspectives that are only accessible using African language concepts that reveal the moral mindset and cultural practices of African people themselves. Keywords in Songhoy-Senni (a language spoken in West Africa) are one resource that can challenge the dominant canard in historical scholarship that reduces the historical complexity to the half-truth that "slavery" was endemic to Africa, and Africans themselves were, therefore, responsible for the transatlantic "slave trade" as well. In Songhoy-Senni, however, "*baanya*," the word for "slave," means "one who does not even have a mother"—referring to lineageless persons who had lost their freedom in war or as punishment for crime (instead of the European practice of imprisonment). Indeed, there is no indigenous word for prison in Songhoy-Senni and other African languages (DeWolf, 2008; Maiga, 2010). Thus, it is important to consider a more democratic understanding of teachers' cultural competence that includes autochthonous perspectives on what is taught to incorporate not just knowledge and dialogue *about* culture, but also what teachers need to know, be able to do, and be like to teach *through* students' cultures (Goodwin & Swartz, 2004). In Brazil, which we consider next, and in Belizean examples that follow, policies to achieve more equitable educational systems have yet to embrace these aspects of culture as an asset for teaching and learning.

Ethnic-Racial Relations and Education for Equity and Diversity in Brazil

> It must be stressed that there is still no consensus among the Brazilian elite, or even among Brazilian social scientists, that Brazil suffers from significant and systematic racial discrimination . . . [Will] Afro-Brazilians come to see their life situation as being determined to a significant degree by racial discrimination . . . will they translate that consciousness into collective action?
>
> Thomas Skidmore, 1992

A brief review of "ethnic-racial" relations in Brazil begins with the two major events that challenged Brazilians after the abolition of slavery in 1888 and the advent of the Brazilian Republic in 1889: to build a nation and a national identity that included the formerly enslaved African population and to turn them into citizens holding rights and duties. With few exceptions, the ideology of biological determinism influenced the majority of the intellectuals who dedicated themselves to the task of defining a unique identity for the nation.

For example, eugenics (the applied science that aimed to "ameliorate" the human race) had wide support among both liberals and conservatives before the Nazis appropriated it in the 1930s. This "scientific racism" included a growing belief that Black people were genetically inferior to whites and mulattos were degenerate (Outhwaite & Bottomore, 1996, p. 289). Eugenicists argued that "race mixing" would eliminate Black people and lead gradually to a purely white Brazilian population (Nascimento, 1979). "Whitening" the population, or miscegenation, according to this ideology, was seen as the only possible alternative. The idea that white blood "would purify, dilute and exterminate" black blood (Heringer, 1995, p. 219) opened the possibility for mestizos in Brazil to ascend to the "civilized" stage (Guimarães, 1999, p. 50).

Scholars suggest that the writing of social historian Gilberto Freyre (1933), who promoted this ideology, "provided a sanitized version of Brazil's long history of colonization and slavery," turning the negative image of miscegenation into a positive phase of nation building (Twine, 1997, p. 6). According to Freyre, Brazilian society was free from the racism that afflicted other nations, and in Brazil slavery and race relations were more benign than in the United States. Thus, the myth of "racial democracy," which was documented by the Black American sociologist, E. Franklin Frazier (1942), became one of the central tenets of Brazilian national identity and continues to exalt the idea that individuals from all social classes and ethnic groups live together harmoniously (De Sousa & Nascimento, 2008). As Heringer (1995) noted, "a sense that racial discrimination is more than isolated actions of individuals" is missing in Brazilian society (p. 205). This national ideology that also has been a pillar of the education system allows dominant elites to obscure racial discrimination and blocks non-white Brazilians' consciousness of their victimization and any sense of group identity (Munanga, 1999, p. 80).

Historically, the Black Movement has played an important role in opposing the myth of racial democracy in Brazil, exposing the social exclusion that Afro-Brazilians—who comprise, arguably, half the population—suffer as a result of racial discrimination and racism (Rocha, 2000).[6] The contemporary Black Movement identifies the subaltern integration of the Black population as the main indicator of the persistence of racism. Black Movement activists recognized that "race" could be used to mobilize society toward the democratization of social relations. The

Movement's long struggle for attention to racial issues in educational policy was vindicated by Federal Law No. 10,639 that was approved in 2003, and mandated the study of "Afro-Brazilian and African History and Culture" throughout the education system.[7] Also, in 2004, the National Council of Education/Plenary Council (CNE/CP) approved Edict 3/2004 that created the National Curricular Directive for Education for Ethnic Racial Relations and the Study of Afro-Brazilian and African History and Culture, and the objectives of a new Secretariat of Continuing Education, Literacy, and Diversity (SECAD) included "valuing the richness of our ethnic and cultural diversity." These initiatives constitute important developments for Brazil's national agenda.

Paradoxically, when the educational system, which has had a eugenic orientation and homogenization as fundamental principles (Dávila, 2003), finally began to address diversity, it became one of the main arenas for the diversity debate, for the mobilization of social movements to challenge racial discrimination, and one of the most important contexts for national development that democratizes social relations.[8] Next, drawing on our own action-research experiences and observations, we describe how a municipality and university-based Black Movement scholar-activists partnered to support policies that advance education for improving ethnic-racial relations in one community in Brazil.

Policy for Diversity: The Case of São Carlos, Brazil

The administration of the City of São Carlos (City Hall)[9] that was elected in 2001[10] demonstrated its commitment to equity and diversity in pioneering and innovative ways by establishing specific governmental objectives related to human rights (for children, youth, older people, women, and for Brazilians of African descent in particular). Given that São Carlos represents Brazil's social conservatism, the election of a democratic government demonstrated that the population wanted change. To guarantee the rights of groups considered to be "minorities," in 2001 the city formed the *Session* for the Fight Against Racism and Discrimination within the Citizenship and Social Assistantship Secretariat (SMCAS). Between 2002 and 2008 successful educational approaches were recognized and rewarded by non-governmental community agencies that promote education for ethnic-racial relations. In 2008 an administrative reform established a Division of Policies for Racial Equality the objective of which was to actively promote ethnic-racial equality through collaboration with the other municipal Secretariats, foundations, *Autarquias* (an autonomous, de-centralized unit that indirectly assists in federal public administration), and Civil Society organizations, particularly on behalf of Afro-descendants.

To implement this municipal policy in the schools of São Carlos, it was necessary to prepare teachers, school directors, pedagogy coordinators, students, and families, as well as other education professionals to understand the meaning of ethnic-racial relations in education. The objectives of the continuing education academic courses offered for teachers included developing instructional materials, analyzing textbooks and images in existing materials, and the preparation of an introduction to African history and culture. The *Nucleus* (Center) for Afro-Brazilian Studies (NEAB) at the Federal University of São Carlos also offered a course in "Afro-Brazilian and African Cultural Studies." In addition, teachers, professors, school staff, as well as students and their families participated in two- to three-hour thematic workshops focused on teaching about ethnic-racial relations as part of the Work Schedule of the Pedagogy Collective (*Horários de Trabalho Pedagógico Coletivo*).

As noted previously, Federal Edict 3/2004 mandated teaching "Afro-Brazilian and African History and Culture" in public and private education. However, public sector teachers in São Carlos, motivated by the ongoing curricular reform policy City Hall had previously initiated, had already taken steps since 2001 to promote education for ethnic-racial relations. Teachers who implemented the policy reform reported a number of positive outcomes that were important not only for students and teachers, but also for the community at large. For example, accepting and understanding positive ethnic-racial relations strengthened Black students' self-esteem and teachers noticed behavior and attitude changes such as a decline in bullying and name-calling among Black and non-Black students.

Educational activities for ethnic-racial equality in São Carlos have not been limited to municipal schools. In 2006, to commemorate the legacy of *Zumbi*, the leader of the *Quilombo dos Palmares*, the historic maroon community that is an important symbol of resistance to slavery in Brazil, the City of São Carlos, with the Federal University of São Carlos, inaugurated the Odette dos Santos Afro-Brazilian Municipal Cultural Center.[11] This Cultural Center showcases educational projects for the entire community mainly through arts and cultural expression of African origin. It includes a hip-hop studio for dancers, DJs, B-Boys, and B-Girls,[12] graffiti arts, the Dance Project, which offers urban "street" dancing, African dance and classical ballet classes, and an Art Exhibitions Room. An "Africanities" (African Heritage) Room dedicated to research and exhibitions on Afro-Brazilian and African history and culture, first initiated at the Federal University of São Carlos in 1999, by Professor Petronilha B. Gonçalves e Silva, as part of a UNESCO Laboratory for Human Rights program and transferred to the City of São Carlos, includes interactive presentations, traveling exhibitions, workshops for students and teachers, and support-related research. The Africanities Room is open to anyone interested in investigating and gaining knowledge about the culture and history of the African continent and African migration. Both permanent and temporary African and Afro-Brazilian culture and history collections serve all ages, educational levels, and research interests, as well as public and private schools from kindergarten to high schools and higher education.

Finally, in addition to its educational, pedagogic, and scientific role, the Cultural Center's programs strengthen the African identity of Afro-Brazilians in the context of education for ethnic-racial relations. Many city residents, including teachers, have revealed their lack of knowledge of and surprise to learn about the people of the African continent and about African people's migrations to other continents. It is also interesting to note that Black visitors and program participants gain a feeling of self-worth when learning about their origins in Africa and the value of the contributions of their ancestors to the development of humankind and to the Brazilian nation. Many return to the Cultural Center as volunteers, which is an indirect indication of the impact of this facility in the community.

In 2008, when the municipal government changed, there was a lack of continuity and coherence in the implementation of the city's educational policies. That officials believed "diversity" had already been achieved and that this presumed "success" was not documented indicates the prevalence of the myth of racial democracy and how a simplistic understanding of diversity blocks critical awareness and any propensity toward gathering empirical data to evaluate the results of significant policy reform efforts. Thus, those who want to maintain advantages for certain social and ethnic-racial groups can undermine reform policies established to respond to the demands of social movement groups to address discrimination and diversity. While not a direct consequence of the lack of knowledge of education activists and teachers, it is worth noting that educators in schools and classrooms are often not able to critically analyze the obduracy of the social inequity ethnic-racial realities in Brazil engender. That is why collaboration among scholar-activists and Movement activists is so important. However, without short-, medium-, and long-term objectives, supported by adequate funds, material conditions, and professional training for those responsible for the policy, it will remain a mere intention that does not go beyond a written document. As Edict 3/2004 (which mandated, teaching Afro-Brazilian and African history and culture) states:

> The success of federal, institutional and pedagogic public policies that aim to repair, recognize and valorize the identity, culture and history of Black Brazilians depends necessarily, on physical, financial, material, intellectual and affective conditions favorable to teaching and learning; in other words, all black and non-black students, as well as their teachers, need to feel valued and supported.
>
> (Brazil Ministry of Education, 2004, p. 13)

Thus, the São Carlos example also suggests that merely creating public policy to support diversity, either through laws and/or mandatory programs, projects, etc., is not enough to guarantee their implementation or institutionalization. Still, Secretariats, educational directives, and school programs constitute learning spaces that inform and sensitize teachers, pedagogy coordinators, administrative employees, and other school staff. Implementing public policies that support racial equality, that is, education for ethnic-racial relations or teaching Afro-Brazilian, African, and Indigenous history and culture, directly addresses Brazilian national identity and recognizes and valorizes the nation's ethnic-racial roots.

Reserved Places at Public Universities

Brazilians, especially at public universities, are living in the midst of momentous societal change created by new investments in the public sector that are expanding the number of available places at the University and creating reserved places (or "quotas") for minorities.[13] In 2001, the state universities of Rio de Janeiro (Universidade do Estado do Rio de Janeiro) and Universidade Estadual do Norte do Fluminense) were the first Brazilian public universities to reserve 40% of their places for "self-declared blacks" (*negroes*) and browns (*pardos*). In 2004, the University of Brasilia became the first federal university to implement an affirmative policy for Black and indigenous people in Brazil.[14] These policies are intended to overcome the social and ethnic-racial inequalities among white, Black, and indigenous students who graduated from public and private high schools, participants in social movements, the politically "exiled," and other disadvantaged citizens (Htun, 2004).

In this context of mandated access to public universities, we reviewed the progress several Brazilian universities are making toward achieving diversity goals by examining their websites in order to review their undergraduate and graduate educational programs (e.g., all course curricula, short courses, professional meetings, conferences, etc.). First, we found a number of programs and courses that are not part of the formal course of study. Black professors or researchers who specialize in ethnic-racial relations teach some of these optional course subjects, and some continuing education courses were also designed for community members outside the university. Second, we also found a record of presentations at scientific meetings, seminars, conferences, and lectures organized by graduate and undergraduate students and professors associated with Afro-Brazilian Studies groups and national associations of researchers and graduate students that have focused on ethnic-racial relations. Between 1998 and 2007 the Association of Graduate Studies and Research in Education (ANPED), with the Educative Action group and financial support from the Ford Foundation commissioned early career researchers to study issues related to "Blacks and Education." Three M.A. theses and one doctoral dissertation were completed between 2003 and 2009. ANPED also created the Afro-Brazilians and Education Working Group, which presented various studies on this topic at the annual meeting of the National Association of Graduate Studies and Research in the Social Sciences conference (ANPOCS) (Fleuri, Bittencourt, & Schucman, 2002).

Finally, education programs identified through this review of university websites included those that were organized before Edict 3/2004, which, like this legislation, resulted from the Black Movement's collaboration with higher education institutions as well as independent activities. For example, the Center for Afro-Oriental Studies (CEAO) at the Federal University of Bahia has existed for the past 50 years and the NEAB has been in existence at the Federal University of São Carlos for 18 years. While these universities, among others, had already sponsored or organized educational activities for improving ethnic-racial relations; most of the time, however, these initiatives, including continuing education programs for teachers and political education for social movement militants and other activists, benefited communities outside the university.

Considering the historic inattention to racial discrimination and racism in education in Brazil, broad-based public education strategies are needed to undo the ideology of racial democracy (Hanchard, 1999). Tavolaro (2008) discusses the form of "affirmative action" that has emerged in Brazil as part of the "discourse on race." Education policies, practices, and strategies for racial-ethnic equality must be continuously and conscientiously monitored and evaluated, especially as these initiatives are being debated. Thus, there is an important role for engaged research/ers because attention to such issues risks being transformed into merely focusing on content and teaching methods, which does not necessarily mean addressing the fundamental and systematic reformulation of the educational principles, objectives, and methodologies that contribute to ethnic-racial inequity.

The next section of the chapter examines two education policies in Belize that influenced how ethnicity and national identity are incorporated into the social studies curriculum and teacher preparation programs. Based on teacher interviews in Belize and a selected review of relevant scholarship and research on educational change in this postcolonial Central American nation, this discussion argues for professionalization of teacher preparation in higher education.

Teacher Education and Diversity in Belize

> Beginning with the Black Power movement of the late 1960s and early 1970s, middle- and working-class Creole youth increasingly adopted an Afrocentric cultural consciousness that distinguished them both from their elders and other ethnic groups in Belizean society.
>
> R. George Daniel, 2006

Belize, formerly British Honduras, is an ecological and archeological wonder. The country lies south of Mexico, east of Guatemala, and north of Honduras, with the Caribbean Sea as its western border. Belize also boasts of the longest barrier reef in the western hemisphere and is the center for ecological tourism on the isthmus. Its position at the intersection of local and global identification is reflected in the field of education. While international and regional organizations have imposed their structure on its government and education, Belize continues to exert its foundational belief in the strength of diversity.[15] Emerging from over three centuries of British colonial domination (from 1862 to 1981), this self-proclaimed pluralistic society—composed of many cultures speaking many languages—went to great lengths to define itself and its culture (Peedle, 1999). A fuller analysis of Belize's colonial history, current state of race and class relations, and anti-Black and anti-Indian racism would consider the Belizean "myth of racial harmony" (i.e.,"race-mixing," associating "degeneracy" with blackness, etc.). For example, Appelbaum, Macpherson, and Rosemblatt (2003) argue:

> Middle-class Belizean Creoles suppressed their own mixed-race lineages by removing the black mother and her mixed-race offspring from the founding moment of the Creole nation . . . [thus] their fitness to legislate. By associating themselves with whiteness without explicitly claiming to be white, middle-class Creoles presented themselves as authentic natives [versus indigenous Maya] who, as Britain's partners in governance, could secure a racially harmonious and loyal colonial nation.
>
> (p. 109)

Nationalism and pluralistic education goals co-exist in Belize and have influenced educational policy, national identity, and academic curricula while the professionalization of teacher education lags behind. While policy mandates have resulted in a greater variety of higher education programs to certify teachers, teacher preparation in Belize needs to be professionalized to fulfill national development expectations, as well as educational policies. Belize (like many postcolonial societies) maintains a practice of hiring citizens, even if they do not have teacher preparation or formal training (Thompson, 2008). However, the policy and practice of non-traditional preparation and on-the-job training ill equips teachers to deliver the national curriculum effectively (Mullens, Murnane, & Willett, 1996). This is especially crucial for national goals given the need to address the nation's diversity through a sound curriculum approach.

The diversity of Belize's population mirrors its diverse landscape. Each of Belize's 12 ethnic groups has deep cultural connections to the land (Peedle, 1999). Not surprisingly, themes of race, ethnicity, and nationalism have been embedded in the national mission, goals, and objectives

for education. Educational policy adheres to the same nationalist principles and cultural policies implemented after independence in 1983. The
National Culture Policy Council initiative of 1993 remained committed
to pluralism, as it was deemed necessary to realize the goal of national
unity (Grant, 1976). Education was used to transmit these ideas (Post,
1995). Pan-ethnic nationalist identity and individuals' ethnic cultures
are introduced in primary schools to foster both national and individual identities. (The term Pan-ethnic nationalist identity denotes ethnicity
and Belizean citizenship.) Essentially, to be Belizean entails ethnic group
membership (Haug, 1998).[16]

The Belizean social studies curriculum has absorbed this national
goal, emphasizing the teaching of ethnicity in the context of nationalism (Oestrich, 2002). The history of the nation was depicted through a
political prism that guided content selection. Efforts to transition from
colonial education to Belizean education resulted in additions to, and
deletions from, this curriculum. Since independence, local Belizean history has replaced British history (Rutheiser, 1990). Initially, however,
ancient history of the region was not included in the social studies curriculum this policy. For example, the Garinigu people were included in the
curriculum with the exclusion of the (indigenous) Maya. Progressively,
the curriculum grew to incorporate ancient Mayan history, as well as the
contributions of Belize's diverse ethnic groups. However, ethnicity was
celebrated through surface multicultural activities, such as the observance
of national holidays, participation in cultural events, and display of ethnic clothing, all of which researchers have deemed ineffective (Banks &
Banks, 1989; Howard, 2006; Nieto, 2000). In addition, conversations
among teachers about racial inequalities, privilege, prejudice, and their
economic impact are unlikely because of a lack of training in general and
regarding such important issues, in particular. Nor can student goals of
personal development, social responsibility, and citizenship in the context
of social justice and peace be realized without trained teachers who have
a level of relevant professional knowledge and critical knowledge of the
nation's history (Howard, 2006; King, 2006).

A scarcity of resources continues to impact teacher education negatively.
Teacher education in Belize was developed in the context of colonialism
and continues to reflect vestiges of that past (Thompson, 2008). In addition to schools established by the state, religious groups were allowed
to set up schools to assist in educating Belize's youth. Missionaries and
teachers trained in Britain staffed schools funded by churches. As Belize
transitioned to self-government and eventually to independence, the
administration of church and state schools was transferred to Belizeans
(Phillips, 1998). These schools were, and still are, curricularly and profes-
sionally disjoined (Bennett, 1999). The daunting task of staffing schools
resulted in the practice of hiring teachers without certification or training.
Sixth form graduates, who have the equivalent of an Associate's degree,

are hired to educate the nation's elementary school youth and are allowed a four to five-year grace period within which to enroll in a formal teacher education program to obtain a bachelor's degree (Thompson, 2008). This non-traditional route toward teacher preparation undermines the field's professionalism and contributes to a high teacher turnover rate—a trend that continues despite Government Legislation of 2000 mandating teacher licensure (Belize Ministry of Education, 2000).

In August 2000, Belize's Ministry of Education introduced new legislation that required elementary and secondary school teachers to have a teaching license issued by the state (Belize Ministry of Education, 2000). This mandate increased the number of teachers enrolled in post-secondary teacher training programs, but it has nevertheless been slow to change the field of teacher education. School administrators, government policy, and teacher education programs themselves have contributed to this lag. As a result, untrained teachers continue to be hired. For example, school administrators in church and state schools did not encourage applicants to seek post-secondary training prior to employment. Employed teachers enjoyed the benefit of receiving a full salary while preparing for college entrance exams. Teacher preparation programs only admitted teachers with classroom experience, and the government fully financed the cost of their education on a sabbatical basis.

There existed two institutions with teacher training programs, Belize Teacher's Training College and the University of Belize. While the University provided training programs, Belize Teacher Training College was solely dedicated to training elementary school teachers (Thompson & Crossley, 1999). Belize Teachers' Training College adhered to these policies by excluding admission for pre-service teachers. However, since the 2000 legislation, the college has enlarged their admissions to include pre-service teachers into the program. The government also accredited junior colleges to prepare citizens for teacher training programs. Presently, there exist in excess of seven junior colleges designed to feed into one of the two college or university training programs. Licensure, as defined by the state, not only requires coursework, but also passing a battery of exams.[17]

Professionalizing the field of education in Belize would provide a plethora of educational benefits at every level, including higher education. Initially training teachers is a benefit to students. Many inexperienced teachers are learning the profession on the job at the expense of students and national development. Professionalization will increase the pool of trained teachers, decrease turnover, and enable career teachers to inform teaching strategies and enhance resource materials. Additionally, higher education can play an enhanced role in the nation through multicultural teacher education that prepares teachers, for example, to draw upon the nation's rich diversity as a resource in writing curriculum that fulfills national goals. While professionalizing the field of education is not a cure for all the ills of Belizean education, it is a start that has promise. The

Ministry of Education has provided a foundation of pluralistic policies for the education of its citizens, but does not provide fiscal or executive support or rewards to fully implement and assess the effectiveness of this policy framework. Governmental legislation has created the stimulus to increase licensure and professionalism in the field of education, but continues to lack enforcement. Thus, the great resources of diversity and history in Belize remain repressed and under-utilized in so far as education is concerned by a lack of training, leadership, execution, adequate funding, and evaluation.

Conclusion: "Just Who Are We?"

> Sylvia Wynter: I knew nothing about my own historical reality, except in negative terms that would have made it normal for me, as Fanon points out, both to want to be a British subject and in so wanting, to be anti-black, anti-everything I existentially was. I knew what it was to experience a total abjection of being.
>
> David Scott, 2000

In the United States, Brazil as well as Belize (and other nations) where linkages have existed between "whiteness and civilization . . . [and] among blackness, hybridity and degeneracy" (Appelbaum et al., 2003, p. 109), African-descent youth need opportunities to recover and to identify with their African heritage, which encompasses more than slavery and popular music culture and images of urban youth that globalized corporate media project worldwide. Youth in Brazil and Belize are increasingly "fascinated" and identify with Black popular culture. Educators use a hip-hop dance studio in São Carlos's Afro-Brazilian Municipal Cultural Center to reach youth and develop their cultural identity and group pride. However, if education in the increasingly globalizing world of the 21st century is to mean preparation for *cultural citizenship*, that is, incorporation into one's cultural or ethnic community and *cultural democracy*, what is and is not taught about Africa and African people's heritage—in the curriculum and in teacher education—is vitally important for curriculum and teacher education policy, practice, theorizing, and for engaged research/ers.

This perspective on globalization and diversity is absent from the literature on effective strategies for "preparing teachers for the global age"(Longman Foundation, 2008). Research and evaluation of education policy for equity are needed to address professional preparation in which the definition of "quality teaching" is expanded to incorporate pedagogical practices that enable teachers to nourish cultural democracy by affirming students' group consciousness as well as their national identity. Banks (2008) notes that Carter G. Woodson (1933/1977) had "made a case for cultural democracy," as opposed to the "miseducation" of students and teachers, "when he argued that a curriculum for African American students should reflect their history and culture". This observation applies to youth in other nations as well. In addition, what is ultimately at stake, as the AERA Commission on Research in Black Education emphasized, is the cultural well-being of African Americans as a requirement for human freedom (King, 2005).

While educators and activists in Brazil emphasize "race" to press for the democratization of society, the Brazilian model of "racial democracy" and increasing references to a "post-racial" America since President Barack Obama's election suggest a possible convergence toward the "Latin Americanization" of the United States. However, one commentator laments, "Just Who Are We?" observing that a younger generation of Black Americans "believ[es] that 'change' has already come, is more apt to embrace 'nationality' over 'race' and is unwilling to wage a continued struggle for retention of their African identity" (Russell, 2009). Black people in the United States, and elsewhere, need education for global consciousness, that is, opportunities to rescue our ethnic identity—and African legacy—in order to build truly multiracial societies in which other groups can join in the struggle for real democracy that values diversity and racial justice.

Notes

1 In 1991, Joyce King and Petronilha Beatriz Gonçalves e Silva offered a citywide professional development course—the first on this topic—for teachers and a community workshop for parents, both on "Racism and Discrimination in Education" in São Carlos, Brazil.

2 U.S. racism defined Black identity in rigid black-white binary terms of the "one-drop rule" of Jim Crow segregation and white *supremacy*. Brazil's "colorism" exists in a multiracial "ternary" (black, white, mixed) context with more fluid ethnic identification but also racial ambiguity and white *superiority* (Daniel, 2006; also, Telles, 2004).

3 Amistad Commissions are state-appointed panels that examine how African American history and culture are being taught in public schools. The aim is to ensure that the history and legacy of slavery are not neglected. See State of New Jersey, 2010.

4 The AERA Commission on Research in Black Education recommended: "Public policy development informed by international comparative research that enhances the education, survival, and advancement of African descent people [including] assessing the impact of African language, culture, and heritage study in motivating student effort and engagement as well as teacher knowledge and development in various African and Diaspora contexts" (King, 2005, p. 355).

5 A history textbook locates Egypt in "North Africa, Southwest Asia and Central Asia"—a "region" that includes Algeria, Saudi Arabia, Turkey, Pakistan, Uzbekistan, etc.—that appears separated from the "sub-Saharan" part of the African continent. See Richard G. Boehm et al., *Exploring Our World* (Columbus: Glencoe/McGraw-Hill, 2008).

6 J. Rocha (2000) reported that "blacks are almost totally absent from positions of power—from all levels of government, from congress, the senate, the judiciary, the higher ranks of the civil service and the armed forces." This is so "even in Salvador . . . where blacks make up more than 80% of the population . . ." (see Rocha, 2000). Telles (2002) noted: "according to the 1991 Census, the population of Brazil is 52 per cent white, 41 per cent brown, 5 per cent black . . ." Such statistics may reflect "inflated whiteness" (Twine, 1997) or self-identification within Brazil's complex (ternary) racial/ skin-color classification system, e.g., *branco*/white, *pardo*/brown, *preto*/black, the more ambiguous *moreno*/brunette, etc. (Telles, 2004).

7 Since the 1988 Federal Constitution to the current government, mainly up to 2003, the Brazilian Ministry of Education created various "spaces" for diversity such as: the National Curricular Parameters (*Parâmetros Curriculares Nacionais*, PCNs) on "cultural plurality"; the *References and National Curricular Parameters for Indigenous Schools*; and *Diversity in the University*, etc.

8 One indicator of the importance of difference and cultural identity issues in educational research is the work presented at the National Society of Graduate Studies in Education 25th annual meeting. Of 491 studies submitted,70 discussed questions related to diversity and difference in education (Fleuri et al., 2002, p. 1).

9 Located in São Paulo State 235 km from the capital, São Paulo, and recognized as the "National Capital of Technology," the city of São Carlos hosts several technology enterprises, two nationally and internationally recognized public universities—Universidade Federal de São Carlos (UFSCar) and Universidade de São Paulo (USP). The Black population is a minority.

10 The current administration is the third popularly elected democratic government in São Carlos: 2001 to 2004; 2005 to 2008; and 2009 to 2012.

11 Odette dos Santos, a black woman who was admired and honored in São Carlos, created the city's first Samba School. Brazilian Samba schools, volunteer musical groups that organize traditional Carnival floats/displays, also function as neighborhood associations that address various community needs (e.g., medicine, education, etc.).Eventually "Odette and her Samba School" became the "Samba School of May Flower." The "familiar and entertaining" May Flower Club, an important social and benevolent organization established May 4th 1928 by Black railway workers of the Paulista Company. Odette was the daughter of the club's founders. In 2009 Odette would have been 81 years old.

12 B-boys/B-girls refers to the "break-boys/girls" who engage in improvisational hip-hop or break-dancing.

13 In *University World News*, Simon Schwartzman (2009) reported the Brazilian Congress was discussing legislation, introduced by the government of President Luiz Ignázio Lula da Silva, requiring federal (public) higher education institutions to introduce a 50% quota for poor, Black, and indigenous descent public school graduates. This legislation is currently under review by the Supreme Court.

14 Lilia G. M. Tavolaro (2008). Affirmative action in contemporary Brazil: Two institutional discourses. *International Journal of Politics, Culture, and Society, 19*(3–4), June, pp. 145–160. Published online at DOI: 10.1007/s10767–008–9022-z

15 UNESCO funding to the postcolonial nation was accompanied by educational reforms in curricula and teacher education. In addition, American universities excavated Mayan ruins and prescribed relevant curricular modifications. Belize administers the Caribbean-based examinations instead of British exit exams.

16 The 1980 Census listed 39.7% of the population as Creole (English speakers largely descended from enslaved Africans). The Creole (Kriols), Afro-Caribbean, and Garifuna (Garinigu, Black Caribs) form the majority of the Afro-Latin Americans in Central America. See "The Cultural Diversity of Belizean Society." Retrieved August 25, 2010, from http://countrystudies.us/belize/23.htm

17 English teachers interviewed in Orange Walk Town, Belize, revealed that prospective teachers are required to take a battery of at least three tests for certification. Teachers also stated that pursuit of a Bachelor's degree in education required two years away from family.

References

Appelbaum, Nancy, Macpherson, A. S., & Rosemblatt, K. A. (2003). *Race & nation in modern Latin America*. Chapel Hill: University of North Carolina Press.

Asante, Molefi K. (1991). Afrocentric curriculum. *Educational Leadership, 49*(4), 28–31.

Banks, James A. (2008). Diversity, group identity, and citizenship in a global age. *Educational Researcher, 37*(3), 129–139.

Banks, James A., & Banks, Cherry A. (1989). *Multicultural education: Issues and perspectives*. Needham Heights, MA: Simon and Schuster.

Belize Ministry of Education. (2000). *Handbook of policies and procedures for school services*. Belmopan: Author.

Bennett, J. Alexander. (1999). *Belize primary education development project: Improving quality on the provision of education for all in Belize*. An examination of the impact of a Basic Education Project. UNESCO report. Retrieved October 8, 2010, from http://www.unesco.org/education/wef/countryreports/belize/contents.html

Brazil Ministry of Education. (2004). Parecer No. 003. *Diretrizes Curriculares Nacionais para a Educação das Relações Étnico-Raciais e para o Ensino de História e Cultura Afro-Brasileira e Africana*. Brasília: Author.

Chavous, Tabbye M., Bernat, D. H., Schmeelk-Cone, K., Caldwell, C H., Kohn-Wood, L., & Zimmerman, M. A. (2003). Racial identity and academic attainment among African American adolescents. *Child Development, 74*(4), 1076–1090.

Daniel, G. Reginald. (2006). *Race and multiraciality in Brazil and the United States: Converging paths?* University Park: Penn State Press.

Dávila, Jerry. (2003). *Diploma of whiteness, race and social policy in Brazil, 1917–1945*. Chapel Hill: Duke University Press.

De Sousa, Leone C., & Nascimento, Paulo. (2008). Brazilian national identity at a crossroads: The myth of racial democracy and the development of Black identity. *International Journal of Politics, Culture, and Society, 19*(3–4), June, pp. 102–215.

DeWolf, Thomas N. (2008). *Inheriting the trade: A northern family confronts its legacy as the largest slave-trading dynasty in U.S. history*. Boston: Beacon.

Fishman, Gustavo E., & Gandin, Luis, A. (2009). Pedagogies of inclusion: Lesson from Escola Cidadã. In Soula Mitakidou, Evangelia Tressou, Beth Blue Swadener, & Carl A. Grant (Eds.), *Beyond pedagogies of exclusion in diverse childhood contexts: Transnational challenges* (pp. 65–80). New York: Palgrave.

Fleuri, Reinaldo M., Bittencourt, Silvana. M, & Schucman, Lia V. (2002). *A questão da diferença na educação: Para além da diversidade. 25th annual meeting of ANPEd. Caxambu, Brazil.* Retrieved July 10, 2009, from http://www. anped.org.br/25/sessoesespeciais

Frazier, E. Franklin. (1942). The Negro family in Bahia, Brazil. *American Sociological Review, 7*(4), 465–478.

Freyre, Gilberto. (1933). *Casa grande and senzala.* Rio de Janeiro: Schmidt.

Gonçalves e Silva, Petronilha B. (2005). A new millennium research agenda in Black education: Some points to be considered for discussion and decision. In Joyce E. King (Ed.), *Black education: A transformative research and action agenda for the new century* (pp. 301–308). Mahwah, NJ: Erlbaum.

Goodwin, Susan, & King, Joyce E. (2007). *A curriculum framework and criterion standards for contextualized teaching and learning about people of African descent.* Rochester, NY, and New York: RTA Press and National Urban League.

Goodwin, Susan, & Swartz, Ellen. (2004). *Teaching children of color: Seven constructs of effective teaching in urban schools.* Rochester, NY: RTA Press.

Grant, Carl H. (1976). *The making of modern Belize.* Cambridge, MA: Cambridge.

Guimarães, Antônio Sérgio A. (1999). A. *Racismo e anti-racismo no Brasil.* São Paulo: Editora 34.

Hanchard, Michael. (Ed.). (1999). *Racial politics in contemporary Brazil.* Chapel Hill: Duke University Press.

Haug, Sarah W. (1998). Ethnicity and ethnically "mixed" identity in Belize: A study of primary school age children. *Anthropology & Education Quarterly, 29,* 44–67.

Heringer, Rosana. (1995). Introduction to the analysis of racism and anti-racism in Brazil. In Benjamin P. Bowser (Ed.), *Racism and anti-racism in world perspective* (pp. 203–226). Thousand Oaks: Sage.

Howard, Gary R. (2006). *We can't teach what we don't know: White teachers, multiracial schools.* New York: Teacher's College Press.

Htun, Mala. (2004). Affirmative action: Changing state policy on race in Brazil. *Latin American Research Review, 39*(1), 60–89.

King, Joyce E. (2006). "If justice is our objective": Diaspora literacy, heritage knowledge and the praxis of critical studyin' for human freedom. In A. Ball (Ed.), *With more deliberate speed: Achieving equity and excellence in education—Realizing the Full Potential of Brown v. Board of Education* (pp. 337–360). National Society for the Study of Education 105th Yearbook, Part 2. New York: Ballenger.

King, Joyce E. (Ed.). (2005). *Black education: A transformative research & action agenda for the new century.* Mahwah, NJ: Erlbaum.

King, Joyce E. (1995). Culture-centered knowledge: Black studies, curriculum transformation and social action. In James A. Banks, & Cherry M. Banks, (Eds.), *The handbook of research on multicultural education* (pp. 265–290). New York: Macmillan.

King, Joyce E. (1992). Diaspora literacy and consciousness in the struggle against mis-education in the Black community. *Journal of Negro Education, 61*(3), 317–340.

King, Joyce E. (1991). Dysconscious racism: Ideology, identity and the miseducation of teachers. *Journal of Negro Education, 60*(2), 133–146.

King, Joyce E., & Williams, Gwendolyn. (in press). "Heritage knowledge, cultural citizenship, and quality teaching: A call for liberatory urban teacher leadership development. *Souls.*

Lee, Carol D. (2008). Synthesis of research on the role of culture in learning among African American youth: The contributions of Asa G. Hilliard, III. *Review of Educational Research, 78*(4), 797–827.

Longman Foundation. (2008). *Teacher preparation for the global age.* Silver Spring, MD: Author.

Maiga, Hassimi. (2010). *Balancing written history with oral tradition: The legacy of the Songhoy people.* New York: Routledge.

Mullens, John, Murnane, Richard J., & Willett, John B. (1996). The contribution of training and subject matter knowledge to teaching effectiveness: A multilevel analysis of longitudinal evidence from Belize. *Comparative Education Review, 40*(2), 139–228.

Murrell, Peter C. (2009). Identity, agency, and culture: Black achievement and educational attainment. In Linda C. Tillman (Ed.), *The Sage handbook of African American education* (pp. 89–106). Thousand Oaks, CA: Sage.

Munanga, Kabengele. (1999). *Rediscutindo a mestiçagem no Bras il: identidade nacional versus identidade negra.* Petrópolis: Vozes.

Nascimento, Abdias do. (1979). *Mixture or massacre: Essays in the genocide of a Black people.* Buffalo, NY: Puerto Rican Studies and Research Center, State University of New York.

Nieto, Sonia. (2000). *Affirming diversity: The sociopolitical context of multicultural education. Third Edition.* New York: Longmann.

Oestrich, J. B. B. (2002). Social studies curriculum development in Belize: 1950–2001. Unpublished dissertation. The University of Texas at Austin.

Outhwaite, William, & Bottomore, Tom. (1996). *Dicionário do pensamento social do século XX.* (Eduardo Francisco Alves, & Álvaro Cabra, Trans). Rio de Janeiro: Jorge Zahar. (Original work published, 1994).

Peedle, Ian. (1999). *Belize: A guide to the people, politics and culture.* New York: Interlink.

Phillips, Melissa. (1998). Nationalism and cultural change in Belize. Unpublished dissertation. The University of Chicago.

Post, David. (1995). Education and the national question today. *Comparative Education Review, 39*, 211–218.

Rocha, J. (2000, April 19). Analysis of Brazil's 'racial democracy,'*BBC News.* Retrieved July 8, 2009, from http://news.bbc.co.uk/2/hi/americas/719134.stm

Russell, Carlos, E. (2009, July 16). President Obama's African Speech . . . Shades of the "Gunga Din" Syndrome. Retrieved July 10, 2009, from http://www.blackcommentator.com/333/333_obama_african_Tellspeech_russell_guest.html

Rutheiser, Charles. (1990). Culture, schooling and neocolonialism in Belize. Unpublished dissertation. The Johns Hopkins University.

Schwartzman, Simon. (2009, June 21). Brazil: Student quotas—the policy debate. *University World News,* Issue # 0081. Retrieved, September 9, 2010, from http://www.universityworldnews.com/article.php?story = 20090618190531212

Scott, David. (2000, September). The re-enchantment of humanism: An interview with Sylvia Wynter. *Small Axe, 8*, 119–207.

Seck, Ibrahima. (2005). Worldwide conspiracy against black culture and education. In Joyce E.

King (Ed.), *Black education: A transformative research and action agenda for the new century* (pp. 285–290). Mahwah, NJ: Erlbaum.

Skidmore, Thomas. (1992). Fact & myth: Discovering a racial problem in Brazil. Working Paper #173, W. W. Kellogg Foundation.

State of New Jersey (2010). *Amistad Commission.* Retrieved, September 13, 2010, http://www.nj.gov/state/divisions/amistad and Amistad Commission Interactive Textbook, http://www.njamistadcurriculum.com/

Tavolaro, Lilia G. M. (2008, June). Affirmative action in contemporary Brazil: Two institutional discourses on race. *International Journal of Politics, Culture and Society, 19*(3–4), 145–160.

Telles, Edward E. (2004). *Race in another America: The significance of skin color in Brazil* Princeton: Princeton University Press.

Telles, Edward E. (2002). Racial ambiguity among the Brazilian population. *Ethnic and Racial Studies, 25*(3), 415–441.

Thompson, Cynthia. (2008). The role of early experience in the development of a professional knowledge-base and identity as a teacher investigating teacher preparation in Belize. Unpublished dissertation. Florida State University.

Thompson, Cynthia, & Crossley, Michael. (1999). Reforming teacher education in a small state: Problems and potential for distance education in Belize. In Teame Mebrahtu, Michael Crossley, & David Johnson (Eds.), *Globalization, education reconstruction and societies in transition* (pp. 137–156). Oxford: Symposium Books.

Twine, Frances Winddance. (1997). *Racism in a racial democracy: The maintenance of white supremacy in Brazil.* New Brunswick, NJ: Rutgers University Press.

Woodson, Carter G. (1933/1977). *The miseducation of the Negro.* Washington DC: Associated Publishers.

13 Teaching and Administrative Development in Southern Africa: Illustrations from Mozambique and Angola

Mouzinho Mario and Beverly Lindsay

In June 2009, the Woodrow Wilson International Center for Scholars convened a conference entitled, "South Africa and United States Relations" that concentrated on South Africa in view of the then new administration of President Barack Obama's foreign policies and international relations toward the African continent. Featured speakers were Assistant Secretary of State for Africa Ambassador Johnnie Carson and the South African Minister of Science and Technology Naledi Grace Pandor, who had also served as the Minister of Education. As anticipated Ambassador's Carson's remarks focused on geopolitical and economic relations coupled with the need for diplomatic and strategic partnerships (Woodrow Wilson International Center for Scholars, 2009a). Diplomatic relations encompass health matters such as HIV/AIDS, scientific and technological collaboration, and cooperative educational enterprises with universities and other bodies.

Similarly Minister Pandor emphasized the critical importance of science, technology, engineering, and mathematics (STEM) fields within South Africa, among Southern African nations, and with the United States as the African countries strive toward regional economic development and peace and security (Pandor, 2009). Indeed, the Southern African Development Community (SADC)—composed of South Africa, Angola, Botswana, Democratic Republic of Congo (DRC), Lesotho, Madagascar, Malawi, Mauritius, Mozambique, Namibia, Seychelles, Swaziland, Tanzania, Zambia, and Zimbabwe—collectively articulates aims and objectives that include achieving economic growth and eliminating poverty; promoting peace and security; and supporting the development of human resources to include educational opportunities (SADC, 2010). Toward educational objectives, the Southern African Regional Universities Association (SARUA) operates to revitalize regional universities and foster leadership and progress to respond to SADC developmental challenges. Further, enhancing post-secondary opportunities for students and individual universities via consortium programs include the ability of students from one SADC nation to matriculate in another country's universities (Woodrow Wilson International Center for Scholars, 2009b; SARUA, 2010). While consortium opportunities exist, it is difficult for non-South African baccalaureate degree students to enroll in South Africa universities, arguably among the best in terms of physical infrastructure, library resources, and scientific and information technology equipment, due, on the one hand, to the language barrier, for non-English-speaking member states, and to a lack of equivalence, harmonization, and standardization of university entrance requirements of the education and training systems in the region, on the other (SADC, 1997).

This dilemma is coupled with the ever-present need to enhance human resources to foster regional development to bolster SADC's geopolitical and international relations. Of special note are the Portuguese-speaking nations of Mozambique and Angola that are often overlooked in the global policy and higher education scholarly literature. Thus our chapter focuses on Mozambique's and Angola's endeavors for training teachers and education administrators in order to move toward development in an evolving globalized region as "education should try to counterbalance negative effects and extend the potentialities for all in a democratic fashion" (Papastephanou, 2005, p. 537) for the second and third largest Portuguese-speaking nations in the world.

Portuguese-Speaking Nations

Throughout the developing world, governments are reforming their educational systems in order to enhance their ability to respond effectively to changing domestic, global, and international environments and contexts. Repeated calls for better educated, responsible citizens, under rapidly growing school enrollments and serious financial constraints, have led governments to recruit large numbers of teachers with little or no professional preparation. In view of this, since the 1990s many education reforms in developing nations have focused on improving the quality of teachers through both initial and in-service teacher education and training (Martin, 1999; Wideen, Grimmet, & Andrews, 2002; Cheng, Chow, & Mok, 2004; OECD, 2005; Kruss, 2008).

This chapter highlights structural arrangements that facilitate or hamper the initial and continuing education as well as work of teachers, and examines the roles of universities in the preparation of baccalaureate teachers, educational administrators, and leaders in Portuguese-speaking nations. We are concerned with how administrators address a range of endeavors to help teachers facilitate conditions that may affect current and future students' interactions with the larger environment. In essence, we seek to explore answers to: How do or can universities play a meaningful role in the preparation of teachers, educational administrators, and leaders who are able to function effectively in both national and global environments in these countries?

Although Portuguese-speaking nations comprise significant parts of the African, European, and South American continents and are organized as a Community of Portuguese-Speaking Countries (CPLP) they are often overlooked. For example, there are nearly 200 million inhabitants in Brazil (U.S. Department of State, 2010b), over 20 million in Mozambique (U.S. Department of State, 2010c), about 17 million in Angola (U.S. Department of State, 2010a), and approximately 11 million in Portugal (U.S. Department of State: Portugal, 2010d)—that is, close to 250 million people in the most populous Portuguese-speaking countries with educational challenges. Although a common formal and official language is prevalent, there are significant variations of language, education, ethnicity, race, and political affiliation among them.

Mozambique and Angola share other features. Both gained independence from Portugal in 1975, after long years of armed struggle and soon chose socialist paths of development, which, under geopolitical "cold war" conditions, cost them protracted periods of armed conflict and economic and social instability. Armed struggle lasted for 16 years in Mozambique and for 27 years in Angola. Finally, both Angola and Mozambique are undergoing processes of democratization in a context of peace and reconciliation, political stability, and market economy.

This chapter draws from available body of research as well as official and unofficial documents and policy papers produced over the last decade to highlight the emerging structures and models of initial and in-service education and training of teachers and administrators in Mozambique and Angola (Ministério da Educação, 2005; Ministry of Education and Culture, 2005; Mario, 2006). Research so far has shown that both nations suffer from chronic deficiencies in the provision of qualified teaching and administrative staffs, particularly at primary and secondary levels (Ministério da Educação, 2005, 2008b, 2008c; Banco Mundial, 2005; Ministry of Education and Culture, 2005).

Throughout the chapter, we maintain that in developing nations like Mozambique and Angola, where the supply and maintenance of basic material, textbooks, equipment, and furniture are highly problematic, well-prepared and motivated teachers and professionals are essential to improving and sustaining the quality of student learning in schools (Dove, 1986; Hardman et al. 2009). In line with Darling-Hammond (2006, pp. 7–8), we also maintain that teacher education programs in these countries should be both *learning-centered* and *learner-centered*. In practical terms, this means that in addition to preparing teachers to perform well in standard, quiet classrooms, teacher education programs in these countries should also prepare teachers who are able to expand students' expectations and achievements and, in doing so, enhance educational opportunity and social justice within the nations and the SADC.

Mozambique

Challenges and Expansions

In Mozambique, expanding school enrollments, nonexistent or insufficient educational infrastructure, inadequate funding, and a lack of effective policies that articulate and stimulate initial and continuing teacher education within the framework of decentralized decision-making are listed among the most salient factors explaining continuing deficiencies in the provision of qualified teaching and administrative staffs, particularly at primary and secondary levels. In addition, the debilitating effects of HIV/AIDS also play an important role (Ministério de Educação, 2004; Banco Mundial, 2005; Conselho de Ministros, 2006).

The Mozambican education system is undergoing a period of rapid expansion, which began in 1992, when a peace agreement between the Frelimo Party Government (in power since independence) and the *Resistência Nacional Moçambicana* (RENAMO) put an end to a 16-year-long armed conflict. Since then, the government of Mozambique along with its national and international partners has made remarkable efforts in ensuring equitable access to all levels of the education system, particularly to primary education, improving quality and relevance of educational provision, and building institutional capacity.

Thus between 1992 and 2008, EP1 (first 5 years of primary education) and EP2 (last 2 years of primary education) enrollments rose from 1.3 million to 4.8 million, and over the same period the number of schools grew from 2,836 to 10,060. The Gross Enrollment Rate (GER) in grade 1 increased from 59% to 160% in the same period. At the EP2 level GER has also risen substantially. However, the absolute number of students at this level is much smaller (704,506 in 2008, compared to over 4 million for EP1) and transition from EP1 to EP2 remains a major problem (INE, 2009; República de Moçambique, 2008). Many primary schools, especially in the countryside, do not offer the full 7-year primary education cycle (EP1 and EP2), they offer only the first 5 years of primary education (EP1); so continuation in EP2 often requires many children to walk long distances from home or to leave their families in order to join relatives in the cities, or live in precarious boarding conditions (Banco Mundial, 2005). As one would expect, this constitutes a major access barrier for girls and certainly a driving force towards rural exodus (Mario, 2005).

The consequences of the phenomenal expansion were enormous for teacher preparation and teacher supply. In 2006 there were 60,000 primary teachers (EP1 and EP2) and 8,000 secondary teachers. In order to cope with the pressure of fast-growing enrollments and under serious financial constraints, the Ministry of Education has relied on massive recruitment of the so-called contracted teachers. These are largely untrained or under-qualified teachers, recruited from amongst Grade 10 school leavers, who start teaching after short "emergency" courses in survival skills of up to 21 days. As a result, the proportion of nonqualified teachers and the pupil/teacher ratios have increased over the years. The proportion of nonqualified to qualified teachers in EP1 grew from 26.6% in 1992 to 42.2% in 2004. In EP2 the growth of the proportion of unqualified teachers was even higher: from 6.4% in 1992 to 34.6% in 2004. Pupil/teacher ratios in EP1 have been increasing as well, from 62:1 in 1999 to 74:1 in 2005, whereas the average class size has increased from 83 in 1999 to 90 in 2005. Under these conditions, overcrowded, teacher-centered classrooms, and double shifts, particularly in large cities, are no longer an exception within the school system (Conselho de Ministros, 2006). Also arising from the need for rapid expansion, many different kinds of teacher preparation programs designed to satisfy the demand for primary and secondary teachers have emerged. By contrast, adding to the disappointment and frustration among teachers, opportunities for in-service training and continuous professional development have been relatively scarce.

Sites for Teacher Training

The current teacher education landscape in Mozambique is both complex and problematic. Since independence, from 1976 onwards, the Ministry of Education has implemented many different models of teacher education, but at present it does not have a single, unified model for the entire system (Passos, 2009). Most initial teacher education, especially for primary schools, is currently undertaken by the *Centros de Formação de Professores*—CFPPs (Teacher Training Centers), the *Institutos de Formação de Professores*—IFPs (Teacher Training Institutes), and the *Ajuda de Desenvolvimento de Povo para Povo*—ADPP (People to People Development) Colleges. The CFPPs and IFPs are public, whereas the ADPP Colleges are private. The CFPPs offer a three-year training program after Grade 7 (7+3 model). Based on entrance qualifications and number of years of training teachers are classified as basic, middle, or upper level teachers. The basic level group includes teachers who have attended a CFPP after Grade 7; the middle level group comprises those who have attended a teacher training college after Grade 10, and upper level teachers are those who have attended a higher education institution after Grade 12. Basic level teachers qualify to teach in EP1 schools, whereas only middle level teachers qualify to teach in both EP1 and EP2 schools (Passos 2009, p. 28). For the purposes of remuneration teachers are further ranked N1 (top level) through N5 (bottom level).

In 1997 the Ministry of Education introduced the *Institutos do Magistério Primário* (IMAPs). The IMAPs offered a two-year program and recruited students following completion of Grade 10 (10+2 model). Both the CFPP and the IMAP are college-based programs, where pedagogical training is provided concomitantly with training in the primary curriculum subjects. Teachers graduating from the IMAPs are classified as N3 teachers and are qualified to teach in both EP1 and EP2 schools.

In 2007 the IMAPs were renamed *Institutos de Formação de Professores* (IFPs). Like the IMAPs, the IFPs recruit Grade 10 students; however, their program has been transformed and reduced to one year only (10+1 model). A significant step toward reducing contractual teachers within the system, this model, however, is unlikely to equip teachers with adequate subject knowledge, pedagogical skills, and motivation needed for professional integration, stability, and retention, unless adequate resources are made available for their continuous professional development (Duarte & De Bastos, 2009). In addition, given the necessity to provide potential teachers with intermediate skills, little time is devoted to issues of globalization and international matters within SADC.

A fourth model of initial teacher education is provided by the NGO-based *Ajuda de Desenvolvimento Povo para Povo* (ADPP) Colleges. ADPP started operating in Mozambique in 1993. Candidates for the ADPP program must hold a Grade 10 certificate, and are expected to undergo an integrated college-based and school-based program for two and half years (10+2.5 model). Pedagogical training at ADPP Colleges is consecutive to the training in the primary curriculum subjects. Teachers graduating from the ADPP colleges are classified as N3 and qualify to teach in EP1 and EP2 schools (Mario 2005; 2006).

There are significant inequalities and a lack of parity of esteem between the four kinds of institutions responsible for delivering initial teacher education. Such inequalities and disparities are, in turn, perceived to be at the heart of the present low status of teachers and the teaching profession in Mozambique (Government of Mozambique, 2005).

At secondary level (Grades 8–12), in theory, the university sector is responsible for the preparation of teachers. Since 1986 the main provider at this level has been the Pedagogical University (UP); however, in 2001 the Eduardo Mondlane University's (UEM) Faculty of Education (FoE) started offering a secondary teacher education program as well. In both universities the entry requirement is completion of Grade 12, and the duration of the program is four years. UP also undertakes a training of trainers program for those wishing to teach in the CFPPs and IFPs. The entry requirement for this program is Grade 12, and the program is of three-year duration. Due to the limited number of secondary school teachers graduating from UP and UEM, or who pursue a teaching career, in practice many graduates from the IMAPs/IFPs are being recruited as secondary school teachers.

At UEM the pre-service curriculum includes subjects such as Foundations of Education, Sociology of Education, School Organization and Administration, Curriculum Development and Teaching Models, Assessment of Student Learning, and Teaching Practice. Some of the modules (e.g., Sociology of Education, and Curriculum Development and Teaching Models) focus primarily on generic competencies and skills, while others emphasize specific, problem-solving skills at school and classroom levels. However, some of the modules devoted to the development of generic competencies cover global and regional topics and issues as well. For instance, while the Sociology of Education module's main focus is the study of the relationship between the school and society, and the school as an organization, it also exposes students to concepts for understanding the relationship between education systems and their national and global environments and concerns, particularly in terms of access, quality, equity, opportunity, and the role of education in national, regional, and global integration. The Curriculum Development and Teaching Models module also includes topics and issues of regional and international relevance, and it discusses different models and strategies of curriculum implementation and change from a comparative and international perspective (Faculdade de Educação, 2009).

Opportunities for in-service training (INSET) and continuing professional development (CPD) are scarce. In addition to the institutions and programs designed for initial primary teacher education described earlier, new opportunities have been created for nonqualified or poorly qualified teachers to upgrade their qualifications. For a long time this has been accomplished through a distance education program in the *Instituto de Educação à Distância e Aberta*—IEDA (Institute for Open and Distance Education), the *Zonas de Influência Pedagógica*—ZIPs (Zones of Pedagogical Influence), and the *Cursos de Reforço Escolar: Contínuos, Experimentais e Reflexivos*—CRESCER (*Courses for School Strengthening: Systematic, Continuous, Experimental and Reflexive*) (Da Costa et al., 2005; Conselho de Ministros, 2006; Passos, 2009; Pessula, 2009).

IEDA was established in 1996 as an institution for the upgrading of primary school teachers and its mission is to provide in-service training and upgrading through distance learning to those teachers who entered the profession with less than Grade 7. Those teachers who were classified as N5 teachers would be upgraded to N4 upon successful completion of a 50-module program, covering the whole primary curriculum, and get a salary increase. During distance learning, students receive support through a system of *Núcleos Pedagógicos*—NPs (Pedagogical Nuclei), which have been established in selected schools. A facilitator, usually a senior teacher recruited from a local primary school, who receives specific training in the new role, serves the NPs (Ministério da Educação, 2004; Da Costa et al., 2005).

The ZIPs are not a recent innovation in the postcolonial history of Mozambique. They were established in 1978 as a focal point for a school cluster where teachers were expected to meet regularly (at least once in a month) in order to plan together or attend prescribed training activities under the oversight of a tutor or mentor (Mario, 2005). On the one hand, a lack of a coherent policy for the ZIPs, as administrative and pedagogical structures that provide resources and support to curriculum innovation and classroom practice, and a lack of financial resources, on the other, have limited the role of ZIPs in teachers' CPD (Duarte and De Bastos, 2009).

Based on past and ongoing INSET activities and experiences in different parts of the country, the Ministry of Education introduced a new school-based and ZIP-based system of teacher education provision, known as CRESCER. The system claims to follow the cascade model of training, with flexible, participatory, and cyclical implementation. Each training institution is expected to develop training activities in the various subjects of the school curriculum, in close collaboration with the schools and ZIPs. The starting point of the system are small groups of teachers who meet regularly to discuss, assess and reflect on their own experiences of implementing teaching strategies, methods and materials in the classroom. Regular attendance of training sessions by the teachers, at ZIP level, and regular monitoring visits by INSET providers are part of this training system (Da Costa et al., 2005, p. 6). Despite these provisions, confused and contradictory perceptions about the nature of CRESCER persist at different levels of implementation. As a 2005 evaluation of the CRESCER system has found, most teachers view the program as a course, very few view it as a system. There are also teachers who view it simply as a methodology, as the new curriculum, as distance education or, simply, as the unification of teacher training (Government of Mozambique, 2005, p. 11). Apparently, a major source of this confusion lies in the Ministry's unfortunate attempt to combine the development of a national system for the provision of INSET and CPD, on the one hand, with a course that is intended to provide minimum level of training to untrained teachers, on the other, at the same time.

Angola

Challenges and Expansions

Following 27 years of civil war, the peace agreement in April 2002 provided Angola a much-needed opportunity to rebuild and reform its education system. According to the Angolan Ministry of Education's estimates, in 2005 nearly half of the total number of the existing schools at independence had been destroyed or seriously damaged during the war. As a result, in 2005, only 62% of school age children had a place in schools (Castiano, 2007).

In view of this situation the Government of Angola with support from several partners such as UNICEF and the European Union designed and implemented an Emergency Program. The purpose of this program was to rebuild the schools destroyed by the war, increase the number of children in schools, and employ emergency teachers. As a result, over 28,300 new classrooms were built in the country between 2002 and 2008, and 81,388 new teachers were recruited in the same period. Available data indicates that in 2008, more than 167,989 primary school teachers taught 3,757,677 children in primary schools compared to 1,733,549 in 2002. Available data also indicates that 64% of the teachers are unqualified or underqualified, and less than 10% of the teaching force in 9 of the 18 provinces of Angola have adequate academic and professional qualifications (Banco Mundial, 2007; Ministério da Educação, 2007; Ministério da Educação, 2008a).

As the aforementioned figures clearly indicate, the Angolan education system is expanding rapidly. These figures also indicate the need for the rethinking and planning for the system's growth. However, in view of the severe damage caused by the prolonged war and the subsequent need for fast recovery, the reform of the education system appears to have taken place without a clear understanding of how teacher training could be developed in a systematic way. Indeed, aspects such as quality of education, management of the human resources, and, most importantly, the intervention of domestic and international donors and partners in education, especially at primary level, lacked adequate coordination and harmonization to ensure rational use of the scarce resources (Castiano, 2007).

Under these circumstances, it is no surprise that the Angolan education system is confronted with serious shortages of qualified teachers, which is, and will certainly remain for many years, one of the biggest challenges to making universal basic education a reality, particularly in rural areas (Nsiangengo & Diasala, 2008).

Although the Decree 30/91 that approves the statutes of non-university teaching staff prescribes that a primary teacher should take charge of one morning or one afternoon shift only and his/her total workload should not exceed 26 contact hours per week, confronted with the growing demand for education and shortage of qualified teachers many schools are forced to run three rather than two daily shifts.

The average pupil/teacher ratio is 44:1 (Ministerio da Educação, 2008). However, this national average has been difficult to maintain. During the first author's school visits and classroom observations in different parts of Angola, he observed classes ranging from 40 to over 90 children per teacher. In many schools, this situation is often worsened by the presence of large numbers of administrative staff being counted as teaching staff (Mario, 2008).

Sites for Teacher Training

Two types of public institutions provide initial teacher preparation in Angola: the middle level institutions and the higher level institutions.

Middle level institutions comprise the *Escolas do Magistério Primário* (EMP), and *Institutos Médios Normais* (IMNs) (also known as *Escolas de Formação de Professores do 1º Ciclo* (EFP). Higher level institutions comprise the *Insitutos Superiores de Ciências da Educação* (ISCED) and the *Escolas Superiores de Educação* (Ministério da Educação, 2010). The EMPs (teacher training colleges) qualify primary teachers for Grades 1 to 6. The EMPs recruit students with Grade 9 and the training lasts for 4 years. Only six of these institutions are currently operating in the country. The *Institutos Médios Normais* (IMNs) train teachers for the 1st cycle of secondary education (Grades 7–9). They recruit students with Grade 9 and train them for 4 years as well. In both the EMPs and the IMNs the training is free of charge. The academic and pedagogical training and teaching practice are offered simultaneously during the 4-year training program (concomitant model). There is at least one IMN in each province. Teacher training is also provided by the ADPP Escolas de Professores do Futuro (EPF). Like their Mozambican counterparts, EPFs are associated with the Danish ADPP. The EPFs prepare teachers for Grades 1 to 6 for rural and semi-rural schools primarily, and recruit students from Grade 10. The duration of the training is 30 months (Banco Mundial, 2007; Nsiangengo and Diasala, 2008).

The training of teachers for the 2nd Cycle of General Secondary Education (Grades 10–12) is the responsibility of the Higher Pedagogical Institutes, attached to Agostinho Neto University (*Universidade Agostinho Neto* [UAN]), and the Schools of Higher Education (*Escolas Superiores de Educação* [ESE]). The UAN Higher Pedagogical Institutes offer a 4-year licenciatura program, whereas the Schools of Higher Education offer a 3-year bachelor's program (Ministério da Educação, 2010).

A number of difficulties associated with poor management of the training process appear to affect negatively the exit profile of graduates from the IMNs. First, critics claim that the training provided by these institutions is too general, theoretical, and abstract. In their opinion, such training is dominated by normative, prescriptive, and descriptive approaches (INIDE, 2005b, p. 8). Second, the teaching and learning conditions are very poor, the curricula offer compartmentalized training and are repetitive, leaving no room for self-study and independent work. Third, most of the lecturers in the IMNs have no specialized training in education (*agregação pedagógica*). These are viewed as factors that contribute to poor integration of the graduates from these institutions within the school system (*ibidem*), and limited ability to address international and global concerns.

In order to cope with these problems, in addition to reducing the number of years of initial teacher training, the government of Angola has relied heavily on INSET and distance learning (Ministério da Educação, 2004; 2005). INSET and CPD are provided through *cursos de agregação pedagógica* (specialized training for teaching) and *cursos de superacão* (upgrading courses). The *agregação pedagógica* provides fast professional training to Grade 12 graduates who teach with poor or no pedagogical preparation. The EMPs are responsible for this type of training. The upgrading courses *(cursos de superação)* provide supplemental academic and professional training to underqualified teachers. This type of training was first organized in the so-called Provincial Upgrading Centers *(Centros Provinciais de Superação*—CPSs) that were later transformed into *Centros de Formação Local*—CFLs (Local Training Centers). Some of the upgrading programs have been supplied through a distance learning mode (Banco Mundial, 2007). It should be noted, however, that despite the diversity of INSET programs that teachers have gone through, none of them has led to professional certification (Campos, 2006, pp. 159–222, quoted by Banco Mundial, 2007).

Educational Administrators

Universities and other postsecondary institutions throughout the world are expected to play pivotal roles in preparing educational administrators who are able to provide sound leadership and managerial capacity, at different levels of the education system (Hoy and Miskel, 2009; Lindsay, 2005a; Otaala, 2006). Moreover, such administrators are to be able and willing to work collaboratively with students and other professionals to resolve the tensions and ambiguities that emerge from the interaction between multiple, and often conflicting, global and domestic realities. We present detailed examples from Mozambique and a succinct one from Angola since the former nation apparently has programs further developed than those in the latter country.

One of the major weaknesses of the Mozambican and Angolan education systems and in the public sector are their limited pools of qualified administrators, planners, and executives who are capable of translating the goals, policies, and strategies of the potential reforms into operational plans, strategies, and actions that may, in turn, be monitored and evaluated (Mario, 2008). As Lindsay (2008) observes, for schools and colleges to function efficiently and effectively, the contributions of quality administrators that are firmly grounded on sound principles of administration, curriculum design, and assessment, *inter alia*, are essential.

After 15 years of temporary closure, the FoE at UEM finally reopened its doors in 2001. From the outset, the FoE expressed willingness to become a leading center of reflection and knowledge production in the field of education in Mozambique (Faculdade de Educação, 2009) especially since it was the only institution that offered postgraduate training for the entire nation. For that reason it has focused its activities on postgraduate education, research, and service to schools and other components of the education and public sector systems. It also has stressed the importance of assisting the University administration in its efforts to improve the pedagogical competencies and skills of emerging lecturers and other academic staff members who have never learned how to teach properly and assess and support student learning in higher education institutions. Thus, the FoE, in addition to delivering the educational component of the teacher training program (*ramos educacionais*) to various constituents within and external to UEM, is also offering a postgraduate diploma and a master's degree in several areas including educational administration and management. Students are expected to hold a *Licenciatura* degree (i.e., a 4-year bachelor's degree) and at least two years of work experience. After one year of full-time study they earn a Postgraduate Diploma of Education. Those who qualify for the master's level, after another year of study, are awarded a master's degree (Faculdade de Educacão, 2009).

Since sound administration and management is indispensable for effective schools, teacher training institutes, and universities that are affected by international and global conditions, UEM opted to work closely with the American Embassy to secure Fulbright and other senior professionals with substantive international experience to develop courses and modules in administration. Both of the authors worked collaboratively, for example, as a special comprehensive course was developed for graduate students from the University of Pedagogy, several national Ministries, UEM professionals, and select school faculty. We were cognizant that the course needed to address individual and institutional capacity development present in developing countries, but especially those requiring special attention after prolonged civil conflict and war. The course entitled, "Administration, Planning, and Budgeting," concentrated on academic and strategic planning, fiscal resource acquisition and management, and human resource development—areas that are vital to administrators in various roles (Lindsay, 2007a). A blend of local, provincial, domestic, national, and Southern African phenomena were integrated into the curriculam. Aspects of educational features in the SADC nations and those from French-speaking areas such as the DRC, Burundi, and Rwanda were incorporated, especially since the former nations have consortium arrangements and the immigrants from the latter nations are present in educational settings in Mozambique and other SADC member states.

Within this course, students were exposed to concepts, tenets, and theories of administration and planning, engaged in applied solutions to administrative problems, and posited paradigms for current and likely future administrative and planning of Southern African challenges. Administrative and policy literature regarding academic and strategic planning, for example, from Africa, Australia, England, and the United States, was used in order to expose students to domestic and global frameworks so administrators could enhance students' and teachers' options in the evolving Mozambique, Angola, and SADC (Lindsay, 2007a). Critical actual and simulated task force projects were assigned to students in light of school enrollment patterns, teacher and school personnel qualifications, and finite financial resources. Since the postgraduate students were professionals in postsecondary institutions and government ministries, assignments encompassed civil and professional interactions among domestic and SADC ministries and international donor organizations. Their task force projects posited frameworks and paradigms for current problems and those likely to appear on the educational landscapes such as human resource development to address increasing necessity for additional English-language instruction since English is the *lingua franca* in SADC.

Aware of the challenges associated with educational administration, the Ministry of Education in Angola and its partners have devised a national strategy for ensuring the provision of INSET for educational administrators and school managers. With financial support from the European Union and technical support from UNICEF and UNESCO, the strategy is under implementation since 2008 and is known as Project for the Support of Primary Education (*Projecto de Apoio ao Ensino Primário* [*PAEP*]). Four areas of intervention have been prioritized: (1) improving the system of statistical data collection; (2) strengthening planning and budgeting systems; (3) strengthening supervision and school management systems; and (4) improving the training of trainers (Minstério da Educação, 2008a). It is hoped that this effort, along with other activities being carried out in the context of the Master Plan for Teacher Training (Ministério da Educação, 2008c) will have a lasting impact on the quality of education in Angola.

The Synthesis for Current and Future Endeavors

As deans and executives reflecting upon the material presented in our chapter, we continue to envision fundamental challenges that have been partially addressed and those looming on the horizon. In order to help move Mozambique and Angola forward in their national development and as proactive members of the SADC and global communities—via educational enterprises—we identify four thematic and policy motifs for consideration. All entail cooperation and partnerships.

First, within Mozambique and Angola, fundamental problems revolve around absent conditions for quality education such as expansive enrollments and unqualified or underqualified teachers and administrators. Current and/or alternative structural and pedagogical arrangements are needed which may appear via cooperative arrangements among educational entities and ministries.

Two, since Mozambique and Angola are SADC members, cooperative arrangements with other member nations could enhance options for selective educational and policy borrowing. Some undergraduate and certainly many graduate students at UEM are fluent in Portuguese, English, and an African language. One day in the midst of the second author's teaching a graduate seminar, the translator was called suddenly from the classroom. While continuing to talk, she hoped that the translator would return momentarily to share comments. During a pause, a graduate student leapt to his feet and translated for the few students who did not comprehend English (Lindsay, 2007b). His English skills had been enhanced by extended time spent in South Africa on various SADC-related assignments.

Three, our chapter discussed a special Fulbright course designed for educational and public administrators that was developed by Mozambican and American educational professionals. Such cooperative arrangements lead to an infusion of new concepts and practices tailored to local conditions, but in light of international and global realities. This Fulbright endeavor was also an illustration of a program from a G-8 nation with an emerging one where indigenous needs were paramount, yet coupled with domestic and international cooperative activities. Such programs operationalize the diplomatic and policy perspectives of Minister Pandor and Ambassador Carson voiced at the Woodrow Wilson Conference.

Fourth, while information and communication technology are constantly evolving, the globalization of technology can enable members of SADC to communicate and share best practices so all university students are beneficiaries. Moreover, teachers, school personnel, and public ministry professionals can employ modern technology as observed during the second author's Fulbright in Mozambique. Contemporary technology is bypassing old modes as nations leap toward innovative educational communications. Certainly, we observed the leap to an ultra-modern environment as UEM graduate students recorded lectures using cell phones, prepared PowerPoint presentations, used flash drives, and sent text messages routinely. These are common technological features associated with Western globalization. That is, the aspects of globalization that include the flow of knowledge and ideas regardless of geographical boundaries (Knight, 2008; Watson, 2007) are undertaken by technological modes and can be transmitted to educational professionals in both rural and urban milieus.

As we engage collaboratively on the aforementioned with university professionals, we could paraphrase former South African President Nelson Mandela's statement that universities are charged with the responsibility of leading themselves and the continent in the world of the 21st Century so innovative policies can contribute to a cherished rebirth of African academic excellence (Mandela, 2006). Academic excellence produces knowledge and contributes to the domestic and global flow of ideas benefitting Mozambique, Angola, and the SADC.

References

Banco Mundial. (2007). *Qualificação e Emprego de Professores em Angola* (Versão para Comentários). Washington, DC: Banco Mundial.

—— (2005). *Moçambique: Análise de Pobreza e Impacto Social.* Relatório N29423—MZ Banco Mundial.

Campos, Bártolo P. (2006). *Estratégia para o Desenvolvimento Profissional de Professores do Ensino Primário em Angola.* Luanda: União Europeia/República de Angola (Projecto N7. ACP.ANG.083).

Castiano, José P. (2007). *Reconstruction of the Education System in Angola: Improving the Quality of Teacher Education.* Midterm Evaluation Report. Luanda.

Cheng, Yin C., Chow, King W., & Mok, Magdalena M. C. (2004) *Reform of Teacher Education amid Paradigm Shift in School Education.* The Netherlands: Springer.

Conselho de Ministros. (2006). *Plano Estratégico de Educação e Cultura 2006–2010/11.* Aprovado pela 14ª Sessão Ordinária do Conselho de Ministros, de 13 de Junho de 2006. Maputo: Author.

Da Costa, D. Daniel., Hooker, Mary, Lauchande, Carlos, Magacelane, E., Nivagara, D., Saar, H., Ostertag, M., & Ussene, A. (2005). *CRESCER: Um Manual de Provisão de Formação em Serviço de Professores Primários.* Maputo: Ministério da Educação e Cultura.

Darling-Hammond, Linda. (2006). *Powerful teacher education: Lessons from exemplary programs.* San Francisco: Jossey-Bass.

Dove, Linda. (1986). *Teachers and teacher education in developing countries: Issues of planning, management and training.* Beckenham: Croom Helm.

Duarte, Stela M., & De Bastos, Juliano N. (2009). Tendências da Formação de Professores: Subsídios à Reforma Curricular da Universidade Pedagógica. In S. M. Duarte, H. N. Dias, & M. Cherinda (Orgs.) *Formação de Professores em Moçambique: Resgatar o Passado, Realizar o Presente, Perspectivar o Futuro.* Maputo: Universidade Pedagógica.

Faculdade de Educação. (2009). *Programas de Pós-Graduação em Educação 2009/2010.* Maputo: Author.

Hardman, Frank et al. (2009). Changing pedagogical practices in Kenyan primary schools; the impact of school-based training. *Comparative Education, 45*(2), 65–86.

Hoy, Wayne K., & Miskel, Cecil G. (2009). *Educational Administration: Theory, Research, and Practice.* Boston: McGraw Hill.

INE (Instituto Nacional de Estatística). (2009). *Anuário Estatístico/Statistical Yearbook 2008.* Maputo: Author.

INIDE (Instituto Nacional de Investigação e Desenvolvimento da Educação). (2005a). *Currículo de Formação de Professores do Ensino Primário: Reforma Curricular.* Luanda: Author.

—— (2005b). *Currículo de Formação de Professores do 1° Ciclo do Ensino Secundário: Reforma Curricular.* Luanda: Author.

Knight, Jane. (2008). *Higher education in turmoil: The changing world of internationalization.* Rotterdam: Sense Publishers.

Kruss, Glenda. (2008). *Teacher Education and Institutional Change in South Africa.* Cape Town: Human Sciences Research Council. Retrieved February 8, 2010, from www.hsrcpress.ac.za

Lindsay, Beverly. (2008). Cosmopolitan perspectives of challenges in commonwealth countries: Toward alternative educational administrative paradigms. Paper presented at the annual meeting of the American Educational Research Association, New York, NY.

Lindsay, Beverly. (2007a). Educational Administration, Planning, and Budgeting. Faculty of Education, Eduardo Mondlane University—Autumn–Winter 2007, Maputo, Mozambique. Retrieved May 1, 2010, from http://www.ed.psu.edu/educ/cshe/people/beverly-lindsay-ph.d

Lindsay, Beverly. (2007b). Mozambique. Center for International Exchange of Scholars. Retrieved June 30, 2009, from www.cies/org/specialists/stories/ss_blindsay2.htm

Lindsay, Beverly. (2005a). Initiating transformation of realities in African and African American universities. In Joyce King (Ed.) *Black education: A transformative research and action agenda for the new century* (pp. 183–194). Washington DC: American Educational Research Association and Mahwah, NJ: Lawrence Erlbaum Associates.

Lindsay, Beverly. (2005b). *An indispensable link for national and social development: Developing and enhancing educational administration, planning, and policy research.* Faculty of Education, Eduardo Mondlane University—Autumn–Winter 2007, Maputo, Mozambique.

Mandela, Nelson. (2006). *Nelson Mandela Metropolitan University Mission and Vision.* Retrieved from http://Africanhistoryabout.com/odmandelanelson

Mario, Mouzinho. (2008). *Análise das Linhas Estratégicas do UNICEF no Novo Programa para 2009–2011: Oportunidades e Constrangimentos à Implementação do Compromisso Relativo à Educação Primária da Criança Angolana.* Luanda: UNICEF.

Mario, Mouzinho. (2006). *Models of teacher preparation in post-conflict Mozambique: A critical assessment.* Presentation to Doctoral Students of the University of Pretoria Faculty of Education, within the framework of Module 6: Comparative Dimensions of Education Policy and Policy Implementation, Maputo.

Mario, Mouzinho. (2005). *O papel da educação na luta contra a pobreza e a exclusão social em Moçambique: Contradições e Desafios.* Paper presented at the Conference on Education and Development in Africa. Fundação Calouste Gulbenkian & Centro de Estudos Africanos, ISCTE. Lisboa.

Martin, Michaela. (1999). *The role of the university in initial teacher training: Trends, current problems and strategies for improvement.* IIEP Contributions N32. Paris, UNESCO: International Institute for Educational Planning.

Ministério da Educação. (2010). *Mapa de Escolas de Formação de Professores, Magistérios Primários/ADPP em Angola.* Luanda: Author.

Ministério da Educação. (2008a). *Evolução da Educação e Ensino em Angola, 2000–2008.* Luanda: Author.

Ministério da Educação. (2008b). *Projecto de Apoio ao Ensino Primário (PAEP).* Luanda: Ministério da Educação & Fundo Europeu de Desenvolvimento.

Ministério da Educação. (2008c). *Plano Mestre de Formação de Professores em Angola 2008–2015.* Luanda: Author.

Ministério da Educação. (2007). *Plano de Desenvolvimento a Médio Prazo 2009–2013.* Luanda: Ministério da Educação, Gabinete de Estudos.

Ministério da Educação. (2005). *Plano Nacional de Educação para Todos, 2001–2015: Educação de Qualidade para Todos.* Luanda: Author.

Ministério da Educação. (2004). *Estratégia para a Formação de Professores 2004–2015.* Maputo: Author.

Ministry of Education and Culture. (2005). *Evaluation of the Impact of*

Technical and Financial Support to the Implementation of Initial, In-service and Continuing Professional Development of Teachers Including the Crescer *System*. Draft Report. Maputo: Author.

Nsiangengo, Pedro, & Diasala, Andre J. (2008). O Programa Escola dos Professores do Futuro para a Formação de Professores em Zonas Rurais em Angola. *Perspectivas, 38,* 103–118.

OECD (Organization for Economic Cooperation and Development). (2005). *Teachers Matter: Attracting, Developing, and Retaining Effective Teachers.* Paris: OECD. Retrieved February 17, 2010, from www.oecd.org/edu/teacherpolicy

Otaala, Bernard. (2006). African tertiary institutions' response to the HI/AIDS epidemic. In Carl A. Grant, & Liane M. Summerfield. Humanizing Pedagogy, (pp. 242–267). Boulder: Paradigm Publishers.

Papastephanou, Marianna. (2005). Globalization, globalism and cosmopolitanism as an educational ideal. *Educational Philosophy and Theory, 37(4),* 533–551.

Passos, Ana F. J. (2009). A comparative analysis of teacher competence and its effect on pupil performance in upper primary schools in Mozambique and other SACMEQ countries. Unpublished PhD Dissertation, Pretoria, RSA: University of Pretoria.

Pessula, Pedro A. (2009). Reforma Curricular a Formação de Professores Primários. Análise do Plano Curricular e do Programa de Metodologia de Educação Física. In Stella M. Duarte, H. N. Dias, & M. Cherinda (Orgs.) *Formação de Professores em Moçambique: Resgatar o Passado, Realizar o Presente e Perspectivar o Futuro.* Maputo: Universidade Pedagógica.

República de Moçambique. (2008). *Plano Económico e Social 2009.* Maputo: Author.

SADC (Southern Africa Development Community). (2010). SADC Profile. Retrieved January 15, 2010, from www.SADC.int/

SADC (Southern African Development Community). (1997). *Protocol on Education and Training.* Retrieved February 17, 2010, from www.ub.bw/p/documents/1997_SADC_protocol.pdf

SARUA. (2010). About Us. *Southern African Regional Universities Association.* Retrieved February 8, 2010, from www.sarua.org/?q=content/about-us

Tabulawa, Richard Tjombe. (2009). Education reform in Botswana; Reflections on policy contradictions and paradoxes. *Comparative Education, 45(1),* 87–107.

U.S. Department of State. (2010a). *Background note: Angola.* Retrieved October 1, 2009, from http://www.state.gov/r/pa/ei/bgn/6619.htm

U.S. Department of State. (2010b). *Background note: Brazil.* Retrieved January 15, 2010, from http://www.state.gov/r/pa/ei/bgn/35640.htm

U.S. Department of State. (2010c). *Background note: Mozambique.* Retrieved January 15, 2010, from http://www.state.gov/r/pa/ei/bgn/7035.htm

U.S. Department of State. (2010d). *Background note: Portugal.* Retrieved January 15, 2010, from http://www.state.gov/r/pa/ei/bgn/3208.htm

Watson, David. (2007). *Managing civic and community engagement.* London: Open University Press.

Wideen, Marvin, Grimmet, Peter, & Andrews, Ian. (2002). International Teacher Education: From Dilemmas to Principles. In E. Thomas (Ed.) *Teacher education: Dilemmas and prospects.* London: Kogan Page.

Woodrow Wilson International Center for Scholars. (2009a). South Africa and United States Relations: Remarks by Amb Johnnie Carson. Retrieved November 1, 2009, from www.wilsoncenter.org/index.cfm?

Woodrow Wilson International Center for Scholars. (2009b). South Africa and United States Relations: Remarks by Minister Naledi Pandor. Retrieved November 1, 2009, from www.wilsoncenter.org/index.cfm?

Part IV

Global Environments and Diversity

14 Universities and Global Diversity: Movement toward Tomorrow

Wanda J. Blanchett and Beverly Lindsay

Access to higher education and the availability of an educated and skilled global workforce that can work effectively with individuals whose backgrounds, religions, politics, experiences, and worldviews differ from their own is essential to the overall well-being and sustainability of humanity. How our society, and specifically universities and colleges, responds to diversity in a global context is one of the most significant challenges facing higher education in the 21st Century. In fact, according to Smith (2009), "Globally, diversity continues to play a significant role in relation to many political structures, irrespective of whether those structures are democratic" (Smith, 2009, p. 7). Without question, the world is changing (Stewart, 2007) and some have argued that globalization is responsible for creating a new world order that is "Post-American" (Zakara, 2009). Regardless of whether one agrees with this assertion or not, we are indeed experiencing historical levels of global interdependence in terms of our economies, foreign policies, politics, technologies, services, and higher education systems. Given that the U.S. mortgage crisis—also known as the "Great Recession"—caused a global economic downturn, the world's economies have never been more interdependent than they are today (Douglass, 2010). What is most astonishing about the Great Recession is how far reaching its impact has been—all regions of the world and all sectors within our society have been impacted. For instance, a significant number of countries, nations, and states have been literally thrown into a struggle for their very survival as currency values have plummeted, financial institutions have collapsed (Moore, 2007), and multi-billion dollar construction projects halted in some of the richest and most powerful nations in the world (Fox, 2007). While this crisis has created pandemonium throughout the world, we cannot help but wonder what impact this crisis will have on developing countries that were already experiencing significant hardships and are impacted by this crisis through no fault of their own (McCord, 2010). For example, as discussed in Chapter 13, by Mario and Lindsay, what will be the impact on Mozambican and Angolan citizens and their educational systems that were already experiencing "nonexistent or insufficient educational infrastructure, inadequate funding" and the "debilitating effects of HIV/AIDS" (p. 230). More importantly, as members of a global society, we must ask what is our role in making sure that some of the poorest and least well served among us do indeed survive this crisis and have an opportunity to thrive (Watson, 2007).

To deal with this economic crisis, countries and nations are trying to make adjustments to their spending and the services provided to their citizens. Historically, in times of financial crisis, Higher Education Institutions (HEIs) in the United States have played a significant role in educating or re-educating the workforce to support the next wave of innovation, but the most recent economic woes seem to be sparing no sector of American society—including higher education (Douglass, 2010). Therefore, we are concluding this volume at a time of tremendous uncertainty and ambiguity worldwide concerning the state of our global economy and the impact that the recession will have on institutions of higher education and the practice of higher education throughout the world. Several states (e.g., California, Arizona, Florida, Michigan) within the United States have already made significant cuts in their support for public universities and college reducing these HEIs' budgets (The Chronicle of Higher Education, 2008). While not as drastic, and seemingly far more strategic, we have heard talks of potential higher education budget reduction measures being implemented in other countries around the world (Douglass, 2010). According to Douglass, these conversations appear to be far less significant globally and aimed at protecting higher education investments and funding as a component of some foreign countries', nations', and states' overall economic, political, and educational strategies. However, others such as Hickling-Hudson and Sidhu, in Chapter 9, would disagree with his perspective. Nonetheless, there is growing concern that the United States is not being as strategic in its approach to higher education funding during these difficult financial times and some states are actually treating higher education funding as "low hanging fruit" in the recession. Unfortunately, these budget reduction measures are coming at a time when our society is more diverse than ever before (Smith, 2009) and when universities and colleges have developed missions and identified strategic priorities aimed at becoming more diverse and global in their scope.

Even in uncharted economic times, we contend that HEIs are of ". . . vital importance for sociocultural and economic development, and for building the future, for which the younger generations will need to be equipped with new skills, knowledge and ideals" (UNESCO, 1998, p. 1). Ironically, this statement was made over a decade ago looking into the future when the economy was strong, but it is still relevant today. As if the global recession is not enough, there are other geopolitical issues that our society and universities must contend with and be responsive to. For example, we are keenly aware that as we write this concluding chapter, individuals, families, and businesses are experiencing great devastation as the British Petroleum (BP) oil leak continues to spill; according to some estimates, anywhere from 10,000 to 60,000 barrels of oil a day into the Gulf Coast (Broder et al., 2010). BP's oil spill is causing great harm and wreaking havoc on the environment as well as the seafood, shellfish, and tourism industries along the Gulf Coast while raising serious questions about who will be ultimately held responsible for this global partnership. For instance, the lines of responsibility are unclear with regard to BP's responsibilities and those of the U.S. government related to this environmental disaster and the costs associated with the cleanup and recovery activities (Broder, Robertson, & Krauss, 2010). Needless to say, universities have to be able to respond to these and other geopolitical issues in a timely and effective manner.

HEIs by their very *raison d etre* are driving forces for creating the new knowledge that will lead to new skills and ideals that will spur global economies, lead to technologies that prevent unnecessary environment disasters (for example, oil spills), and prepare citizens to embrace fully diversity in a global context (Chirea-Ungureanu & Danila, 2009; Smith, 2009; Stewart, 2007). As stated over a decade ago in the 21st Century Vision declaration, higher education has an explicit responsibility to support both the economic and sociocultural well-being of our society. While the economic component often receives considerable attention, the sociocultural aspects are also critically important and may include, but are not limited to, an obligation to prepare future generations to recognize, acknowledge, appreciate, and be responsive to diversity. As Smith (2009) states, "For higher education—as for our society—diversity is not only its challenges but also its future" (p. 254). Despite recognition that this is a valid assertion, both our society and higher education have experienced incredible challenges in being able to respond appropriately. Given that the primary purpose of universities and higher education is to prepare current and future generations to meet and appropriately address the most significant challenges of their day, it is reasonable to pose the question of what is the role of universities and higher education in the preparation of the next generation(s) to embrace global diversity.

Our volume builds upon and expands Dodds' (2008) work, which provided a critical review of the existing literature pertaining to globalization in higher education. In her review, Dodds offered a synthesis of the various conceptualizations of globalization found in the literature while also offering an analysis of the impact of globalization on higher education. She categorized the conceptualizations of globalization into three areas (that is, globalization as "global flows" and "pressures," globalization as trends: marketization, and globalization as ideology). Additionally, she identified four prevalent themes that emerged in the literature when exploring the impact of globalization on HEIs including: ". . . globalization as leading to a concentration of linguistic and/or economic power, to increased competition between HEIs, to HEIs being viewed as a means of stimulating national competitive advantage, and to changes in the nature of information and, relatedly, culture" (p. 510). Our volume seeks to articulate and analyze universities' roles in preparing professional educators for changing global diversity via explications of current trends in selected geographical regions and nations and positing paradigms to ameliorate global challenges. Our concluding chapter offers a synthesis of the major recurrent themes throughout the volume organized as follows: 1) Universities' movement toward globalization: Varying definitions and conceptualizations; 2) Universities' movement toward globalization: Impact of/on the practice of higher education; 3) Universities' movement toward globalization: Impact on unique colleges and universities; and 4) Universities and global diversity: Implications and conclusions.

Universities' Movement toward Globalization: Varying Definitions and Conceptualizations

Knight argues that as higher education practice has evolved in relation to the nature of global engagement, the terms and concepts used to illustrate the movement from internationalization to globalization in higher education reflects this evolution. However, another possible explanation of the evolution, or use of different terminology, is that the terms are "responsive to changing views of political correctness" as Lindsay (2011) suggests. In clarifying the difference between internationalization and globalization, Knight refers to internationalization as "the process of integrating an international, intercultural, or global dimension into the purpose, functions or delivery of higher education at the institutional and national levels" (Knight, 2008, p. xi, 21, and 82, as cited in Lindsay, 2011). Knight also referred to globalization as "the process that is increasing the flow of people, culture, ideas, values, knowledge, technology, and economy across borders, resulting in a more interconnected and interdependent world" (Knight, 2008, p. x, 4, and 83, as cited in Lindsay, 2011).

As the existing literature (for example, Dodds, 2008; Knight, 2003) in the area of globalization/internationalization and higher education illustrates, these two terms are often used interchangeably and there are varied meanings and conceptualizations of what constitutes globalization in higher education. Applying Knight's and Dodd's conceptualizations of globalization, we explored the intersection of globalization with diversity to analyze the global interconnectivity and responsibility of universities, particularly administrators and faculty, by taking into account the changing dynamics of globalization and the relationship to diverse demographic groups and regions. Like Watson (2007), we assert that universities have both a local and global commitment to civic engagement through the preparation of their students to participate in a globally diverse society. Thus, our volume explored how global diversity is conceptualized in matters of higher education through a variety of perspectives and within a wide-range of universities in select G-20 and G-8 countries and nations and other regions such as the Middle East and the Caribbean.

In their comparative study of the United States and Russia, Stromquist and Smolentseva (Chapter 2) suggested that internationalization and global diversity in higher education present a unique opportunity for global solidarity if it were,

> interpreted as the process that brings to the fore the problems of other, mostly developing, countries and tries to incorporate in the curriculum the knowledge needed to address those problems as well as to raise social awareness. Under this definition, regions such as Sub-Saharan Africa and Western Asia would receive attention.
>
> (p. 37)

Such a definition of global diversity would employ a global social justice lens to bring attention to gross inequities in developing countries and it would seek to subsequently address these inequities. Despite the benefits of conceptualizing globalization through a broad global social justice lens, few universities have adopted such a definition of conceptualization in practice though many in North America have in theory. In fact, the authors posed that U.S. universities' international activities have focused on just the opposite; and thus, have centered on developing relationships with prestigious universities and centers in wealthy developed countries with little or no attention given to addressing global social problems in less developed countries where such actions are sorely needed. This conclusion suggests that many U.S. universities have largely conceptualized globalization as "global flows," "globalizations as trends: marketization," and "globalization as ideology" as asserted by Dodds (2008). Although it is logical and practical to expect that globalization in higher education would lead HEIs to engage in such activities to transform their curriculum, this does not seem to always be the case. Stromquist and Smolentseva argue that few U.S. universities are actually leveraging their international relationships as a means of re-conceptualizing and enriching their own curriculum to reflect global perspectives, introspective analyses of American culture and higher education, or individual and national geopolitical self-awareness. This perception of an unwillingness to internationalize U.S. universities' curriculum coupled with many U.S. universities appearing to have less interest in internationalizing themselves and more interested in homogenization and imperialism, has been cited by Yang (2002) as a negative effect of globalization in higher education. To be sure, we are not arguing that an end product of globalization in higher education is homogenization and imperialism, but rather, we are asserting that when HEIs are not willing to internationalize themselves and their curriculum, the benefits are not mutual and their acts can have negative connotations and effects.

In their exploration of the conceptualization of globalization that applies to globalizing higher education efforts in the Middle East, Khoury and Lindsay (Chapter 4) found that six U.S. universities' (for example, Carnegie Mellon University) development of Education City in Qatar has been met with mixed reactions ranging from perceptions of possible homogenization and imperialism to a belief that such a partnership has national significance. They came to this conclusion because there are two major assertions regarding prestigious American universities involvement in higher education in Qatar depending upon whether local or global individuals support the effort. Accordingly, they concluded that "Those who vehemently oppose Education City will point to the obvious examples of how local and Islamic cultures are being overshadowed in favor of an American worldview," and "[t]hose who favor American education will assert that the quality of an American education and the possibilities for intercultural understandings supersede any implications of an imperialist agenda." However, the authors noted that in other parts of the Middle East, there were different conceptualizations of the purpose and value of globalization of higher education. For instance, the authors noted that at Sultan Qaboos University, "globalization is seen as both a positive and a threatening force that needs to be both welcomed and challenged. A highly globalized world is one that benefits Oman by bringing Oman to the world and the world to Oman." Consequently, what is happening in the Middle East pertaining to globalization in higher education does not fit neatly into the categories of globalization offered by Dodds (2008), but due to their differing geopolitical context, globalization is conceptualized differently even in the same region of the world. Like Sultan Qaboos University, the University of the West Indies (UWI) has also expressed a commitment to globalization.

In Chapter 5, Lindsay stated that, ". . . the UWI asserts that its enduring mission is to propel the economic, social, political and cultural development of West Indian society through teaching, research, innovation, advisory and community services and intellectual leadership" (Office of Planning and Development, 2007, p. 6 as cited by Lindsay, p. 94). Additionally, Lindsay also noted that higher education administrators were keenly aware of the pressing need to better prepare Jamaican citizens, who are indeed the majority in their home country, for immigration to the U.S. and other countries where they will likely experience racism, white privilege, and be assigned a minority status. This realization is forcing the UWI to focus more attention on the preparation of its citizens to participate in a globally diverse society where they will encounter racial/ethnic, cultural, and other forms of diversity and possible discrimination. While most definitions and conceptualizations of globalization discussed in our volume focused on the local or regional context, a national conceptualization and focus on globalization was also discussed in Chapter 11.

In her discussion of "European Union Universities and Teacher Preparation," Florian states, "Globalization of education refers to both a process of alignment of national systems for purposes of comparability, collaboration and exchange, and a process of differentiation for the purposes of competition and marketization" (p. 200). In Chapter 12, in an analysis of how nations with a shared legacy of African enslavement, King et al. discuss the complexity of globalization in this context, and offer a way of defining and responding to globalization that takes into consideration this historical complexity. King et al. stated the following when defining globalization, "Globalization refers to the most recent phase of the worldwide economic system of interlocking interests, power structures, and institutions of domination that transcend national borders . . . (King & Goodwin as cited in King et al., p. 209). These authors also highlighted the importance of the higher education curriculum, especially in these settings, to be truthful, robust enough to prepare educators who are culturally competent, and that will support the development of "our identity and consciousness as African descent people to overcome racial injustice"(p. 207). Therefore, their conceptualization of a globally diverse curriculum included both the development of new knowledge, skills, and dispositions while also helping to heal wounds caused by racism, discrimination, and white privilege. In Chapter 9, "The internationalization of universities is understood as the 'integration of an international, intercultural or global dimension into the teaching, research and service functions of the university'" (Knight, 2003, as cited by Hickling-Hudson & Sidhu, p. 158). As illustrated earlier, this conceptualization of internationalization also acknowledges the importance of creating a sense of social awareness and development of self-identity in relation to Australia's indigenous populations while also preparing higher education students for a global context.

Universities' Movement toward Globalization: Impact of/on the Practice of Higher Education

Universities' movement toward globalization is also impacting the practice of higher education. While we assert that universities' engagement in globalization is a natural fit due to their unique mission of contributing to the production of new knowledge and ideals and preparing future generations accordingly, it seems that there are many motivating factors that contribute to universities' decisions to internationalize. A significant factor includes competition among universities and the growing need for universities to increase and diversify their sources of revenue in a global climate of decreased government and state support of higher education (Douglass, 2010; Rhoads, 2006). As a result, many universities are looking to foreign students, study abroad programs, foreign exchange programs, and even dual degree programs as a means of branding and revenue generation. As Stromquist and Smolentseva observed in their comparative study of Russian and U.S. universities, increasing enrollment to counter decreases in government funding has lead to almost doubling the number of schools in Russia's Moscow State University over the last decade. They also highlight the fact that instead of simply expanding existing academic program areas, Moscow State University has almost doubled the number of schools within colleges and has created new programs in the areas of "business, public auditing, television, and translation and interpretation" (p. 32). While similar trends were not noted in U.S. universities, the authors did point to "branding" being employed by U.S. universities; a method of presenting "one's university as unique in a particular way Such academic areas as medicine, engineering, law, business administration, and the hard sciences were cited as "hot issues from the marketing perspective" (p. 33). Branding in these supposedly hot disciplines appears to be leading to large research and government contracts for some universities. Because many U.S. universities view internationalization as an alternative revenue stream during a time of unpredictable and declining higher education budgets, a number of them are establishing offices in foreign countries and have hired or plan to hire high-level executives (for example, associate provost) whose responsibilities are globally centered. According to Stromquist and Smolentseva, "International responsibilities call for a constant scanning of the external environment, contacting potential partners, establishing networks, recruiting international students, and recruiting stellar faculty who can transfer their fame and resources to their new university" (p. 59).

While some universities seem to be new to the internationalization of higher education game, Australia is not new to this game as demonstrated by their 20 plus year history in the international education industry, which is believed to be valued at $15.5 billion Australian dollars—prior to applying expenses and their distribution model. According to Hickling-Hudson and Sidhu, ". . . the economic rationale for internationalizing the student body has remained important for Australia's universities to help them to cope with the burden of underfunding by the state" (p. 151). It seems that a deliberate and concerted effort was made in the 1980s through the adoption of "market-driven policies . . . to transform Australia from a heavily protected economy reliant mainly on mineral and agricultural commodities, to one that embraced knowledge-intensive services" (p. 159). This move made possible the establishment of an education export industry that moved public universities from their initial base of domestic students to an increased reliance on "income from international student fees as their operating budgets were reduced by governments of all political persuasions, part of a broader policy to steer the public sectors towards the market" (p. 159) The movement of the higher education system into a market economy has had two unpredicted effects. The first is the "proliferation of private higher education institutions supported by student fees" (p. 159). Second, the authors concluded that, "the policy has attracted some students for whom education is of secondary importance—their primary goal being to achieve permanent residency" (p. 160).

Similarly, Russia's decision to join the Bologna declaration was partially attributed to their desire to increase internationalization by moving to the European bachelor-master. Sung (in Chapter 3), also cited national and regional interests as contributing to Korea's and China's movement toward internationalization. Specifically, Sung asserts that "Given that the current mobilization of materials and information is only possible through technology and the use of English language, both Korea and China invest tremendous efforts and resources to teach the English language to their students" (Kim & Jeon, 2005 as cited in Sung, p. 47) During the 2005/2006 academic year, China and Korea, respectively, sent the second and third largest number of students to the United States to study (National Institute for International Education, 2002, as cited by Sung, p. 51). These moves suggests that "Globalization has influenced the adoption of internationalization practices at national, regional, and individual levels through such norms of international students, international contracts, joint projects, and exchanges" (Stromquist and Smolentseva, p. 40).

Universities' Movement toward Globalization: Impact on Unique Colleges and Universities

It seems that there is indeed a role for unique colleges and universities to play related to globalization, but globalization in these settings might look different from what has been undertaken by large prestigious research universities to date. Unique colleges and universities are just that—unique because of their particular missions. However, being unique does not shield them from the growing demands and realities of globalization in higher education. As Lindsay and Scales Williams points out in Chapter 6, even Historically Black Colleges and Universities (HBCUs) in the United States whose primary mission is to educate African Americans are experiencing an increase in students from other ethnic/racial backgrounds and a growing number of international or foreign-born students. They further highlight that in the wake of the devastation caused by Hurricane Katrina, HBCUs in New Orleans are contending with an influx of diverse workers and their families from across the U.S., as well as from other countries as new residents have come to New Orleans seeking employment and to play a role in the rebuilding of the region.

Similarly, when discussing the Indigenous-controlled or tribal colleges and universities (TCUs) that serve Native Americans, Tippeconnic and Faircloth (Chapter 7) argued that despite tribal colleges and universities' unique mission of providing "an education that is more accessible and culturally appropriate than mainstream institutions, or those public and private colleges and universities in the United States that provide educational opportunities to the general public," TCUs already operate in a global context. To make their argument, they illustrated the three ways that TCUs are globally engaged, including the fact that these HEIs are holistic in their approach to education—not just focused singularly on education, but for preparation of students for life and the world outside of the indigenous community—and that TCUs as a movement are engaged in higher education activities throughout the world. In discussing the implications of globalization for Commuter Urban Public Universities (CUPUs), Abbate-Vaughn and DeGennaro highlighted the fact that engaging in global activities is indeed a balancing act for these universities due to their missions focused on the production of local knowledge and delivery of services to address local and regional challenges. Therefore, to stay true to their unique missions, CUPUs have, "begun to increasingly engage in the process of glocalization" (Robertson, 1995 as cited by Abbate-Vaughn & DeGennaro, p. 145), which refers to "thinking globally, but primarily acting locally" (p. 145).

Universities' and Global Diversity: Implications and Conclusions

Without question, we live in a globally diverse world, but despite this reality our society and HEIs are not prepared for this level of diversity. Up until recently, discussions about globalization have mainly focused on the economic opportunities afforded the U.S. and other countries through the expansion and opening up of their higher education trade markets to the world (Rhoads, 2006). Therefore, it has only been in the last several years that we have begun exploring the implications of globalization for higher education. Now that globalization in higher education is gaining more attention, much of the attention centers on what globalization will mean for HEIs, which places HEIs in a rather passive role versus an active role in determining how they will respond to and lead in the context of globalization (Dodds, 2008). However, we concur with Dodds that globalization presents a tremendous opportunity for HEIs to define and disseminate exemplary models for how HEIs can and are engaged in globalization. This opportunity moves our engagement from being simply an additional source of revenue to activities that are literally transforming higher education curriculum; preparing students to be full and active participants in our globally diverse society.

To begin this process, we will share a few examples of what is occurring among university students and colleges/schools of education to push HEIs toward a more active role in the pursuit of global diversity. While there are a number of HEIs approaching global diversity, exposing university and college students to curriculum experiences that will prepare them for global citizenship appears to be a step in the right direction. In Chapter 10, Meyer et al. analyze their international survey of higher education students' perception of world-mindedness and global citizenship. Their findings are astonishing and illustrated that overall students from a variety of disciplines are entering universities in Australia, England, New

Zealand, and the United States, even though these are English-speaking countries with ". . . positive or somewhat neutral understandings and dispositions about constructs related to international and intercultural interactions" (p. 187). Their findings have several implications for future research and HEIs future practice relative to global diversity. First, they noted some differences in students' global-mindedness depending upon their disciplines or majors, as well as some differences based upon which countries they were from. Since this study employed quantitative methodologies, the researchers recommended that qualitative interviews be conducted with these and other students to explore further the cross-national findings. Second, they highlighted the importance of ensuring that the curriculum in HEIs builds upon and expands students' global-mindedness versus simply re-exposing students to what they came to HEIs already knowing. Last, there is a dearth of research that provides insights into higher education students' current level of preparation and openness to learning more about global diversity and global citizenship. Therefore, to close this gap, Meyer et al. suggested that as HEIs and programs take on this issue, it is critically important that they carefully document and conduct ongoing research on their efforts.

A potential national model for approaching global diversity in HEIs was offered by Florian in Chapter 11 in her descriptive analysis of how the European Union (EU) universities are collectively responding to global diversity. Specifically, she chronicles how, ". . . the movement of people both as a result of economic migration and refugee status has led to new meanings of multiculturalism within the countries of the EU and a new agenda for social inclusion across Europe" (p. 202). The EU model is built upon the notion that providing support to the member states will enable them to meet the challenges presented by global diversity in their society and local schools. For instance, "A 2007 report of the Commission of the European Communities cited a European Council report that found 'Education and training are critical features to develop the EU's long-term potential for competitiveness as well as for social cohesion'" (Florian, p. 203). Although the model was discussed in our volume within the context of the higher education teacher education programs and their effort to revise their practice in an attempt to be responsive to the historical and changing demographics of the EU student population, the fact that this is a national commitment that is tied to the EU's long-term goals is helpful. More importantly, this model illustrates commitment to global diversity that is not an add-on to existing practice(s), but instead, has the potential to improve practice at multiple levels; including but not limited to, national higher education, and the local individual school and classroom levels. Given that this model is still early in its implementation, ongoing research is needed to actually determine how their most diverse and underserved population fare going forward.

In summary, when we embarked upon this project, we set out to answer several critical questions related to universities and global diversity such as how are universities around the world defining and conceptualizing global diversity, and are they operating from some common understandings of what it means to prepare students and educators for global diversity. We were also interested in determining what global diversity in higher education looked like in practice and the identification of models that might serve to better inform our work and efforts in this area. Given that global diversity in higher education is still evolving, there are many questions, other areas of education, and a number of geopolitical issues that we were not able to address in this volume that are pertinent to these discussions and should be addressed in future discussions of global diversity. However, going forward, it is essential that we commit to a conceptualization that embodies the complexity of this important work. Clearly, HEIs are not simply impacted by global diversity, but they have the unique responsibility of preparing students for the new and changing world, which includes understanding the complexity of a variety of peoples, and a commitment to social justice, such that those with the greatest need receive the greatest benefit. As universities move towards tomorrow within the context of global diversity, HEIs and their faculty should indeed set the parameters for globalization by being cognizant of the interactive roles of such settings with the larger society. Globalization is not on the horizon, it is here and HEIs must play a role in determining its success.

References

Broder, John, M., Robertson, Campbell, & Krauss, Clifford. (2010). Amount of oil spill could escalate, company admits. Retrieved June 25, 2010 from *The New York Times*. http://www.nytimes.com/2010/05/05/us/05spill.html

Chirea-Ungureanu, Carmen & Danila, Oonela. (2009, September). *International standards and development cooperation in higher education or what shall we do next?* Proceedings of the 2009 EMUNI Conference on Higher Education and Research. Porotoz, Solvenia.

Dodds, Anneliese. (2008). How does globalization interact with higher education? The continuing lack of consensus. *Comparative Education, 44*(4) 505–517.

Douglass, John Aubrey. (2010, April). *Higher education budgets and the global recession: Tracking varied national responses and their consequences.* Research & Occasional Paper Series: CSHE.

Fox, Justin. (2007). Cracks in the economy. *Time, 170*(13), 46–51.

Knight, Jane. (2003). *Internationalization of higher education practices and priorities: 2003 IAU survey report.* Paris, France: International Association of Universities.

Lindsay, Beverly. (2011). International and global phenomena: Continuing excellence or enhancing elitism in higher education? *Comparative Education.*

McCord, Anna. (2010). The impact of the global financial crisis on social protection in developing countries. *International social security review, 63*(2), 31–45.

Moore, Matt. (2007). U.S. Homeowner woes felt around world. *The Huffington Post.* Retrieved June 25, 2010 from http://www.huffingtonpost. com/huff-wires/20070812/global-contagion

Rhoads, Robert. (2006). University Reform in Global Times: Opportunity and challenges. *Chung Cheng Educational Studies, 5,* 1–24.

Smith, Daryl, G. (2009). *Diversity's promise for higher education: Making it work.* Maryland, Baltimore: The Johns Hopkins University Press.

Stewart, Vivien. (2007). Citizens of the world: The future is here. It's multiethnic, multicultural, and multilingual. But are students ready for it? *Educational Leadership, 64*(7), 8–14.

The Chronicle of Higher Education. (2008). Bad economy could get even worse, hurting spending on higher education. *The Chronicle of Higher Education,* Retrieved August 3, 2010 from http://chronicle.com/article/ Bad-Economy-Could-Get-Even/41757/

Watson, David. (2007). *Managing civic and community engagement.* England, Open University Press.

UNESCO. (1998). World Declaration on higher education for the twenty-first century: Vision and action. Retrieved June 11, 2010 from http://www.unesco. org/education/educprog/wche/declaration_eng.htm

Yang, Rui. (2002). University internationalisation: Its meanings, rationales and implications. *Intercultural Education, 13*(1), 81–95.

Zakara, Fareed. (2009). *The post-American world.* New York, New York: W.W Norton & Company, Inc.

Contributors

Jorgelina Abbate-Vaughn (Ph.D., Boston College) is an Associate Professor of Teacher Education at the University of Massachusetts Boston. Her scholarship, published in national and international journals, in both English and Spanish, centers on urban education challenges and issues of diversity as they affect teaching, learning, and equal access. She has taught in various areas within the United States and in her native Argentina in a variety of capacities within the Prek-graduate school pipeline, and in the Dominican Republic as a Fulbright Scholar. Her early experiences in the United States as a working-class immigrant mastering English fuel her commitment to urban universities.

Wanda J. Blanchett (Ph.D., Pennsylvania State University) is Dean of the School of Education and Ewing Marion Kauffman/Missouri Endowed Chair in Teacher Education at the University of Missouri, Kansas City. She is the immediate past Associate Dean and Associate Professor in the School of Education at the University of Colorado, Denver. She specializes in urban and special education. Currently, she is the immediate-past Chair of the Global Diversity Committee of the American Association of Colleges of Teacher Education. She has published numerous scholarly articles and presented extensively at annual conferences of the American Educational Research Association and the American Association of Colleges of Teacher Education. Her research focuses on equity issues including urban teacher preparation, issues of race, class, culture, gender, disproportionate representation of students of color in special education, severe disabilities, and issues of sexuality for students with disabilities.

Regina Conceição (M.A.) is a doctoral student in Education at the Federal University of São Carlos, Brazil whose research focus is effective teaching in public schools. She has worked with teachers using oral history, memory, anti-discrimination approaches and develops programs in a joint city-university Afro-Brazilian Cultural Center. Since 2001 she has been responsible for implementing public policy in race relations in the São Carlos Municipal Office of Education.

Donna DeGennaro is an Assistant Professor at the University of Massachusetts Boston. Her current research interests center on youth technology practices and interactions in informal learning environments. The research draws on theories from cultural sociology to examine the interrelationship between culture, history, and social interactions and how they inform emergent learning designs. She has recently returned from a summer fellowship in the Dominican Republic where she worked with disadvantaged female youth to increase their technology skills.

Susan Faircloth (Ph.D., Pennsylvania State University) is an Associate Professor of educational leadership and co-director of the Center for the Study of Leadership in American Indian Education, in the College of Education at the Pennsylvania State University. Her research focuses on the education of culturally and linguistically diverse learners, particularly American Indian and Alaskan Native students. She also studies issues related to the preparation of educational leaders. Faircloth's recent publications include "Collaborating with Tribal Communities and Families to Improve the Social, Emotional, and Linguistic Competence of Young Indigenous Children" in *Perspectives on Communication Disorders and Sciences in Culturally and Linguistically Diverse Populations* (with R. Pfeffer). Faircloth previously served as the Director of Policy Analysis and Research with the American Indian Higher Education Consortium in Alexandria, Virginia.

Lani Florian (Ph.D., University of Connecticut) is Professor of Social and Educational Inclusion at the University of Aberdeen (UK). Her research interests include categorization of children, models of provision for meeting the needs of all learners, and teaching practice in inclusive schools. She has written extensively on inclusive education and has consulted on special needs education and inclusion internationally. She is co-author of *Achievement and Inclusion in Schools*, winner of the 2008 NASEN/TES academic book award and co-editor of *Promoting Inclusive Practice*, winner of the NASEN/TES academic book award in 1999.

Petronilha Beatriz Gonçalves e Silva (Ph.D.) is a Full Professor in the field of Teaching-Learning and Ethnic-Racial Relations at the Federal University of São Carlos (UFSCar), a researcher in the university's Afro-Brazilian Studies Group, chairperson of the UFSCar Affirmative Action Program, and a member of the Higher Education Chamber of the National Council of Education from 2002 to 2006.

Anne Hickling-Hudson (Ph.D., University of Queensland) is a professor in the Faculty of Education at Queensland University of Technology (Australia). She specializes in cross-cultural and international education, and has earned her undergraduate and graduate degrees at the

Universities of the West Indies and Hong Kong, respectively. She served as president of the World Council of Comparative and International Education Societies from 2001 to 2004. Anne has been a pioneer in applying postcolonial theory to the comparative analysis of educational policy and national development. She has been involved in designing and implementing an Australian teacher educational curriculum in "Teaching the Studies of Asia," which has been adopted by a dozen Australian universities as part of their postgraduate degree programs. She is currently involved in cross-cultural policy and curriculum research on how educators in Papua New Guinea, the Caribbean, and Africa are helping to counter the crisis of HIV/AIDS.

Garry Hoban (Ph.D., University of British Columbia) is Associate Professor of Science Education and Teacher Education at the University of Wollongong, Australia. His dissertation focused on teachers' professional learning in Canada. He is the author of *Teacher Learning for Educational Change* (Open University Press, 2002), editor of *The Missing Links in Teacher Education Design* (Springer, 2005), co-author of *Action Learning in Schools* (Routledge, in press), and has published over 70 refereed journal articles, book chapters, and conference proceedings.

Issam E. Khoury is a doctoral candidate at the Pennsylvania State University, pursuing a dual-title Ph.D. in Higher Education and Comparative and International Education, and a Masters degree in International Affairs. A Palestinian native, Issam earned Bachelors degrees at Virginia Tech and a Masters degree at Ohio State. He has worked in Residence Life at American University and with the Department of State's International Visitor Program. He is the coauthor, with Beverly Lindsay and Suzie Hickey, of "Democracy and Terrorism: What Role for Universities" which appeared in *Research in Comparative and International Education*.

Joyce King (Ph.D., Stanford University) is the Benjamin E. Mays Endowed Chair of Urban Teaching, Learning and Leadership at Georgia State University, where she is also Professor of Educational Policy Studies. Joyce has served as a Senior Academic Affairs Officer at Spelman College, Medgar Evers College, and the University of New Orleans. Her publications include *Teaching Diverse Populations* and *Black Education: A Transformative Research and Action Agenda for the New Century*. Recent publications include: "If Justice is Our Objective: Diaspora Literacy, Heritage Knowledge, and the Praxis of Critical Studying" in the *National Society for the Study of Education Yearbook*, and "Critical & Qualitative Research in Teacher Education: A Blues Epistemology for Cultural Well-Being and a Reason for Knowing" in the *Third Handbook of Research on Teacher Education*.

Beverly Lindsay (Ph.D., American University; Ed.D., University of Massachusetts, Amherst) is an Invited Visiting Professor at the Institute of Education (University of London) and Inaugural University Fellow and Professor at Dillard University in New Orleans. Her scholarship examines comparative and international education policy issues and international affairs; and her publications include *Ralph Johnson Bunche: Public Intellectual and Nobel Peace Laureate* (Senior Author and Editor) and *The Quest for Equity in Higher Education* (with Manuel Justiz). She has produced six books and nearly 100 scholarly and policy publications. Her work in international higher education has taken her to six continents to work in executive and faculty development. She has served as a Dean of International Policy Studies at Hampton University and Pennsylvania State University, and has held senior positions at the University of Georgia and the United States Department of State's Bureau of Educational and Cultural Affairs. Distinguished Fulbright Fellowships have been awarded to South Korea, Zimbabwe, and Mozambique where she taught graduate courses and engaged in research on peace and conflict resolution and presented invited lectures to the diplomatic community. In 2008 and 2009, she was a Visiting Professor at the University of the West Indies, Jamaica. She is a Professor and Senior Scientist of Higher Education and International Policy Studies at Pennsylvania State University.

Mouzinho Mario (Ph.D., University of Pittsburgh) is currently an Associate Professor in the Department of Educational Administration and Management at Eduardo Mondlane University, Mozambique and a Senior Researcher with UNICEF in Angola. He is the immediate former Dean of the Education Faculty at Eduardo Mondlane University. His areas of interest include teacher education, higher and adult education, and national and international development. He has written several articles and research reports, and is the co-author of *Higher Education in Mozambique: A Case Study*, and of *Reviews of National Policies for Education: South Africa*. He has served as an education consultant for DFID, the Ford Foundation, OECD, and UNESCO.

Luanna H. Meyer (Ph.D., Indiana University— Bloomington) is Director of the Jessie Hetherington Centre for Educational Research and Professor of Education (Research) at Victoria University of Wellington (New Zealand). Her research has focused on inclusive education, attitudes towards diversity and multicultural education, effective interventions for challenging behavior, and higher education initiatives to promote global mindedness. She has published over 200 books, journal articles, and book chapters and been invited to speak in several countries and over 30 U.S. states.

Evaldo Ribeiro Oliveira (M.A.) is a Doctoral Student in Education at the Federal University of São Carlos, Brazil. His research interests include Black intellectuals and Black education. As an active member of the university-based Afro-Brazilian Studies Group (NEAB/UFSCar), his professional experience includes teacher training, staff development, and educational materials development to support ethnic-racial relations.

Hyun-Sook Park (Ph.D., University of California— Berkeley) is Professor of Special Education in the Connie L. Lurie College of Education at San Jose State University in California, where she prepares teachers to work with students with disabilities from diverse cultural and linguistic backgrounds. Her areas of expertise and research interests have been social development of students with disabilities, transition, multicultural special education, and research methods. She has received many federal grants and has widely published in these areas, including books, book chapters, peer-reviewed journal articles, and monographs.

Tatiane Cosentino Rodrigues, M.A., is Doctoral student in Education at the Federal University of São Carlos, Brazil. Her master's thesis in Sociology is titled "The Black Movement in the Brazilian Scene: Struggles and Contributions to Educational Policies 1980–1990." She is an active member of the Afro-Brazilian Studies Group (NEAB/UFSCar) and is working on a research project focused on "The Rise of Diversity in Contemporary Educational Policies."

Ravinder Sidhu is a Post-Doctoral Fellow at the School of Education, University of Queensland, Australia Her research interests are in the sociology of transnational education, comparative and international education and student mobilities. She is the author of *Universities and Globalization: To market, to market* (Mahwah, NJ: Lawrence Erlbaum Associates). Before commencing her doctoral studies, Ravinder worked in the areas of educational aid and international student advising.

Christine E. Sleeter (Ph.D., University of Wisconsin—Madison) is Professor Emerita at California State University Monterey Bay, where she was a founding faculty member. Her research focuses on antiracist multicultural education and multicultural teacher education. She has published over 100 journal articles and book chapters, and several books, including *Unstandardizing Curriculum* (Teachers College Press, 2005), *Facing Accountability in Education* (Teachers College Press, 2007), and *Doing Multicultural Education for Achievement and Equity* (with C. A. Grant, Routledge, 2007).

Anna Smolentseva (Ph.D., Moscow State University) is a Senior Research Fellow at the Institute for Studies of Education at Moscow State University, Russia. Her research interests involve globalization and internationalization of higher education, academic profession, research universities, doctoral education, and educational sociology. Anna Smolentseva is an author of over 30 publications on higher education in English and Russian.

Pete Sorensen is a Lecturer in Education at the University of Nottingham, England, where he teaches on postgraduate courses in education and has led developments in flexible approaches to initial teacher education, including the use of e-learning and multiple school practicum placement models. He has researched extensively on collaborative approaches to professional development, peer learning and routes to teacher accreditation, with publications including a co-edited book, *Issues in Science Education* (Routledge, 2000), and many journal articles and conference proceedings.

Nelly P. Stromquist (Ph.D., Stanford University) is professor of comparative and international education in the College of Education at the University of Maryland. Dr. Stromquist specializes in issues related to international development education and gender, which examines from a critical sociology perspective. She has considerable experience in formal and non-formal education, particularly in Latin America and West Africa. Her research interests focus on the dynamics among educational policies and practices, gender relations, social justice, and societal change. More recently, she has been studying how the processes of globalization are shaping structures and functions of education, especially at the higher education level. Her most recent books are: Feminist Organizations and Social Transformation in Latin America (Boulder: Paradigm, 2006), and (Ed.) The Professoriate in the Age of Globalization (Rotterdam: Sense Publishers, 2006). She has served as associate editor of the Comparative Education Review and is on the editorial board of various journals in the U.S., U.K., Spain, South Africa, and Brazil. She was selected as a New Century Fulbright Scholar in Higher Education.

Kiwan Sung (Ph.D., Pennsylvania State University) currently teaches at the School of English Language & Culture at Kyung Hee University in Yong-in, Korea. His teaching and research interests include English teaching methods, multimedia-assisted language teaching, and critical theory and pedagogy. He has been involved in curricular and instructional revisions and evaluations at both local and national levels and also engaged in international collaborative work over the years. He also serves as secretary general for the Korea Association of Teachers of English, vice president at the Korea Association of Multimedia-Assisted Language Learning, and a board member for the Korean chapter of Asia TEFL and the Society of Teaching English through Movies. He has extensively presented both in national and international conferences including AERA, Asian TEFL, etc.

John Tippeconnic III (Ph.D., Pennsylvania State University) is a Professor of Education in the Educational Leadership Program at the Pennsylvania State University. He is also the director of the American Indian Leadership Program and co-director of the Center for the Study of Leadership in American Indian Education. He has over 30 years of experience in education at the national, state, local and tribal levels. His research interests include educational policy, leadership, school reform, higher education, and American Indian higher education. He is a member of the Connache Tribe. He is the co-author of the book *Next Steps: Research and Practice to Advance Indian Education* and the recent chapter with Saunders *Policy Issues in the Education of American Indians and Alaska Natives* in the book, *Multicultural Education Policies in Canada and the Unites States.*

Melissa Speight Vaughn, M.A., is a doctoral student in Educational Policy Studies at Georgia State University. Her research interests include investigating how educational policy and globalization affect teacher education programs in Anglophone Caribbean countries, interactions between dynamics of cultural maintenance and global education initiatives in the Anglophone Caribbean and Brazil, and how community-based citizenship education affects student learning and community involvement.

Tara Scales Williams (Ph.D., Penn State University) is the Director of Multicultural Education and Affiliate Faculty of Higher Education at Penn State University. She has published in a range of outlets such as the *Journal of Black Studies* and presented numerous papers at the annual conferences of the American Sociological Association, American Educational Research Association, and the Association for the Study of Higher Education.

Kenneth Zeichner (Ph.D., Syracuse University) is Boeing Professor of Teacher Education and at the University of Washington where he teaches graduate courses in the study of teacher education and directs the teacher education program. He is the author of many books and papers on teacher education including most recently *Teacher Education and the Struggle for Social Justice* (Routledge, 2009).

Index